The Passions of Law

CRITICAL AMERICA
General Editors: Richard Delgado and Jean Stefancic

Negrophobia and Reasonable Racism:
The Hidden Costs of Being Black in America
Jody David Armour

Black and Brown in America:
The Case for Cooperation
Bill Piatt

Black Rage Confronts the Law
Paul Harris

Selling Words:
Free Speech in a Commercial Culture
R. George Wright

The Color of Crime:
Racial Hoaxes, White Fear, Black Protectionism, Police
Harassment, and Other Macroaggressions
Katheryn K. Russell

The Smart Culture:
Society, Intelligence, and Law
Robert L. Hayman, Jr.

Was Blind, But Now I See:
White Race Consciousness and the Law
Barbara J. Flagg

The Gender Line:
Men, Women, and the Law
Nancy Levit

Heretics in the Temple:
Americans Who Reject the Nation's Legal Faith
David Ray Papke

The Empire Strikes Back:
Outsiders and the Struggle over Legal Education
Arthur Austin

Interracial Justice:
Conflict and Reconciliation in Post–Civil Rights America
Eric K. Yamamoto

Black Men on Race, Gender, and Sexuality:
A Critical Reader
Edited by Devon Carbado

The Passions of Law

EDITED BY

Susan A. Bandes

New York University Press

NEW YORK AND LONDON

NEW YORK UNIVERSITY PRESS
New York and London

Library of Congress Cataloging-in-Publication Data
The passions of law / edited by Susan Bandes.
p. cm.—(Critical America)
Includes bibliographical references and index.
ISBN 0-8147-1305-x (cloth: acid-free paper)
1. Law—Psychological aspacts. 2. Emotions. I. Bandes, Susan,
1951–II. Series.
K346 .P37 1999
340'.1´9—dc21   99–6525
                            CIP

Manufactured in the United States of America

10 9 8 7 6 5 4 3 2 1

To Stephen, Daniel, and Andrew, who bring me joy.

Contents

Acknowledgments

I want to thank Richard Delgado and Jean Stefancic first of all. It was Richard and Jean who, upon reading my earlier work in law and emotion, conceived the idea for this anthology. I then had the great fortune to work with a group of scholars whose creativity and insight are well known, and whose collegiality and warmth made them a delight to work with. Thanks to Danielle Allen, Cheshire Calhoun, John Deigh, Dan Kahan, Toni Massaro, Bill Miller, Martha Minow, Jeffrie Murphy, Sam Pillsbury, Richard Posner, Austin Sarat, and Bob Solomon. I reserve special thanks for Martha Nussbaum, whose work in this field has been a beacon for me and so many others, and whose generosity I deeply appreciate. The conference she hosted on this book's subjects at the University of Chicago gave us an opportunity for a true exchange of ideas and made the book better than it might otherwise have been. Thanks also to Niko Pfund, whose patience and insight and support for this project made it all possible. And of course, to Stephen, Daniel, and Andrew, for everything.

Contributors

Danielle S. Allen is Assistant Professor of Classics at the University of Chicago and has written on various aspects of ancient Greek penal practice and theory. Her book *The Politics of Punishing in Democratic Athens* is forthcoming with Princeton University Press.

Susan A. Bandes is Professor of Law at DePaul University, where she teaches criminal procedure, federal jurisdiction, and law and literature. She has published widely in these areas in journals, including the law reviews of the University of Chicago, Stanford University, and the University of Michigan. Her articles include "Empathy, Narrative and Victim Impact Statements," in the *University of Chicago Law Review*, on the role of emotion theory in the law. She is currently writing a book on narrative, anecdote, and systemic governmental misconduct.

Cheshire Calhoun is Professor of Philosophy at Colby College, Waterville, Maine. She is coeditor with Robert C. Solomon of *What Is an Emotion? Classical Readings in Philosophical Psychology*. She is currently working on a book on the structure of gay/lesbian subordination and the non-identity of gay/lesbian and feminist politics. She has also published essays on forgiveness, integrity, responsibility, and moral failure.

John Deigh is Professor of Philosophy at Northwestern University, where he teaches moral and political philosophy. He is the author of *The Sources of Moral Agency*, a collection of philosophical essays in moral psychology, and the editor of Ethics.

Dan M. Kahan is Professor of Law at Yale Law School. He graduated in 1989 from Harvard Law School, where he was president of the *Harvard Law Review*, and thereafter clerked for Judge Harry T. Edwards of the U.S. Court of Appeals for the D.C. Circuit and for Justice Thurgood Marshall of the U.S. Supreme Court. He has been a visiting member of the faculties at Yale Law School and Harvard Law School, and a member of the

University of Chicago Law School faculty from 1997–1999. His publications on criminal law have appeared in journals such as the *Harvard Law Review*, the *Columbia Law Review*, and the *Georgetown Law Journal*, and in the *Wall Street Journal* and the *Washington Post*.

Toni M. Massaro is Professor of Law at the University of Arizona, where she holds the Milton O. Riepe Chair in Constitutional Law. She teaches law and procedure and has written several articles on shame penalties in criminal law as well as other works on constitutional issues and procedure.

William Ian Miller teaches at the University of Michigan Law School. He is the author of *Humiliation* (Cornell University Press, 1993) and *The Anatomy of Disgust* (Harvard University Press, 1997), as well as books and articles on the sagas of medieval Iceland.

Martha Minow, Professor at Harvard Law School, is the author of *Between Vengeance and Forgiveness: Facing History after Genocide and Mass Violence* (Beacon Press, 1998); *Not Only for Myself: Identity, Politics, and Law* (New Press, 1997); and *Making All the Difference: Inclusion, Exclusion, and American Law* (Cornell University Press, 1990).

Jeffrie G. Murphy is Regents Professor of Law and Philosophy at Arizona State University. He is the author of numerous books and articles on moral and legal philosophy, including *Kant: The Philosophy of Forgiveness and Mercy* (with Jean Hampton) and *The Philosophy of Law: An Introduction to Jurisprudence* (with Jules Coleman). His third collection of essays, *Character, Liberty and Law: Kantian Essays in Theory and Practice*, appeared in 1998.

Martha C. Nussbaum is the Ernst Freund Distinguished Service Professor of Law and Ethics at the University of Chicago, with appointments in the Law School, the Philosophy Department, and the Divinity School, and an Associate appointment in the Classics Department. Her most recent book is *Sex and Social Justice* (Oxford University Press, 1999).

Samuel H. Pillsbury is Professor of Law and William Raines Fellow at Loyola Law School, Los Angeles. He is the author of numerous works on criminal law and punishment, most recently *Judging Evil: Rethinking the Law of Murder and Manslaughter* (New York University Press, 1998).

Richard A. Posner is Chief Judge of the U.S. Court of Appeals for the Seventh Circuit and Senior Lecturer at the University of Chicago Law

School. He has written extensively on legal and jurisprudential issues. His latest book, *The Problematics of Moral and Legal Theory*, was published in 1999.

Austin Sarat is William Nelson Cromwell Professor of Jurisprudence and Political Science at Amherst College. He is president of the Law and Society Association and chair of the National Working Group on Law, Culture, and the Humanities. His recent books include *Divorce Lawyers and Their Clients: Power and Meaning in the Legal Process* (coauthor); *Cause Lawyering: Political Commitments and Professional Responsibilities* (coeditor); *Everyday Practices and Trouble Cases* (coeditor); and *Law in the Domains of Culture* (coeditor). His current projects include *The Cultural Lives of Law* and *When the State Kills: Capital Punishment and the American Condition*.

Robert C. Solomon is Quincy Lee Centennial Professor at the University of Texas at Austin. He is the author or editor of nearly thirty books, among them *The Passions* (Doubleday, 1976), *From Hegel to Existentialism* (Oxford University Press, 1988), *About Love* (Simon and Schuster, 1988), *A Passion for Justice* (Addison-Wesley, 1990), *Ethics and Excellence* (Oxford University Press, 1992), and, with Kathleen Higgins, *A Short History of Philosophy* and *A Passion for Wisdom* (both by Oxford University Press, 1997). He regularly visits at the University of Auckland in New Zealand.

Introduction

Susan A. Bandes

Emotion pervades the law. This isn't an entirely surprising notion. We know that witnesses bring emotion into the courtroom, and that courtroom drama can be powerfully evocative. We've had many opportunities recently to watch the raw emotion of witnesses, barely suppressed by the legal filters designed to mute its force. We've heard the heartbreaking testimony of the victims, or families of victims, of the Oklahoma City bombing, which evoked widely shared sorrow and compassion. Louise Woodward's trial for killing a baby in her charge raised questions about Woodward's state of mind when baby Matthew was hurt, about whether his mother was sufficiently devoted to him, about whether the judge was properly detached or the prosecutor sufficiently compassionate, and about the role of national and international emotion—in this case a roller coaster of compassion, sadness, revulsion, and outrage at the act, the verdict, and the sentence. The trial of O. J. Simpson for the murder of his former wife, Nicole, and her friend Ron Goldman gave us more evidence than we might have desired about the difficulty of keeping the courtroom free of emotion. We witnessed the anger of Goldman's parents, heard reports of Simpson's past anger toward his onetime spouse (and of the uncertainty about whether the jury could consider it), and perhaps felt strong emotion of our own—anger at the police tactics or anger at the verdict. Widespread rage at the acquittal of the four police officers accused of beating Rodney King provided dramatic evidence that legal choices are sometimes made in an emotional minefield.

We know that jurors, witnesses, and defendants have feelings, but the conventional story of law is that before judgment these feelings will be categorized as admissible or inadmissible, and disregarded when necessary.

We take it for granted that jurors sometimes bring compassion and mercy, or anger and a desire for vengeance, to their deliberations, but we may think of jurors' tendency toward such feelings as illegitimate—steps on the path to jury nullification. We are aware that the law sometimes explicitly mentions emotion, and that defenses like "heat of passion" or even categories of conduct like "hate crime" grant the language of emotion some legitimacy in the arid, formalistic discourse of law. But we may assume either that the law can provide definitive, neat definitions of unlawyerlike terms like *passion* and *hate*, or that for law to traffic in emotion at all is unwise and suspect.

In the conventional story, emotion has a certain, narrowly defined place in law. It is assigned to the criminal courts. It is confined to those—like witnesses, the accused, the public—without legal training. In this story, there is a finite list of law-related emotions—anger, compassion, mercy, vengeance, hatred—and each emotion has a proper role and a fixed definition. And it is portrayed as crucially important to narrowly delineate that finite list and those proper roles, so that emotion doesn't encroach on the true preserve of law: which is reason.

The essays in this volume tell a far more unruly, complex, and emotional story about the place of emotions in the law. The law, as they illustrate, is imbued with emotion. Not just the obvious emotions like mercy and the desire for vengeance but disgust, romantic love, bitterness, uneasiness, fear, resentment, cowardice, vindictiveness, forgiveness, contempt, remorse, sympathy, hatred, spite, malice, shame, respect, moral fervor, and the passion for justice. Emotion pervades not just the criminal courts, with their heat-of-passion and insanity defenses and their angry or compassionate jurors but the civil courtrooms, the appellate courtrooms, the legislatures. It propels judges and lawyers, as well as jurors, litigants, and the lay public. Indeed, the emotions that pervade law are often so ancient and deeply ingrained that they are largely invisible.

In the criminal courts, emotion seems most visible. Anger, mercy, and the desire for vengeance are close to the surface. Certainly when the death penalty is at issue, the law finds itself speaking of emotion with an unaccustomed explicitness. Judges instruct juries on the role of mercy (acceptable) and the role of sympathy (unacceptable). The role of vengeance in capital cases is not addressed explicitly, though maybe it should be, since the question of vengeance is never far from the surface. Perhaps the most explicit recognition of vengeance in the courtroom comes from victim impact statements, in which relatives of murder victims tell the capital jury about the devastation caused by the crime and, in some jurisdictions, about the sentence they would like to see imposed. Media coverage, more often than not, provides the explicit discussion of vengeance.

In this volume the role of vengeance receives careful attention from Jeffrie Murphy, Danielle Allen, and Robert Solomon. Their wide-ranging discussions of the complex emotional makeup and problematic moral utility of vengeance introduce some of the most important themes of the volume. They illustrate the impossibility of treating this or any emotion as a monolithic, easily definable entity. In addition, they illustrate the need to treat each emotion contextually, a point that is underscored by Martha Minow's discussion of vengeance in the very different context of crimes by the state. I will return to the important themes of the contextuality and complexity of emotions shortly.

The death penalty engages the popular imagination. Austin Sarat's essay examines the ways in which popular culture, both in a film and book like *Dead Man Walking*, and in real-life dramas like the execution of Karla Faye Tucker, treats the remorse of the defendant.[1] As he reminds us, the proper role of remorse and the ability of the law to measure it are pervasive questions that haunt not only high profile death penalty cases but drier provinces, such as the Federal Sentencing Guidelines. Sam Pillsbury's discussion of the Louise Woodward trial illustrates the pull that even a noncapital criminal case can have on the public imagination. His dissection of the opinion in that case shows a judge's understandable confusion about what place emotion—the defendant's, the grieving parents', the public's, the prosecutor's, and his own—ought to play in decisions about indictment, the conduct of the trial, verdict, and sentencing. The confusion is understandable largely because the conversation has been off-limits. It threatens the conventional story about judicial and prosecutorial dispassion and the law's ability to cordon off emotion.

The questions of emotional content, though most obvious in the courtroom, pervade the law at a much earlier point in its development. There is the question, for example, of what should be criminalized. Should the emotions evoked by various acts be relevant to whether those acts are declared unlawful? Martha Nussbaum, taking issue with Bill Miller's thesis in his groundbreaking book on disgust,[2] proclaims that disgust is one emotion that has no redeeming value in the legal arena. She argues that disgust has led societies—ours and others—to treat homosexuals, women, Jews, and other marginalized groups as if they were less than human. Judge Posner takes issue with her conclusion, finding disgust and revulsion legitimate and valuable barometers of societal morality. Social constructionists like Dan Kahan would go further, arguing that law can shape the cognitive content of emotion—for example, leading us to feel disgust for certain genuinely heinous but underpunished acts—such as racial violence.[3] Toni Massaro, in her discussion of shame and disgust, offers a skeptical critique of the social constructionist account. She finds its assumptions about the nature of the emotions themselves oversimplified. She also questions the account's version of what evokes emotions like shame and disgust, and of what actions these emotions lead to once they are evoked.

Once it is decided what ought to be criminalized, there is the question of when emotion should ameliorate or exacerbate a finding of criminal conduct. Criminal codes must deal with the unavoidably emotional questions of which accompanying states of mind render criminal acts most punishable. Should crimes be deemed more reprehensible because they are fueled by racial hatred? Should crimes be deemed less reprehensible because they were done in the heat of passion rather than calmly planned? Judge Posner notes that sometimes the worst crime is the one committed by the defendant who is shockingly devoid of emotion. If he was provoked, he's often viewed as less culpable. Sam Pillsbury's discussion of the verdict in Louise Woodward's case focuses on the sub-rosa psychological and moral distinctions judges make when they decide which motivation for killing a baby is worthy of greater punishment: rage, or fright and confusion mixed with anger. But what provocations and mitigating emotional states should the law recognize? How, for example, do we avoid the slippery slope toward recognizing disgust directed at those different from us as a sufficient provocation?

There are other basic questions in criminal law as well. One is peculiar to criminal law: Why do we punish? The other overlapping question applies in the civil arena as well: Why do people obey the law? The question of why we punish is carefully explored in this volume, as is the related question of what emotions we hope to evoke in those we punish. Robert Solomon explores vengeance as a reason to punish, asking whether vengefulness is an emotion the criminal law should seek to satisfy, and whether it is a rational emotion. Like much of the scholarship in this collection, Solomon's dissection of vengefulness makes it impossible to think of it as a monolithic, acontextual emotion again. Jeffrie Murphy achieves something similar with the retributive emotions, in his essay revisiting (and revising) the thesis of his brilliant book with Jean Hampton.[4] He essentially offers a *diagnosis* of retributivists, asking *why* they favor punishment on such grounds. He focuses, in part, on a refutation of the assertion that retribution is grounded in guilt, and that guilt is an emotion that leads toward moral correctness rather than moral error.

Danielle Allen also does a diagnosis of sorts. She asks not so much why we punish as why we feel such a deep and abiding unease (or as she terms it "dis-ease") about punishing. She argues that the unease stems from an inability to find a satisfying justification for punishing and suggests that the justification lies in a more communitarian notion of punishment's goals. Martha Minow studies another aspect of the community's need to punish—the question of what types of punishment and what emotions engendered by those punishments can heal the wounds caused by such unimaginable state-inflicted harm as terrorism, mass violence, and genocide.[5] How, she asks, can any legal proceeding express the proper level of outrage while respecting the bedrock notion of human dignity?

Toni Massaro and Austin Sarat both explore the question of what emotions we seek, or should seek, to evoke in those we punish. Massaro's essay continues her study of the role of shame in punishing.[6] She describes the tremendously complex nature of shame, and the wide divergence in views about what it constitutes, what causes it, and how it manifests itself. As she emphasizes, shame is an emotion that varies according to who experiences it and in what context. She questions both the possibility and the wisdom of institutionalizing the evocation of shame in offenders. Sarat, like Massaro, is skeptical of the ability of legal institutions to require particular emotional reactions. He wonders how we can measure the sincerity of the required remorse, and whether a showing of remorse is worth requiring if we can't be sure of its sincerity.

In civil law, the emotional content may seem less salient, more . . . civilized. But this very lack of obviousness renders the effect of emotion in the civil context insidious, and all the more important to identify. There are basic questions about law and lawmaking that apply in both the criminal and civil realms. For example, how do legislatures decide what conduct is worthy of legal protection or in need of legal proscription? The role of emotions like disgust is evident in debates about obscenity ordinances, and in the decision whether to extend certain protection to gay men and lesbians. But as Cheshire Calhoun illustrates, it is not only the play of "negative" emotions like disgust and intolerance but also "positive" emotions like romantic love that have consequences for legislation on issues like gay rights. For example, particular socially constructed notions of romantic love have led to proscriptions against gay marriage.

Determining what conduct the law should regulate raises a basic question: Why do people usually obey the law? John Deigh posits that the decision to obey authority depends on the existence of an emotional bond, and explores the nature of that bond. He suggests that obedience to law requires not only fear and vulnerability but some positive emotions as well—perhaps respect, conscience, or commitment to the collective good. Bill Miller suggests less hopefully that implicit in the message of any law—criminal or civil—is the element of fear. A related question is why people invoke the protection of the civil law. That is, why do people sue? Robert Solomon suggests that anger, resentment, and vindictiveness are the motivating forces behind the persistence and even ruinousness of many civil lawsuits. And indeed, the notion of punitive damages suggests the civil recognition of a desire for some measure of vengeance.

Finally, there is the question of the emotional effect the law has on litigants. Does it contribute to their emotional well-being? Could it be reformed to do so? For example, what of those who must use civil law during one of the most emotional times of their lives—a divorce? Divorce court, as Martha Minow reminds us, has a way of exacerbating bitterness rather than channeling it constructively. She asks how law can be used to channel emotions like bitterness or the desire for revenge constructively rather than simply to replicate and exacerbate them.

There is another basic question underlying both criminal and civil law: What motivates judges? To what extent can or should judges factor emotion out of their legal decision making? Even when the law concedes that jurors and litigants are human and recognizes that attorneys are not only human but institutionally directed to be partial, it holds out the last bastion of emotionless reason: the jurist. The judge is expected to be impartial, distant, and detached, and to let passion play no part in his decision making. Is it possible for the judge to make decisions without doing so through the lens of selective empathy and a particular system of values? I would argue that it is not. Rather, there are grave dangers for the judge, the litigant, and the judicial system in general arising from the illusion that judges operate in an emotionless realm that transcends individual emotions and moral choices.[7]

What accounts for the law's insistence on neutral, emotionless judging? More generally, what accounts for the law's devotion to the myth of an emotionless, cognition-driven legal system? The mainstream notion of the rule of law greatly overstates both the demarcation between reason and emotion, and the possibility of keeping reasoning processes free of emotional variables. It has had to maintain this insistence in the face of insights reached in psychology, philosophy, anthropology, and neurobiology concerning the complex interplay between emotion and cognition. These fields generally portray emotion and cognition as acting in concert to shape our perceptions and reactions. But more than that, they assume that it is not only impossible but *undesirable* to factor emotion out of the reasoning process. By this account, emotion in concert with cognition leads to truer perception and, ultimately, to better (more accurate, more moral, more just) decisions.

The reasons for law's devotion to an emotionless cognitive sphere are interesting to contemplate. Here are a few speculations, admittedly overgeneralized. In part, it is an unfortunate by-product of the law's well-known insularity and unwillingness to learn from other disciplines that legal scholars are so far behind in understanding how knowledge is acquired and how and why people act on it. It is also likely that emotion, by its very nature, threatens much of what law hopes to be. To the extent legal systems thrive on categorical rules, emotion in all its messy individuality makes such categories harder to maintain. Rules (for example, rules of punishment) based on tidy assumptions about how people will react to certain penalties may be threatened by more complex evidence about motivations. Law is wary of ambiguity, and likes predictable outcomes. The notion of the rule of law is based, at least in part, on the belief that laws can be applied mechanically, inexorably, without human fallibility.

The essays in this volume move beyond the debate about *whether* emotion belongs in the law, accepting that emotional content is inevitable. They focus on the important questions: How do we determine which emotions deserve the most weight in legal decision making and which emotions belong in which legal contexts? The essays begin from the premise that law needs to incorporate the widely shared insights developed in other fields. The development of law—of its content, its structures, its actors, and the dynamics among them—has been harmed and stunted by the failure to heed the lessons learned in every discipline that has studied emotions. One clear lesson is that the law cannot understand and incorporate emotion theory on its own. Since the law has no choice but to traffic in emotions, it needs to understand and evaluate them. This is a truly interdisciplinary endeavor, and thus this volume brings together many of the most highly influential and, indeed, groundbreaking scholars of emotion theory, in fields that include philosophy, classics, psychology, religion, ethics, law, and social thought.

As Toni Massaro succinctly puts it, the difficulty is in navigating between the dangers of reductionism and paralysis. The need for interdisciplinary discussion is evident. If it wasn't evident before (even in the face of disastrous attempts to craft an insanity defense without regard for psychiatric knowledge), it is becoming increasingly so as the law's flirtation with shaming penalties and institutionalized remorse heats up, and as a capital jurisprudence is built around largely unacknowledged emotions like mercy, compassion, vengefulness, and racial animus. But the discussion needs to proceed very carefully for two reasons. First, it is too easy to oversimplify or even misinterpret insights gleaned from other disciplines. As these essays so well illustrate, emotion theory is a tremendously complex endeavor. It isn't even really a field but, rather, several overlapping fields, generating multiple theories. It sometimes seems like a theoretical smorgasbord, from which each scholar can choose the definitions or concepts most amenable to her particular legal argument. Legal scholars (as well as lawyers, legislators, judges) need to guard against this temptation to pillage other fields without regard for their full complexity and to use the spoils selectively to make legal arguments. Legal choices have consequences that include the loss of property, livelihood, liberty, and even life.

This leads to the second reason to be careful: the danger of paralysis. As we try to avoid the hubris of oversimplifying or rejecting the knowledge of other disciplines, it is also true that law has its own set of purposes, demands, and limitations. Apart from the (considerable) joy of learning itself, the knowledge we gain about emotion is usable in a legal context only if it can be translated in light of law's requisites. For example, what if we conclude that an emotion like shame or remorse is so complex in its origins and workings that it simply can't be pinned down? And what if we conclude that the stimuli that cause shame and the reactions to shame vary so much that we can't generalize beyond each individual? These recognitions would be important correctives to the legal tendency to treat emotions as monolithic, obvious, and self-defining. They would be important pieces of knowledge for those who seek to legislate based on shame. Perhaps, as Toni Massaro argues, they would help lead to the decision that shaming penalties are unworkable. But at some point, the law needs to categorize and simplify for its own purposes. Though we can't definitively pin down the essence of vengefulness or compassion, for example, these emotions will continue to influence sentencing decisions. And the judicial system will continue to sentence. At some point, we need to take what we know, with a large dose of humility, and incorporate it into our decision making processes.

The incorporation must be done with a keen awareness that the role of a particular emotion in, for example, the therapeutic context, will differ from its role in the legal realm. I have written about the need for this awareness in regard to empathy.[8] It is sometimes too easy to speak of a "benign" tool for understanding like empathy, as if it is an unmitigated good, regardless of context. The empathy that serves as an important tool for therapists does not easily translate into a necessarily positive emotional tool for legal actors, such as judges. The goals of judging are not necessarily consonant with the goals of therapy. The judge, unlike the therapist, seeks not just to understand but to pass judgment. In the criminal context this requires sentencing—often followed by imprisonment or even loss of life.

In therapy, it is important both to understand emotions and, as a way toward that understanding, to express them. Is expressing emotion equally important in law, say, in a court of law? It depends on what goal we seek to achieve. Kahan argues that there are several valuable reasons for emotion to be expressed. If a judge feels an emotion, such as racial hatred, he argues, we are better off knowing that he does feel it. It enables us to identify decisions wrongly based on such emotion, and also to take action against the judge if necessary. Moreover, he argues, if the emotion isn't expressed judicially, it will surface elsewhere, perhaps in a less desirable place. Massaro responds that expressions of disgust by a judge may give others implicit license to act upon them—for example, license to wreak physical violence on homosexuals or women. There is a related question of whether a judge or a defendant ought to be expected to express ritualized emotions. For example, does it help enforce societal norms to encourage a judge to express disgust toward those who commit heinous murders, or does it become a hollow ritual? Is it beneficial for defendants or victims to express remorse at their crimes, or does it raise the question Murphy and Sarat both struggle with—how can we evaluate the sincerity of such expressions, and what is their worth without a means of gauging sincerity?

The problem of gauging the sincerity of expressions of remorse exemplifies another difficult hurdle in translating emotional knowledge into law. Can law deal with emotions at all, or only with their physical manifestations? Whereas the subtleties of emotions like fear or shame may be endlessly fascinating to psychologists and philosophers, of what use are they to the law, unless they can be outwardly measured? Miller's discussion of the military codes attempting to outlaw and punish cowardice raises this question. It arises not only because those with cowardice in their hearts don't always act upon it but, conversely, because sometimes those with courage in their hearts may find their bodies unwilling to cooperate. What, asks Miller, ought the law to do in that situation?

In a sense, this is simply the familiar criminal law question about whether the law can ever punish state of mind alone, or state of mind only if it leads to bad acts, or bad acts even without the accompanying state of mind. But it leads directly to the core moral question of whether the law should be directed at the act or the actor. Are we disgusted at the act, or is the person disgusting? Is it ever permissible, as Murphy argues it is, to hate the sinner as well as the sin—at least if the sin betrays the character of the sinner? Both Nussbaum and Allen warn of the dangers of treating the offender as a disgusting being, a being outside society and unlike the rest of us, rather than as a person who has done a disgusting act but is also part of a community. Allen shows the evolution from the concept of punishment as a means of addressing the anger caused in the community by the transgressions of one of its members, toward the use of punishment as a means of purging the community of that anger by purging it of the wrongdoer. Ought wrongdoers to be purged from the community, or quarantined? Is this, for example, an assumption underlying the "three strikes, you're out" laws—that after a certain number of bad deeds, the wrongdoer has shown himself to be irredeemably bad and worthy of quarantine?

Underlying all the questions raised above is the first, intractable problem—the one that could cause any scholar of emotions to lose heart—the problem of how to define emotion. The problem may be intractable but not insuperable. Emotion theorists have never come close to agreeing on a definition of *emotion*; indeed, there seems to be widespread agreement on the impossibility of finding one. Emotions may be active or passive, reducible to physical processes or psychological states, rational or nonrational, voluntary or involuntary. They are variously described as motives, attitudes, character traits, moods, or feelings. The depth of the disagreement on how to define *emotion*, however, has not seemed to inhibit the rich interdisciplinary debates that make up emotion theory. The question, then, is whether this particular discussion—on emotion's role in the law—can proceed despite the lack of definition.

The range of definitions is evident from a comparison of Judge Posner's article with Sam Pillsbury's. Judge Posner, perhaps alone among the contributors to this volume, holds out the possibility of carving out areas in which emotion is unwelcome and does not intrude. (Although his discussion of the emotions of judges betrays a generous definition of the term: he notes with approval that judges bring emotions like wonder, pride, and delight to their solving of judicial problems.) Sam Pillsbury, in his study of the emotions driving the jurisprudence of Justices Oliver Wendell Holmes and John Marshall Harlan, posits a broad definition that includes in the realm of emotion the passion for justice and the commitment to principle. Does it matter whether, for example, we call commitment to principle an emotion or view it as purely cognitive? To what extent do we need to agree on what counts as an emotion in order to have a useful dialogue? And to what extent do definitions that are useful in other fields help with the tasks of law?

There are several answers to these questions. Most important, in my opinion, is to avoid the trap of calling "emotional" that which is different, or that which law wishes to marginalize. It is important to keep the functional, strategic, and political consequences of defining *emotion* in sight. Emotion tends to seem like part of the landscape when it's familiar, and to become more visible when it's unexpected. The law perpetuates the illusion of emotionless lawyering and judging by portraying certain "hard" emotions or emotional stances as objective and inevitable. Even a legal process devoid of such "soft" emotions as compassion or mercy is not emotionless; it is simply driven by other passions. But the passion for predictability, the zeal to prosecute, and mechanisms like distancing, repressing, and isolating one's feelings from one's thought processes are the emotional stances that have always driven mainstream legal thought. As a result, they avoid the stigma of emotionalism. That derogatory term is reserved for the "soft emotions": compassion, caring, mercy. One of the most important functions of these essays is to challenge the notion of a neutral, emotionless baseline and to identify such invisible emotions. When emotions remain invisible, they remain impervious to evaluation or change.

When discussing whether a particular emotion has a place in law, we may also be led into error if we overlook the fact that there are different ways of thinking about emotion, each with its own set of (sometimes unarticulated) assumptions. Massaro, for example, makes this point in her discussion of the role of shame in sentencing. She argues that discussions of the role of shame often rely upon particular yet unidentified theories of emotion. She gives as examples assumptions that law can shape the content of our emotions, which flow from social constructionist accounts of emotion, and assumptions that an emotion suppressed in one venue will appear in another, which flow from Freudian accounts. In short, it may not be necessary to choose a theory of emotion, but it is important to recognize the theoretical premises underlying one's assumptions.

The nature of an emotion may matter very much if the law determines to use emotion to accomplish certain ends. If we are going to use shaming penalties based on assumptions about the nature of shame, what causes shame, and what shame propels people to do, then we need to be clear about what definition we are using and we ought to be willing to evaluate it. What do we need to know about hate in order to decide whether to penalize hate crimes? Judge Posner asserts that hate is a cognition rather than an emotion, and therefore to penalize it is to penalize thought processes. Nussbaum asserts that disgust embodies destructive cognitions that the law should not condone,[9] whereas Kahan calls it a thought-provoking sentiment that can positively influence community norms.

Context is crucial in arguments for the propriety or desirability of a particular emotion. How we define *emotion* may, legitimately, depend on why we need to know, or on the context in which the question arises. Is the desire for vengeance an emotion that belongs in the legal realm? It would be difficult to tell the survivor of a ghastly murder, the mother of a murdered daughter for example, that she has no right to desire vengeance against the killer. What follows from this? It does not necessarily mean that the judge or jury presiding over the killer's trial is entitled to base his verdict or sentence on vengeance. It says little about the role of vengeance in a civil trial against the killer. It doesn't even resolve the question of whether the survivor ought to be permitted to express her desire for vengeance in the criminal or civil case. Each context presents very different considerations, and each argument must consider those differences carefully.

Another difficult definitional issue arises in the translation of emotion theory into the legal realm. Of what use is an emotion to law if it doesn't manifest itself in action? Murphy talks about the "problem of other minds." How can a trier of fact ascertain what emotion an offender feels? Does the law really mean to determine whether a confession is the product of free will, or only whether the objective indicia of consent are present? Is it sensible to require a showing of remorse, given what Judge Posner calls the problem of "forensic resourcefulness?" Is it possible to legislate against cowardice and faintheartedness in battle? Is there such a thing as an unconscious emotion, and if so, asks Miller, what should the law do about unconscious cowardice that manifests itself in legs that just won't cooperate?

When policy is made and consequences are affixed based on understandings of emotions, definition becomes more than a matter of academic interest. There is the problem that law cannot accommodate the endless subtleties and variations that might exist among emotional states, and among those who experience particular emotions. It is error of a sort to assume a blanket definition of any emotion, as these essays so well illustrate. It is also an oversimplification to assume that any emotion will be experienced in the same way by any two people. At what point do these variables render the translation into the legal context impossible? We might conclude that shaming penalties cannot work because the variations among defendants are too great to allow for any predictable outcomes. But we don't have the luxury of deciding not to think about the role of anger and vengeance in sentencing because the emotions persist despite our failure to grapple with them. Can penal theory be fine-tuned to accommodate philosophical and psychological insights? How much categorization and simplification is acceptable in crafting penalties, given the impracticalities of individuation and the law's commitment to equality of treatment? These are difficult questions, but they are not made easier by ignoring the insights of philosophy and psychology.

If we can agree that emotions may be defined differently, and evaluated differently, according to the context, how do we decide whether a particular emotion is appropriate in a given legal context? Is there a hierarchy of emotions? Are some better than others, or even irrevocably wrong in the legal context? Do some emotions lead judges or juries to make bad decisions, or lead them into moral error? Are some emotions debilitating to societal harmony?

Nussbaum makes such an argument for disgust, an emotion she would like banished from the legal lexicon. Kahan defends disgust as an effective means of shaping desirable norms of conduct. Murphy takes issue with the influential argument that resentment is another such "low-order" emotion, and Solomon, similarly, seeks to rehabilitate vengefulness. Judge Posner finds the desire for vengeance both morally neutral and a fact of life. Minow agrees that it cannot be eliminated but worries that it leads to debilitating hatred. Despite these deep disagreements, there is common ground. One of the most important shared insights of the essays in this volume is that evaluating emotions is an inherently normative enterprise. One must not become mired in easy generalizations about "good" emotions like compassion or mercy, or "bad" emotions like anger or the desire for revenge. Having said that the appropriateness of particular emotions is a contextual matter, and that the nature of emotions is complex and variable, there is still room to argue that some emotions are generally more desirable than others. The key proviso is that the arguments need to be supported. As these essays so well illustrate, the discussion of the appropriateness and desirability of various emotions will draw from philosophy, psychology, religion, history, ethics, classics, biography, social thought, popular culture, and a host of other sources. (Indeed, one overriding message of these essays is the fragility of the intersection among the moral, religious, political, and emotional realms.) There are many possible normative measures—the central point is that the normative discussion must take place. No particular emotion is inherently value-laden.

If there are desirable emotions, or at least emotions that are more desirable than others in particular contexts, are emotions educable? The recent literature on emotions in philosophy, psychology, and neurobiology essentially agrees that emotions are not merely instinctive and uncontrollable but also partially cognitive. If emotions have cognitive components, does this mean they are open to evolving cognitive understandings—to new information and experiences? If so, it might be possible to mitigate the limitations of one's own perspectives and to consciously split off some of the factors—say, blind spots, prejudices, and fears—that inappropriately interfere with judgment. These are crucial questions for lawmakers, jurists, and legal scholars.

For example, the shaming penalties Kahan advocates assume that offenders can learn from their feelings of shame. Can individual conduct be shaped in this way? Calhoun demonstrates that restrictive laws against same-sex marriage depend on certain notions of romantic love. Can legislative or societal notions of romantic love evolve? To understand legal decision making, and the evolution of law in general, we need to explore the extent to which the emotions of legal actors are open to new understandings. If emotions are educable, where should the information come from, and what forms can it take? Can emotion shape law? Can law, in turn, shape emotion? And are these even coherent questions, given the infinite variability of emotions, the people who experience them, and the situations in which they arise?

The rich, complex, even anarchic field of emotion theory seems an odd subject for a field like law, which values—or thinks it does—finality, predictability, accuracy, logic, rationality. But emotion pervades law, and always has. It's just that sometimes it's more visible than others. The essays in this volume make it impossible to think of law as a solely cognitive, emotionless zone again. They take the conversation about emotion far beyond easy platitudes about the desirability of compassion, mercy, and love or the dangers of vengeance and resentment. The questions, most of them, remain, but the sources available for addressing them are now far richer.

NOTES

1. The narratives of death (murder and execution) are themes that Sarat has explored extensively. See, e.g., Austin Sarat, Speaking of Death: Narratives of Violence in Capital Trials, 27 L. & Soc'y. Rev. 19 (1993).

2. William Ian Miller, The Anatomy of Disgust (Cambridge: Harvard University Press, 1997).

3. Kahan builds on a substantial body of work on social construction theory. See, e.g., Dan M. Kahan, What Do Alternative Sanctions Mean? 63 U. Chi. L. Rev. 591 (1996); Dan Kahan, Social Influence, Social Meaning and Deterrence, 83 Va. L. Rev. 349 (1997).

4. Jeffrie Murphy and Jean Hampton, Forgiveness and Mercy (Cambridge: Cambridge University Press, 1988).

5. She expands on these themes in her recently released book. See Martha Minow, Between Vengeance and Forgiveness: Facing History after Genocide and Mass Violence (Boston: Beacon Press, 1998).

6. See, e.g., Toni Massaro, The Meanings of Shame: Implications for Legal Reform, 3 J. Psych. Public Policy & Law 645 (1997).

7. Susan Bandes, Empathy, Narrative and Victim Impact Statements, 63 U. Chi. L. Rev. 361, 377–79 (1996).

8. Id. at 390–410.

9. See also Martha Nussbaum, Upheavals of Thought: A Theory of the Emotions (Cambridge: Cambridge University Press, forthcoming), in which Nussbaum continues her brilliant exploration of the cognitions embodied in various emotions and the means we ought to use to evaluate these cognitions.

Part I

Disgust and Shame

Chapter One

"Secret Sewers of Vice"
Disgust, Bodies, and the Law

Martha C. Nussbaum[1]

The Professor of Gynaecology: He began his course of lectures as follows: Gentlemen, woman is an animal that micturates once a day, defecates once a week, menstruates once a month, parturates once a year and copulates whenever she has the opportunity. I thought it a prettily-balanced sentence.

> W. Somerset Maugham, *A Writer's Notebook*

Was there any form of filth or profligacy, particularly in cultural life, without at least one Jew involved in it? If you cut even cautiously into such an abscess, you found, like a maggot in a rotting body, often dazzled by the sudden light—a kike!

> Adolf Hitler, *Mein Kampf*

If a man had been able to say to you when you were young and in love: "An' if tha shits an' if tha pisses, I'm glad, I shouldna want a woman who couldna shit nor piss . . ." surely it would have helped to keep your heart warm.

> D. H. Lawrence to Ottoline Morrell, quoting from
> *Lady Chatterley's Lover*

I. Disgust and Lawmaking

Disgust is a powerful emotion in the lives of most human beings.[2] It shapes our intimacies and provides much of the structure of our daily routine, as we wash our bodies, seek privacy for urination and defecation, cleanse ourselves of offending odors with toothbrush and mouthwash, sniff our armpits when nobody is looking, check in the mirror to make sure that no conspicuous snot is caught in our nose-hairs. In many ways our social relations, too, are structured by the disgusting and our multifarious attempts to ward it off. Ways of dealing with repulsive animal substances such as feces, corpses, and spoiled food are pervasive sources of social custom. And most societies teach the avoidance of certain groups of people as physically disgusting, bearers of a contamination that the healthy element of society must keep at bay.

Disgust also plays a powerful role in the law. It figures, first, as the primary or even the sole justification for making some acts illegal. Thus, sodomy laws have frequently been defended by a simple appeal to the disgust that right-thinking people allegedly feel at the thought of such acts. The judge at Oscar Wilde's trial said that he would prefer not to describe "the sentiments which must rise to the breast of every man of honour who has heard the details of these two terrible trials," but his violent repudiation of the defendants made his disgust amply evident.[3] Lord Devlin famously argued that such social disgust was a strong reason to favor the prohibition of an act, even if it caused no harm to others; he applied his conclusion explicitly to the prohibition of consenting homosexual acts.[4] In his recent work on disgust, legal theorist William Miller, while not supporting Devlin's concrete policy recommendations, gives support to his general line by arguing that the degree of civilization in a society may properly be measured by the barriers it has managed to place between itself and the disgusting.[5] Legal barriers, in such a view, could easily be seen as agents of the civilizing process.

One area of the law in which judgments of the disgusting are unequivocally central is the current law of obscenity: the disgust of an average member of society, applying contemporary community standards, has typically been taken to be a crucial element in the definition of the obscene. The Supreme Court has noted that the etymology of the word "obscene" contains the Latin word for filth, *caenum*, and that two prominent dictionaries include the term "disgusting" in their definition of the term.[6]

The disgust of society also figures in legal arguments about categories of acts that are already considered illegal on other grounds. The disgust of a criminal for a homosexual victim may be seen as a mitigating factor in homicide.[7] The disgust of judge or jury has frequently been regarded as relevant to the assessment of a homicide where potentially aggravating factors are under consideration.

On one view of these matters, the emotion of disgust is highly relevant to law and a valuable part of the legal process. For Devlin, society cannot defend itself without making law in response to its members' responses of disgust, and every society has the right to preserve itself. Every society, therefore, is entitled to translate the disgust-reactions of its members into law. For Miller, a society's hatred of vice and impropriety necessarily involves disgust, and cannot be sustained without disgust. Disgust "marks out moral matters for which we can have no compromise."[8] It should follow that for Miller disgust plays a legitimate role in the criminal law, and perhaps in other areas of law as well. For Dan M. Kahan, discussing Miller's book, disgust ought to be permitted to play a larger role in the criminal law than most legal theorists currently want it to play. Disgust is "brazenly and uncompromisingly judgmental,"[9] indeed "necess[ary] . . . for perceiving and motivating opposition to cruelty."[10]

These are plausible theses, which should not be easily dismissed. Nor should they be dismissed by a blanket condemnation of all appeals to emotion in law, or by the strong and misleading contrast between emotion and reason that we all too frequently hear when legal theorists discuss appeals to sympathy, or indignation, or overwhelming fear.[11] If, as seems plausible, all these emotions involve complex evaluative cognitions,[12] then they cannot be called "irrational" as a class. Instead, we must evaluate the cognitions they embody, as we would for any class of beliefs, asking how reliable they are likely to be given their specific subject matter, their typical process of formation, and so forth. There seem to be no reasons to think that the cognitions involved in emotion are generally and ubiquitously unreliable.[13]

It is not even clear that we can say of any entire emotion-type that it is totally unreliable in the sense that it always gives bad guidance in matters of importance. The questions we are most likely to ask about fear, anger, grief, and sympathy are: do they have the right view of their object or not? Does the emotional person correctly assess the situation and the values contained in it, or not? Are her emotions those of a reasonable person, or not? And these questions will usually be asked well only in the concrete. Anger as a whole is neither reliable nor unreliable, reasonable or unreasonable; it is only the specific anger of a specific person at a specific object that can coherently be deemed unreasonable.

We may sometimes judge, however, that a particular emotion-type is al-

ways suspect or problematic, in need of special scrutiny, given its likely aetiology, its specific cognitive content, and its general role in the economy of
human life. One might argue, for example, that envy is always suspect, in
the sense that it is likely to be connected to social hierarchy and the unwillingness to accept the equal worth of people; or that jealousy is always suspect, given its links to the desire for possession and control. This is the type
of argument I shall be making about disgust. I shall argue that the specific
cognitive content of disgust makes it always of dubious reliability in social
life, but especially in the life of the law. Because disgust embodies a shrink-
ing from contamination that is associated with the human desire to be non-
animal, it is more than likely to be hooked up with various forms of shady
social practice, in which the discomfort people feel over the fact of having
an animal body is projected outwards onto vulnerable people and groups.
These reactions are irrational, in the normative sense, both because they
embody an aspiration to be a kind of being that one is not, and because, in
the process of pursuing that aspiration, they target others for gross harms.

Where law is concerned, it is especially important that a pluralistic democratic society protect itself against such projection-reactions, which
have been at the root of gross evils throughout history, prominently including misogyny, antisemitism, and loathing of homosexuals. Thus while
the law may rightly admit the relevance of indignation, as a moral response
appropriate to good citizens and based upon reasons that can be publicly
shared, it will do well to cast disgust onto the garbage heap where it would
like to cast so many of us.

In specific terms, I shall argue that the disgust of a defendant for his alleged victim is never relevant evidence in a criminal trial; that disgust is an
utter red herring in the law of pornography, occluding the salient issues of
harm and even colluding in the perpetuation of harms; disgust is never a
good reason to make a practice (for example sodomy) illegal; that even
where one homicide seems worse than another because it is unusually disgusting, this disgust-reaction should itself be distrusted, as a device we employ to deny our own capacities for evil.

II. The Cognitive Content of Disgust

Disgust appears to be an especially visceral emotion. It involves strong bodily reactions to stimuli that often have marked bodily characteristics. Its
classic expression is vomiting; its classic stimulants are vile odors and other

objects whose very appearance seems loathsome.[14] Nonetheless, important research by Paul Rozin[15] has made it evident that disgust has a complex cognitive content, which focuses on the idea of incorporation of a contaminant. His core definition of disgust is "[r]evulsion at the prospect of (oral) incorporation of an offensive object. The offensive objects are contaminants; that is, if they even briefly contact an acceptable food, they tend to render that food unacceptable."

Rozin does not dispute that disgust may well have an underlying evolutionary basis; but he shows that it is distinct from both *distaste*, a negative reaction motivated by sensory factors, and (a sense of) *danger*, a rejection motivated by anticipated harmful consequences. Disgust is not simple distaste, because the very same smell elicits different disgust-reactions depending on the subject's conception of the object. Subjects sniff decay odor from two different vials, both of which in reality contain the same substance; they are told that one vial contains feces and the other contains cheese. (The real smells are confusable.) Those who think that they are sniffing cheese usually like the smell; those who think they are sniffing feces find it repellant and unpleasant. "It is the subject's conception of the object, rather than the sensory properties of the object, that primarily determines the hedonic value."[16] In general, disgust is motivated primarily by ideational factors: the nature or origin of the item and its social history (e.g. who touched it). Even if subjects are convinced that ground dried cockroach tastes like sugar, they still refuse to eat it, or say it tastes revolting if they do.

Nor is disgust the same as (perceived) danger. Dangerous items (e.g. poisonous mushrooms) are tolerated in the environment, so long as they will not be ingested; disgusting items are not so tolerated. When danger is removed, the dangerous item will be ingested: detoxified poisonous mushrooms are acceptable. But disgusting items remain disgusting even when all danger is removed. People refuse to eat sterilized cockroaches; many object even to swallowing a cockroach inside an indigestible plastic capsule that would emerge undigested in the subjects' feces.

Disgust concerns the borders of the body: it focuses on the prospect that a problematic substance may be incorporated into the self. For many items and many people, the mouth is an especially charged border. The disgusting has to be seen as alien: one's own bodily products are not viewed as disgusting so long as they are inside one's own body, although they become disgusting after they leave it. Most people are disgusted by drinking from a glass into which they themselves have spit, although they are not sensitive to saliva in their own mouths. The ideational content of disgust is that the self will become base or contaminated by ingestion of the substance that is viewed as offensive. Several experiments done by Rozin and colleagues indicate that the idea involved is that "you are what you eat": if you ingest what is base, this debases you.

The objects of disgust range widely, but Rozin has confirmed experimentally that "all disgust objects are animals or animal products," or objects that have had contact with animals or animal products—a major source being contact with "people who are disliked or viewed as unsavory." It is difficult to explain why plant products (apart from decayed and moldy specimens) are not disgusting,[17] but research suggests that the motivating ideas have to do with our interest in policing the boundary between ourselves and non-human animals, or our own animality. Hence tears are the one human bodily secretion that is not found disgusting, presumably because they are thought to be uniquely human, and hence do not remind us of what we have in common with animals.[18] Feces, snot, semen, and other animal bodily secretions, by contrast, are found contaminating: we do not want to ingest them, and we view as contaminated those who have regular contact with them. (Thus "untouchables," in the Indian caste system, were those whose daily function was to clean latrines; oral or anal reception of semen, in many cultures, is held to be a contamination and a mark of low or base status.) Insofar as we eat meat without finding it disgusting, we disguise its animal origin, cutting off skin and head, cutting the meat into small pieces.[19]

Rozin tentatively concludes that the core idea in disgust is a belief that if we take in the animalness of animal secretions we will ourselves be reduced to the status of animals. We can extend this thought by adding, along lines suggested by Rozin's research, that we also have disgust-reactions to the spoiled or decaying, which, on this picture, would make us mortal and decaying if ingested. Disgust thus wards off both animality in general and the mortality that is so prominent in our loathing of our animality. Indeed, we need to add this restriction in order to explain why some aspects of our animality—for example, strength, agility—are not found disgusting. The products that are, are the ones that we connect with our vulnerability to decay and become waste products ourselves. Thus in all cultures an essential mark of human dignity is the ability to wash and to dispose of wastes. (Rozin points to analyses of conditions in prisons and concentration camps that show that people who are forbidden to clean themselves or use the toilet are soon perceived as subhuman by others, thus as easier to torture or kill.[20] They have become animals.)

A prominent feature of disgust is the idea of "psychological contamination." The basic idea is that past contact between an innocuous substance and a disgust substance causes rejection of the acceptable substance. This contamination is mediated by what Rozin, plausibly enough, calls laws of "sympathetic magic." One such law is the law of *contagion*: things that have been in contact continue ever afterwards to act on one another.[21] Thus, after a dead cockroach is dropped into a glass of juice, people refuse to drink that type of juice afterwards. A second is "similarity": if two things are alike, action taken on one (e.g. contaminating it) is taken to have affected the other. Thus, a piece of chocolate fudge made into a dog-feces shape is rejected, even though subjects know its real origin; subjects also refuse to eat soup served in a (sterile) bedpan, or to eat soup stirred with a (sterile) flyswatter.

Disgust appears not to be present in infants during the first three years of life. It is taught by parents and society. This does not show that it does not have an evolutionary origin; many traits based on innate equipment take time to mature. But it does show that with disgust, as with language, social teaching plays a large role in shaping the form that the innate equipment takes. Usually this teaching begins during toilet training; ideas of indirect and psychological contamination are usually not firm until much later. Both parental and social teaching are involved in these developments. (The disgust levels of children correlate strongly with those of their parents,[22] and disgust objects vary considerably across cultures.)

Disgust, as Rozin says, is an especially powerful vehicle of social teaching. Through teaching regarding disgust and its objects, societies potently convey attitudes toward animality, mortality, and related aspects of gender and sexuality. Although the cognitive content and aetiology of disgust suggests that in all societies there are likely to be certain primary objects of disgust—feces and other bodily fluids—societies have considerable latitude in how they extend disgust reactions to other objects, which objects they deem to be relevantly similar to the primary objects. Thus, although it seems right in a sense to say that there are some "natural" objects of disgust, in the sense that some broadly shared and deeply rooted forms of human thinking are involved in the experience of disgust toward primary objects, many objects become objects of disgust as a result of highly variable forms of social teaching and tradition. In all societies, however, disgust expresses a refusal to ingest and thus be contaminated by a potent reminder of one's own mortality and animality.

III. Disgust and Indignation

Disgust is therefore distinct not only from fear of danger but also from anger and indignation. The core idea of disgust is that of contamination to the self; the emotion expresses a rejection of a possible contaminant. The core objects of disgust are reminders of mortality and animality, seen as contaminations to the human. Indignation, by contrast, centrally involves the idea of a wrong or a harm. Philosophical definitions of anger standardly involve the idea of a wrong done—whether to the person angered or to someone or something to whom that person ascribes importance. Thus, the standard Stoic definitions are "desire to avenge a wrong," "desire to punish one by whom one believes oneself to have been wronged," and "desire for retaliation against someone by whom one believes oneself to have been wronged beyond what is appropriate."[23] Notice that the idea of a (believed) wrong is so important that the last Stoic definition includes it twice over, by adding "beyond what is appropriate" to the word "wronged." Most subsequent definitions of anger and indignation in the Western philosophical tradition follow these leads,[24] and psychology has taken a similar line.[25]

It has been frequently remarked that indignation rests on reasons that can be publicly articulated and publicly shaped. Thus Aristotle's *Rhetoric* gives the aspiring orator elaborate recipes for provoking indignation in an audience, by presenting reasons they can share with regard to a putative wrong. He also gives the orator recipes for taking indignation away, by convincing the audience that they had not in fact been wronged in the way they thought. The reasons underlying a person's indignation can be false or groundless; but if they stand up to scrutiny, we can expect our friends and fellow citizens to share them. In that way, as Adam Smith remarked, indignation is very different from romantic love:

> If our friend has been injured, we readily sympathize with his resentment, and grow angry with the very person with whom he is angry. . . . But if he is in love, though we may think his passion just as reasonable as any of the kind, yet we never think ourselves bound to conceive a passion of the same kind, and for the same person for whom he has conceived it.[26]

This is not to say that many reasons for indignation are not bad reasons. Most of the philosophers who write about this emotion note that it is a function of the intensity of our evaluative investment in "external goods" such as money, honor, and possessions. People often overinvest in these externals, and to that extent their indignation at damages to them may be an unreliable public reason. But the emotion itself, in its nature, is well suited to ground public action in a society that aims to base its judgments on the public exchange of reasons.

Disgust is very different. Although some disgust-reactions may have an evolutionary basis and thus may be broadly shared across societies, and although the more mediated types of disgust may be broadly shared within a society, that does not mean that disgust provides the disgusted person with a set of reasons that can be used for purposes of public persuasion. You can teach a young child to feel disgust at a substance—by strong parental reactions, and by other forms of psychological influence. But imagine trying to convince someone who is not disgusted by a bat that bats are disgusting. There are no publicly articulable reasons to be given that would make the dialogue a real piece of persuasion. All you could do would be to depict at some length the alleged properties of bats, trying to bring out some connection, some echo with what the interlocutor already finds disgusting: the wet greedy mouth, the rodentlike body. But if the person didn't find those things disgusting in a visceral way, that's that.

Again, imagine trying to convince someone who didn't find gay men disgusting that they are disgusting. What do you do? As the campaign in favor of Amendment 2 in Colorado showed, you can do two things. On the one hand, you can try shifting from the ground of disgust to the ground of more reason-based sentiments such as fear (they will take your children away from you) or indignation (they are being given "special rights"). On the other hand, if you remain on the ground of disgust, you will have to focus on alleged properties of gay men that inspire disgust: they allegedly eat feces and drink raw blood.[27] But such appeals to revulsion are not public reasons on which differential treatment under law can reasonably be based.[28]

Disgust is problematic in a way that indignation is not, because it concerns contamination rather than damage; because it is usually based on magical thinking rather than on real danger;[29] and because its root cause is our ambivalent attitude to what we are, namely mortal animals. It may well be that all known societies police the borders of human animality with this strong emotion; it may even be that in our evolutionary history such policing proved valuable, by bounding off a group against its neighbors and promoting clannish solidarity. Perhaps even today societies need this policing in order to flourish, because people cannot endure the daily confrontation with their own decaying bodies. But it cannot be denied that the policing itself works in ways that cannot stand the scrutiny of public reason. There is something wrong with disgust as a basis for law in principle, not just in practice.

The boundary between disgust and indignation is sometimes obscured by the fact that disgust can come packaged in a moralized form. The judge at Wilde's trial represents himself as expressing a moral sentiment about the badness of sodomy, as we shall later see; to that extent he took himself to be offering a type of public reason. And there are examples of disgust that lie even closer to indignation. Because I am so critical of disgust in this paper, for the sake of fairness let me illustrate this point with an example of disgust that deeply moves me, and with which I identify, namely the famous "cry of disgust" in the third movement of Mahler's Second Symphony. Words cannot fully capture this musical experience, but, to cite Mahler's own program, the idea is that of looking at "the bustle of existence," the shallowness and herdlike selfishness of society, until it "becomes horrible to you, like the swaying of dancing figures in a brightly-lit ballroom, into which you look from the dark night outside. . . . Life strikes you as mean-ingless, a frightful ghost, from which you perhaps start away with a cry of disgust."[30] This disgust, we might think, is a valuable moral response to the deadness of social interactions, very close to an emotion of indignation at the wrongs done to people by hypocrisy, stifling ossified customs, and the absence of genuine compassion. Mahler's response to it, in the next move-ment, is to focus on pure compassion for human suffering, embodied in a text from folk poetry and music that alludes centrally to Bach.[31] Doesn't this mean that there is a type of disgust that offers some very good public reasons to criticize some social forms and institutions?

I believe not. However close the "cry of disgust" lies to indignation, its content is anti-social. Its content is, "I repudiate this ugly world as not a part of me. I vomit at those stultifying institutions, and I refuse to let them become a part of my being." Indignation has a constructive function: it says, "these people have been wronged, and they should not have been wronged." In itself, it provides incentives to right the wrong; indeed it is typically defined as involving a desire to right the wrong. By contrast, the artist who runs away from the world in disgust is at that moment not a po-litical being at all, but a romantic anti-social being. Thus Mahler's turning to compassion in the ensuing movement does not grow directly out of his disgust; in fact, it requires him to overcome disgust, as he dramatizes by depicting the compassionate sentiments as embodied in the mind of a young child, who simply lacks that emotion. "O small red rose, humanity lies in the greatest need," begins the lyric: and the figure of the delicate flower is its own antidote to the disgust that has preceded. We are now viewing humanity as delicate, vulnerable, flowerlike: we have overcome the momentary temptation to vomit at its imperfections. Thus I would argue, with Mahler, that even the moralized form of disgust is an emotion that must be surmounted on the way to a genuine and constructive social sympathy.

IV. Disgust, Exclusion, Civilization

If disgust is problematic in principle, we have all the more reason to regard it with suspicion when we observe that it has throughout history been used as a powerful weapon in social efforts to exclude certain groups and persons. So powerful is the desire to cordon ourselves off from our animality that we often don't stop at feces, cockroaches, and slimy animals. We need a group of humans to bound ourselves against, who will come to exemplify the boundary line between the truly human and the basely animal. If those quasi animals stand between us and our own animality, then we are one step further away from being animal and mortal ourselves. Thus throughout history, certain disgust properties—sliminess, bad smell, stickiness, decay, foulness—have repeatedly and monotonously been associated with, indeed projected onto, groups by reference to whom privileged groups seek to define their superior human status. Jews, women, homosexuals, untouchables, lower-class people—all these are imagined as tainted by the dirt of the body. The stock image of the Jew, in antisemitic propaganda, was that of a being disgustingly soft and porous, receptive of fluid and sticky, womanlike in its oozy sliminess, a foul parasite inside the clean body of the German male self.[32] When Jews were depicted in fairy tales for children, they were standardly represented as disgusting animals who had these same properties.[33] Thus for Hitler (and not only for him), the Jew is a maggot in a festering abscess, hidden away inside the apparently clean and healthy body of the nation.

Notice that in such cases disgust is socially engineered rather than rooted in broadly shared human responses; it is summoned up as a way of putting some group down, distancing it from the dominant group, causing it to occupy a status between the fully human and the merely animal. It is not because in some intrinsic way Jews were actually or "originally" found disgusting that they came to be associated with stereotypes of the disgusting. The causality is more the other way round: it is because there was a need to associate Jews (or at any rate *some* group, and for various reasons Jews came readily to mind) with stereotypes of the animal, thus distancing them from the dominant group, that they were represented and talked about in such a way that they came to be found disgusting, and it was actually believed that their bodies were in crucial ways unlike the bodies of "normal people."[34]

Similar disgust properties are traditionally associated with women, as receivers of semen and as closely linked, through birth, with the mortality of the body.[35] Otto Weininger made this idea explicit: the Jew is a woman. (Jewish women, accordingly, were doubly disgusting, hyper-animal beings who exercise a fascinating allure but who must be warded off.)[36] And women in more or less all societies have been vehicles for the expression of male loathing of the physical and the potentially decaying. Taboos surrounding sex, birth, menstruation—all these express the desire to ward off something that is too physical, that partakes too much of the secretions of the body. William Miller describes these male attitudes to women as inevitable aspects of male sexuality, although he also views them as connected with political discrimination against women.[37] Because the woman received the man's semen, she "is what she eats" (whether in the sense of oral or vaginal incorporation); she becomes the sticky mortal part of him from which he needs to distance himself.[38] Consider the professor of gynecology, quoted by Maugham in my epigraph: for him woman is emblematic of all the bodily functions; she is, in effect, the male's body, and her receptive sexual eagerness is the culmination of her many disgusting traits.

Consider, finally, the central locus of disgust in today's United States, male loathing of the male homosexual. Female homosexuals may be objects of fear, or moral indignation, or generalized anxiety, but they are less often objects of disgust. Similarly, heterosexual females may feel negative emotions toward the male homosexual—fear, moral indignation, anxiety—but again, they rarely feel emotions of disgust. What inspires disgust is typically the male thought of the male homosexual, imagined as anally penetrable. The idea of semen and feces mixing together inside the body of a male is one of the most disgusting ideas imaginable—to males, for whom the idea of non-penetrability is a sacred boundary against stickiness, ooze, and death. The presence of a homosexual male in the neighborhood inspires the thought that one might oneself lose one's clean safeness, one might become the receptacle for those animal products. Thus disgust is ultimately disgust at one's own imagined penetrability and ooziness, and this is why the male homosexual is both regarded with disgust and viewed with fear as a predator who might make everyone else disgusting. The very look of such a male is itself contaminating—as we see in the extraordinary debates about showers in the military. The gaze of a homosexual male is seen as contaminating because it says, "You can be penetrated." And this means that you can be made of feces and semen and blood, not clean plastic flesh.[39] (And this means: you will soon be dead.)

Both misogynistic and homophobic disgust have deep roots in (mostly male) ambivalence about bodily products and their connection with vulnerability and death. These reactions still involve learning, but they are likely to be broadly shared across cultures in a way that disgust at Jews is not. We don't have the sense in these cases, as we do in the case of antisemitic disgust, that the actual physical properties of the group were more or less totally irrelevant to their choice as disgust object: a broadly shared anxiety about bodily fluids finds expression in the targeting of those who receive those fluids. On the other hand, disgust in these cases is surely compounded by the element of deliberate construction that characterizes antisemitic disgust. The interest in having a subordinate group whose quasi-animal status distances the dominant group further from its own animality leads, here too, to a constructing of the woman, or the gay man, as disgusting by the imputation of further properties found disgusting. Bad smell, sliminess, eating feces—these are projected onto the group in ways that serve a political goal.

William Miller, following Freudian psychoanalyst Norbert Elias, argues that the more things a society recognizes as disgusting, the more advanced it is in civilization.[40] He holds this thesis even though he grants Rozin his distinction between disgust and genuine danger, and even though he grants everything I have just said about the connection between disgust and the hatred of Jews, women, homosexuals, and other groups who become emblematic of the animal. Nor does he confine his claim to cases of moralized disgust like my Mahler example; it is at least arguable that we might measure social progress by the degree to which people learn to be disgusted by racism and other forms of social injustice. But Miller's focus is simply on the bodily. His claim is that the more we focus on cleanliness and the more intolerant we become of slime, filth, and our own bodily products, the more civilized we are.

This claim seems utterly unconvincing. It seems plausible enough that as society advances it will identify more things as physically dangerous, and so protect itself better against germs and bacteria. But that is not Miller's claim. His claim is that the magical thinking characteristic of disgust is itself a sign of social progress.

If any such sweeping thesis can be entertained, surely the more plausible thesis is that the moral progress of society can be measured by the degree to which it *separates* disgust from danger and indignation, basing laws and social rules on substantive harm, rather than on the symbolic relationship an object bears to anxieties about animality and mortality. Thus the Indian caste system was less civilized than the behavior of Mahatma Gandhi, who cleaned latrines in order to indicate that we share a human dignity that is not polluted by these menial functions.[41] Similarly, the behavior of D. H. Lawrence's character Mellors to Lady Chatterley is much more civilized than the behavior of all the upper-class men around her. They evince disgust at her body and its secretions; Mellors tells her that he would never like a woman who did not shit and piss. Lawrence remarks to Ottoline Morrell that such attitudes help to "keep [the] heart warm": they help constitute the relationship between male and female as deeply reciprocal and civilized, rather than based on self-loathing and consequent denigration of the female.

We might, with Walt Whitman, go still further: the really civilized nation must make a strenuous effort to counter the power of disgust, as a barrier to the full equality and mutual respect of all citizens. This will require a re-creation of our entire relationship to the bodily. Disgust at the body and its products has collaborated with the maintenance of injurious social hierarchies. The health of democracy therefore depends on criticizing and undoing that social formation. The job of the poet of democracy therefore becomes that of singing "the body electric," establishing that the locus of common human need and aspiration is fundamentally acceptable and pleasing—still more, that it is the soul, the locus of personal uniqueness and personal dignity. Slave's body, woman's body, man's body, all are equal in dignity and beauty:

> The male is not less the soul nor more, he too is in his place. . . . The man's body is sacred and the woman's body is sacred. No matter who it is, it is sacred—is it the meanest one in the laborer's gang? . . . Each belongs here or anywhere just as much as the well-off, just as much as you, Each has his or her place in the procession.

Whitman sees that the realization of this idea requires an elaborate undoing of disgust at the parts of bodies that we typically find problematic: hence the remarkable long conclusion of the poem, in which he enumerates the parts of the body from top to bottom, outside to in, depicting them all as parts of the soul, all as clean and beautiful, to be encountered with "the curious sympathy one feels when feeling with the hand the naked meat of the body." Curious sympathy takes the place of disgust, and the traversal of the body triumphantly ends:

> O I say these are not the parts and poems of the body only, but of the soul,
> O I say now these are the soul![42]

Whitman makes it clear that this recuperation of the body is closely linked to women's political equality. Because misogyny has typically seen the female as the site of the disgusting, a decontamination of the body, especially in its sexual aspects, is an essential part of undoing sex-based inequality (and the closely related inequality of the homosexual male). Responses to Whitman's poetry on its publication show us the depth of the problem. In a fashion typical of the American puritanism of the time, reviewers could not describe the poetry's focus on the sexual without describing it as disgusting. Thus the defenders against the charge of filth proceeded by denying the poems' sexual content: "I extract no poison from these leaves," wrote one Fanny Fern, contrasting Whitman's poems with popular romances in which "the asp of sensuality lies coiled amid rhetorical flowers." Edward Everett Hale, praising the book's "freshness and simplicity," insisted, "There is not a word in it meant to attract readers by its grossness."[43] What is striking about these reviews is their total lack of any way to talk about sexual longing other than in the language of disgust.

Whitman's response, throughout his career, was to represent the receptive and "female" aspects of sexuality as joyful and beautiful, indicating at the same time that in present-day America this joy can be realized only in fantasy. Thus in section 28 of *Song of Myself* he offers what he calls a "parable." By placing it immediately after an account of a slave's body, he invites us to ponder its connection to the theme of political equality:

> Twenty-eight young men bathe by the shore,
> Twenty-eight young men and all so friendly;
> Twenty-eight years of womanly life and all so lonesome.
> She owns the fine house by the rise of the bank,
> She hides handsome and richly drest aft the blinds of the window.
> Which of the young men does she like the best?
> Ah the homeliest of them is beautiful to her.
> Where are you off to, lady? for I see you,
> You splash in the water there, yet stay stock still in your room.
> Dancing and laughing along the beach came the twenty-ninth
>   bather,
> The rest did not see her, but she saw them and loved them.
> The beards of the young men glisten'd with wet, it ran from

> their long hair,
> Little streams pass'd all over their bodies.
> An unseen hand also pass'd over their bodies,
> It descended tremblingly from their temples and ribs.
> The young men float on their backs, their white bellies bulge
>   to the sun,
> They do not ask who seizes fast to them,
> They do not know who puffs and declines with pendant and
>   bending arch,
> They do not think whom they souse with spray.   (SM 11)

These lines depict female sexual longing, and the exclusion of the female, by morality and custom, from full sexual fulfillment, and from public recognition as a sexual being. Their placement invites us to see the
woman as a figure for the excluded black man, who must also hide his desire from the white world, who also runs the risk of being seen as a
metaphor for the feared intrusion of the sexual. But there is another excluded party who also hides behind the curtains. In the depiction of the
woman's imagined sexual act, linked, as it is, to other oral-receptive imagery in other poems about the allure of the male body, Whitman also
refers to the exclusion of the male homosexual, whose desire for the bodies
of young men must be concealed even more than must female desire. The
easy joy of these young men depends on their not knowing who is watch-
ing them with sexual longing; and this is true of the situation of the homosexual male in society, at least as much as it is of the black man gazing erotically at the white woman, or the female gazing erotically at the male. As he
says in *Calamus*: "Here I shade and hide my thoughts, I myself do not expose them, / And yet they expose me." The woman, then, is also the poet,
caressing in fancy bodies that in real life shun his gaze.

The woman's gaze, like the gaze of the poet's imagination in the earlier
section, is tenderly erotic, caressing the bodies in ways that expose their
naked vulnerability, their soft bellies turned upward to the sun. And she caresses something more at the same time. The number twenty-eight signifies the days of the lunar month and also of the female menstrual cycle. The
female body, in whose rhythms Whitman sees the rhythms of nature itself,
is immersed in finitude and temporality in a manner from which the male
body and mind at times recoils. (Havelock Ellis, writing eloquently about
this passage, cites the elder Pliny's remark that "nothing in nature is more
monstrous and disgusting than a woman's menstrual fluid.") In caressing
the twenty-eight men, the woman caresses her own temporality and mor-

tality, and at the same time sees it in them, approaches and makes love to it in them, rather than turning from it and them in disgust.

Whitman suggests that the willingness to be seen by desire entails a willingness to agree to one's own mortality and temporality, to be part of the self-renewing and onward flowing currents of nature. It is because it touches us in our mortality that sex is deep and a source of great beauty. In the final poem of *Leaves*, he imagines embracing a male comrade, and says, "Decease called me forth." The deep flaw in Whitman's America, then, the flaw that for him lies at the heart of hatreds and exclusions, is disgust at one's own softness and mortality, of the belly exposed to the sun; the gaze of desire touches that softness, and must for that reason be repudiated as a source of contamination. Over against this flawed America Whitman sets the America of the poet's imagination, healed of disgust's self-avoidance, therefore truly able to pursue liberty and equality.

Whitman's America is an ideal fiction. No real society has triumphed over disgust in the way depicted here. But it is plausible to take this vision as a regulative ideal when we ask what role disgust should play in our political institutions.[44] With Whitman, I have argued that there are reasons both general and specific for such a critical attitude to disgust. Let us now turn to specific legal issues to see whether we can uncover there the signs of the problems we have found, and to see whether our critical attitude will offer useful legal guidance.

V. Disgust and the Offender:
The "Homosexual Provocation" Defense

Should a criminal's reaction of disgust ever help his cause, when he has committed a violent crime? The defense of "reasonable provocation" appeals to the emotion of the offender in order to argue for a reduction in level of homicide from murder to voluntary manslaughter.[45] Usually, however, the emotional state invoked is anger. To win a reduction, the defendant must show that he acted "in the heat of passion" after a provocation by the victim of the crime, that the provocation was "adequate," and that the emotion he exhibited was that of a "reasonable man." The sheer intensity of the defendant's emotional excitation will not suffice to mitigate crime; such a policy would reward people for "evil passions."[46] A person of "a cruel, vindictive, and aggressive disposition, will seize upon the slightest provocation to satisfy his uncontrolled passions by forming a design to kill."[47] For this reason, evidence of the defendant's emotional state is standardly not admitted into evidence unless the provocation meets a standard legal definition of reasonableness. As one judge remarked, "Suppose then we admit testimony that the defendant is quick-tempered, violent and revengeful; what then? Are these an excuse for, or do they even mitigate crime? Certainly not, for they result from a . . . neglect of self-culture that is inexcusable."[48] The account of what would provoke a "reasonable man" to violence has shifted over time, but it always involves some serious aggression and harm done to the defendant by the victim: bodily assault, adultery with the person's wife, and domestic abuse are three salient examples. This is in keeping with the fact that the emotional focus of the law is on outrage, an emotion that responds to damage or harm. The idea behind the defense is that if the reasons for being angry are good enough, and such as to command broad public agreement, then a reduction in level of crime is warranted. What counted as an adequate provocation used to be defined as a matter of law. More recently, jurors have been given some latitude to judge the offense for themselves; but courts still sometimes define certain types of provocation as insufficient as a matter of law, refusing to let the jury hear this emotional evidence.[49]

Does a person's disgust at the mere presence of a homosexual fulfill the legal criteria for a provocation defense? One would think not, if my reasoning is correct. Just by being in the world as a homosexual, the homosexual has not committed an aggressive or harmful act against the offended person. If a person's psychology is such that the mere physical proximity of such a homosexual person feels like an assault, the solution of a "reasonable" such person (if such there can be!) would be to get out of the area, not to kill the victims. Violence is no more defensible than it would be if someone shot someone because he didn't like the person's face, or smell, or skin color.

Stephen Carr, a drifter, lurking in the woods near the Appalachian Trail, saw two lesbian women making love in their campsite. He shot them, killing one of them. At trial he argued for mitigation to manslaughter on grounds of reasonable provocation, arguing that his disgust at the sight of their lesbian lovemaking provoked his response. He sought to introduce psychiatric evidence to explain, on the basis of his childhood history, this unusually strong disgust reaction. The judge refused to admit such evidence, and rightly: "[The law] does not recognize homosexual activity between two persons as legal provocation sufficient to reduce an unlawful killing . . . from murder to voluntary manslaughter. . . . A reasonable person would simply have discontinued his observation and left the scene; he would not kill the lovers."[50] Carr's disgust was inadmissible as a matter of law, because it did not fulfill the legal criteria, which require harmful and aggressive action.[51]

Carr's case is unusually clear, because the women did nothing at all in relation to Carr, and indeed were not aware of his presence.[52] More legally problematic has been a group of cases in which defendants seek mitigation on grounds of an alleged homosexual advance committed by the victim, which allegedly occasioned a disgust that led to the ensuing violence. Although judges have sometimes refused to admit evidence of such alleged provocation, quite a few such defendants have been able to present this defense and have gotten a reduction to voluntary manslaughter or a very light sentence for murder.[53] Does such an advance ever justify a violent reaction?

An initial problem with such defenses is that the facts are usually very difficult to establish. There may be many witnesses to a physical assault and to a history of domestic battery. The homosexual advances that such defendants allege typically occur without witnesses, and there may be more than a shadow of a suspicion that the defendant has used the victim's sexual orientation as a convenient occasion to allege an advance in order to seek mitigation. But let us stipulate that the facts are all true as the defendants narrate them, considering only non-coercive and non-threatening forms of sexual approach. Does disgust at an attempted homosexual seduction provide a legally adequate basis for mitigation?

Jerry Volk and his friend John Hamilton arrived in Minneapolis broke, with no place to stay.[54] They planned to pose as gay prostitutes, pick up a homosexual man, and rob him. They picked up Traetow. Some hours later Traetow was found shot dead in his own apartment; his hands and legs had been taped. Volk's thumbprint was on a broken vodka bottle on the floor. Volk admitted being present at the scene, and at least being an accomplice in the homicide (although there remained a disagreement between Volk and Hamilton as to which of them actually shot Traetow). His story was that when Traetow made a homosexual advance to him, he was "revolted" and provoked to homicide. Hamilton also described Volk as "pretty disgusted." On appeal, Volk claimed that the trial court improperly refused to instruct the jury on a heat of passion manslaughter defense. The court disagreed. "Assuming for argument the truth of these circumstances, there was no provocation sufficient to elicit a heat of passion response. A person of ordinary self-control under like circumstances would simply have left the scene." In other words, seduction is not assault or gross harm, so long as there is neither intimidation nor duress. If a sexual advance is found disgusting, just leave, don't kill the seducer.

The law of voluntary manslaughter is rational and consistent. It offers perfectly clear reasons why some emotional reactions are relevant to mitigation, while others are not. Indignation is relevant under certain circumstances, where it is a reasonable response to an adequate provocation. Disgust is totally irrelevant, because feeling contaminated or "grossed out" by someone is never a sufficient reason to conduct oneself violently against that person. On my account of the two emotions, this is as it should be: society has wisely recognized that people's disgust is totally irrelevant to the justification of violence. We see the wisdom of this judgment, when we think of disgust directed against Jews, or women, or blacks, or the mentally or physically handicapped. In none of these cases would we even briefly entertain the thought of a "heat of passion" defense for someone who happens to find members of that group and their romantic advances disgusting. In other times and places, this would not have been so. Indeed, we can all too easily imagine the loathsomeness of a Jew's advances being used in exactly the way Volk used the alleged advance by Traetow. The fact that, as a society, we are conflicted about the disgust issue as applied to homosexuals shows us that this group is currently a focus of our desire to cordon ourselves off from the viscous, the all-too-animal. That, I would argue, is an even stronger reason for us to be skeptical of those emotional responses, and to refuse as a matter of law to admit them into evidence.

VI. Disgust and the "Average Man": Obscenity

Should disgust ever be a central factor in rendering a practice illegal? We can begin our consideration of this question with the law of obscenity, which makes some of the salient issues especially clear. Legal accounts of the obscene standardly refer to the disgusting properties of the work in question, as they relate to the sensibilities of a hypothetical "average man." The legal standard set by *Miller v. California*[55] in 1972 holds that a work may be subject to state regulation "where that work, taken as a whole, appeals to the prurient interest in sex; portrays, in a patently offensive way, sexual conduct specifically defined by the applicable state law; and, taken as a whole, does not have serious literary, artistic, political or scientific value." This determination is to be made from the point of view of "the average person, applying contemporary community standards." Disgust enters the picture in two ways: as a way of articulating the notion of the "patently offensive," and also as a way of thinking about what "prurient interest" is: it is to be understood as a "shameful or morbid interest in nudity, sex, or excretion."[56]

In order to make these connections clearer, the Court analyzes the concept of obscenity in a fascinating and significant footnote. Criticizing an earlier decision for not offering a precise definition of the obscene,[57] the Court discusses the etymology of "obscene" from Latin *caenum*, "filth." Next, Justice Burger cites the *Webster's Third New International Dictionary* definition of "obscene" as "disgusting to the senses . . . grossly repugnant to the generally accepted notions of what is appropriate . . . offensive or revolting . . ." and the *Oxford English Dictionary* definition of "obscene" as "[o]ffensive to the senses, or to taste or refinement, disgusting, repulsive, filthy, foul, abominable, loathsome."[58]

This, however, is not the end of the matter. The note now adds that the material being discussed in this case is "more accurately defined," as "pornography" and "pornographic materials." In other words, the concept of the "obscene" now undergoes further refinement and analysis via the concept of the "pornographic." The etymology of "pornography" from the Greek term for "harlot," or female "whore," is now discussed, and pornography is defined (via Webster's dictionary) as "a depiction of licentiousness or lewdness: a portrayal of erotic behavior designed to cause sexual excitement."

The mingling of ideas in this account is truly fascinating. In order to offer a "precise" account of the *Roth* notion of "prurient interest," the Court brings in the concept of the disgusting, as it is used in dictionary definitions of obscenity. But this concept, in turn, is rendered "more accurately" by reference to the concept of the female whore and the related idea of a "portrayal of erotic behavior designed to cause sexual excitement." In other words, that which appeals to prurient interest is that which disgusts, and that which disgusts is that which (by displaying female sexuality) causes sexual excitement. But why this linkage? Aren't disgust and sexual arousal very different things?

The nexus has in fact caused some legal conundrums. In a 1987 case in the Fourth Circuit concerning films depicting intercourse with animals, the defense argued that the materials in question were not obscene because they were surely not sexually arousing to the "average man"; indeed, the "average man" would find films like "Snake Fuckers," "Horsepower," and "Horny Boar" pretty revolting.[59] Undaunted by this difficulty, the unanimous three-judge panel responded that the obscene *is* the disgusting, and it surely would be inconsistent with the spirit of the law to find milder materials obscene because they arouse average people, and to let more deeply revolting materials off because they disgust average people:

> [T]he offensiveness requirement in the Miller test is more than minimally met, however, the greater the number of people who would react to the material with revulsion and disgust. Surely Guglielmi is right that the reaction of most people to these films would be one of rejection and disgust, not one of sexual arousal, but that cannot lead to the conclusion that the most offensive material has constitutional protection while less offensive material does not.[60]

In this collision between the averagely arousing and the averagely disgusting, the disgusting takes precedence for purposes of interpreting the *Miller* standard: for surely the worse cannot get more protection that the less bad, and the disgusting is surely worse than the merely arousing.

The two standards suggested in *Miller* do not always point in the same direction, clearly, and they leave many problems of interpretation for courts to sort out. But why, we might ask, should one ever have supposed that these ideas would go together? What is sexy about the disgusting, and what is disgusting about the activities of a female whore? The answer should by now be all too evident. In this confused nexus of concepts we discern the time-honored view that sex itself has something disgusting about it, something furtive and self-contaminating, particularly if it is the body of a female whore (receptacle of countless men's semen) that inspires desire. Justice Burger records and endorses a conceptual linkage crafted by the long tradition of misogyny and misanthropy that I discussed in section III, a tradition brilliantly described by such disparate writers as William Miller and Andrea Dworkin.[61] The female body is seen as a filthy zone of stickiness, sliminess, and pollution, disgusting to males because it is the evidence of the male's own embodiment, animality, and mortality. Disgust for oneself as animal is projected onto the "female whore" whose activities typify, for Justice Burger, the sexually arousing and hence the disgusting. In Smith's words, "When we have dined, we order the covers to be removed." The presence of that reminder of "our" (meaning male) sexuality is disgusting if it remains around in the community to haunt us.

This conceptual nexus is ubiquitous in the post-Victorian period in attacks on sexually explicit artworks. Typical is an early review of Joyce's *Ulysses*:

> I have read it, and I say that it is the most infamously obscene book in ancient or modern literature. The obscenity of Rabelais is innocent compared

with its leprous and scabrous horrors. All the secret sewers of vice are canalized in its flow of unimaginable thoughts, images and pornographic words. And its unclean lunacies are larded with appalling and revolting blasphemies directed against the Christian religion and against the holy name of Christ— blasphemies hitherto associated with the most degraded orgies of Satanism and the Black Mass.[62]

The attack on the novel focused on Molly Bloom's monologue, whose frank depiction of a woman's non-marital sexual desires—combined, as they are, with ruminations about her menstrual period, deflationary thoughts about the penis, and memories of love—are indeed shocking to those in the grip of the disgust-misogyny I have outlined. Indeed, we can see the operations of disgust-misogyny in the very strange response of this reader (hardly unusual) to the work he purports to have read.

Joyce believed that our disgust with our own bodily functions lay at the root of much social evil—nationalism, fanaticism, misogyny. Like Lawrence he held that a healthy society would be one that comes to grips with its own mortal bodily nature and does not shrink from it in disgust. Joyce's novel, of course, is the opposite of disgusting to one who reads it as it asks to be read. Like Lawrence's *Lady Chatterley*, it presents the body as an object of many emotions—desire, humor, tender love, calm acceptance. But one emotion that is conspicuously absent from both writers (and the invitation they give to their readers) is the emotion of disgust. The novels of Joyce and Lawrence were found disgusting precisely because the society that read them was so deeply in the grip of a kind of loathing of its own animality that it could not actually read the works. Writers who wish to present the body without disgustingness have standardly encountered such reactions. They are found threatening precisely because they ask their readers to look at the body; the reader's antecedent disgust with the body (especially the female body) gets projected back onto the work, as a way of warding off the challenge it poses.

We have good reasons, then, to doubt whether the disgust of the "average man" would ever be a very reliable test for what might be legally regulable in the realm of art. If indeed disgust is frequently a defensive projection stemming from a fear of confronting the naked body, especially when the body is presented in a non-disgusting way, then we have some reason to fear that loathing of sexuality and animality may render unreliable many judgments that are made about works of art. Any society that pursues sex equality should be deeply skeptical of this conceptual nexus, and protective of works that seek to separate the arousing from the disgusting. Were it true that the "average man" feels disgust at such works, a society committed to equality should worry about the "average man" and his education, rather than about the works to which he reacts.

In short: the legal definition of obscenity actively colludes with misogyny, has the root concepts of misogyny embedded in it.

It seems to me that Catharine MacKinnon and Andrea Dworkin are entirely right in their argument that the serious moral issue posed by pornographic materials is not the issue of sexual explicitness, and the alleged disgusting excitingness of that. The issue that a society committed to the equality of its female citizens should take seriously is the issue of subordination, humiliation, and associated harms. Much pornography, it is no news to say, depicts sexuality in a way designed to reinforce misogynistic stereotypes, portraying women as base and deserving of abuse, as wanting and asking for abuse, and as gratifying outlets for the male's desire to humiliate and abuse. It is this that we should take seriously, both in moral argument and in legal discussion of the regulation of pornographic materials. But of course this feminist concept of the pornographic is profoundly at odds with the legal concept of the obscene. It doesn't just reorient "our" thought, it implicitly shows up the misogyny inherent in "our" previous thought. Exactly what the consequences of this reorientation should be for the law is a question that may be disputed.[63] But there can be no doubt, I believe, that their reorientation of the moral debate has been extremely salutary, a welcome redirection of political thought to the issue of women's equality, rather than to the alleged inherent disgustingness of sex (and of women).

But, Kahan will now ask, doesn't disgust have a valuable role to play even in this revised feminist program of scrutiny? Let us consider a case in which the pornographic materials in question are patently offensive to feminists and an assault on women's equality. We might call them "disgusting," using the term in a richer moral sense. Even in such cases, I would argue, the emotion of disgust is a confusion and a distraction from the serious moral issues that ought to be considered. In 1984, *Hustler Magazine* published features depicting Andrea Dworkin in a derogatory manner:

The February Feature is a cartoon, which, as described in the plaintiffs' complaint, "depicts two women engaged in a lesbian act of oral sex with the caption, 'You remind me so much of Andrea Dworkin, Edna. It's a dog-eat-dog world.'" The March Feature is a ten-page pictorial consisting of photographs of women engaged in, among other things, acts of lesbianism or masturbation. Some of the photographs depict obviously staged scenes that include posed violence and phony blood. One photograph, supposedly of a Jewish male, has a caption stating: "While I'm teaching this little shiksa the joys of Yiddish, the Andrea Dworkin Fan Club begins some really serious suck'n'squat. Ready to give up the holy wafers for Matzoh, yet, guys?" The December Feature was included in the "Porn from the Past" section of the magazine. It shows a man performing oral sex on an obese woman while he masturbates. A portion of the caption states: "We don't believe it for a minute, but one of our editors swears that this woman in the throes of ecstacy [*sic*] is the mother of radical feminist Andrea Dworkin."[64]

I shall not comment here on the central legal issues in the case, which concern the definition of the concept of a public figure for the purposes of the law of libel and slander and the distinction between statements of fact and privileged statements of opinion. What interests me is a side-argument in which the Court considers the issue of obscenity. The Court's conclusion is that the materials in question involve political speech and thus cannot be obscene under the *Miller* test: "Because the Features expressed opinions about matters of public concern, they did not lack 'serious literary, artistic, political, or scientific value.' It follows that they are not obscene." Again, I shall leave to one side, for purposes of my argument here, the question whether this claim of political value is plausible.

What interests me is that on the way to her conclusion, and immediately prior to her description of the features attacking Dworkin, Judge Hall feels it important to express her disgust with the materials in the case and the periodical in general. "Hustler Magazine is a pornographic periodical. Much of its content consists of what we have recently described as 'disgusting and distasteful abuse.'" So the features attacking Dworkin are "disgusting," and thus might have been candidates for obscenity had the political-speech issue not intervened. The question is, what is this disgust about, and is it relevant to the serious issues in this case?

On one reading, we may call it the Kahan reading, the disgust felt by the judge at *Hustler* and the Dworkin features is a tough, uncompromising moral sentiment that should be honored as highly relevant to the legal regulation of expression, even if, in the present case, other arguments prevented this reaction from determining the outcome. I believe that Kahan ought to take this position. But I am dubious. The morally salient issue in the case, it seems to me, is one of harm, humiliation, and subordination. Dworkin is being treated as a plaything of male fantasies of humiliation and domination; in retaliation for her feminist criticism of men, *Hustler* is taking pleasure in portraying her as both disgusting and contemptible. The appropriate reaction to these assaults on Dworkin is outrage and indignation, not disgust. We don't vomit at subordination and inequality, we get mad.

What is found disgusting here, I believe, is the physical grossness of what is depicted—both the grossness of the men's depicted behavior and, I can't help thinking, the grossness of the image of Andrea Dworkin so displayed. *Hustler* is disgusting, in short, because it shows obese people copulating, inviting our disgust at their obeseness. The response of disgust is exactly what the periodical solicits and reinforces: male disgust at the obese body of Andrea Dworkin. The whole idea of the features is to humiliate feminists and feminism by showing Andrea Dworkin's body as disgusting, in a very traditional misogynistic sense. When the judge says "disgusting," then, she is at least in part colluding in the magazine's project. It is difficult to believe that she would use the same words of a slender model of the *Playboy* type. Insofar as she does distance herself from the magazine, she does so in a way that expresses class-based disdain for the lower-class males depicted in *Hustler*: she finds their appearance and behavior disgusting. And this, too, colludes in the magazine's enterprise: for it standardly portrays itself, with pride, as the sex-magazine for "regular guys," guys who would be scorned and found disgusting by the readers of up-market porn like *Playboy*. In neither case does her disgust record an emotion that is morally relevant to what is really going on in the case. At worst, she joins in the humiliation of Dworkin. At best, she makes some disdainful comments about lower-class men that are altogether irrelevant to the legal issues before her.

In short: the really significant moral issues raised by pornographic materials are issues of equality, subordination, and humiliation. To violations of the equality of a fellow citizen, the appropriate response is anger, not disgust. If Kahan thinks this anger too fragile to survive without disgust, he should think harder, I believe, about the ambiguity of the disgust-response and its tendency to reinforce precisely those harms to which anger responds.

VII. Disgust as a Reason for Illegality: Sodomy, Necrophilia

But is Lord Devlin ever right? Is widespread disgust at a practice ever sufficient reason to make it illegal? Most responses to Devlin's argument have been very broadly focused: Ronald Dworkin, for example, treats all negative emotions as similarly irrational, arguing that none of them is ever a sufficient basis for making a practice illegal. But if we have a cognitive account of the emotions, we are unlikely to take this line. The cognitions involved in indignation, as we have seen, are highly relevant to making practices illegal—where they are true and well reasoned. The very *belief* that a certain type of conduct causes gross harms is not all by itself reason to render a practice illegal; for of course that belief might be groundless and false. But where such reasons are true and convincing, then we at least have a *prima facie* case for legal regulation. We will then have to debate whether the harm is large enough, whether we want to apply legal sanctions only to harmful practices that affect nonconsenting third parties or also to some forms of harming that do not involve nonconsenting parties (suicide, driving without a seatbelt, boxing), and whether the harm is of a type that it makes sense to regulate by law.

Where disgust is concerned, however, I would argue that we never have even a *prima facie* case for legal regulation. Revulsion is not a harm in the legally relevant sense: if the acts of A revolt B, here as in the homicide case, there is no justification for retaliation on the part of B (including legal retaliation) because A has not, by his very existence, trespassed against or harmed B. We need to say more about this view of the necessary conditions for legal regulability: harm has to be more carefully defined, and the type of intentional activity requisite for a judgment that a harm has been done.[65] Nor will the view command universal agreement. I would argue, however, that it is in this way that we best make sense of our desire to live together in a combination of liberty and safety. Where our safety is not threatened by another, the presumption should be in favor of liberty.

On this view of things, sodomy laws cannot be justified, nor can any laws criminalizing consensual sexual relations.[66] For no showing has ever been convincingly made that sodomy harms people. It is fascinating to observe that whenever restrictions on homosexual conduct are contemplated, a parade of witnesses standardly comes forward to testify about alleged harms of such conduct. In the trial of Amendment 2 in Colorado, the state introduced testimony on psychological self-harm, on child abuse, on various types of alleged subversion of the civic fabric—all in order to show what possible "compelling interest" the state might possibly have in preventing homosexuals from enjoying the protection of non-discrimination laws. Similarly, in *Baehr v. Lewin* a vain attempt was made to show that gay couples cause psychological harm to children, in order to support the claim of compelling state interest in denying gays access to marriage. In both cases, all such testimony was shown up as pathetically weak, and the issue came down to disgust. It became clear, indeed, that disgust lay behind the success of Amendment 2: for its proponents reluctantly admitted under oath that they had circulated materials that alleged that gays eat feces and drink raw blood—propaganda very similar to antisemitic propaganda from the Middle Ages.[67] The effort to introduce the harm testimony shows that the proponents of anti-gay measures themselves recognize that disgust is a weak reed on which to hang legal restrictions. A showing of serious harm is necessary; if the real motive has been disgust, one must put on a show to make people think it has been something else.

Let us now return to the third trial of Oscar Wilde; for it shows this point in an especially fascinating way. In his famous speech at sentencing, Mr. Justice Wills spoke as follows:

> Oscar Wilde and Alfred Taylor, the crime of which you have been convicted is so bad that one has to put stern restraint upon one's self to prevent one's self from describing, in language which I would rather not use, the sentiments which must rise to the breast of every man of honour who has heard the details of these two terrible trials. . . . I hope, at all events, that those who sometimes imagine that a judge is half-hearted in the cause of decency and morality because he takes care no prejudice shall enter into the case, may see that that is consistent at least with the utmost sense of indignation at the horrible charges brought home to both of you.
>
> It is no use for me to address you. People who can do these things must be dead to all sense of shame, and one cannot hope to produce any effect upon them. It is the worst case I have ever tried. . . .
>
> I shall, under such circumstances, be expected to pass the severest sentence that the law allows. In my judgment it is totally inadequate for a case such as this. The sentence of the Court is that each of you be imprisoned and kept to hard labour for two years.[68]

Mr. Justice Wills maintains that decency prevents him from describing his real sentiments, which are also those of "any man of honour." A description would require "language which I would rather not use." He thus strongly hints that the emotion is a violent disgust that could find appropriate expression only in indecent language, like a kind of vomiting in speech.[69] He treats the prisoners as objects of disgust, vile contaminants who are not really people, and who therefore need not be addressed as if they were people. (At the conclusion of the speech, Wilde called out, "And I? May I say nothing, my lord?" His lordship made no reply, simply gesturing to the warders to remove the prisoners.) At the same time, however, Mr. Justice Wills appeals to public reason by claiming that he has combined judicial impartiality with "the utmost sense of indignation at the horrible charges brought home to you." Indignation is the public face worn by an unspeakable disgust.

On what, we might now ask, could indignation be plausibly based? Wilde was convicted for "gross indecency." He had had oral sex with a number of working-class men well above the legal age of consent (the youngest was eighteen and most were in their twenties). All sought out relationships with him, often in order to advance careers in literature and the theatre; he treated them with generosity, taking them on trips and buying them lavish presents.[70] Had the Justice attempted to show reasons for indignation that any person could share, it would have been very hard for him to point to wrongs done by this conduct, far less to show that it is "the worst case I have ever tried." Disgust hides behind the screen of indignation, but it is clearly disgust, not indignation at harm, that is driving the sentencing. What is really being said is: these are two slimy slugs who ought to be squashed before they insinuate themselves into our bodies.

There is one apparently harmless sexual practice that seems to be an exception to my general claim that disgust has no legal relevance. For we feel this practice should be illegal, and we seem to have no reason behind this but our disgust. This practice is necrophilia, in the words of one judge "the most loathsome, degrading and vile sexual activity imaginable."[71] The history of legislation regarding this practice is uneven. Most states have some laws against desecration of the corpse, but sexual desecration, though viewed as especially disgusting, is usually not singled out for especially harsh punishment. Indeed, some corpse-desecration statutes may not cover it at all: California's statues uses the words "willfully mutilates," and it is unclear whether this language applies to the damage done to the corpse during intercourse.[72] Rape statutes, meanwhile, have typically been interpreted to require a live victim, except in cases where the defendant mistakenly believes the person to be alive at the time of rape; even in alleged felony murders in which the murder is a prelude to a desired act of necrophilia, it has standardly been held that the defendant can be convicted only of attempted rape, not rape.[73] Necrophilia in which the perpetrator is not involved in the victim's death appears to be legally unprovided for in many jurisdictions; this state of affairs is sometimes defended on the grounds that necrophilia is a victimless crime.[74]

Here Kahan will be ready to step in. Surely my position against the legal relevance of disgust requires us to conclude that necrophilia should not be a crime; but surely our moral intuitions tell us otherwise. Here, then, may be a case in which our disgust is highly relevant to the determination that a practice should be illegal.

To answer this I must discuss the more general question of damage to corpses. We view these wrongs as grave wrongs primarily on account of the harm they cause to relatives and loved ones of the deceased. The corpse is the property of the living, and it is an especially valuable and intimate type of property, like a precious sentimental or religious artifact. Where the dead person is without relatives and friends, we view necrophilia as an insult to the life of the person that was, and as an assault on religious or personal meanings that the state, by taking that person's corpse as its property, undertakes to protect from desecration. In so judging we do not take any stand on the metaphysical issues connecting corpse and person; it is enough for us that people have religious beliefs and other deeply rooted ethical and emotional beliefs that are offended by the practice in question, and a right to complain in virtue of the fact that the corpse is their property. In this sense, laws against corpse-mutilation are closely related to laws against the desecration of churches and religious artifacts: they are not just property crimes but an especially grave type of property crime, because they express a disregard for religious meanings that we have agreed, as a society, to protect. Even when they do not have such meanings, they may have emotional meanings that are especially central to the survivors. Necrophilia is especially horrible to us, especially outrageous, because we feel that use of these religiously charged objects for sexual purposes involves an especially deep profanation of their religious or emotional meaning (like the sexual profanation of a religious sanctuary).

A further issue is that of consent. We understand a recent corpse to have an especially intimate connection with the person who was, and therefore, just as we abhor rape, we also abhor sexual violation of the corpse. (This would include violations by relatives with whom the deceased did not have a sexual relationship, and would thus support prohibitions against necrophilia even by people who have lawful custody of the corpse.) We also view such violations as a sign that this person does not care about consent or even sentience. Someone to whom sex with an inert object is exciting seems to reveal an extreme tendency to treat a sexual partner as a mere thing. These two thoughts pull in opposite directions when the necrophilic act is with a former consensual sexual partner, such as a dead spouse. Here we do not have the sense that consent is being violated, but we do view the act as saying something unpleasant about the person.

It seems to me that such considerations are the ones most relevant to the legal treatment of necrophilia. They are probably sufficient to justify some criminal penalties, including penalties that define necrophiliac violations as somewhat more severe than lesser forms of corpse desecration and vandalism of tombs. Necrophilia is altogether different from consensual sodomy. There is no live person whose consent can make sexual conduct acceptable, and instead there is a piece of precious property that has been vandalized in an especially outrageous way, without consent. Sodomy laws are wrong because they enact in law a disgust that neighbors feel toward the consensual practices of people whose lives are no business of theirs; necrophilia penalties are right because the treatment of the corpse is the perfectly legitimate concern of whoever holds it as property, whether the state or private individuals, and because only those individuals can represent the dead person's interest in consent. Another way of putting it is that people don't become other people's property until they are dead.

Given this analysis, once again it would appear that disgust by itself is not the driving force. What we feel when a religious sanctuary is violated is outrage: outrage because the protection of religion is a value to which we have deeply committed ourselves as a society. We may also feel disgust, but the reasons for the law are contained in our response of outrage. It is the wrong done to religious people, not the sense we have that we are contaminated by vile sexual practices, that explains the legitimacy of some criminal penalties.

VIII. Disgust and the Jury: "Horrible and Inhuman" Homicides

So far, however, I have not considered a class of cases especially pertinent to Kahan's pro-disgust argument. These are cases in which a jury is asked to consult reactions of disgust in order to determine whether a homicide is "especially heinous, atrocious, or cruel,"[75] a determination that many state statutes make relevant to the potential applicability of the death penalty. A salient example is a Georgia statute that permitted a person to be sentenced to death if the offense "was outrageously or wantonly vile, horrible and inhuman."[76] We can easily see that this sort of language, while not explicitly mentioning the term "disgust," invites jurors to consult their disgust-reactions when considering aggravating circumstances. It is plausible enough to think that here disgust plays a central and also a valuable role, in identifying an especially heinous class of homicides.

The first and most obvious problem with this, the problem that the Court has repeatedly noted, is that this language is so vague that it virtually ensures that the death penalty will be applied in "an arbitrary and capricious manner." Such was the holding in *Godfrey* concerning the Georgia language. "There is nothing in these few words, standing alone," the Court wrote, "that implies any inherent restraint on the arbitrary and capricious infliction of the death sentence. A person of ordinary sensibility could fairly characterize almost every murder as 'outrageously or wantonly vile, horrible and inhuman.'"[77] Similar was the finding in the Oklahoma case, in which a unanimous Court found the language "especially heinous, atrocious, and cruel," unconstitutionally vague, offering insufficient guidance to the jury. What has emerged as constitutional is a "limiting construction" or set of such constructions that give jurors far more concrete description of aggravating circumstances: felony murder, for example, and murder with torture.[78] But if we have such descriptions we can leave disgust to one side; we really don't need it to tell us whether torture was used. And the emotion clearly doesn't correctly identify the class of murders that are typically understood to involve aggravating circumstances. Many felony murders will not typically elicit the reaction of disgust: for example, the shooting of a bank officer during a holdup will standardly be found very bad, but rarely disgusting. On the other hand, some murders that seem disgusting to at least many jurors may not involve constitutionally defined aggravating circumstances: the Court is surely right that many jurors will react with disgust to many if not all murders, when bloody or gory circumstances are precisely described. Bloodiness and goriness are the usual elicitors of disgust. But many especially vile murders lack these features, and many murders that have these features are vile only in the sense that any murder is vile.

There is also a problem about the type of disgust that places the murderer in a class of heinous monsters more or less outside the boundaries of our moral universe. This is, that the further we place him (or her, but it is almost always a him) at a distance from us, the less obvious it is that this is a moral agent at all, and the less obvious it consequently is that this person deserves the penalty we reserve for fully responsible agents. No matter how we define insanity for legal purposes, when we turn someone into a monster we immediately raise the issue of sanity. Aristotle already held that certain individuals (for example Phalaris, who boiled people in cauldrons) were so weird that they were not even vicious, because we think that such extreme pathology shows that someone isn't really a chooser of ends at all. No matter what psychological concepts we use, we have a hard time not getting into a similar difficulty, when we try to combine a strong ascription of moral responsibility with an account appealing to disgust at the alleged monstrousness of the person's deeds. Perhaps this difficulty can be solved; but it needs to be squarely faced. Disgust, far from shoring up the moral borders of our community, may actually make them harder to police.

There is a deeper point that we should now consider. Frequently, I have argued, our disgust at a group signals a desire to cordon ourselves off from something about ourselves that this group represents to us. This diagnosis is especially clear in the areas of misogynistic and homophobic disgust, but I believe that it applies to our response to evil as well. We very often tell ourselves that the doers of heinous wrongs are monsters, in no way like ourselves. This tendency plays a strong role, for example, in writing and reading about the Nazis and the Holocaust. The tremendous enthusiasm for Daniel Goldhagen's recent book,[79] both in Germany and the United States, cannot easily be explained either by its novelty or by its quality. What does explain it, I believe, is the desire of many people (including present-day Germans, who are carefully exonerated by Goldhagen) to believe that the culture that gave birth to the horrors of Nazism was a monstrosity, an aberration. Unlike other books that stressed the commonness of the evil deeds of Nazi perpetrators (in different ways, Hannah Arendt, Christopher Browning),[80] or books that stressed the role of cultural ideology in building a Nazi mentality (in different ways Raul Hilberg,[81] Omer Bartov[82]), Goldhagen's book argues that the Germany that produced the Nazis was *sui generis*, a "radically different culture" to be viewed "with the critical eye of an anthropologist disembarking on unknown shores."[83] These people were not made by factors that can easily be replicated in other times and places, and they are not acting out deeply shared human capacities for destruction. They are unique disgusting monsters. We are nothing like this, and we could not possibly create anything like this.[84] When we see Nazis in this "anthropological" way, whether in works of history or in films and novels, we are comforted: evil is outside, alien, has nothing to do with us. Our disgust creates the boundary: it says, this contamination is and must remain far from our bodies. We might even say, in this case again, that we call disgust to our aid: by allowing ourselves to see evil people as disgusting, we conveniently distance them from ourselves.

By contrast, when we see Nazis depicted without disgust, as human beings who share common characteristics with us—whether the emphasis is on the capacity of all human beings for evil or on a universal submissiveness to distorting ideologies—this is alarming, because it requires self-

scrutiny, warning us that we might well have done the same under comparable circumstances. It alerts us to the presence of evil (whether active or
passively collaborative) in ourselves, and requires us to ask how we might
prevent similar phenomena from materializing in our own society. We have
to confront the fact that we might become them; but this means that in a
significant sense we already are them—with the fearfulness, weakness, and
moral blindness that go to produce such evils. Because this response is so
much more psychologically troubling and politically challenging than the
response elicited by Goldhagen, it is not surprising that Goldhagen's book
has been embraced with warm approval. It permits us to forget the atrocities U.S. military officers perpetrated in Vietnam, the atrocities perpetrated
against slaves and Native Americans (not to mention Jews, who were hardly
well treated, even if they were not exterminated) in our own history. No,
monsters cause evil, and that sort of evil could only happen over there.[85]

I believe that a similar thing happens when we are urged to react with disgust at the criminal acts of a murderer. We are being urged to see that person as a monster, outside the boundaries of our moral universe. We are
urged precisely *not* to have the thought, "there, but for . . . go I." But in reality, it seems likely that all human beings are capable of evil, and that many if
not most of the hideous evildoers are warped by circumstances, both social
and personal, which play a large and sometimes decisive role in explaining
the evil that they do. If jurors are led to think that evil is done by monsters
who just were born different, are freaky and inhuman, they will be prevented
from having thoughts about themselves and their own society that are
highly pertinent, not only to the equal and principled application of the law
but also to the construction of a society in which less evil will exist. If we
classify murders as involving "aggravating circumstances" by some reasoned
account—for example, by enumerating aggravating conditions such as torture and felony murder—we permit such useful thoughts to come forth and
not to be stifled: for such a classification requires us to ask why we think torture bad, and to reflect about the strong social reasons we have for seeking
to deter it. (Emotions of indignation will frequently be connected with such
a reflective process.) If we classify by disgust, I would argue, we stifle such
thoughts and comfort ourselves where comfort is not due.

We should now consider one more specific case, since it figures prominently in Kahan's pro-disgust argument. A murderer named Beldotti apparently killed in order to gratify sadistic sexual desires.[86] He strangled his
female victim, cut off her nipples, and stuffed her into trash bags. Police recovered from his home numerous post-mortem photographs of the de-

ceased, posed with dildos penetrating her vagina and anus. The jury found that Beldotti's crime showed "extreme atrocity and cruelty," and sentenced him to life in prison without parole. While in prison, Beldotti requested that the dildos, photos of the victim, the trash bags in which she had been placed, and other sexual paraphernalia be returned to his representatives outside prison. The State opposed this request, arguing that giving these items back, even if not to Beldotti himself, would "justifiably spark outrage, disgust, and incredulity on the part of the general public." It urged that the property be put in the trash, and the Massachusetts Court of Appeals agreed, concluding that returning the property would be "offensive to basic concepts of decency treasured in a civilized society."

Kahan argues that the Beldotti case shows that disgust plays an ineliminable role in criminal law by shoring up community morality: the result in the case, and what is good about it, cannot be explained without giving disgust the central role. Kahan argues that no concern with rehabilitation or specific deterrence could explain the result (given Beldotti's life sentence), and that a concern with general deterrence would not explain the State's refusal to surrender these particular items. The only remaining explanation, Kahan concludes, is disgust. If it had granted Beldotti's request, the State itself would be "tainted" by the contamination his relics would import. The request to put the items "in the trash can where they belong" is an unmistakable expression of disgust, and the case shows that this emotion is central to protecting society's moral boundaries.

First of all, I am not persuaded by Kahan's arguments about general deterrence. Obviously enough, to surrender to a murderer the paraphernalia he used in a murder would be a treatment so indulgent that it could well lessen the deterrent effect of his life sentence. By contrast, giving his relatives back his keys or his wallet would have little tendency to make other sex murderers think that Beldotti had gotten away lightly; that would be a perfectly unremarkable thing to do with a prisoner's effects, and it probably would never be publicly commented on or reach the ears of other sex murderers.

But the heart of the issue surely is that Kahan has forgotten about retribution. The most natural way to view the State's refusal is as a retributive quid pro quo: you took a woman's life with these sex toys, so to punish you we are going to refuse you the things that give you sexual pleasure.[87] The State mentioned not one reaction, but three: "outrage, disgust, and incredulity." Kahan focuses only on disgust and contamination. But surely the first and third responses are also highly significant, and they go closely together. Outrage expresses the idea that it is unreasonable and wrong to reward Beldotti in just that area where he should be most severely punished. Such a reward would not only be astonishing—the response of "incredulity"—it would be a profound injury and disrespect to the dead, to anyone who cares about her, and to society itself. This sense of outrage is highly cognitive, expressing a reasoned judgment that can be publicly shared.[88] Its cognitions are not focused, as are those of disgust, on contamination to the self; they focus on the harm or wrong that has occurred. Outrage is thus closely linked to the idea of retributive punishment, to the thought that (instead of rewarding this guy by returning his murder weapons) we should be punishing him by denying him access to the tools he used to commit his hideous crime.[89]

Disgust is clearly in the picture; no doubt the State is right that the public would react with disgust (expressing a sense of contamination and defilement) as well as with outrage and incredulity, were the State to grant the request. But outrage is sufficient to explain the result and why it is correct; we do not need to rely on disgust, as Kahan suggests. And outrage, as I have argued, is a moral sentiment far more pertinent to legal judgment, and far more reliable, than disgust. It contains reasoning that can be publicly shared, and it does not make the questionable move of treating the criminal like an insect or a slug, outside of our moral community. Instead, it firmly includes him within the moral community and judges his actions on a moral basis. Thus it avoids any tendency to portray the criminal as a monster, one whom none of us can possibly be.

Indeed, I believe it is clear that in the actual case outrage is not only the sounder response to Beldotti, it is also more explanatory of the outcome and the opinions. For neither the State nor the court does treat Beldotti as an alien or a monster, with the eye of an "anthropologist disembarking on alien shores." They treat him as a perfectly sane person who has made an absolutely outrageous request. They react with "incredulity" because they assume that Beldotti is not a monster, but a sane human being, and must know that his request is outrageous. Were they thinking of him as like a slug or a heap of vomit, they would not be so outraged by the request, they would just see it as lunatic pathology. But they don't: they know he is a human being with recognizable rationality, and that is why the right response to the request is anger. Disgust is there, but it is in considerable tension with outrage and incredulity. I suggest that the judgment in the case followed, rightly, the moral sentiment of outrage and indignation, which, unlike disgust, is worthy of guiding public choice.

Disgust is a deeply embedded response. All adult human beings acquire it in some form, and all known societies teach it in some form. It may even be that many or even most human beings need some of it in order to live, because they cannot endure too much daily confrontation with their own decay and with the oozy stuffs of which their bodies are made. But we should not conclude from this fact that disgust is a valuable response for legal and political purposes. Many responses that are deeply embedded in human nature are morally questionable and unworthy of guiding public action. Disgust, I have argued, collaborates with evil; it offers us nothing to keep our political hearts warm.

NOTES

1. I am most grateful to Sonia Katyal for excellent research assistance, to Rachel Nussbaum for valuable discussion of Nazi Germany, and to Kate Abramson, Marcia Baron, Peter Cicchino, Dan M. Kahan, Andy Koppelman, Ariela Lazar, Catharine MacKinnon, Michelle Mason, Jeffrie Murphy, Rachel Nussbaum, Richard Posner, and Cass Sunstein for comments on a previous draft. The title of this paper is taken from a review of James Joyce's *Ulysses*, which I discuss in the text.

2. See the masterful treatment of the topic in William Ian Miller, *The Anatomy of Disgust* (Cambridge: Harvard University Press, 1997), which I reviewed in *The New Republic*, November 17, 1997, pp. 32–38. I am grateful to Miller for provoking this further response.

3. Mr. Justice Wills, Sentence, quoted in *The Three Trials of Oscar Wilde*, ed. H. Montgomery Hyde (New York: University Books, 1956), 339.

4. Devlin, *The Enforcement of Morals* (1959, repr. 1965), p. 17.

5. Miller, chapter 7.

6. *Miller v. California*, 413 U.S. 15, 93 S. Ct. 2607 (1973), footnote 2, majority opinion written by Chief Justice Burger. The Court here corrects the definition of obscenity in *Roth v. U. S.*, 354 U.S. 15, 487 S. Ct. at 1310 (1957), which mentions only appeal "to prurient interest." This definition, the Court argues, "does not reflect the precise meaning of 'obscene' as traditionally used in the English language." The dictionary definitions are further discussed in section VII below.

7. See Robert B. Mison, "Comment: Homophobia in Manslaughter: The Homosexual Advance as Insufficient Provocation," *California Law Review* 80 (1992), 133–78.

8. Miller, 194. It is far from clear, in Miller's argument, why disgust alone should allegedly play this role, rather than indignation, or horror, or a sense of tragedy.

9. Kahan, "*The Anatomy of Disgust* in Criminal Law," *Michigan Law Review* 96 (1998), at 1624.

10. Kahan, *Id.* at 1652. Kahan, like Miller, does not make it sufficiently clear why disgust alone should have this role, rather than other moral sentiments. But if other moral sentiments do play some of the roles Kahan imputes to disgust, then it becomes less clear on what grounds he wishes to claim that disgust is "necessary."

11. Such a blanket condemnation of all appeals to "irrational emotion" seems to be involved in Ronald Dworkin's otherwise valuable argument against Devlin in "Liberty and Moralism," in *Taking Rights Seriously* (Cambridge: Harvard University Press, 1977), 240–58. For a criticism of it, see my *Poetic Justice* (Boston: Beacon Press, 1996), chapter 3.

12. See my *Upheavals of Thought: A Theory of the Emotions* (Cambridge: Cambridge University Press, forthcoming), and Dan M. Kahan and Martha C. Nussbaum, "Two Concepts of Emotion in Criminal Law," *Columbia Law Review* 96 (1996), 269–374.

13. The Stoics thought that there were such reasons, but this is because they believed that all "external goods" were totally without value and they argued, correctly, that emotions ascribe worth to things outside the self that we do not fully control. They recommended this radical view as one that would free us from the tyranny of such objects and events. If we accept their recommendation we do have some reasons for thinking all emotions unreliable; but then we have no reasons for caring about law, whose focus is the relationship between persons and "external goods." I shall assume the falsity of the normative Stoic thesis for the purposes of this paper: in other words, I shall assume that at least some things and persons outside the self have worth, and that the law should acknowledge this worth.

14. By "classic" Rozin and I mean both that these are ubiquitous occasions of disgust and also that these are the central paradigm cases to which people typically turn in explaining disgust or why a particular thing is disgusting.

15. Rozin has published many articles on aspects of disgust, but a comprehensive account of his views is in Rozin and April E. Fallon, "A Perspective on Disgust," *Psychological Review* 94 (1987), 23–41.

16. Rozin and Fallon, p. 224 n. 1.

17. Jeff Murphy tells me that he finds okra disgusting, and suggests that this may be because it has "what seems like a mucous membrane" and thus strikes him as animal-like. I recall having a similar reaction as a child, although now okra (a staple of Indian cuisine, where it typically loses its mucosity by being stir-fried) is one of my favorite dishes both to eat and to cook.

18. Rozin, p. 28, citing Sherry Ortner.

19. Rozin, p. 28, citing research by A. Angyal.

20. Rozin, citing T. Despres.

21. This law has a positive side, in our eagerness to possess or even touch objects that have been the property of celebrities, to sleep where they have slept, etc.

22. See Paul Rozin, April Fallon, and R. Mandell, "Family Resemblance in Attitudes to Foods," *Developmental Psychology* 20 (1984), 309–14.

23. Seneca, *De Ira*, 1.3.3, 1.2.3b; the first is Seneca's version of the Aristotelian view, the second is Posidonius' version; the third is in Diogenes Laertius and Stobaeus: see *Stoicorum Veterum Fragmenta* III.395–97.

24. Thus Spinoza: "Indignation is hatred towards one who has injured another": *Ethics* III, *Definition of the Emotions*, 20.

25. See Richard Lazarus, *Emotion and Adaptation* (New York: Oxford University Press, 1991), pp. 217–34, defending and developing Aristotle's account of anger and showing that it is supported by recent experimental work. See also A. Ortony, G. L. Clore, and A. Collins, *The Cognitive Structure of Emotions* (Cambridge: Cambridge University Press, 1988), defining anger as involving "disapproving of someone else's blameworthy action" (148); James Averill, *Anger and Aggression: An Essay on Emotion* (New York: Springer-Verlag, 1982), stressing the role of socially shaped norms in anger.

26. Adam Smith, *The Theory of Moral Sentiments*, I.ii.2.1.

27. Testimony of Will Perkins, trial of Amendment 2, heard personally by me, October 1994.

28. The proponents of Amendment 2 seemed well aware of this, and thus were reluctant to admit to the tactics they had used. Their direct testimony focused on "special rights" and dangers to society; it was the plaintiffs, on cross-examination, who introduced evidence of the campaign's appeal to disgust into the record.

29. It is important to recall at this point the difference between disgust and a response to danger: disgust is insensitive to information about risk, and not well correlated with real sources of harm: see Rozin above.

30. Mahler, letter to Max Marschalk, cited in Deryck Cooke, *Gustav Mahler* (Cambridge: Cambridge University Press, 1980).

31. I discuss this movement of the symphony in *Upheavals of Thought: A Theory of the Emotions*, Cambridge University Press, forthcoming.

32. See Otto Weininger, *Sex and Character* (trans. from 6th German edition, London and New York: William Heinemann and G. P. Putnam's Sons, date not given), pp. 306–22. "... some reflection will lead to the surprising result that Judaism is saturated with femininity, with precisely those qualities the essence of which I have shown to be in the strongest opposition to the male nature." Among the Jewish/feminine traits explored here is the failure to understand the national State as the aim of manly endeavor: thus Jews and women have an affinity for the ideas of Marxism. They also fail to comprehend class distinctions: they are "at the opposite pole from aristocrats, with whom the preservation of the limits between individuals is the leading idea" (311).

33. See the remarkable exhibit of such children's books in the Historisches Museum in Berlin. Similarly, untouchables, in the traditional Indian caste system, were viewed as quasi animals, soiled by the pollution of the animal aspects of their betters.

34. See, for example, Sander Gilman, *The Jew's Body* (New York: Routledge, 1991).

35. For a valuable treatment of these aspects of disgust, see the essays "Repulsion" and "Dirt/Death" in Andrea Dworkin, *Intercourse* (New York: The Free Press, 1988), from which the first two epigraphs in this paper were taken. Compare Weininger, p. 300: "Woman alone,then, is guilt; and is so through man's fault. . . . She is only a part of man, his other, ineradicable, his lower part."

36. Unpublished paper by Rachel Nussbaum, based on research on the Jewish woman in antisemitic novels of the 1920s and 1930s. Weininger also has this idea: if the Jew is a woman, the Jewish woman is accordingly the most sensual and bodily, the "odalisque." There are related stereotypes of black women.

37. Miller, *Anatomy*, chapter 6. I comment further on the politics of Miller's book in my review.

38. This idea is evident, too, in the apparently widespread distaste of straight men for cunnilingus after ejaculation; although it is difficult to find anything beyond anecdotal evidence on this point, the aversion seems to be connected to an idea of being made "womanly." A gay man who read this paper writes: "Interestingly, both in my own experience and that of my gay male friends, I have found no such aversion to semen whether one's own or that of others (apart from a reasonable concern with safe-sex practices and the transmission of HIV)."

39. Thus it is not surprising that (to males) the thought of homosexual sex is even more disgusting than the thought of reproductive sex, despite the strong connection of the latter with mortality and the cycle of the generations. For in heterosexual sex the male imagines that not he but a lesser being (the woman, seen as animal) received the pollution of bodily fluids; in imagining homosexual sex he is forced to imagine that he himself might be so polluted. This inspires a stronger need for boundary drawing.

40. Miller, *Anatomy*, chapter 7. See David Papineau's 1998 review of two books on cloning in *The New York Times Book Review*, Sunday, September 6: he shrewdly notices that the view of disgust in regard to human cloning taken by the ultraconservative thinker Leon Kass is really the same as that taken by Miller in his essay in *Clones and Clones*, ed. M. Nussbaum and C. Sunstein (New York: Norton, 1998), although Miller presents himself as a culture theorist and not at all as a conservative thinker.

41. Gandhi also noted that in terms of real danger, the upper castes were less clean than the lower. During a plague, he went round to inspect the toilet habits of the various residents of his area, and found that the untouchables were doing fine, because they defecated in the fields, far from dwelling places, while upper-caste families disposed of the contents of chamber pots in gutters that ran alongside the house, and were thus at high risk for infection. See *Autobiography*.

42. *I Sing the Body Electric*, section 9.

43. See David S. Reynolds, *Walt Whitman's America: A Cultural Biography* (New York: Knopf, 1995), 346ff.

44. I do not mean to suggest that I find every aspect of Whitman's social vision appealing: see my longer discussion in chapter 13 of *Upheavals of Thought: A The-*

ory of the Emotions (Cambridge: Cambridge University Press, forthcoming). His emphasis on the interchangeability of erotic objects leaves too little room for the risks and vulnerabilities involved in deep personal love.

45. See Kahan and Nussbaum, 306–23, for an extensive discussion of this issue.

46. *Maher v. People*, 10 Mich. 212, 220 (1862).

47. *Rivers v. State*, 78 So. 343, 345 (Fla. 1918).

48. *Small v. Commonwealth*, 91 Pa. 304, 306, 308 (1879).

49. See Kahan and Nussbaum.

50. *Commonwealth v. Carr*, 580 A.2d 1362, 1363–65 (Pa. Super. Ct. 1990). See generally Claudia Brenner, *Eight Bullets: One Woman's Study of Surviving Anti-Gay Violence* (Ithaca, NY: Firebrand Books, 1995).

51. Adultery has typically been considered adequate grounds for mitigation when a man kills either the paramour or the unfaithful wife in the heat of passion reasonably shortly after the discovery. But the theory underlying this tradition is that adultery is an extremely grave aggressive act against the husband and against his property: in fact "the highest invasion of [his] property" by another man, *Regina v. Mawgridge*, 84 Eng. Rep. 1107, 1115 (1707). For this reason, discovery of a fiancée's adultery has typically not counted as adequate provocation: see *Rex v. Palmer*, 2 K.B. 29, 30–31 (1913).

52. Carr is an exception to my general claim, above, that male disgust targets male rather than female homosexuals. Often, indeed, female same-sex lovemaking is found arousing by males, and it is a staple of pornography aimed at males. Carr's psychological history—which allegedly included a lesbian mother, as well as a history of rejection by women—presumably would explain this anomaly.

53. See Mison, "Homophobia" (above n. 7). Consider, for example, *Schick v. State*, 570 N. E. 2d 918 (Ind. App. 1991). A young man, out drinking with his friends, hitched a ride home with another man, the victim. Together they drove around looking for women for sex. After a while the young man asked, "Where can I get a blow job?" The victim replied, "I can handle that." They drove around some more, then went to a baseball field at a local school. The victim pulled down his pants, but the young man kicked him and stomped on him, took his money, and left him to die on the baseball field. Before leaving he carefully wiped the victim's car clean of his fingerprints. At trial the defense argued that the homosexual advance was sufficient provocation to explain the killing; the prosecutor did not object, and the judge permitted the defense. (The theft and the wiping of fingerprints were described as afterthoughts.) The jury convicted the young man of voluntary manslaughter. See Mison, 134–35. See also Gary David Comstock, "Dismantling the Homosexual Panic Defense," *Law and Sexuality* 2 (1981), 81–102; but the "homosexual advance" defense should be distinguished from the "homosexual panic" defense, which involves the idea that the violence is the psychotic reaction of a latent homosexual.

54. *State v. Volk*, 421 N.W. 2d 360 (Minnesota 1988).

55. 413 U.S. 15, 93 S. Ct. 2607 (1973).

56. *Miller* n. 1, quoting from the California Penal Code.

57. *Miller* n. 2; the definition in *Roth v. U. S.*, which mentions only that appeal to "prurient interest," "does not reflect the precise meaning of 'obscene' as traditionally used in the English language."

58. *Miller*, n. 2.

59. *U.S. v. Guglielmi*, 819 F. 2d 451 (1987). The defense added the argument that even were the standard relativized to zoophiliacs, we could not even conclude that the materials were arousing to "the average zoophiliac," since there was no such thing. They introduced expert testimony on zoophilia that stated that zoophiliacs differ in their preferences for different animals, and most have a preferred animal; thus there was no "average" member of that class for whom the contested materials as a group would be found sexually arousing.

60. *Ibid.*, 454.

61. Miller, *Anatomy*; Dworkin, "Repulsion" and "Dirt/Death."

62. James Douglas, *Sunday Express*.

63. See my "Rage and Reason," *The New Republic* August 11/18, 1997, pp. 36–42, also in Nussbaum, *Sex and Social Justice* (New York: Oxford University Press, 1998), discussing arguments for and against the MacKinnon/Dworkin proposal for a civil ordinance under which women damaged in the making or use of pornography can sue its purveyors for damages.

64. *Dworkin v. Hustler Magazine, Inc.*, 867 F. 2d 1188, 9th Cir. (1989).

65. In obvious ways, the view follows Mill, although it does not rule out legal regulation of acts that physically endanger the self. Mill's "harm principle" is itself notoriously difficult to interpret.

66. The case for regulation is much stronger for adultery than for sodomy, since adultery has traditionally been viewed as a gross harm by the adulterous male against the cuckolded male. However, that view (which underlay the "heat of passion defense," see above) was based on an archaic and objectionable view of the woman as a piece of property, rather than as an agent capable of consent: see discussion of *Regina v. Mawgridge* above.

67. Testimony of Will Perkins, October 1994, which I heard in person. On the similarity between U.S. prejudice against homosexuals and mediaeval anti-semitism, see Richard Posner, *Sex and Reason* (Cambridge: Harvard University Press, 1992), p. 346; John Boswell, "Jews, Bicycle Riders, and Gay People: The Determination of Social Consensus and Its Impact on Minorities," *Yale Journal of Law and Humanities* 1 (1989), 205–28.

68. *The Three Trials of Oscar Wilde*, p. 339.

69. Similarly, the Marquess of Queensbury repeatedly used the language of disgust to refer to Wilde's conduct with his son and with others: he referred to "disgusting conduct" and a "disgusting letter" (from Wilde to Bosie): see Richard Ellman, *Oscar Wilde* (London: Penguin, 1987), p. 447. At the conclusion of the second criminal trial, he wrote a letter to the press in which he said that Wilde should be

treated as "a sexual pervert of an utterly diseased mind, and not as a sane crimi-nal"—thus distancing him even more thoroughly from the normal human com-munity (Ellman, p. 478).

70. The men were typically not actual prostitutes; their occupations included groom, newspaper seller, office boy, clerk, manservant, and bookmaker. Several had literary or theatrical aspirations. Wilde's presents to them included nice clothes, sil-ver cigarette cases, walking sticks, theatre tickets, and first editions of his books. The Parker brothers, introduced to Wilde by Taylor, were more like call-boys. Charles Parker, one of the leading witnesses against Wilde, was an unemployed manservant; after his link with Taylor ended, he went into the army. Repeatedly the prosecution alluded to the low social class of these young men, in order to impugn the rela-tionships as improper. Disgust for the working classes was in this way interestingly mixed with disgust at same-sex conduct. One exchange: "Did you know that one Parker was a gentleman's valet, and the other a groom?" "I did not know it, but if I had I should not have cared. I didn't care twopence what they were. I liked them. I have a passion to civilize the community."

71. *Locke v. State*, 501 S. W. 2d 826, 829 (Tenn. Ct. App. 1973) (dissenting opinion, dissenting from the conclusion that "crime against nature" includes cunnilingus, reasoning that even necrophilia has never been illegal in Tennessee). See Tyler Trent Ochoa and Christine Newman Jones, "Defiling the Dead: Necrophilia and the Law," *Whittier Law Review* 18 (1997), 539–78.

72. See *People v. Stanworth*, 11 Cal. 3d 588, 604 n. 15, 114 Cal. Rptr. 250, 262 n. 15, 522 P.2d 1058, 1070 n. 15 (1974) (holding that the crime of rape requires a live victim, but that dead bodies are protected under the "mutilation" provision of the Health and Safety Code. Other case law, however, defines "mutilation" as requiring the cut-ting off of a limb or some other essential part of the body. See Ochoa and Jones, p. 544.

73. *People v. Kelly*, 1 Cal. 4th 495, 3 Cal. Rptr. 677, 822 P.2d 385 (1992). Rape, the court held, is a crime whose essential element "'consists in the outrage to the per-son and feelings of the victim of the rape'. . . . A dead body has no feelings of out-rage." The court held, however, that the defendant was guilty of felony murder: "A person who attempts to rape a live victim, kills the victim in the attempt, then has intercourse with the body, has committed only attempted rape, not actual rape, but is guilty of felony murder and is subject to the rape special circum-stance."

74. See Ochoa and Jones, p. 549 n. 63, citing interview with a California prose-cutor.

75. Language from the Oklahoma statute in question in *Maynard v. Cartwright*, 486 U.S. 356, 108 S. Ct. 1853 (1988).

76. *Godfrey v. Georgia*, 446 U.S. 420, 100 S. Ct. 1759, 64 L. Ed. 2d. 398 (1980).

77. Ibid. at 428–29, 100 S. Ct. at 1764–65.

78. See *Maynard v. Cartwright*, 1859.

79. Daniel Jonah Goldhagen, *Hitler's Willing Executioners: Ordinary Germans and the Holocaust* (New York: Knopf, 1996).

80. C. Browning, *Ordinary Men* (New York: HarperCollins, 1992), stressing the role of ordinary human reactions such as yielding to peer pressure, the desire not to be thought cowardly, not to lose face, etc.

81. Hilberg, *The Destruction of the European Jews* (New York: Holmes and Meier, 1985), stressing the psychological importance of a deliberate ideologically motivated treatment of Jews as similar to vermin, or even to inanimate objects.

82. Bartov, *Hitler's Army* (New York: Oxford University Press, 1991), stressing the role of ideology in creating a group capable of carrying out atrocities. See also Bartov, *Murder in Our Midst: The Holocaust, Industrial Killing, and Representation* (New York: Oxford University Press, 1996).

83. Goldhagen, p. 15.

84. See Omar Bartov's "Ordinary Monsters," a review of Goldhagen, in *The New Republic*, April 29, 1996, 32–38, which sees the falsely comforting message of Goldhagen's work as a possible reason for its enthusiastic reception despite its scholarly faults. See further the exchange between Goldhagen (TNR, December 23, 1996) and Bartov and Browning (TNR, February 10, 1997); also Bartov's review of *The Concentration Camp* by Wolfgang Sofsky, TNR, October 13, 1997.

85. See Bartov, pp. 37–38: "We are left with the thesis that the Germans were normally monsters, and that the only role of the Nazi regime was to furnish them with the opportunity to act on their evil desires. . . . Goldhagen is actually appealing to a public that wants to hear what it already believes. By doing so, he obscures the fact that the Holocaust was too murky and too horrible to be reduced to simplistic interpretations that rob it of its pertinence to our own time." For discussion of these issues I am grateful to Rachel Nussbaum.

86. *Beldotti v. Commonwealth*, 669 N. E. 2d 222 (Mass. Ct. App. 1996).

87. The fact that the items would presumably never again be in Beldotti's possession is no more problematic for this interpretation than it is for Kahan's, since both of us think, plausibly, that giving them back to his agents in accordance with his wishes is a way of letting him have his way concerning them.

88. See C. Sunstein, D. Kahnemann, and D. Shkade, "Assessing Punitive Damages (with Notes on Cognition and Valuation in Law)," 107 *Yale Law Journal* 2071 (1998), on the reliability and predictability of judgments of outrage in punitive damage cases.

89. This is not inconsistent with my claim, above, that giving him back his money or other property would not occasion outrage, even though he might have used money or other property to commit his crime. The sex paraphernalia were intimately connected with the specific nature of the crime and its terrible brutality, in a way that other items of property were not.

Chapter Two

The Progressive Appropriation of Disgust

Dan M. Kahan

1

Disgust is regarded as a paradigmatically *illiberal* sentiment. Mercy, because of its perception of individuals' vulnerability to forces outside their control, is unambiguously congenial to liberal values such as dignity and autonomy. Indignation and fear are at least potentially redeemable in liberal terms because they take as their objects external harms or threats to the person. Even guilt (if not shame) is thought to have a place in a liberal jurisprudence to the extent that individuals are educated to experience it when they interfere (or contemplate interfering) with the rights of others. But disgust, which embodies only our aversions to alien values and ways of life, is thought to furnish no legitimate ground for coercion in a state dedicated to liberal principles. Indeed, to date, the most important accounts of disgust in law are to be found in socially conservative defenses of public morals offenses and in liberal critiques of the same.[1]

I am unsatisfied with this alignment. My aim in this essay is to redeem disgust in the eyes of those who value equality, solidarity, and other progressive values. It would certainly be a mistake—a horrible one—to accept the guidance of disgust uncritically. But it would be just as big an error to discount it in all contexts. There are indeed situations in which properly directed disgust is indispensable to a morally accurate perception of what's at stake in the law. Even more important, disavowing even properly directed disgust cedes the powerful rhetorical capital of that sentiment to political reactionaries, who'll happily make use of *improperly* directed disgust to entrench illiberal regimes.

2

The conception of disgust that I mean to defend is the one identified by William Miller in his masterful book, *The Anatomy of Disgust*.[2] For Miller, disgust is not an instinctive and unthinking aversion but rather a thought-pervaded evaluative sentiment (pp. 7–9). It embodies the appraisal that its object is low and contaminating, and the judgment that we must insulate ourselves from it lest it compromise our own status (pp. 8–9). Disgust, according to Miller, gets its distinctive content from hierarchic social norms, which are themselves reinforced by our feelings and expressions of disgust (pp. 18, 50, 80, 194, 217).

Although Miller himself doesn't address criminal law in any detail, I believe his book supplies a critical remedy to the inattention that criminal law theorists have shown this sensibility. That's the nerve of an essay published elsewhere, in which I use Miller's account to illuminate the influence of disgust across a wide array of institutions and doctrines—from capital punishment, to shaming penalties, to hate crimes, to voluntary manslaughter.[3]

In this essay, however, I will focus on only two of Miller's claims, which I believe vindicate the normative value of disgust in criminal law.[4] The first can be called *the moral indispensability thesis*. According to Miller, disgust is an indispensable member of our moral vocabulary. "It signals seriousness, commitment, indisputability, presentness, and reality" (p. 180); "it marks out moral matters for which we can have no compromise" (p. 196), "harms that sicken us in the telling, things for which there could be no plausible claim of right" (p. 36). No other moral sentiment is up to the task of condemning such singular abominations as "rape, child abuse, torture, genocide, predatory murder and maiming"; bare indignation, for example, is too self-centered, too obsessed with "setting the balance right" for perceived slights to one's own person, to motivate the impassioned desire to punish such wrongs even when visited upon strangers (pp. 36, 186, 195). Indeed, we cannot "put cruelty first among vices," writes Miller drawing on Judith Shklar,[5] unless we treat properly directed disgust as one of our virtues (p. 202).

The second claim can be called *the conservation thesis*. Although the objects of disgust vary across places and times, *all* societies inevitably make use of disgust to inform their judgments of high and low, worthy and unworthy. This is so not only for aristocratic regimes, in which distinctions of class are uncontested, but also for egalitarian democratic ones, which are "based less on mutual respect for persons than on a ready availability of certain styles of contempt to the low that once were the prerogatives of the high" (p. 21).

The conservation of disgust across distinct and evolving modes of social organization explains why groups that are low in status seek to appropriate rather than annihilate the idiom of disgust, and why disgust, rather than disappearing, becomes a salient focal point for political contention within socially fluid, pluralistic societies. "In the hurly-burly of anxious competition for status," different groups aggressively market their favored conceptions of disgust "either to maintain rank already achieved, to test whether it ha[s] been achieved, or to challenge for its acquisition" (p. 217).

We see this dynamic at work in critiques of "hierarchies based on race, ethnicity, gender, physical and mental handicap, sexual orientation" and the like, movements that are at least as concerned with securing "changes in the emotional economy" as they are with securing "equal rights" (p. 235). To whose sensibilities should the law defer—the heterosexual soldiers who are disgusted by the idea of sharing barracks with gays or opponents of the gay-soldier ban who are disgusted by homophobia?[6] With whom should we be disgusted—the National Endowment for the Arts for funding sacrilegious art or conservative congressmen for proposing to screen NEA grant applications for offensiveness?[7] The question is never whether a society should organize itself around emphatic ideas of high and low, worthy and worthless, but only what the content of those animating hierarchies will be.

Together, the moral indispensability thesis and the conservation thesis suggest we shouldn't reject the guidance of disgust wholesale. If Miller is right that properly directed disgust is essential to perceiving cruelty, then attempting to banish it risks making the law morally blind. Likewise, if the conservation thesis is right—if disgust inevitably perseveres as social norms change—then opposing it will be both futile and self-defeating. We won't make any genuine progress in extirpating it; indeed, by disclaiming disgust, we'll only be denying ourselves a resource to fight those who, with no embarrassment, are willing to use it to advance illiberal causes. These are the arguments that I'll now develop.

3

Start with the moral indispensability thesis. It's tempting to seek support for this claim in the capital cases applying the "outrageously or wantonly vile, horrible, or inhuman" standard,[8] which says, in effect, that capital sen-

tencers (typically juries) should trust their own disgust sensibilities to identify which murderers deserve to die. These cases involve tales that "sicken us
in the telling" (p. 36).[9] They are the stories of men who gang rape an eleven-
year-old girl in the woods, poke sharp sticks through her vagina into her
abdominal cavity, and then smash her skull with a brick, while she begs for
her life;[10] who cut out the vocal cords of a witness to a crime and then am-
putate his feet and hands with an electric saw;[11] who leave the scene of a ter-
rifying nighttime burglary with the eighty-year-old victim dying in prayer,
a knife protruding from her eye socket.[12] (As Miller observes—in a much
more prosaic context—it is impossible to write of disgusting things without becoming disgusting oneself [p. 5]). These cases graphically bear out
Miller's contention that we cannot "put cruelty first among vices" without
counting properly directed disgust as a virtue (p. 202): it is not enough to
become angry when one hears of these atrocities; one must want to retch.

Nevertheless, I don't want to lay all my emphasis on the "horribly-vile"
standard. For one thing, condemnation in such cases is overdetermined:
wholly apart from whether they revolt us, killers who mutilate and torture,
who savor the suffering and degradation of their victims, warrant severe
punishment for purposes of deterrence and incapacitation. What's more,
for many—myself included—the lessons that such cases can teach us seem
clouded by the morally problematic status of the death penalty itself.

What we need to test the indispensability thesis, then, is a noncapital
case in which disgust seems both necessary and sufficient to remark the
cruelty of an offender's behavior. For this consider the request of Dennis
Beldotti.[13]

Beldotti committed murder to gratify his sadistic sexual appetites. His
female victim, strangled and stuffed into trash bags, was found in the bath-
room of his home. Bruises and cuts covered her body. Her nipples had been
sliced off. Incisions rimmed her pubic area. From Beldotti's bedroom, the
police recovered numerous nude photographs of the victim: some of these
had belonged to the victim and her husband and had apparently been
stolen by Beldotti from the victim's home; others of these snapshots had
been taken by Beldotti himself, after the victim's death, and showed dildos
penetrating her vagina and anus.[14] Based on these and other facts, the jury
found that Beldotti's crime reflected "extreme atrocity and cruelty," a factor
justifying life imprisonment without parole.[15]

Massachusetts law provides that at the conclusion of criminal proceedings the property seized and used in evidence should be dealt with in a
manner consistent with "the public interest."[16] Beldotti requested that the

state return certain items of his to his representatives outside prison. These included "four dildos"; "bondage paraphernalia"; "one plastic encased photo of the victim"; "female undergarments"; "one broken 'Glad Heavy Weight Trashbag' box"—presumably the one containing the bags he used to wrap his victim; "twenty-four magazines depicting naked pubescent and prepubescent girls and boys"; and scores of pornographic tapes and magazines "bearing such titles as 'Tamed & Tortured,' 'Tit & Body Torture,' and 'Tortured Ladies.'" The state opposed Beldotti's request on the ground that surrendering these items "would justifiably spark outrage, disgust, and incredulity on the part of the general public."[17] "The overwhelming public interest here," the state's attorney argued, "is that [the requested materials] be thrown in the trash can where they belong. . . . This has nothing to do with free expression. It has to do with the degradation of a young woman by a depraved individual."[18]

The Massachusetts Court of Appeals agreed. "Although property may not be forfeited simply because it is offensive or repugnant," the court observed,

> we see a connection between the property that Beldotti seeks to have returned to him and the crime he committed. The murder for which Beldotti is serving his life-term was particularly gruesome; he photographed the victim's naked torso after inserting dildos into her vagina and anus and after sexually mutilating her body. The items that Beldotti seeks to have returned to him can be seen as being directly related to those acts, as having influenced his behavior, or as being relevant to an understanding of the psychological or physical circumstances under which the crime was committed.

"In these circumstances," the court concluded, "to return the property would be so offensive to basic concepts of decency treasured in a civilized society, that it would undermine the confidence that the public has a right to expect in the criminal justice system."[19]

My guess is that this decision will strike nearly everyone as indisputably correct. What I want to argue is that there is in fact no viable basis for that intuition other than the one the court gave—namely, the disgustingness of Beldotti's request.

What other rationale could there be? The idea that possession of such items would undermine Beldotti's "rehabilitation" makes no sense, insofar as he was serving a term of life without parole. Perhaps inmates shouldn't be allowed to possess such materials, all of which could cause disruption inside a prison, and some of which could actually be used to torture other prisoners. But Beldotti sought to have the materials released only to his representatives outside prison; whether Beldotti himself could take possession of the items, the court recognized, was a separate issue that would have been addressed in the first instance by prison administrators.[20]

It might be thought that no one—in or out of prison—should be allowed to possess legally obscene materials. But preventing the consumption of obscenity would hardly be a disgust-neutral ground for the decision. What's more, as the court recognized, the mere possession of seized magazines and tapes, as opposed to the distribution of them, would not have violated state law.[21]

Forfeiture of the property might be defended as a punitive measure aimed at promoting general deterrence. But deterrence doesn't explain why Beldotti should be made to forfeit *these* particular articles rather than some others. Assume that imposition of a fine of a certain size could deter as effectively as the forfeiture of Beldotti's dildos and trash bags, his picture of the victim, and his "Tit & Body Torture" magazines and tapes. Would it then be acceptable—morally—to let Beldotti have his toys after all in exchange for a payment of that amount? If the answer is no, deterrence can't be the reason why. What grounds do we have, anyway, for thinking that the forfeiture of Beldotti's property adds *any* marginal deterrence to that achieved by sentencing him to life imprisonment without parole? If our confidence in the intuition that *Beldotti* was correctly decided outstrips our access to the empirics that would substantiate the deterrent benefits of forfeiture of his property, then something else besides deterrence explains the intuition.

That something *is* disgust. As the court recognized, the items Beldotti wanted bore the unmistakable aura of his crime. Bureaucratically processing his request—treating it as if it were no more remarkable than a claim for a stolen wallet or an impounded automobile—would have trivialized the unfathomable cruelty of his deeds. Indeed, because the atrocity of his crime consisted largely in the satisfaction he took in defiling his victim, restoring these items to his control, and thereby facilitating even his vicarious (for now) enjoyment of them, would have allowed Beldotti, as the state argued, to continue degrading her after death. By connecting the denial of Beldotti's request to "public confidence" in the law, moreover, the court recognized that enabling Beldotti to satisfy his tastes would inevitably have made the *state itself* complicit in his depravity. The *only* way to avoid being tainted by his request was to throw Beldotti's misogynistic magazines and his trash bags and his dildos and his kiddy porn "in the trash can where they belong"—rhetorically, if not literally.

I don't mean to exaggerate the significance of this analysis. Obviously, showing the indispensability of disgust to the result in one case doesn't prove Miller's claim that disgust is essential to our perception of, and opposition to, cruelty. But I do see *Beldotti* as an appropriate challenge to put to those who might advocate a disgust-free conception of criminal law. In effect, it turns the questions with which I started this section completely around: What besides disgust (and "just so" stories) can really explain the perception that granting his request would be wrong?[22] And if nothing else does, what could possibly justify committing ourselves to a regime that quiets so urgent a moral instinct?[23]

4

So far I've been arguing, consistently with the moral indispensability thesis, that there will indeed be circumstances in which disgust is essential to accurate moral perception. I now want to take up the significance of the conservation thesis, which, again, holds that disgust inevitably persists, notwithstanding shifts in social norms.

The progressive opponents of what I would regard as improperly directed disgust in law have in fact taken the lesson of the conservation thesis to heart. In the face of racist and homophobic violence, for example, they haven't been content to argue for mere tolerance; instead they have fought disgust fire with disgust fire. Supporters of hate-crime legislation want the public to understand not just that the "hate" killers are wrong to be disgusted by their victims, but that they themselves are "twisted," "warped," "sick," and "disgusting," and as a result properly despised as outsiders.[24] Severe punishment is the idiom that the criminal law uses to get that message across. Indeed, advocates for gays, women, African Americans, Jews, and others perceive severe punishments as *conferring* the high status that violence against them seeks to deny—which is exactly why political contention surrounding hate crimes is so intense.[25]

Consider here another disgust-crime story. To show a friend how easy it would be to get away with killing, Gunner Lindberg, a self-proclaimed white supremacist, picked out Vietnamese-American Thien Minh Ly from a crowd of roller skaters at a high school playground and stabbed him some fifty times in the body and neck.[26] Writing later to a cousin, Lindberg boasted of "kill[ing] a Jap a while ago."

I walked right up to him and he was scared. I looked at him and said, "Oh, I thought I knew you," and he got happy that he wasn't gonna get jumped, then I hit him. I stabbed him in the side about seven or eight times. He rolled over a little, so I stabbed his back 18 or 19 times. Then he lay flat and I slit . . . his throat on his jugular vein.[27]

For this crime, Lindberg (who wore a Dallas Cowboys football jersey every day at trial to mark that team's Super Bowl victory on the day of the attack)[28] earned the distinction of becoming the first offender sentenced to death under a California law authorizing capital punishment for racially motivated killings.[29] Civil rights advocates—including some who ordinarily oppose the death penalty—hailed the sentence on the ground that it appropriately remarked society's *disgust* for Lindberg and his deed. "It was an incredibly disgusting tale of torture and mutilation," the chairman of the Orange County Human Relations Commission noted in support of the sentence. "There's no question this is a sick act of a really troubled mind."[30]

As the conservation thesis predicts, then, those committed to using criminal law to raise the status of historically subordinated groups have not disavowed disgust but, rather, have sought to appropriate and redirect it against their opponents.[31] The liberal antidisgust position says that they are making a mistake to do that, that they should instead avail themselves of theories and styles of argument that are themselves free of disgust and hence free of that sentiment's sad historical association with unjust hierarchy.[32]

The insights of liberalism do indeed give us just as much reason to be wary of disgust—indeed, of all emotions[33]—in criminal law. The moral worth of emotional insight is never any better than the moral value of social norms and meanings that construct it. Nevertheless, drawing on the conservation thesis, I want to suggest that renouncing the guidance of disgust in criminal law altogether would in fact defeat, rather than advance, liberal ends.

The strongest version of this argument objects on principle to the perceived opposition between liberalism and hierarchy. It's true that liberal regimes renounce (at least in theory) rankings of a particular sort—such as those based on race, gender, and class—but they haven't renounced all perceptions of high and low, noble and base, worthy and unworthy. Even egalitarians hold pedophiles and sadists in low esteem, for example, not just because such persons threaten physical harm but because their values reveal them to be despicable. Indeed, as Miller points out, those who seek to raise the status of historically subordinated groups seek to reshape our "emotional economy" so that we'll come to see racists, sexists, and homophobes, among others, as debased in exactly the same way (p. 235). On this account, the proper course for liberalism is not to obliterate disgust but to reform its objects so that we come to value what is *genuinely* high and to despise what is *genuinely* low.

The criminal law has traditionally been seen as performing a "moral educative" function of this sort.[34] Punishment is thought to discourage criminality not only by raising the "price" of such misconduct but also by instilling aversions to it.[35] It's no surprise that legal moralizing of this sort has been, and continues to be, an instrument for entrenching reactionary regimes. But it can just as well furnish a weapon for attacking them.[36] Erecting a liberal counterregime of disgust, I've tried to show, is exactly the aim behind "hate crime" laws, which seek to make the proponents of illiberal species of hierarchy the object of our revulsion.

This is, as I've indicated, the *strongest* response to the liberal critique of disgust in criminal law; I want to lay more emphasis, however, on a weaker and more pragmatic rejoinder. This position views liberal opposition to disgust not as defective in principle but as self-deluding and self-defeating in practice.

To begin, the liberal opposition to disgust risks lulling progressives into a state of rhetorical vulnerability. After all, reactionaries will be completely unmoved by principled arguments against disgust because reactionaries are, by hypothesis, the group least inclined to show respect to their fellow citizens. Consequently, if progressives disclaim disgust in their public rhetoric, they will more often than not be restraining themselves unilaterally, allowing their adversaries exclusive access to this rich species of expressive capital.[37] To put this point in more concrete and partisan terms, if we give up on enhanced penalties for gay bashing, *they* will still insist on the Defense of Marriage Act.[38] Under these circumstances, forgoing disgust in the name of progressive values is not principled; it's just naïve.

In addition, styles of criminal law theorizing that purport to dispense with disgust do nothing in reality to mute its influence. They merely *disguise* it, and in so doing prolong the life of outmoded and illiberal norms in the law.

The dominant forms of criminal law theory both have liberal antecedents. *Voluntarism*, which derives from Kantian moral philosophy, treats punishment as justified if, and to the extent that, the offender's behavior stems from choice.[39] *Consequentialism*, which derives from utilitarian theory, views punishment as warranted if, and to the extent that, visiting suffering on the offender promotes desired states of affairs.[40] Consistent with the liberal bias against public moralizing, neither theory assigns intrinsic normative significance to the valuations that construct disgust or any other emotional sensibility.[41]

Neither theory, however, has succeeded in banishing such evaluations from the law. Voluntarism seeks to mute the influence of disgust sensibilities by making excuses depend not on the quality of offenders' emotional evaluations but, rather, on the destructive effect of emotions (or "impulses") on offenders' choice capacities; its focus is not on who is too virtuous but on who is too sick to be punished. Yet juries are notoriously resistant to excusing mentally unbalanced offenders who commit heinous crimes, no matter how obvious the origins of such behavior in pathology:[42] "[t]he muddle-headed reformers who seek to make crime a matter of illness rather than culpable intention," Miller writes, "fail to realize that we do not cease blaming just because someone is sick" (p. 203). At the same time, if we insist that decision makers speak in a mechanistic rather than an evaluative idiom, then we can expect them to describe as "sick" the offenders who are too virtuous to be held accountable for their crimes. Hence, the historic use of the "irresistible impulse" conception of insanity as a vehicle for excusing all manner of virtuous outlaws, from the cuckold to the battered woman.[43] And if their disgust sensibilities tell decision makers that a particular offender, such as the homophobe, deserves solicitude, we can expect them to see him as excusably "sick," too, a lesson taught to us in the selective receptivity of the law to the "homosexual panic" defense to charges of murdering gay men.[44]

The same story can be told about consequentialism. It attempts to suppress evaluative appraisals by connecting excuse to the relative dangerousness of an impassioned or impulsive offender.[45] But which impassioned offenders juries and judges see as dangerous necessarily depends on which victims they see as valuable enough to be protected from harm: cuckolds/battered women aren't all that dangerous, unless one happens to be a paramour/tyrannical man.[46] And if disgust sensibilities tell the decision maker that homosexuals are worth little, then that decision maker will predictably see the killing of one as a "one-time tragedy," committed by an otherwise normal person who the decision maker can be "confident . . . w[ill] not kill again."[47]

In short, the criminal law theories associated with modern liberalism don't genuinely purge the law of disgust. They only push disgust down below the surface of law, where its influence is harder to detect.

And *that's* bad. It should be clear that there's no way to guarantee that decision makers will be guided by liberal rather than illiberal disgust sensibilities.[48] But their sensibilities are likely to deviate least from the moral ideal when the evaluations they embody are most fully exposed to view. The prospect of publicly owning up to reliance on anachronistic or illiberal disgust sensibilities can itself shame decision makers into deciding on some other basis. Even more important, when we force decision makers to be open about the normative commitments that underlie their disgust sensibilities, members of the public are fully apprised of what those commitments are. This outcome facilitates the kind of self-conscious competition between liberal and illiberal conceptions of disgust, and between disgust and other moral sentiments, that is the key to making disgust a progressive rather than a reactionary force.

To illustrate, consider a case that Nussbaum and I have written about before. It involves a Texas judge who leniently sentenced a man convicted of killing two men for sport in a gay-bashing crime. "I put prostitutes and gays at about the same level," the judge explained, "and I'd be hard put to give somebody life for killing a prostitute."[49]

The judge's sentence and his remarks were outrageous—indeed, *disgusting*. And they *provoked* public disgust. The judge was formally censured for his remarks, and thereafter defeated in an election in which the support of women and gays for the judge's opponent turned out to be decisive.[50] In the wake of this and other incidents, moreover, the Texas (!) legislature enacted a hate crimes statute that expressly enhances the penalty for crimes motivated by bias against any group.[51] Had the judge cloaked *his* disgust in the rhetoric of voluntarism or consequentialism, it's very unlikely that his decision would have furnished so salient a focal point for rooting out the illiberal sensibilities that the judge's decision embodied.

5

To the two claims I've been discussing—the moral-indispensability and conservation theses—we can now add a third: *the self-delusion thesis*. The kind of hierarchic rankings characteristic of disgust are too durable to be driven from the scene by the morally antiseptic idiom of liberalism. Those who believe otherwise are fooling themselves. If we let them fool us, those who oppose brutal and indefensible hierarchies in law risk becoming their unwitting defenders.

NOTES

I am grateful to the Russell J. Parsons and Jerome S. Weiss Faculty Research Funds at the University of Chicago Law School for generous financial support.

1. This was how the famous Hart-Devlin debate unfolded. *See* H. L. A. Hart, Law, Liberty and Morality (1963); Patrick Devlin, The Enforcement of Morals (1965). An engaging liberal critique of disgust can also be found in Harlon L. Dalton, *"Disgust" and Punishment*, 96 Yale L.J. 881 (1987) (book review).

2. *See* William Ian Miller, The Anatomy of Disgust (1997). I include page citations to Miller's book in textual parentheticals.

3. *See* Dan M. Kahan, *The Anatomy of Disgust in Criminal Law*, 96 Mich. L. Rev. 1621 (1998).

4. Toni Massaro properly warns against "cit[ing] the fact of . . . disgust [in criminal law] as evidence of its moral authority." Show Some Emotions at p. 94; *cf.* Kahan, *supra* note 3, at 1648 ("My aim so far has been to show that disgust does in fact play a central role in criminal law. But nothing I've said implies, necessarily, that this role is morally justified. Indeed, seeing how much consequence the law invests in our disgust sensibilities should make us more intent, not less, on determining whether the law's confidence in that sentiment is warranted."). I agree with her too that the social norms that construct our emotional life aren't *normative* for law; they are susceptible of, and demand, independent moral evaluation. See Dan M. Kahan, *What Do Alternative Sanctions Mean?*, 63 U. Chi. L. Rev. 591, 630 (1996) ("The expressive dimension of punishment helps to describe how deep-seated sensibilities inform a society's institutional choices. But nothing in that phenomenon commits us to accept uncritically either the sensibilities or the institutions that happen to satisfy them."). My only goal here is to show that the foundation of disgust, shame, and related sensibilities in social norms doesn't disqualify them from being pressed into the service of a progressive political agenda. For an extended account of how social criticism can in fact take aim at certain norms at the same time that it appeals to the authority of others, see Michael Walzer, Interpretation and Social Criticism (1987).

5. *See* Judith Shklar, Ordinary Vices (1984).

6. *Compare* Eric Schmitt, *Pentagon Chief Warns Clinton On Gay Policy*, N.Y. Times, Jan. 25, 1993, at A1, col. 3 ("The Joint Chiefs of Staff, headed by Gen. Colin L. Powell, contend that repealing the ban would wreck morale and discipline, undermine recruiting, [and] force devoutly religious service members to resign.") *with* 139 Cong. Rec. H9656 (Nov. 15, 1993) (remarks of Rep. Woolsey) (deriding policy as "offensive" and "appall[ing]"); Suzanne E. Kenney, Letter to Editor, San Fran. Chronicle, Jan. 28, 1993, at A18 ("As a card-carrying feminist, hypersensitive to all forms of discrimination, I am appalled and disgusted by this latest wave of heterohypocrisy.").

7. *Compare* Amei Wallach, *The Funding Fight*, Newsday, Sept. 5, 1989, § II, at 4

(reporting controversy surrounding NEA funding of "Piss Christ," a crucifix submerged in artist's urine) *with* Valerie Richardson, *Helms' Photo in Urine at NEA-Funded Show*, Sept. 12, 1989, Wash. Times, at A1 (reporting controversy surrounding NEA funding of "Piss Helms," a urine-submerged photograph of Sen. Jesse Helms, the sponsor of legislation to ban funding of disgusting art).

8. *See, e.g.*, Ga. Code Ann. § 17-10-30(b)(7); 18 U.S.C. § 3592(b)(6) ("especially heinous, cruel, or depraved"). *See generally* Paul J. Heald, *Medea and the Un-Man: Literary Guidance in the Determination of Heinousness Under* Maynard v. Cartwright, 73 Tex. L. Rev. 571 (1995); Richard A. Rosen, *The "Especially Heinous" Aggravating Circumstance in Capital Cases—the Standardless Standard*, 64 N.C. L. Rev. 941 (1986).

9. Such cases are gruesomely catalogued in Thomas M. Fleming, *Sufficiency of Evidence, for Purposes of Death Penalty, to Establish Statutory Aggravating Circumstance that Murder Was Heinous, Cruel, Depraved or the Like—Post-Gregg Cases*, 63 A.L.R.4th 478 (1988).

10. *See* State v. Brogdon, 457 So. 2d 616, 621–22, 631 (La. 1984).

11. *See* Battle v. Armontrout, 814 F. Supp. 1412, 1416–17 (E.D.Mo.1993), aff'd, 19 F.3d 1547 (8th Cir.1994).

12. *See* Cavanaugh v. State, 729 P.2d 481 (Nev. 1986).

13. *See* Beldotti v. Commonwealth, 669 N.E.2d 222 (Mass. Ct. App. 1996).

14. *Id.* at 224.

15. *See* Mass. Gen. L. Ann. ch. 265 §§ 1–2; Ray Richard, *Beldotti convicted in Needham murder*, Boston Globe, Jan. 26, 1989, at 17.

16. Mass. Gen. L. Ann. ch. 276, § 3.

17. 669 N.E.2d at 225.

18. Patricia Nealon, *X-Rated Materials Held by Court Sought*, Boston Globe, Apr. 2, 1992, at 21 (quoting district attorney).

19. 669 N.E.2d at 225.

20. *See id.* at 224.

21. *See id.*

22. Nussbaum nominates indignation or outrage as an alternative explanation for *Beldotti*. "The most natural way to view the state's refusal is as a retributive quid pro quo: you took a woman's life with these sex toys, so to punish you we're going to refuse you the things that give you sexual pleasure." *"Secret Sewers of Vice": Disgust, Bodies, and the Law*, p. 53. This interpretation, she contends, furnishes not only a superior normative justification for the result but also a more accurate description of it: "[The court and the state's attorney] react with 'incredulity' because they assume that Beldotti is not a monster, but a sane human being, and must know that his request is outrageous. Were they thinking of him as like a slug or a heap of vomit, they would not be so outraged by the request, they would just see it as lunatic pathology." *Id.* at 54. This is unpersuasive. What makes denial of Beldotti's request seem so imperative isn't that we would otherwise be at a loss for ways to get our retributive in-

tentions across; denying him a television set or a nightlight or any other creature comfort—not to mention denying him his liberty for the rest of his life—expresses retributive condemnation quite clearly. Outrage, by itself, doesn't uniquely determine any particular set of deprivations, even if it commits us to imposing deprivations of some sort. The reason Beldotti must be denied the sex toys and photographs and magazines in particular is that our allowing him to have possession of those items would make us complicit in his continuing enjoyment of a distinctly *repulsive species of pleasure*—namely, the defilement and degradation of his victim and her loved ones. Revulsion toward alien and depraved values, intense condemnation of cruelty, and the anxiety to avoid becoming implicated in the same are all native to Miller's conception of disgust as an evaluative sentiment. Nor is there any tension between disgust as an evaluative sentiment and the *intelligibility* of Beldotti's request. In suggesting that we must be experiencing something other than disgust whenever we can understand *why* we are revolted, Nussbaum assumes, inconsistently with her own understanding of emotions, that disgust must be noncognitive.

23. The answer, according to Nussbaum, is the need to avoid a sense of estrangement from the objects of our disgust. To indulge disgust toward the perpetrators of the Holocaust, she maintains, is to see them as "unique disgusting monsters. We are nothing like this. . . . By contrast, when we see Nazis depicted without disgust, as human beings who share common characteristics with us . . . this . . . warn[s] us that we might well have done the same under comparable circumstances." *"Secret Sewers of Vice": Disgust, Bodies, and the Law*, at 51. I find this analysis puzzling. If the argument is that treating Nazis as "disgusting monsters"—as "evil [that] is outside, alien"—is somehow unfair to the Nazis, then I think Nussbaum suffers from an excessive degree of empathy, one that risks denying us the affective resources necessary to *perceive* just how abominable the Nazis' behavior really was. If the argument is the consequentialist one that we might somehow repeat the Nazis' abominations if we indulge our disgust toward them, then I think Nussbaum is guilty of wildly implausible speculation. Why wouldn't a society be *less* likely to engage in genocide if it taught its members to detest those who have perpetrated such atrocities? Why wouldn't a society be *more* likely to turn to genocide if it dedicated itself to making its members see their ultimate moral kinship with the Nazis—to making them see that, after all, "we might well have done the same under comparable circumstances"?! *See generally* Kenworthey Bilz, *Not All Sweetness and Light: The Moral Exclusionary Model in Law and Literature* (unpublished manuscript, Nov. 1997) (arguing that the literary method of appraisal generates morally satisfactory results only when it elicits selective empathy).

24. *See, e.g.,* James Brooke, *Crowd in Denver Rallies Against Skinhead Violence*, N.Y. Times, Nov. 26, 1997, at A20 (reporting speech of Denver mayor: "They [white supremacist 'skinheads'] are not part of Denver's culture. They are not part of Denver's vision. They are not wanted here."); Roger Buckwalter, *Hate Remains a Poison in Society*, Jupiter Courier (Jupiter, Fla.), Sept. 11, 1996, at A4 (describing swastika

graffiti: "This disgusting act by a mental and moral midget . . . was just more evidence—as if any more was needed—that hate continues to infest this free society. . . ."); *Hundreds Mourn Victim of Skinhead, 19, in Denver,* L.A. Times, at A16 (quoting mayor at funeral of hate crime victim: "It's intolerable that something like that happens. It's disgusting to me personally that it happened in our city."); *Neo-Nazis Still Here* (editorial), Seattle Times, Mar. 25, 1997, at B4 (denouncing "[t]he disgusting celebration marking Hitler's birthday that's usually held by [local] neo-Nazis"); John Nichols, *"Time to Stand Up and Be Counted" to Protest the Klan,* Capital Times (Madison, Wis.), Aug. 22, 1995, at 8A (reporting local woman's decision to display pink triangle "to signal disgust with the Klan's homophobia"); *President Starts Anti-Hate Campaign,* Chicago Tribune, June 8, 1997, at 7 (""Voicing disgust over violent bigotry, President Clinton on Saturday ordered a Justice Department review of laws against hate crimes and said he will convene a White House conference on the problem next fall.") Ryan R. Sanderson, Letter to the Editor, Baltimore Sun, July 24, 1997, at 14A (reacting to comment that gay man deserved to be shot: "This is the sickest belief I can imagine.").

25. *See* George P. Fletcher, With Justice for Some 2–4 (1995); Jean Hampton, *The Retributive Idea,* in Jeffrie G. Murphy & Jean Hampton, Forgiveness and Mercy 140–42 (1988); James B. Jacobs & Kimberley Potter, Hate Crimes: Criminal Law and Identity Politics 66–78 (1998); *see also* Randall L. Kennedy, *McCleskey v. Kemp: Race, Capital Punishment, and the Supreme Court,* 101 Harv. L. Rev. 1388, 1393–94,1425 (1988) (describing willingness to execute murderers of African Americans as measure of African American status).

26. *See* Thao Hua, *Murderer Had Troubled Youth, Psychologist Says,* L.A. Times, Oct. 7, at B1.

27. Greg Hernandez, *O.C. Jury Votes Death for Hate Crime Murder,* Oct. 10, 1997, L.A. Times, at A1.

28. *See id.*

29. *See* Cal. Penal Code § 190.2(a)(16); *Supremacist Sentenced To Death For Hate Crime,* L.A. Times, Dec., 13, 1997, at A1.

30. Hernandez, *supra* note 27.

31. This is a well-remarked tactic of social reform movements. *See* Joseph R. Gusfield, Symbolic Crusade: Status Politics and the American Temperance Movement 206 (2d 1986); Joseph R. Gusfield, *On Legislating Morals: The Symbolic Process of Designating Deviance,* 56 Cal. L. Rev. 54, 56–57, 73 (1968).

32. See Nussbaum, *"Secret Sewers of Vice."*

33. Obviously, disgust is not the only emotion ever to have served the cause of hierarchy. Indignation, too, is constructed by and reinforces status norms, which at different times and places—indeed, in all times and places—have been hierarchical. *See generally* Gusfield, *supra* note 31, at 112 (defining "[m]oral indignation [as] the hostile response of the norm-upholder to the norm-violator where no direct, personal advantage to the norm-upholder is at stake," and giving as ex-

amples indignation directed at homosexuals, bohemians, drug addicts, and social radicals). Indeed, the common law paradigm of righteous indignation belongs to the dishonored cuckold, who is afforded mitigation when he kills his unfaithful wife or her paramour—a legal convention clearly rooted in hierarchical
gender norms. *See generally* Donna K. Coker, *Heat of Passion and Wife Killing:
Men Who Batter/Men Who Kill*, 2 Rev. L. & Women's Studies 71 (1992); Jeremy
Horder, *Provocation and Responsibility* (1992). Nussbaum argues, contra Miller,
that indignation is capable of doing all the legitimate work that disgust does in
remarking and motivating opposition to cruelty. *See* Nussbaum, *"Secret Sewers of
Vice,"* at 28. But whether or not she is right about that, she is wrong to think that
the "historical . . . use[] [of disgust] as a powerful weapon in social efforts to exclude certain groups and persons," id. at 15, gives us a reason to prefer indignation.

34. *See, e.g.,* John Andenaes, *General Prevention—Illusion or Reality?*, 43 J. Crim.
L., Criminology, & Police Sci. 176, 179 (1952); Jean Hampton, *The Moral Education
Theory of Punishment*, 13 Phil. & Pub. Affairs 208, 212 (1984).

35. *See* Kenneth G. Dau-Schmidt, *An Economic Analysis of the Criminal Law as
Preference-Shaping Policy*, 1990 Duke L.J. 1.

36. *See, e.g.,* Katherine Baker, *Sex, Rape, and Shame* 79 B.U. L. Rev. 663 (1999)
(advocating use of shaming penalties to attack the social meaning of sex as con-
quest on college campuses).

37. Offering her own pragmatic argument, Toni Massaro warns of the danger
that progressives who trade on disgust, shame, and related sensibilities risk inciting
a reactionary backlash. See *Show (Some) Emotions*, at 99. But insofar as reactionaries are already fully aware of the power of these sensibilities, how does the progressive appropriation of them make things worse? Indeed, why should progressives refrain from invoking them in the absence of any enforceable assurance that their adversaries will do likewise? Massaro's arguments are important, and I do not claim
to have fully answered them here. I attempt a more comprehensive response in Dan
M. Kahan, *The Secret Ambition of Deterrence*, 113 Harv. L. Rev. (forthcoming Dec.
1999).

38. *See* Pub. L. 104–199, § 2, 110 State. 2419 (1996) ("No State, territory, or possession of the United States, or Indian tribe, shall be required to give effect to any
public act, record, or judicial proceeding of any other State, territory, possession, or
tribe respecting a relationship between persons of the same sex that is treated as a
marriage under the laws of such other State, territory, possession, or tribe, or a right
or claim arising from such relationship.").

39. The most influential voluntarism account is that of H. L. A. Hart. See H. L.
A. Hart, Punishment and Responsibility 46–49 (1968).

40. This is the position associated with Jeremy Bentham. *See* Jeremy Bentham,
An Introduction to the Principles of Morals and Legislation, reprinted in The Utilitarian 162 (1961), and his successors, *see, e.g.,* Gary Becker, *Crime and Punishment:*

An Economic Approach, 76 J. Pol. Econ. 169 (1968); Richard Posner, *An Economic Theory of Crime*, 85 Colum. L. Rev. 1193 (1985).

41. *See* Dan M. Kahan & Martha C. Nussbaum, *Two Conceptions of Emotion in Criminal Law*, 96 Colum. L. Rev. 269, 301–5 (1996); *see also* Claire O. Finkelstein, *Duress: A Philosophical Account of the Defense in Law*, 37 Ariz. L. Rev. 251 (1995) (discussing "voluntarist" and "welfarist" theories of criminal law).

42. Empirical evidence, for example, suggests that juries, no matter how instructed on the definition of insanity, give little weight to the condition of the defendant's psyche and focus instead on a cluster of factors relevant to the defendant's culpability. *See, e.g.*, Norman J. Finkel & Sharon F. Handel, *How Jurors Construe "Insanity,"* 13 Law & Hum. Behav. 41, 57 (1989); James R. P. Ogloff, *A Comparison of Insanity Defense Standards on Juror Decision Making*, 15 Law & Hum. Behav. 509, 521, 526 (1991).

43. *See* Kahan & Nussbaum, *supra* note 41, at 345–50.

44. See Gary David Comstock, *Dismantling the Homosexual Panic Defense*, 2 Law & Sexuality 81, 96–97 (1992); Robert B. Mison, Comment, *Homophobia in Manslaughter: The Homosexual Advance as Insufficient Provocation*, 80 Cal. L. Rev. 133, 167–69 (1992).

45. *See, e.g.*, Herbert Wechsler & Jerome Michael, *A Rationale of the Law of Homicide: II*, 37 Colum. L. Rev. 1262, 1280–82 (1937).

46. *See* Kahan & Nussbaum, *supra* note 41, at 311–12.

47. *See Judge Draws Protest After Cutting Sentence of Gay Man's Killer*, N.Y. Times, Aug. 17, 1994, at A15. (reporting comments of judge explaining lenient sentence for man who hunted down and then shot between the eyes a gay who had earlier propositioned him).

48. Nor is there any way to guarantee this about any other emotion, including indignation. *See supra* note 33.

49. *See* Kahan & Nussbaum, *supra* note 41, at 364.

50. *See* Lisa Belkin, *Gay Rights Groups Hail Defeat of Judge in Texas*, N.Y. Times, Dec. 4, 1992, at B20, col. 5.

51. See Tex. Penal Code Ann. § 12.47 (West 1994); Tex. Code Crim. Proc. Ann. art. 42.014 (West Supp. 1996); see also Clay Robison, *Richards Signs Hate Crimes Bill into Law*, Houston Chronicle, June 20, 1993, State section, at 3 (noting that purpose of the legislation is to enhance "criminal offenses motivated by the victims' race, religion, ethnicity, sexual orientation or national origin").

Chapter Three

Show (Some) Emotions

Toni M. Massaro

I

Social norm theory is a strand of behavioral economics that analyzes social norms, status competition, and social meaning, and the ways in which all three influence individual behavior.[1] This literature complements (or offers a "friendly amendment" to)[2] neoclassical, rational-choice models of individual behavior, by adding social context and human emotions that help explain individual conduct that otherwise might appear inexplicable and irrational.[3] The aim is to beef up economists' unrealistically thin account of human behavior, while still preserving the relative simplicity and predictive power of the economics model.

The esteem of others, some of this literature suggests, is a powerful incentive to observe norms: losing social status hurts enough that the mere threat of loss can elicit behaviors that may otherwise seem contrary to one's self-interest.[4] This status sensitivity may induce cooperation with norms that may serve the collective but that may be of little use to any one person. This status sensitivity is driven in turn by two emotions—shame and pride—which can motivate humans to observe social norms in ways that are not captured fully by neoclassical models of rational choice.

To illustrate the point, the social norm literature sketches familiar scenes—such as that of restaurant patrons who leave tips in restaurants far from home[5]—that betray the limitations of traditional models of rational choice, wealth-maximizing behavior. People *do* tip in these situations, we realize. Isn't it *irrational* to tip when miserly behavior pays more (in terms of wealth) and costs nothing (in terms of status)? *Why* do they tip when no one will see them (and thus think less of them) if they don't?

We then are told that the answers are rather simple and may still fit within the basic rational-choice model of human behavior, if one considers two points. The first is that status matters in ways that are comparable to wealth, and the second is that status norms, once internalized, have an emotional dimension that motivates individual behavior in persistent ways that can produce behavior that departs from both a simple, wealth-maximizing model's predictions and a simple status-maximizing model's predictions. Violating an internalized social norm can trigger a negative emotion—shame, or the fear of it—which can deter norm violation, even when the external constraints that initially helped to instill them such as an observant, present "other" who notices, declaims, and threatens to (or does) broadcast the norm default are absent. A well socialized patron thus will *feel bad* if he stiffs the waiter because he has internalized the norm of tipping, and tipping therefore does make "economic" sense, even when no norm police are present, once the costs of these negative emotions are taken into account.[6] Norm policing is both an inside *and* an outside job; indeed, the omnipresent, internal panoptic, with its emotional arsenal, is a more vigilant and effective deterrent to norm deviation than the most officious neighborhood snitch. The better that this process is understood, therefore, the easier it may be to deter norm deviance.

Thus it is no surprise that social norm literature, along with this "sociofunction-of-emotions" component, has caught the eye of legal scholars.[7] Several writers have applied this literature to constitutional law,[8] tort law,[9] contract law,[10] and criminal law.[11] The criminal law scholars among them—whose work is my focus here—are recasting the social order and deterrence models that dominated criminal law theory in the 1940s–1960s[12] into the social norm vocabulary of social meaning and social influence.[13]

Applying a social norm model, the criminal law scholars argue that criminal law can alter the social meaning of criminal behaviors (e.g., from "acceptable" to "unacceptable"), which in turn may influence status-conscious citizens to avoid the behavior themselves, to withdraw approval of others who engage in it, and to thereby shore up the social norm underlying the law.[14] For example, if law criminalizes nonconsensual intercourse between married partners, then it expresses condemnation of the act, which may help shift the social meaning of this behavior from acceptable to reprehensible. Conversely, decriminalizing acts can transform the social meaning of an act by destigmatizing it and making it more socially acceptable. For example, the social meaning of same-sex relationships may change if same-sex sexual relations are decriminalized or same-sex marriage is legalized.[15] Law enforcement strategies should be mindful of the social norm aspect of some criminal behavior and should attempt to disrupt, condemn, or ambiguate social practices that reinforce criminal behavior. For example, police should aggressively enforce ordinances against loitering, panhandling, or prostitution, insofar as these practices signal disorder in the community and broadcast that criminal elements rather than law enforcement have control of public places. It is not enough to arrest and prosecute criminal gang members; law must alter the social context that gives criminal gang activity a certain social status and that makes noncriminal gang members afraid to cooperate with the police, or even to resist participation in criminal gang activity.

Of course, that law has such expressive aims[16] and may alter social meanings is hardly a new concept,[17] as any sociologist would tell us. Indeed, if law *didn't* have some capacity to affect both social meanings and social norms, and to effect some social influence and inflict some emotional harm by denouncing the criminal act and thus conveying disapproval of the offender, it would be pointless, from a consequentialist perspective. Law is widely and properly understood to affect social status, insofar as it constantly draws lines between acceptable and unacceptable behaviors, between law and outlaw, which lines inevitably reflect back on the people who cross them. This social status impact can be explicit, such as in a legal order that expressly assigns social caste and attendant rights and responsibilities, as did the law of slavery and Jim Crow laws.[18] Or it can be fairly implicit, as when the law holds an underage male but not an underage female criminally responsible for consensual intercourse with a minor.[19] What the social norm theory work contributes to these generally understood observations about law, status, and norms, thus are (1) attention to and refinement of a well-known phenomenon; (2) a reduction of the complexities that plague sociological and psychological accounts of this phenomenon, through use of models that consider only a few of the relevant variables, especially "status"; and (3) experimental work that tests in specific contexts our intuition that status anxiety and a desire to maximize our status may induce cooperation.[20] Social norm theory seeks to explain how, exactly, social norms affect human behavior. The criminal law theorists, in turn, seek to translate these social norm descriptive insights into legal reform proposals designed to alter the social norms and thus the relevant behaviors.

Given the sweep of its aims—to explain social norms cross-culturally—the social norm model must be, and is, excessively general and acontextual. It suggests that humans innately and universally seek to maximize "status" but does not define "status," thereby leaving open the possibilities of culturally and individually divergent definitions. That the model is adaptable across social contexts is, of course, both a potential strength and a potential weakness of the model. If viewed at a sufficiently abstract level of analysis, *all* action might be interpreted as arising from some form of "self-interest." Consequently, the abstract insight that all, or even much, human action arises from a self-interested desire to promote one's "social status" may suffer from the fatal deficiency of infinite applicability, unless it can be narrowed in a way that may yield greater meaning and interpretative force.

Can the status, social norm, and shame insights be so narrowed? Or are they too abstract and acontextual to shed meaningful, practical light on concrete legal problems? In particular, does an emphasis on social norms and shame add anything useful to the existing perspectives on criminal penalties or social deviance? Or does it merely restate what is already widely understood about how fear of social disapproval contributes to norm observation in ways that are obviously relevant to criminal law but that are no easier to quantify, to predict accurately, or to control than they were without the specifics of social norm theory? Before turning to these questions, one must consider whether the available literature on human emotions might provide the nuance and contextual sensitivity that the social norm model lacks, and might be combined with social norm theory to make it more precise and thus more powerful.

II

The available literature on human emotions is extremely difficult to summarize, which makes it likewise difficult to determine whether current knowledge about human emotions supports the claims of the social norm model or the legal reforms that are now being proposed on the basis of the social norm model. What is sometimes referred to as "emotion theory" is actually better described as emotion *theories*. The literature is bound only loosely by two unresolved questions: What are human emotions and why do we have them? A rancorous collection of psychologists, biologists, sociologists, neuroscientists, and philosophers have proposed various responses to these foundational questions. The areas of ongoing debate include the extent to which emotions are innate versus learned,[21] the social function of emotions,[22] the physiological genesis of emotions,[23] the moral aspects of emotions,[24] and the role of cognition in emotions,[25] to name only the most visible and profound fault lines within the field.[26] Thus if one proceeds with a theory of human behavior that depends on a particular response to, or interpretation of, these questions, then the theory will be controversial at best among emotion theorists, and quite possibly wrong.

For example, if one focuses solely on shame—the emotion that social norm theory emphasizes—one must recognize that the available literature betrays very little consensus, other than that this emotion is complex and central to a person's sense of self. The ill-understood individual and cultural shadings and variations of the emotion, which are underplayed in the social norm model in order to make universal claims about human behavior, are extensive.

Although individual and cultural variations may not matter to the social norm model, given its general pitch and limited predictive claims, these variations matter quite a bit when one seeks to apply the general model to a specific person or groups of persons, with the hope that a particular external stimulus—like criminal punishment—will elicit or shape these persons' sense of shame, and thereby influence their behavior in predictable, socially desirable ways. What we know about shame makes this hope seem extremely optimistic, if not entirely baseless in many cases.

Most emotion theorists agree that shame is linked with the awareness of an inadequacy, strangeness, limitation, or defeat,[27] but they disagree vigorously about whether it is innate.[28] Notable among those who view shame as innate hardware[29] was the late Silvan Tomkins, who posited that shame is a basic negative affect.[30] According to his account, we may feel shame whenever there is an interruption or barrier to our interest or enjoyment, but that does not completely diminish that interest or pleasure.[31] Shame tends to produce a reduction of one's facial communication by the dropping of one's eyes, eyelids, head, and sometimes the upper body,[32] and, like disgust, "operates ordinarily only after interest or enjoyment has been activated."[33] It is also one of several innate responses that "bias [the human being] to want to remain alive and to resist death, to want to experience novelty and to resist boredom, to want to communicate, to be close to and in contact with others of his species, to experience sexual excitement and to resist the experience of head and face lowered in shame."[34] To say that someone is shameless, according to this account, is incorrect; all human infants arrive neurobiologically "shame ready."[35]

But the line between this purported genetic unfolding and environmental shaping is quite hazy. The shame-ready infant soon learns from his or her personal shame episodes when to feel shame and why, as well as highly individualized avoidance or coping behaviors.[36] Our affect system thus is heavily modulated by our analytical capacities,[37] so that even if the affect of shame is innate (and thus universal), the precise triggers for expressions of shame, even more than other affects, are informed by our experiences (and thus intensely local).[38] These local variations may depend on one's religion,[39] culture, gender,[40] age, family dynamics, and other variables.[41]

This means that shame is not necessarily linked to, or coextensive with, what is normatively *shameful*; rather, it is an "unpathologized"[42] affect that combines with cognition to assist the individual in drawing crucial lines or barriers between what one desires for pleasure (not, necessarily, taboo pleasures)[43] and what one cannot obtain or must forgo to avoid greater pain.[44]

Relinquishing these pleasures can be debilitatingly painful, to the extent that the desires may involve the experienced self,[45] and shame heightens attention to that self and to its limitations.[46] The source of shame, like that of physical pain,[47] may be localized—it typically begins with the face—but its final impact radiates out and embraces the *whole self*.[48]

The shame affect also entails a certain anxious ambivalence. According to some accounts, shame is thwarted interest or excitement that is only *incompletely* overcome.[49] For example, a rebuffed one may turn away in shame with downcast eyes but is still drawn toward the desired one. "'I want, but . . .'" may best express this feature of the shame response.[50]

Shame thus covers tremendous emotional territory, territory that is often divided conceptually into distinct categories of experience.[51] At the level of *affect*, the term *shame* may refer "equally to shyness, defeat, alienation and guilt,"[52] according to some theorists, but at the level of cognitive *experience* these emotions cover a range of experiences that are often codified separately.

That shame can link up so variably to external inputs makes Darwinian sense, insofar as this enables the individual to adapt to his or her social surroundings. Consequently, shame's variability does not necessarily undermine the claim that shame is innate, though it makes it difficult to generalize about the emotion and its manifestations. In a recent work based on "evolutionary psychology,"[53] Robert Wright suggests that humans as a species are chemically addicted to social esteem, in that impressing other people may increase the serotonin (neurotransmitter) level in our brains.[54] In other words, shame and pride are one part of a larger, biologically driven social structure of status and competition that results from the species' struggle for survival.[55] Shame is simply "a way of discouraging the repeat of status-reducing behaviors, however status may be defined by a particular social group."[56]

Some emotion theorists, however, deny that shame, even at the level of affect, is innate or universal.[57] Emotion theorists who argue that "there are some common elements in the contexts in which emotions are found to occur, despite differences due to individual and cultural differences in social learning,"[58] are countered by theorists who express profound skepticism about the existence of any such common elements. Some of the universalism skeptics suggest that our emotions are not "things" or "concepts" at all but "complex narrative struggles that give shape and meaning to somatic and affective experiences . . . [and] whose unity is to be found neither in strict logical criteria nor in the perceptible features of objects, but . . . in the types of self-involving stories they make it possible for us to tell about our feelings."[59] The latter theorists stress the internal contradictions in the emotion literature, noting that "for every William James who claims that the emotions are reducible to feelings of bodily states there is an Errol Bedford who claims that they have nothing to do with feelings or sensations or psychological facts at all, but are rather linguistic ploys for inputting responsibility and blame and for praising and criticizing conduct (as, for example, in 'I hope you are ashamed of yourself,' or 'I sure envy your technique.'")[60]

This ongoing innateness debate casts grave doubt on efforts to map or explain any human emotions. Whether the cartography should entail a charting of neural firings that are genetically predetermined, or a charting of our emotional experiences as we have interpreted them to ourselves, or some combination of both is unclear. The universality of any emotion, including shame, therefore is unresolved, and the literature might best be summarized as follows: The "answer to the question 'Are there basic emotions?' is 'Do not trust anyone who says they really know.'"[61]

Disagreement also persists over the nature of the interests that shame tends to inhibit—that is, what one is ashamed of. Some psychoanalysts, led by Sigmund Freud, have viewed shame as an inhibition of a very particular form of interest: sexual exhibitionism. In their view, shame is a reaction-formation that curbs forbidden pregenital and, later on, genital wishes.

But other theorists describe shame far more generally as a reaction to the tension between one's ego ideal and one's actual performance[62]—that is, between what one desires and what one can attain—that is not limited to defeats in the realms of sex or exhibitionistic desires as Freud suggested.[63] The frustrations that give rise to shame, they note, often erupt from an interpersonal, nonsexual conflict, where "one individual somehow breaks the interpersonal bridge with the other."[64] Thus a common but not exclusive source of shame is the experience of being rejected or unloved by important others.[65] Behind the blush of shame, this account suggests, lurks the fear of contempt and abandonment.[66]

Whether it inhibits sexual desires only, or extends further to inhibit a wide range of pleasures, shame is an undeniably useful response in humans because it helps to curb appetites that may *need* to be curbed. Shame acts as a sentry that assists the individual in respecting others' social and physical borders, thereby protecting the individual from the greater harms these others might inflict. Without a sense of shame, one might proceed heedless of tremendous social and other perils, only to suffer stinging rejection, abandonment, or worse. One who truly felt *no* shame thus would be a radically unsocialized, deeply disturbed individual who lacked a most basic inhibition—so basic that it is likely that very few (if any) utterly shameless individuals exist.

Also clear is that shame involves the whole self in a way that other, closely related experiences do not; for example, many emotion theorists view guilt as a more calibrated, less global, experience than shame.[67] Of course, experiential slippage exists between shame and other closely related emotions, such as guilt, shyness, and embarrassment,[68] but for most theorists, shame is activated by a disturbed sense of oneself that is, if only briefly, *all-encompassing*[69] in ways that these other phenomena are not.[70]

In sum, shame is a potentially devastating incursion into one's idealized sense of self: It is a narcissistic defeat. As one learns to objectify oneself, that is, to see oneself—as an object autonomous of others—one learns to compare oneself to these others.[71] With this stage of development comes the inevitable pain of unfavorable comparisons, as one confronts the hard, developmental truth that there are others who are bigger, stronger, and more competent than oneself, particularly when one is a small child.[72] Self-consciousness thus is shame hell; it expels the child from the Garden of Narcissism, where world and self were coextensive, and infantile grandiosity went unchallenged.[73]

Shame therefore is an inevitable by-product of maturation, even if it is not innate, insofar as it results from the recognition of the limits of the self. All of one's desires for uniqueness or merger simply cannot be fulfilled, even by a vigilant and loving parent. Whether shame is innate remains contested, however, as does the precise role of socialization in creating shame sensitivities. What is not contested is the self-shattering pain that shame can produce in an individual.

Likewise clear is that the same experience may vary widely among individuals, to the extent that cognition and experience mold emotional responses. In general, individuals link up the behavioral indices of shame (lowered head, averted eyes, blushing) with particular *scenes* or *scripts*, whose common theme is failing to attain a desired ideal.[74] Needless to say, however, a wide range of defects may, if observed by others (or by the self-fantasizing exposure of the defect), reveal a nonideal self: one may not be ideally powerful, sexually attractive, moral, intelligent, brave, hygienic, urbane, physically healthy, confident, articulate, and so on.

The nonspecific nature of the affect and its contextual constructions therefore make it extraordinarily difficult to determine whether and how shame will be experienced by a given individual. Parents vary in the barriers that they impose on children's interest and enjoyment,[75] and each child links shame to his or her own life scenes, sometimes in ways the parents did not intend or expect.[76] The result may be that *whatever* emotion triggered the behavior that prompted parental rebuke may be bound to shame, such that the child will feel shame whenever this other affect occurs.[77] A well-meaning parent may, through repeated reprovals of a child's affects, unintentionally teach the child not only that the targeted behaviors are shameful in context, but that the emotions associated with the behavior are too, such that even affectlessness seems shameful,[78] and the child is caught in a hopeless affect pickle.

Children learn about shame responses by observing the shame of others,[79] a mechanism that can transmit shame norms from generation to generation.[80] Such shame legacies promote group or family solidarity,[81] solidarity that can render group members especially vulnerable to vicarious shame,[82] insofar as that solidarity may enhance their empathy for others.[83]

Yet this sparse account of shame—any barrier to interest or enjoyment may trigger the affect of shame—demonstrates why one cannot with confidence predict whether or when an individual actually will experience shame: "The same barrier may produce in different individuals, or in the same individual at different times, counteraction or renunciation or that incomplete reduction of interest and enjoyment which activates shame."[84] Moreover, a barrier to one's interest or enjoyment may arouse multiple affects, further complicating the task of predicting behavior or emotional responses.[85] The plural, contextual, and variable nature of shame therefore makes any effort to *shame* a person, or to elicit shame anxieties in a group of persons, highly uncertain.[86]

Most crucial of all psychological insights about shame, though, in terms of the literature's relevance to legal and social reforms, is that *behavioral re-*

sponses to shame vary in complex ways that can exaggerate or mask its impact, or otherwise make the consequences difficult to predict.[87] For example, children who receive inadequate empathic responses from their parents, or whose idealization of a parent is ignored or rejected by that parent, can become adults in whom shame manifests itself as serious depression, anxiety, anger, or withdrawal.[88] And contrary to assumptions that shame always results in withdrawal from others, remorse, or avoidance of the disapproved behavior, many psychologists instead believe that "[m]any violent children lash out not because of low self-worth but because they are highly prone to shame (that is why so much violence is triggered by acts of disrespect)."[89] Shame can provoke externalization of blame or other responses,[90] including a reduced capacity for empathy.[91]

One simply cannot know in advance what the impact of shame might be in a given case. It can range from no impact, to mild discomfort, to a desire to hide, to a desire to retaliate, to a profound and complete loss of self that inspires a desire to die.

Finally, emotions are not discretely contained phenomena that one can switch on or off precisely. For example, shame is bordered by embarrassment, humiliation, and mortification, in porous ways. If we hope to elicit shame but not the more extreme emotions of humiliation and mortification in a norm violator, then we must realize that any measure aimed at eliciting only shame may often miss the mark, given how labile these related, negative emotions can be.

III

To now return to the questions about whether social norm theory can prove useful to law reform, my first response is that whether or not its insights are *new*, lawyers, judges, and legal scholars should be interested in the literature on social norms, insofar as social norms and emotions plainly do affect one's tendency to obey legal rules. For example, a strong social norm against a behavior may produce negative emotions in response to the behavior, which may deter the behavior among well-socialized individuals who have internalized the norm as much as, or more than, any criminal law against it. Conversely, a social norm of indulging the behavior may undermine any law against it (as well as reduce the chances that such a law will be written or enforced). Knowing in more detail precisely how, when, and why humans observe social norms must matter to a profession that is interested in the operation and efficacy of, and in the need for, legal rules.

But important features of the social norm literature are being lost in some of their translations into specific legal proposals for criminal law reform in ways that make me wary of these proposals. The translation problems stem, in part, from an admirable if somewhat heady zeal to try new ways of responding aggressively and imaginatively to grave social problems, especially to street crimes. Yet this emerging legal literature—which is being heralded as a third way of thinking about and deterring crime,[92]—may lead to a familiar dead end if the writers do not consider the significant limitations of the "status-drive" account of social norms and much social behavior, and the complexities of the emotions that they seek to harness.

A central limitation of social norm theory, of course, is that it presents human emotions in only one, necessarily limited, frame, within which the focus is on only status and shame, and the core assumption is that rational choice explains much, if not all, individual behavior. The model consciously ignores both the many other emotions—such as anger, envy, or love—that motivate individual behavior and other, non-rational-choice frames for this same behavior.

Yet even if one ignores this obvious threshold limitation on the ground that all models sacrifice nuance yet may still be helpful if they have significant predictive value, social norm theory still may not yield much practical insight for criminal law reform. Penologists already *know* that people crave esteem (among other things). What they do not understand fully and what neither social norm theory nor emotion theory catalogues are the variable ways in which this desire is triggered, how it interacts with *other* emotions and desires, and what the behavioral consequences of these desires are.[93]

Particularly as to two aims of criminal law—prediction of specific behaviors in widely varying social contexts, and prescriptions for government interventions to produce certain behaviors—the social norm model may be of little use. Property crimes and sexual offenses, to take only two examples, are far more fraught and complex behaviors than is restaurant tipping. The thinness of the economic accounts, even *with* the social norm additives, thus becomes more problematic. This concern has been noted repeatedly in critiques of economic analysis of criminal behavior and is quickly apprehended if one simply reflects on how complicated it is to understand, let alone to change, a person's personally or socially harmful behaviors,[94] even with heroic, individualized psychotherapeutic and psychopharmacological interventions. The frustrating failures of the rehabilitation model of criminal punishment reflect the profound difficulties that attend government efforts to redirect hands and hearts that seem inclined toward crime.

A second, foreground complication of applying social norm theory to criminal law is that criminal law typically enters where social norms' hold is strongest among nonoffenders but is, for complex reasons, not powerful enough to deter offenders. That is, criminal law deals *primarily* with the people who buck society's most powerful, morally fraught, and prevalent norms, not with those people who have internalized the norms and mind them, for whatever (ill-understood) reasons. The social norm theory descriptions of "normal" social behavior in far-from-home restaurants thus may shed little light on the often gravely antisocial behaviors that are the focus of criminal law.

Third, the variable that social norm theory models studiously avoid defining—"status"—has highly contextual, mobile, ambiguous, and discursive meanings. Compared to the variables that microeconomics and public choice theory typically measure—e.g., wealth (defined as money), reelection, or utility—"social status" and "esteem" are not so observable or intersubjective. One man's status may *well* be a gang member's shame, and vice versa. And as Richard Posner has said, we already know that "different sanctions impose different costs on different people."[95] That is, although most criminal offenders likely do blush—contrary to accounts that exoticize and dehumanize offenders in ways that wrongly assume that they do not blush or feel shame—offenders may blush at different things than nonoffenders, or engage in criminal conduct despite their blushing, for complex reasons not addressed by emotion theory. This work thus sheds only dim light on the emotional makeups, motivations, or behaviors of the law-breaker populations with which criminal law is most visibly and repeatedly concerned. Consequently, we might well concede—indeed, I think we must—that our fear of shame, others' disgust, and loss of social status are very powerful motivations to toe the social norm line; but this may afford us no new insight into what, exactly, that means in a given legal situation.

If one resorts to the vast and internally conflicted psychosocial literature on emotions to fill in the interstices of the bare-frame social norm model, this poses its own problems—especially the "deer-caught-in-the-head-lights-of-complexity" problem. The social norm theorists' insight that the emotion of shame is relevant to social status, social norms, and social influence may be true. But it does not consider how labile, complex, and ill understood this basic emotion is. Yet these complexities become very relevant when one turns from models designed to outline common aspects of human behavior, to reforms designed to produce or change particular behaviors. Full appreciation of the uncertainties, versus an underplaying of them, should make one quite skeptical of reforms based on any *general* model of human motivation.

Emotion theorists, like social norm theorists, aim at generating models of *basic* human emotions and their *common* causes and behavioral consequences. None of this literature purports to comprehensively identify, versus to recognize the existence of, the vast range of specific triggers of these emotions. On the contrary, even evolutionary psychology adherents, who insist that there are basic, innate human emotions that are useful to the propagation of genes, if not to the species, concede that these basic emotions are *highly* adaptable to context.[96]

Still another complication of applying these other literatures to legal reform measures is that law raises a very specific issue that both emotion theory and social norm theory ignore: When is a *governmental* intervention an appropriate or effective means of deterring "stiffing" and encouraging "tipping"? That is, what is the proper role of the government, versus informal means, in shaping social norms and thus our emotional makeups through criminal and civil laws that define what is, or should be, shameful, embarrassing, outrageous, or disgusting? What shape should this governmental intervention take? Should it be punitive? Educational? Therapeutic? Redistributive? What limits do other values, such as liberalism, autonomy, or economic efficiency, place on these governmental strategies?

Finally, neither social norm theory nor emotion theory purports to tell us what *ends* to advance. As Jon Elster has concluded, "There is no single end—genetic, individual or collective—that all norms serve and that explains why there are norms. . . . I do not know why human beings have a propensity to construct and follow norms, nor how specific norms come into being and change. *The problem is closely linked with that of explaining emotions, another poorly understood area of human life.*"[97]

We therefore encounter two threshold perils as we analyze this new legal scholarship: the peril of reductionism inherent in efforts to explain complex human behaviors with compressed, totalizing, cross-disciplinary models, and the peril of paralysis that can accompany refusal to experiment with these cross-disciplinary generalizations unless and until all contextual, cultural, and individual variations are accounted for in the model.

Negotiating these shoals requires that we make a very cautious advance, and consistently test the model's generalizations against the available details, preferably before imposing them on individuals, and particularly before imposing them on individuals (like juvenile offenders) who have the least meaningful political or other means of resisting these legal experimentations. All of the relevant questions obviously cannot be answered before proceeding, but many can, at least, be asked.

IV

Legal scholars should not proceed without contemplating some of these relevant questions nor advance legal reforms based on these models without considering the ways in which the models, which were not designed for law, do not point unambiguously to these reform ends and do not translate unproblematically into legal contexts. This is especially critical in criminal law scholarship, though it applies as well to other fields.

For this reason, reformers must take care in responding to Dan Kahan's influential work on alternative methods of punishing criminal offenders, in which he acknowledges the "people-are-motivated-by-social status" insight of the social norm work and cites important emotion theory work that argues that emotions are socially constructed.[98] Kahan moves from these general observations to a defense of official shaming penalties—such as forcing offenders to wear signs that identify them as convicted criminals—in an effort to produce and exploit this status anxiety.[99]

This shift from the social norm model of human motivation to the specific legal prescription of shaming offenders raises several efficacy and normative concerns, concerns that Kahan acknowledges but that may be underappreciated by others drawn to his proposals for exploiting the link among social status, social norms, social influence, and criminal penalties. For example, both emotion theory literature and common experience suggest that not all offenders will feel shame because of such rituals, and not all audiences for the rituals (assuming they can be identified and actually attend to the penalties) will react to the rituals in uniform ways. Rather, the social meanings and the social-influence effects of shame penalties are not likely to be uniform, predictable, or containable.[100] Moreover, even if stigmatizing criminal behavior does deter crime, this does not tell us how to stigmatize this conduct to achieve deterrence goals without sacrificing other interests. If criminal conviction and the risk of prison or other current punishment methods are not sufficient deterrents, which in many cases seems true, one must wonder whether and why shame penalties or other alternative punishment methods that likewise convey condemnation would be more effective. Invoking the general insight, drawn from social norm theory, that humans are status sensitive simply does not resolve these issues of application. The insight likewise does nothing to help us determine when punishment becomes too severe—i.e., when the withdrawal of social approval is too harsh—or when (and how) social approval should be restored.

A similar elision of important complexities occurs if one identifies crimes that may evoke disgust in others and then enlists the fact of this disgust (that one feels it) as evidence of its moral authority (that one "ought" to feel this emotion). And further, that the government should act on this emotion, through criminal punishment or other legal sanctions, and that the punishment measure should express this emotion as unambiguously as possible. The risk is that any appeal to our disgust, even if bracketed by concerns about its potential misuse,[101] may cause us to move too quickly to severe punishment methods.

Kahan argues that judges in criminal cases should make more textual and explicit the role of disgust rather than downplay the emotion. Downplaying the emotion, he says, may undermine norms, may fail to express or redress fully the harms of some crimes, and, ironically, may make it harder to contain the excesses of our disgust.[102] He describes—in gripping detail—terrible crimes and argues that we punish criminals in part to express outrage and disgust over such crimes. He further asserts that these feelings of disgust justify our punitive instincts,[103] and even shed light on proper punishment methods. We should, says Kahan, "treat disgust with disgust."[104]

In response to a liberalism-based argument against official emphasis on disgust—specifically, because contempt conveys hierarchy, it is inconsistent with liberalism's traditional commitment to egalitarianism—he states: "Why should the proponents of defensible regimes declare a unilateral cease-fire rather than fighting the indefensible ones on their own terms? Erecting a liberal counter-regime of disgust . . . is exactly the aim behind 'hate crime' laws, which seek to make the proponents of illiberal species of hierarchy the object of our revulsion."[105] Revulsion, disgust, and shame thus are wholly compatible with liberal virtues, according to Kahan.

The thrust of Kahan's argument here is, again, the sensible claim that "an expressively effective punishment must make clear that we are in fact disgusted with what the offender has done,"[106] which leads Kahan to reject insufficiently condemnatory sanctions—such as fines or community service—in favor of penalties that are both unambiguous expressions of disgust and less expensive than prison.[107] Criminal penalties *must* tie negative meaning to criminal acts if they are to effect proper social influence over would-be offenders. Penalties *should* increase the social disapproval of offenders because this will increase the cost of the norm deviation, shore up the norm, satisfy retributivist instincts, and better (and less expensively) deter crime.[108]

In this way, the general and simple psychological insight—that people crave status/fear shame—along with the social norm theory insight that people will conform to norms rather than lose status or suffer shame are thus being invoked in support of criminal law measures designed to change the social meanings of acts by various devices. These mechanisms are designed to change social meaning by "tying" one act to another to disambiguate it,[109] to ambiguate it,[110] or to inhibit it,[111] or a mechanism may be an official ritual that tends to undermine or to support a particular social meaning of the act.[112] Shaming penalties, according to this view, can disambiguate acts. For example, colleges may shame date rapists by forcing them to stand in public on campus, in distinctive clothing, and thereby disambiguate acquaintance rape. Coerced sex will become unambiguously bad and not a source of masculine pride.[113] Likewise, official disgust rituals may underscore that the underlying offense is worthy of contempt and disambiguate the meaning of the act.

Yet this series of steps—from the common desire for status, to what we feel about criminal offenders, to what we ought to condemn, and then to specific, potentially severe methods of condemning and shaming these offenders by the state—is mounted very rapidly, so rapidly that it can make the legal proposals' end points seem inevitable. The end points, though, are hardly inevitable; indeed, they may not follow from the prior assertions.

First, the move from any emotion, including disgust, to what "ought" to trigger it must recognize the internal circularity of asserting that law can and should *shape* the cognitive content of our emotions—a social constructionist account—while simultaneously invoking an objective, moral vocabulary to defend these emotional condemnations of particular behaviors and offenders, a vocabulary that is premised, in part, *on these very constructed emotions.* Again, some emotion theory suggests that shame and disgust are basic emotions and do motivate some social and moral linedrawing, but this literature says nothing about what is objectively shame*ful* or disgust*ing*,[114] as I have already said. At most, emotion theory and social norm theory suggest that the emotions of disgust and shame serve universally useful but contextually variable norm-policing functions.

For example, emotion theory suggests that humans "disgust" contaminants and poisonous matter reflexively and universally, as do other animals, such as dogs, and that the accompanying emotion of disgust might be innate.[115] But the literature also explains that *unlike* dogs, humans perform elaborate mental riffs on this primary, physical scene of disgust from contaminating substances, and thereby link the emotion of disgust to other, metaphorical forms of "contamination" and "poisoning." These links may include associating other humans, sometimes entire groups of them, with the feeling of disgust and treating these others as objects—specifically, as objects comparable to disgusting contaminants. This shift from reflexive disgust in response to contaminating substances to disgust over social constructions of what is *like* bad food and thus labeled "disgusting" is crucial. It can lead to the actual expelling and casting aside of what is labeled disgusting, without much reflection on the fact that the offensive object actually is *not* bad food and thus poses no *literal* peril to the body of the one who would expel it.

A similarly shaky progression from our emotions to normative statements about their triggers to punitive responses against those who evoke them may occur with the shame penalty proposals. Shame is best described as a negative emotion triggered by an awareness of one's limitations—a narcissistic defeat—that typically (but not always) causes the rebuffed or defeated one to withdraw. It can also be a particularly devastating emotion insofar as it implicates the self in potentially comprehensive ways. The primary function of shame seems to be that of preventing us from transgressing social (or other) boundaries, which transgressions might trigger physical, social, or other stinging retaliations by others. Shame thus herds us into corrals erected, in part, by the relevant social group and other norm inculcators.[116] Again, however, the emotion is very plastic and undifferentiated, and hence is subject to association with a wide range of external stimuli. (Recall that a shame trigger is merely the perception of *some* limitation or defeat.) Rather obviously, quite different limitations or defeats can be, and are, deemed "shame significant" by different persons or social groups, so that what, *in fact*, will trigger shame in a particular person is highly contextual, and mostly constructed. Consequently, determining what is objectively or normatively "shameful," like determining what is "disgusting," is work that reference to our emotions simply cannot perform.

On the contrary, the social constructionist insight about our emotional makeups—whether drawn from social norm theory, psychology, or common sense—is that our emotions are profoundly malleable; they can be, and are, molded to various ends, *ends that may or may not be normatively sound*. As we come to associate our emotions with particular scenes, of course, these emotions inform our sense of "right and wrong," but only insofar as "right and wrong" are understood to mean what passes for "right and wrong" at a given moment, in a given culture. Reference to our feelings of disgust over an act, then, is simply another way of referring to whatever experiences and norms have given this emotion its cognitive content; it is not an independent means of justifying these norms. A person may feel disgust in the presence of illness, physical weakness, physical disabilities, or uncleanliness, but this disgust does not make any of these triggers of the emotion inherently immoral, blameworthy, or criminal.[117] Indeed, even very widespread disgust over certain behaviors, such as homosexual sodomy, does not translate unproblematically into a good reason to condemn it, let alone to criminalize it. Although Kahan clearly understands this crucial point, others with a less nuanced appreciation of the constructed nature of emotions may not.

Moreover, as stated above, that we feel disgust at an act or would feel shame had we engaged in it tells us nothing at all about how we should punish that act. Even if we deem the act to be criminal, this does not mean that the punishment method should be shaming, ostracizing, or any other method. Reference to emotions thus does not solve, though it may inform, these practical and normative concerns. And embedding disgust, or shame, or other emotions into a social norm framework thus does not resolve the crucial practical and normative issues that plague penologists. Although some social norm literature suggests that social groups develop norms to solve cooperation dilemmas, there is no consensus within the literature about whether the resulting social norms are good, or even if they are always efficient.[118] Likewise, although the social norm literature correctly notes that gossip and other social sanctions play some role in policing "cheaters" and in this fashion can help to secure their cooperation, it doesn't define cheating or claim that these sanctions play an exclusive, efficient, or morally sound role.[119] Finally, nothing at all in the social norm theory discussions of norm policing through gossip and other social sanctions refers to hatred, or to official shaming, or humiliation. Social norm theory refers generally to shame-sensitivity and social status, and to *informal*, social methods of policing disapproved behavior, which are not the same thing. "Down by norms" is not, necessarily, the same as "down by law."

V

But punish we *must*. What is wrong with invoking our admittedly constructed senses of "disgust" or "shame," or our "hatred" in support of these essential acts of cultural line drawing, which are themselves constructed? Even if the criminal law theorists are mistaken in assuming that social norm theory supports the specific reforms they propose, what's wrong with the proposals? Why not have government officials "show some disgust" and say "shame on you" more directly and openly than they now do?

Perhaps the normative agnosticism of our basic emotions and the social norm model should not matter here because American criminal law offers up countless occasions for uncontroversial and legitimate disgust, versus morally illegitimate or irrational expressions of disgust. Simply because there are illiberal, immoral, or insensitive *uses* of shame or disgust does not make our disgust or our constructed sense of shame morally useless or inherently illiberal. To quote Kahan, "[T]he proper course for liberalism is not to obliterate disgust, but to reform its objects so that we come to value what is *genuinely* high and to despise what is *genuinely* low."[120]

Yet several practical reasons to resist an appeal to official disgust and official shaming nevertheless remain, even if one is willing to look past the analytical problems with a reliance on emotion theory or social norm theory as justifications for the reforms, and *even* if one concedes that liberalism can, and does, leave some room for the implicitly hierarchical emotions of disgust and shame.

One reason is that disgust is a comparatively extreme emotion, which sets it apart as especially volatile, consumptive of human energy, and potentially destructive of social peace. The well-documented ways in which group dynamics can quickly transform even fairly cool, moderate feelings into extreme and highly dangerous ones[121] is a sobering caution against official celebration of, or ritualized release of, the already hot emotions of hatred or disgust, however justified these emotional responses might be in response to an act or particular actor, as measured by the relevant normative standard.

In other words, even if we are *sure* that a criminal act is "disgusting," we must consider whether a judge's open expression of that disgust or shaming of an offender might add something particularly unwelcome to the "social meanings" of the criminal act and the official act of punishment, and may evoke more disorder and resistance on the part of offenders. The judge's disgust could imply, among other things, that the community has official license to act on its disgust, which could inspire its members to be far more fierce and punitive to the offender than they might be if responding individually. Armed by the safety of numbers, people often act more violently (and can act with more force) than when they act alone. Underscoring disgust thus could increase the severity of criminal punishment in ways related not to the gravity of the offense but simply to the size and disgust coherence of the group. The risk of disproportionate punishments therefore may become much higher if judges exhort us to express our hatred, revulsion, and disgust through judicial modeling of the intense, negative emotions of anger and disgust. Moreover, release of hot emotions can produce rapid physical responses that are especially difficult to inhibit.[122]

This is especially true if we insist on *unambiguous* expressions of disgust. Like any other form of expression, judicial expression of disgust may have discursive meanings. To best contain the interpretation possibilities and to reduce ambiguity, judges would need to condemn offenders in the clearest possible terms. This could quickly lead to jarringly harsh expressions (though even these might be subject to competing, noncondemnatory constructions by some observers, as the status ambiguities of a prison stint among some subgroups prove).

Consequently, "fighting disgust with disgust," even for crimes that are noncontroversially disgusting, could defeat other, likewise noncontroversial, ends of the legal order, i.e., accurate assessments of blame or fault, proportional punishment, and the preservation of social order. Given our "deep susceptibility for the rhetorical appeals of authoritarian penal policies, we should be very apprehensive about penalties that rely on such rhetorical appeals."[123]

We cannot assume that the release of our suppressed disgust and revulsion toward criminals will inevitably yield more enlightened justice because we will better contain the excesses of our strong emotions if they are exposed to the light of public scrutiny than if they go underground and resurface elsewhere. This description of our inner emotional state, which assumes that unsuccessfully repressed powerful emotions will find their outlet through other, less controllable means if they aren't released properly in formal rituals, hardly derives from the social norm theory accounts of status-seeking, rational-choice-executing citizens that is the premise of the new approach to deterrence of crime. Rather, this psychological description of our submerged, unresolved, and ill-understood emotional conflicts signals another subtle shift, now to a Freudian frame[124] that assumes that the disclosure of a suppressed emotion will help to dissipate it. But as post-

Freudian critiques have lamented and as Freud himself recognized, this is an extremely optimistic account of the immediate (or even long-term) therapeutic value of such revelations. Even if the assumption were valid in the context of an individual, psychoanalytic encounter, it is far from clear that the technique would work comparably well for "society," with the courtroom operating as couch-substitute, and the judge as surrogate for the emotion-releasing analysand. The analysand here is actually the community, but the members of the community are not actually present at the "session"; indeed, they may not know or care very much at all about the courtroom ritual designed to release their outrage.

A final problem with any "fight-disgust-with-disgust" exhortation is that it is so vague. What does this mean, in terms of concrete changes in existing punishment methods? We already deploy life prison sentences and even the death penalty for the most heinous crimes and have a quite rich vocabulary of outrage and disgust for these offenses. If these existing, admittedly extreme, punishment methods are unclear expressions of our outrage and disgust, then how would *other* methods less ambiguously convey these emotions?

Perhaps all judges would be compelled to make public speeches at the moment of sentencing and to refer expressly to the disgust and contempt that our current punishment methods now convey only implicitly. Yet nothing formally prevents judges from making such courtroom speeches at the moment of sentencing, and some do. (That other judges do not is for unclear reasons—reasons I won't speculate about here.) We thus do treat "disgust with disgust," as Kahan notes, through the very fact of deeming certain acts "criminal," through imposing quite harsh, status transforming, and degrading punishments upon the people who commit them, and, in some cases, by speeches that make this disgust explicit when judges sentence offenders.

Perhaps the idea is that mandatory, formalized verbal expressions of judicial disgust, if issued in every appropriate case, would substitute for some of the harsher, physical features of punishment. That is, we might satisfy our expressive ends with less physically severe or lengthy sanctions, and resort to verbal denunciations thus would make punishment less extreme.[125] This possibility is worth exploring, for I see little reason to oppose a change in punishment methods that would satisfy the community's retributive instincts fully with less harsh punishments unless the new methods proved to be significantly less effective at deterring crime. But this is not the apparent rationale for Kahan's "treat-disgust-with-disgust" proposal, which instead seems to be aimed more at persuading liberal theorists to revise their philosophical accounts of criminal punishment than at judges or legislators. Also, Kahan is very careful to reserve his disgust case examples for ones that involve particularly horrific crimes. It is very unlikely that the public would have settled for an aggressive disgust-lashing of any of these violent criminals. More likely is that an official verbal bashing of such offenders would only whet, not sap, the public's appetite for harsher, corporeal complements to the verbal denunciation in the form of life imprisonment, execution, permanent ostracism, physical banishment, or other means, depending on the crime and the crowd.

Alternatively, Kahan may believe that making explicit our outrage and disgust, even without downgrading the penalties we impose, would better convey our commitment to the values implicitly expressed by criminal law in ways that a more dispassionate appeal to this same law cannot.[126] Criminal punishment would therefore become more convincing, both in terms of the message sent to offenders and in terms of the message conveyed to the relevant community. This implies—somewhat inconsistently, given his claim that disgust is already inscribed in our criminal law punishment methods—that we are somehow in peril of missing this message or that current methods aren't expressive enough, despite this modern era of "three strikes," "order-maintenance policing," aggressive "sweep-the-streets" enforcement of antiloitering laws, and the rise in shaming sanctions that attempt to degrade offenders publicly.

The argument that negative emotions are necessary to restore or establish norms against criminal behavior has considerable appeal. Strong emotions rather obviously can have an underlining and amplifying effect on a behavior in ways that can deter it. For example, an apoplectic parent's red-faced, fist-clenched, furious denunciation of misbehavior may convey to a child far more disapproval and commitment to the values underlying the correct behavior than would a calm, affectless explication of why the behavior is off-limits. (Though this won't always be true: if the parent's typical demeanor is very emotionally expressive, a quiet reprimand may actually be far more powerful.) Conveying different levels of negative emotions for different degrees or kinds of misconduct certainly can help others to distinguish between what is merely improper and what is truly beyond the moral pale. Emotional expression may not always be *necessary* to convey these calibrations, but it may be *helpful* in doing so. Yet if this is the point— that emotion helps to signal intensity of feelings associated with certain behaviors and that we ought to show strong emotion when condemning criminals—then I believe it is unnecessary to consult social norm theory literature to make this general point and that significant qualifications are necessary to make any practical use of it: How *much* strong emotion should we convey? In what way? What are the likely other consequences of doing this?

One ironic consequence of ritualizing the expression of an emotion— especially a very strong one—might be that this could deprive it of its underscoring potential. An emotion's authenticity, and thus its power, may be sapped if it seems orchestrated and phony, as mandatory disgust homilies by judges may seem. Although many good trial lawyers, like talented actors, can stage and manipulate emotions believably, this talent is distributed quite unequally among them. Sitting judges are obviously chosen for other skills, and to ask them now to assume this dramatic role may be unreasonable. It would likely be far easier to order judges to feign dispassion than to feign (believable) passion.[127] A second unexpected consequence of formalizing judicial disgust homilies might be that they would lose their shaming power. The sting of a sharp rebuke is far less for one individual if it is routinely administered to others. Rather, shame is typically experienced when a person feels she has been treated both degradingly and differently; when all are shamed, none is.

We simply cannot predict what the wider social effects, if any, of these shaming spectacles and judicial disgust homilies might be. The investigation of, and attempts to measure accurately, the social effects of judicial rhetoric and rulings have proven to be daunting tasks. Penologists who already have tried to assess the social-influence effects of punishment have found that "[t]he difficulties of accurate measurement, the lack of reliable data, and the impossibility of isolating penal variables from other attitude-forming forces, compel them to limit their research to more immediate— and more tangible—penological effects."[128]

Thus, while one may agree completely that "[p]unishment, among other things, is a communicative and didactic institution"[129] and that it does affect social meaning, as the new-wave criminal law theorists would tell us, one should remain very wary of their specific criminal punishment proposals insofar as they assume far more precise knowledge about, and more control over, the intricacies of this communicative and meaning-making process than we currently have, and especially insofar as they would impose controversial models created for one context—individual psychotherapy or psychoanalysis—onto the dramatically different context of criminal trials.

These reforms are particularly worrisome, given the modern shift away from the rehabilitative era's emphasis on treating the *offender* to an effort to renormalize "*society.*" The voice of much modern rhetoric about criminal offenders—dripping with "shame on you's," outrage, and disgust—places very little emphasis on the emotional or physical effect of punishment on offenders.[130] Offenders thus may become, if the new rhetoric about crime and social norms takes hold, social-meaning signposts onto which social messages are inscribed for highly uncertain, pedagogical effect.

As David Garland has said, criminal punishment is "the site at which law and deviance are brought most visibly together, where social anomalies and contradictions are directly addressed, the point at which *purity and danger* dramatically intersect."[131] We are now admonished that the impure (disgusting and shameful) and very dangerous (norm-threatening) criminal should be publicly, officially, and convincingly *condemned.* Moreover, this condemnation cannot be merely implicit in our criminal punishment techniques but is a feature we must *highlight,* through shaming spectacles, judicial disgust homilies, and other methods. In this way, say the criminal law theorists (in a strangely unemotional, cool register) we will "disambiguate" criminal conduct and underscore our commitment to social norms in the most powerful, emotional, unambiguous, and hence effective way.

Yet the social norm frame that props up these proposals has serious limitations, ones that are not effaced by adding emotions to the mix. Indeed, the social norm frame—with its emphasis on status and its emphasis on a functional, strategic account of our emotions—may be an especially dangerous way for criminal law theorists to think about human motivation, social norms, or emotions insofar as it makes very severe punishments seem rational and suggests no limitation on the punishment other than its capacity to degrade offenders and express disgust unambiguously, without shocking dominant political sensibilities. A social norm standpoint, if left unqualified by *other* norms—such as decency and proportionality—offers little reason to oppose *maximally* stigmatic penalties or to contain our outrage and disgust. Shaming, humiliating, and degrading offenders seem supremely logical and warranted, at least for those who commit violent, heinous crimes. Yet this "logic" is illusory, an illusion that may be obscured by the social norm theory's incomplete view of the psychologically complex and normatively complex terrain of criminal punishment.

Conclusion

Adding emotions (and only some of them) to the economics model of social norms is to insert emotions into an already sketched out picture—rather like a color-by-number landscape to which emotion theory adds hues to "create" a preordained picture—one that might have been drawn by a machine. The end result is . . . *emotionless.* Invoking social norm theory, with its emotion theory complement, entitles us to express disgust, shame offenders, and voice our outrage without serious regard for the offender's shame, humiliation, anger, sadness, or indifference. Even more ironically, it permits us to do so without actually consulting the "society" whose norms are allegedly at stake, insofar as *legal* officials are encouraged to undertake a norm-installation task that was first identified as the outcome of organic, informal, social processes.[132] The move from description to prescription, like the move from what "we" feel to what we ought to feel, and to what law ought to condemn and how, must be made cautiously, with full appreciation of the normative complexities.

We surely do need our emotions—all of them—to inform our judgments about right and wrong, good and evil, retribution, and mercy. And our anger, love, outrage, disgust, shame, guilt, compassion, empathy, fear, pride, envy, and jealousy all play some role in why we punish, what we punish, how we punish, whom we punish, and whom we excuse. Nevertheless, while we should try to isolate and attempt to understand these emotions, and to relate them to laws and social norms, we also should be extremely wary of any reform based on an assumption that legal rules or public officials can and should manipulate particular emotions in order to produce predictable behavioral responses. The complexities of our emotions make this premise highly suspect, so that reforms based solely on the premise should be greeted with considerable skepticism. Again this does not mean that these reforms won't "work"—only that they cannot reasonably or persuasively be advanced in the name of one emotion or as supported by "emotion theory."[133] Indeed, one cannot sensibly oppose or defend resort to *any* emotion, as a categorical matter, in criminal law. It will obviously depend—on the crime, the offender, the extenuating circumstances, the culture, and the community.

That our emotions color our thoughts and reason, motivate our actions, and underscore our commitments, and therefore are relevant to criminal law is both undeniably true and hopelessly vague. We might just as easily (and unhelpfully) assert that cognition motivates criminal punishment, and that accordingly we should treat "negative thoughts with negative thoughts."

N O T E S

Thanks to Bernard Harcourt, Genevieve Leavitt, and Catherine O'Neill for clarifying conversations about these issues. Special thanks to Susan Bandes, for her editorial input, to Tanina Rostain, for several discerning reads of the manuscript, and to Dan Kahan, for taking issue with these arguments in ways that helped me better understand his work.

1. *See* Robert H. Frank, *The Strategic Role of the Emotions: Reconciling Over- and Undersocialized Accounts of Behavior* 5:2 Rationality & Society 160, 181–82 (1993) (noting that "emotions are often central" to behavior and "understanding . . . their role will do much . . . to help competing social theories"). *See also* Jon Elster, The Cement of Society: A Study of Social Order (1989); Edna Ullmann-Margalit, The Emergence of Norms (1977); Cristina Bicchieri, *Norms of Cooperation*, 100 Ethics 838 (1990); Jon Elster, *Norms of Revenge*, 100 Ethics 861 (1990); Philip Pettit, *Virtus Normativa: Rational Choice Perspectives*, 100 Ethics 725 (1990); James E. Alt & Kenneth A. Shepsle, Perspectives on Positive Political Economy (1990); Jon Elster, *Social Norms and Economic Theory*, 3 J. Econ. Persp. 99 (1989); James S. Coleman, Foundations of Social Theory (1990).

2. *See* Robert H. Frank, Passions Within Reason: The Strategic Role of the Emotions 258 (1988).

3. For brief but illuminating descriptions of how social norm theory intersects with rational-choice theory, *see* Richard A. Posner, *Social Norms, Social Meaning, and Economic Analysis of Law: A Comment*, 27 J. Legal Stud. 553 (1998); and Tanina Rostain, *The Rise and Fall of Social Norm Theory* (unpublished manuscript on file with author).

4. *See* Elster, Cement of Society, *supra* note 1, at 99–100.

5. *See* Frank, *The Strategic Role of the Emotions*, *supra* note 1, at 169.

6. The far-from-home tipper may be promoting his self-interest in another way: he may want to be known as the type of person who tips—one who honors commitments—to make others more likely to favor him as a trading partner. *Id.* at 170.

7. *See, e.g.*, Lawrence Lessig, *The Regulation of Social Meaning*, 62 U. Chi. L. Rev. 943 (1995); Richard H. McAdams, *The Origin, Development, and Regulation of Norms*, 96 Mich. L. Rev. 338 (1997); Eric A. Posner, *The Regulation of Groups: The Influence of Legal and Nonlegal Sanctions on Collective Action*, 63 U. Chi. L. Rev. 133 (1996); Cass R. Sunstein, *Social Norms and Social Roles*, 96 Colum. L. Rev. 903 (1996); Symposium, 144 U. Pa. L. Rev. (1996); Cass R. Sunstein, *On the Expressive Function of the Law*, 144 U. Pa. L. Rev. 2021 (1996); Symposium, 1997 Wis. L. Rev. 375.

This work in law was predated by Robert Ellickson's influential work on informal law-making. *See* ROBERT C. ELLICKSON, ORDER WITHOUT LAW: HOW NEIGHBORS SETTLE DISPUTES (1991); Robert Ellickson, *Of Coase and Cattle: Dispute Resolution Among Neighbors in Shasta County*, 38 Stan. L. Rev. 623 (1986); Robert Ellickson, *A Critique of Economic and Sociological Theories of Social Control* 16 J. Legal Stud. 67 (1987).

8. *See, e.g.*, Jack Balkin, *The Constitution of Status*, 106 Yale L.J. 2313 (1997); Richard McAdams, *Cooperation and Conflict: The Economics of Group Status Production and Race Discrimination*, 108 Harv. L. Rev. 1003 (1995); Richard L. Hasen, *Voting Without Law?*, 144 U. Pa. L. Rev. 2135 (1996). That the social norm literature has gripped some constitutional and political theorists is unsurprising, given that "status" is linked to caste and to equality, and that "shame" is an inherently debasing or reductive experience that can lower status.

Constitutional law in particular takes status demotions and their stigmatic effects seriously, at least when they are government-inflicted and based on who one is rather than what one has done. For example, "stigma" was central to the Court's decisions in *Brown v. Board of Education*, 347 U.S. 483 (1954) and *Romer v. Evans*, 116 S.Ct. 1620 (1996). *See* James A. Washburn, *Beyond Brown: Evaluating Equality in Higher Education*, 43 Duke L.J. 1115, 1150 (1994) (discussing the context-specific link of racial segregation and stigma). Both cases involved government-reinforced stigma of a particular sort—stigma that undermined the affected group's status as equal citizens—and thus was explicitly and corrosively undemocratic.

Many other government-inflicted status demotions—even ones with "caste" features, such as social or economic status—are not thought to be comparably inconsistent with baseline constitutional equality, thinly conceived. When government penalizes some behaviors, rewards others, and effects a neutral stance toward still others, it *necessarily* places its meaty thumb on the social status scales, to the very uncertain, context-dependent and poorly charted extent that government opprobrium, endorsement, or neutrality affects the social status calculus. Thus, that law does, even with a liberal order, attempt to shape individual preferences to promote socially beneficial outcomes (*see, e.g.*, CASS SUNSTEIN, FREE MARKETS AND SOCIAL JUSTICE [1997]) is irrefutable. The much harder questions remain the normative ones, which include: What counts as a *socially beneficial* outcome? *When* should *government* and not private social forces alone mold the relevant individual preferences? By what *means* should government be allowed to influence our behavior to promote the social good, once we agree on these ends? The new discourse on social norms tells us little about how to resolve these enduring ends/means constitutional questions.

9. Anita Bernstein, *Better Living Through Crime and Tort*, 76 B.U. L. Rev. 169 (1996); Anita Bernstein, *Treating Sexual Harassment with Respect*, 111 Harv. L. Rev. 445 (1997); Cass Sunstein, Daniel Kahneman, & David Schkade, *Assessing Punitive Damages (with Notes on Cognition and Valuation in Law)*, 107 Yale L.J. 2071, 2095–2100 (1998) (discussing role of outrage in punitive damage awards).

10. *See, e.g.,* Janet T. Landa, *A Theory of the Ethnically Homogeneous Middleman Group,* 10 J. Legal Stud. 349 91981); Lisa Bernstein, *Merchant Law in a Merchant Court,* 144 U. Pa. L. Rev. 1765 (1996); Robert D. Cooter, *Decentralized Law for a Complex Economy,* 144 U. Pa. L. Rev. 1643 (1996); Robert D. Cooter, *Structural Adjudication and the New Law Merchant,* 14 Int'l Rev. L. & Econ. 215 (1994).

11. *See, e.g.,* Dan M. Kahan, *Response: Between Economics and Sociology: The New Path of Deterrence,* 95 Mich L. Rev. 2477 (1997) (discussing this merger); Dan M. Kahan, *What Do Alternative Sanctions Mean?,* 63 U. Chi. L. Rev. 591 (1996) (discussing implications of social meaning of punishment alternatives to prison in terms of their expressive effects); Dan M. Kahan & Martha C. Nussbaum, *Two Concepts of Emotion in Criminal Law,* 96 Colum. L. Rev. 269 (1996) (discussing the differences between evaluative and mechanistic theories of emotions, and their implications for criminal law).

12. *See, e.g.,* C. Shaw & H. McKay, Juvenile Delinquency and Urban Areas (1942); Herbert L. Packer, The Limits of the Criminal Sanction (1968). *See also* Fred Du Bow and David Emmons, *The Community Hypothesis,* in Reactions to Crime 167 (Dan A. Lewis, ed. 1981) (tracing the social order movement to Chicago roots).

13. Dan M. Kahan, *Social Influence, Social Meaning and Deterrence,* 83 Va. L. Rev. 349 (1997); Neal Kumar Katyal, *Deterrence's Difficulty,* 95 Mich. L. Rev. 2385 (1997); Paul H. Robinson & John M. Darley, *The Utility of Desert,* 91 Nw. U. L. Rev. 453 (1997); Kenneth G. Dau-Schmidt, *An Economic Analysis of the Criminal Law as a Preference-Shaping Policy,* 1990 Duke L.J. 1; Harold G. Grasmick & Donald E. Green, *Legal Punishment, Social Disapproval and Internalization as Inhibitors of Illegal Behavior,* 71 J. Crim. L. & Criminology 325 (1980). For influential work that discusses the role of shame in encouraging observation of criminal laws, *see* John Braithwaite, Crime, Shame, and Reintegration (1989).

14. For a useful clarification of these terms, as criminal law scholars deploying social norm theory use them, *see* Bernard E. Harcourt, *Reflecting on the Subject: A Critique of the Social Influence Conception of Deterrence, the Broken Windows Theory, and Order-Maintenance Policing New York Style,* 97 Mich. L. Rev. 291 (1998). For an important caution about the social norm theory work as applied to law, *see* Rostain, *supra* note 3.

15. The fear of this very effect inspires some of the opposition to these measures. *See, e.g., Romer v. Evans,* 116 S.Ct. 1620, 1629, 1633 (1996) (Scalia, J., dissenting) (arguing that Colorado's Amendment 2 was inspired by its supporters' desire "to preserve traditional sexual mores" and express "moral disapproval of homosexual conduct").

16. On the expressive aspect of criminal law, the early work of Joel Feinberg has been especially influential. *See* Joel Feinberg, *The Expressive Function of Punishment,* in Doing and Deserving: Essays in the Theory of Responsibility 95–118 (1970) (reprinting the 1965 essay).

17. As my colleague Bernard Harcourt explains, the contemporary notion of so-

cial meanings created by law traces back at least as far as Durkheim and is central to Foucault's work. *See* Harcourt, *supra* note 14. *See also* DAVID GARLAND, PUNISHMENT AND MODERN SOCIETY: A STUDY IN SOCIAL THEORY (1990) (discussing punishment as a psychological, social, and cultural agent). Likewise, much critical legal scholarship analyzes the ways in which legal categories may have significant social meaning and social-status implications. *See, e.g.*, KENNETH KARST, LAW'S PROMISE, LAW'S EXPRESSION, 2–3, 8–15, and passim (1993). Jane C. Murphy, *Legal Images of Motherhood: Conflicting Definitions from Welfare "Reform," Family and Criminal Law*, 83 Cornell L. Rev. 688 (1998); Lisa E. Sanchez, *Boundaries of Legitimacy: Sex, Violence, Citizenship, and Community in a Local Sexual Economy*, 22 L. & Soc. Inquiry 543 (1997).

18. *See* ANDREW KOPPELMAN, ANTIDISCRIMINATION LAW AND SOCIAL EQUALITY 94–95 (1996) (discussing the social meanings conveyed by law).

19. *See Michael M. v. Sonoma County*, 450 U.S. 464 (1981) (upholding California gender-conscious statutory rape status).

20. As one author has said, "Although much has been said about how law shapes social forms, and about how interests shape law, little research has been done on the way that semi-autonomous non-state control forms interrelate with and constitute state law while also being constituted by it." Stuart Henry, *Private Justice and State Law: An Illustration from Labour Law*, in SOCIAL CONTROL AND JUSTICE: INSIDE OR OUTSIDE THE LAW? 13, 20 (Leslie Sebba, ed. 1996).

21. *See* THE NATURE OF EMOTION: FUNDAMENTAL QUESTIONS (Paul Ekman & Richard J. Davidson, eds. 1994) (discussing debate); ROBERT WRIGHT, THE MORAL ANIMAL: EVOLUTIONARY PSYCHOLOGY AND EVERYDAY LIFE (1994) (positing an evolutionary basis for emotions); LEWONTIN, ROSE & KAMIN, NOT IN OUR GENES: BIOLOGY, IDEOLOGY AND HUMAN NATURE (1984) (disputing genetic basis for much human nature, including emotions and behavior); PHILIP KITCHEN, VAULTING AMBITION: SOCIOBIOLOGY AND THE QUEST FOR HUMAN NATURE 230–36 (1985) (critiquing evolutionary basis for human nature as expressed by Wilson and other sociobiologists); THE SOCIAL CONSTRUCTION OF EMOTIONS (Rom Harré, ed. 1986) (discussing social constructionist view of emotions); STEVEN PINKER, HOW THE MIND WORKS (1997) (discussing genetic-survival basis for emotions); HENRY PLOTKIN, EVOLUTION IN MIND: AN INTRODUCTION TO EVOLUTIONARY PSYCHOLOGY (1998) (setting forth modern "evolutionary psychology" theories and their origins).

22. Frank, *The Strategic Role of the Emotions, supra* note 1 (arguing that emotions help solve trust, deterrence, bargaining, and other commitment problems); FRANK, *supra* note 2; Claire Armon-Jones, *The Social Functions of Emotion* in THE SOCIAL CONSTRUCTION OF EMOTIONS, *supra* note 21, at 57 (discussing possible "sociofunctional" role of emotions—including regulation of socially undesirable behavior and promotion of desired social practices, beliefs, values).

23. JOSEPH LEDOUX, THE EMOTIONAL BRAIN: THE MYSTERIOUS UNDERPINNINGS OF EMOTIONAL LIFE (1996) (describing brain and emotions).

24. *See, e.g.*, WILLIAM IAN MILLER, THE ANATOMY OF DISGUST (1997) (discussing political and social functions of disgust).

25. *See* RICHARD S. LAZARUS, EMOTION AND ADAPTATION 8–15 (1991) (discussing cognitivism and emotion); LEDOUX, *supra* note 23, at 49 (noting that "the psychology of emotion, to this day, is mostly about the role of cognition in emotion); EXPLAINING EMOTIONS (Amélie Oksenberg Rorty, ed. 1980) (discussing cognitive aspects of emotions); MARTHA C. NUSSBAUM, POETIC JUSTICE (1995) (discussing evaluative aspects of emotion); Dan M. Kahan & Martha C. Nussbaum, *Two Conceptions of Emotion in Criminal Law*, 96 Colum. L. Rev. 269, 285–89 (1996) (discussing mechanistic versus evaluative accounts of cognition and emotion); Gerald L. Clore, *Why Emotions Require Cognition*, in THE NATURE OF EMOTION, *supra* note 21, at 181; Claire Armon-Jones, *The Thesis of Constructionism*, in THE SOCIAL CONSTRUCTION OF EMOTIONS, *supra* note 21, at 32, 38–39, 41–42 (discussing the argument that emotions are dependent upon cognition).

26. Despite this internal clamor, popular interest in emotions has spiked as books on "evolutionary psychology" and "emotional intelligence" have been pitched at general audiences. *See, e.g.*, WRIGHT, *supra* note 21; DANIEL GOLEMAN, EMOTIONAL INTELLIGENCE (1996).

27. LEON WURMSER, THE MASK OF SHAME 42 (1982) (stating that the central flaws are "weakness, defectiveness, and dirtiness"). Contrast this English expression with the German "Ich schäme mich vor mir selbst" ("I am ashamed of myself"). *Id.* at 49. The German expression captures nicely that "the approval sought is that of the inner censor." *Id.* This description of shame in this section is drawn from an earlier work. Toni M. Massaro, *The Meanings of Shame: Implications for Legal Reform*, 3 J. Psych. Pub. Policy & Law 645, 655–65 (1997).

28. For a helpful review of the psychoanalytical literature on shame, *see* FRANCIS J. BROUCEK, SHAME AND THE SELF 11–24 (1991). The disagreements among emotion theorists about shame reflect deeper divisions about emotions. Consider, for example, one recent work in which the author lists seven different models of human emotion—feeling, behaviorist, physiological, cognitivist, conative, evolutionary, and contextualist—each with a distinctive account of how and why emotions occur. *See* RONALD DE SOUSA, THE RATIONALITY OF EMOTION 37 (1987).

29. *See* DONALD L. NATHANSON, SHAME AND PRIDE: AFFECT, SEX, AND THE BIRTH OF THE SELF 26 (1992), who uses the expressions "hardware, firmware, and software."

30. Affects are "sets of muscle and glandular responses located in the face and also widely distributed through the body, which generate sensory feedback which is either inherently "'acceptable' or 'unacceptable.'" SILVAN S. TOMKINS, AFFECT, IMAGERY, CONSCIOUSNESS, Vol. I: THE POSITIVE AFFECTS 243 (1962); BROUCEK, *supra* note 28, at 6–7.

31. SILVAN S. TOMKINS, AFFECT, IMAGERY, CONSCIOUSNESS: Vol. II: THE NEGATIVE AFFECTS 123 (1963). *See also* NATHANSON, *supra* note 29.

32. Tomkins, *supra* note 31, at 120. Of course, downcast eyes can signal other emotions, such as respect, in cultures that regard direct gazes as confrontational.

33. *Id.* at 123.

34. Tomkins, *supra* note 30, at 169–70.

35. One thus does not learn to feel shame, "any more than one learns to feel pain or to gasp for air." *Id.* at 244.

36. *Id.* at 44. As Tomkins has put it, we are composed of "an ever-changing multi-component set of drives, affects, general and specific amplifiers and alternators. These, along with the transmitting mechanism which transforms messages into conscious form, and the perceptual and memory system, enter into the ever-changing central assemblies, . . . which govern the human organism." *Id.* at 88.

37. As Tomkins says, "Reasons without affect would be impotent, affect without reason would be blind." *Id.* at 112.

38. Klaus Scherer makes this point as follows:

Emotion antecedent situations are *both* universal—with respect to many structural characteristics—*and* culturally specific—due to differences in values, practices, history, interaction patterns, demography, climate, economy, and social structure. One could assume that some basic eliciting themes are very similar, especially for simple emotions like disgust, anger, sadness, and fear. As soon as norms, values, and cultural practices become important, *especially for complex emotions such as shame and guilt*, the eliciting situations and their meaning become vastly more complicated and culture will obviously play a much bigger role with respect to the nature of the eliciting situations.

Klaus R. Scherer, *Evidence for Both Universality and Cultural Specificity of Emotion in Elicitation*, in The Nature of Emotion ,*supra* note 21, at 172, 175 (emphasis added).

39. *See* Gershen Kaufman & Lev Raphael, *Shame: A Perspective on Jewish Identity*, J. Psych. & Judaism, at 30 (Spring 1987).

40. On the gendered aspects of shame, see Barbara L. Fredrickson & Tomi-Ann Roberts, *"Objectification Theory": Towards Understanding Women's Lived Experience and Mental Health Risks*, unpublished manuscript on file with author (forthcoming in Psychology of Women Quarterly) (describing studies that suggest that women experience more shame than men).

41. For example, few adult American males will cry in public, and few adults will throw temper tantrums or publicly hang their heads in shame. Tomkins, *supra* note 30, at 182.

42. Eve Kosofsky Sedgwick & Adam Frank, *Shame in the Cybernetic Fold: Reading Silvan Tomkins*, in Shame and Its Sisters 23 (1995).

43. *Id.* at 22.

44. In Tomkins's words: "Man is not only an anxious and a suffering animal, but he is above all a shy animal, easily caught and impaled between longing and de-

spair." TOMKINS, *supra* note 31, at 185. This midground between our longings—*licit* and *illicit*—and our despair—that our reach exceeds our grasp—is fertile ground for shame. In this respect, Tomkins distinctively avoids the habit in psychological literature of linking shame simply to the prohibited or disapproved. *See* Sedgwick & Frank, *supra* note 42, at 5.

45. TOMKINS, *supra* note 31, at 133.

46. The complete self-involvement and self-consciousness of shame are what give it peculiar power to torment the sufferer. *Id.* at 136.

47. *Id.*

48. Shame is literally an ambivalent turning of the eyes away from the object toward the face, toward the self. *Id.* (emphasis added).

49. "In shame I wish to continue to look and to be looked at, but I also do not wish to do so." *Id.* at 137.

50. *Id.* at 185.

51. *Id.* at 151.

52. *Id.* at 152. Emotion theorists disagree about whether these are offshoots of the same affect, versus distinct emotions. *See* June Price Tangney, Rowland S. Miller, Laura Flicker, & Deborah Hill Barlow, *Are Shame, Guilt and Embarrassment Distinct Emotions?*, 70 J. PERSONALITY AND SOCIAL PSYCH. 1256 (1996) (rejecting Tomkins's account and concluding that shame, guilt, and embarrassment are distinct emotions).

53. *See* WRIGHT, *supra* note 21.

54. *Id.* at 242–44. Cf. Philip Pettit, *Virtus Normativa: Rational Choice Perspectives*, 100 ETHICS 725, 745 (1990) (claiming that "the desire for status ranks with the desire for wealth and power as one of the basic human motives").

55. Wright speculates that "genes may work by instilling drives that, in humans, get labeled 'ambition' or 'competitiveness'; or by instilling feelings such as 'shame' (along with an aversion to it and a tendency to feel it after a conspicuous failure); or 'pride' (along with an attraction to it and a tendency to feel it after doing impressive things). But whatever the exact feelings, if they raise fitness, they will become part of the species 'psychology.'" WRIGHT, *supra* note 21, at 245.

56. *Id.* at 271.

57. *Compare* Paul Ekman, *All Emotions Are Basic, with* Richard A. Shweder, *"You're Not Sick, You're Just in Love": Emotion as an Interpretive System*, both in THE NATURE OF EMOTION, *supra* note 21. *See generally,* LAZARUS, *supra* note 25, at 68–81. For a discussion of this debate as it relates to criminal law, *see* Dan M. Kahan & Martha C. Nussbaum, *Two Conceptions of Emotion in Criminal Law*, 96 COLUM. L. REV. 269, 275–78 (1996).

58. Ekman, *supra* note 57, at 16.

59. Shweder, *supra* note 57, at 37.

60. *Id.* at 33.

61. *Id.* at 43.

62. Gerhart Piers & Milton B. Singer, *Shame*, in GUILT AND SHAME (Herbert Morris, ed. 1971); ANDREW P. MORRISON, SHAME: THE UNDERSIDE OF NARCISSISM 31 (1989).

63. MORRISON, *supra* note 62, at 43.

64. BROUCEK, *supra* note 28, interpreting the work of Gershen Kaufman. *See, e.g.*, GERSHEN KAUFMAN, SHAME, THE POWER OF CARING (3d ed., 1992); GERSHEN KAUFMAN, THE PSYCHOLOGY OF SHAME: THEORY AND TREATMENT OF SHAME-BASED SYNDROMES (1989).

65. BROUCEK, *supra* note 28, at 24.

66. Piers & Singer, *supra* note 62, at 150.

67. *Guilt* typically refers to anxiety over a defective *act or omission*. In contrast, one speaks of being ashamed of one*self*. *See, e.g.*, HELEN MERRELL LYND, ON SHAME AND THE SEARCH FOR IDENTITY 64 (1958); HELEN BLOCK LEWIS, SHAME AND GUILT IN NEUROSIS, 35–37 (1971); SUSAN MILLER, THE SHAME EXPERIENCE 142 (1985).

68. The same deed may provoke both guilt and shame, and some emotion theorists maintain that the affect auxiliary "shame" (that is, the physiological reaction we experience as shame) actually encompasses a wide range of experiences that are at the conscious and contextual level fairly distinct: embarrassment, remorse, shyness, and guilt. *See, e.g.*, NATHANSON, *supra* note 29, at 19 (drawing on the work of Silvan Tomkins).

69. As one writer describes it, "It is as if the ground under one's feet were giving way; depth and spatial relationships may seem altered and one's 'place' in space uncertain, resulting in a kind of vertigo." BROUCEK, *supra* note 28, at 40.

70. Most theorists, too, agree on the following basic elements in the shame experience, drawn from the early, influential work of Helen Merrell Lynd: "the sudden exposure of unanticipated *incongruity*, the seemingly trivial incident that arouses *overwhelming and almost unbearably painful* emotion, the threat to the *core of identity*, the *loss of trust* in expectation of oneself, of other persons, of one's society, and a reluctantly recognized *questioning of meaning* in the work." LYND, *supra* note 67, at 64 (1958) (emphasis added).

71. BROUCEK, *supra* note 28, at 41. Objectification in this sense thus is a healthy, essential developmental step. For an interesting discussion of various positive forms of objectification, *see* Martha C. Nussbaum, *Objectification* 24 PHIL. & PUB. AFFAIRS 249 (1995).

72. BROUCEK, *supra* note 28, at 39–42.

73. This link between shame and self-esteem—indeed, with self-identity—has been argued most vigorously by Andrew Morrison, who maintains that our "shame vulnerability is closely related to narcissistic vulnerability. . . . Narcissistic vulnerability is the "underside" of exhibitionism, grandiosity, and haughtiness—the low self-esteem, self-doubt, and fragility of self-cohesion that defines the narcissistic condition. . . . [S]hame is the principal ubiquitous affect that accompanies and de-

fines that condition." Morrison, *supra* note 62, at 14–12. There is, according to Morrison, a dialectical relationship between shame and narcissism: "[S]hame and narcissism inform each other, as the self is experienced, first, alone, separate, and small, and again, grandiosely, striving to be perfect and reunited with its ideal. Uniqueness and specialness may be imagined in terms of total autonomy and independence, or worthiness for merger with the fantasied ideal." *Id.* at 66 (emphasis added).

74. *Id.*

75. TOMKINS, *supra* note 30, at 212–13. The parent may prevent the child from interacting with the parents as much as the child wishes, may curb the child's physical freedom, may instruct the child to be less boisterous and noisy, or may otherwise limit the child's range of motion—physical, emotional, and in other respects. Each type of resistance may trigger shame, though in different ways.

76. For example, a parent might reprimand a noisy six-year-old in a restaurant by saying "You are acting like a baby! Everyone is looking at you and saying, 'what a bad boy he is being!'" *Id.* at 227.

77. *Id.*

78. *Id.* at 229–30. The point is made beautifully by Tomkins, through a hypothetical shame vignette in which a small boy's parents respond to a series of the boy's affects during dinner in a manner that ultimately renders the boy affectless; yet the parents even reprove him for this resigned, affectless state, saying, "Robert, you could be a little more attentive, you don't have to sit there like a bump on a log. Say something." *Id.* at 230. No affect, even *none*, pleases these parents.

79. *Id.* at 216.

80. *Id.*

81. "[S]hared shame [is] a prime instrument for strengthening the sense of mutuality and community whether it be between parent and child, friend and friend, or citizen and citizen." *Id.*

82. *Id.* at 223. Likewise, group solidarity can be promoted by shared sorrow, shared anger, and so on. *See* LAZARUS, *supra* note 25, at 23–24 (discussing how positive and negative emotions can strengthen social bonds).

83. TOMKINS, *supra* note 30, at 226.

84. *Id.* at 187.

85. *Id.*

86. Consider the following passage from Tomkins, in which he elaborates (with what one suspects is autobiographical energy) on the multiple ways in which a single aspect of life work may be a complex, highly individualized source of shame:

> If my investment of interest and enjoyment is in work which has a characteristic level of difficulty, I can be shamed by a radical deviation from this optimal level. . . .
>
> If I wish to have my work remain private, I can be ashamed if it is opened to public scrutiny. If, however, I wish my work to be widely known and it re-

mains unknown, this can evoke shame because affect is still invested in publicity but encounters the wall of the unconsciousness of others of my work.

If I wish the initiation or continuation of my work to be demanded by others, their indifference can evoke shame. If, however, I wish the initiation or continuation of my work to be entirely my own decision, even the enthusiastic clamor of others for my work may seem coercive and evoke shame. . . .

If I wish to diversify my investments of affect in many objects . . . then I may be shamed if there is disproportionate time and energy demanded by my work which threatens liquidation of other affect investments. If, however, I wish to dedicate all my energies to work, the demands of family, friends and play may evoke shame because they interfere with the monopolistic pursuit of my work. . . .

If I am a bright housewife, I may be ashamed because too much of my work is exclusively muscular. If I am mesomorphic academic, I may be ashamed because my work is too much cerebral and too little somatotonic. . . .

If I am a pure scientist but I also wish my work to make a direct, immediate contribution to social welfare . . . I may feel ashamed. If, however, I am an applied scientist who wishes also to make a contribution to knowledge but whose work is . . . more useful than illuminating, then I may also experience shame.

If I am an individual whose work is very imaginative, rich and suggestive, but who wishes also that this work be precise, rigorous and beyond question, then I may be shamed by any suggestion of error. If I am an individual whose work is precise, rigorous, and correct, but I also wish it to be imaginative, rich and suggestive, I may be shamed by any suggestion of sterility or restriction of scope. (*Id.* at 189–90)

This passage also may explain some of the emotional complexities of workplace relations, where shame issues, along with other emotional issues, affect interactions among employees in subtextual, sometimes baffling ways.

87. The difficulties in interpreting one's own emotions, or in reading others' accurately, have led some emotion theorists to conclude that the only reliable means of detecting emotional responses accurately is by hooking individuals up to machines that measure changes in their physiological states. The detection/interpretation problem is obviously compounded when the emotion itself is embarrassing or shameful, as shame is for may people.

88. Shame not only rims these adults' emotional lives in a developmentally normal way, it comes to define them in an unhealthy way. Therapeutic attempts to undo these harmful emotional effects of childhood often founder because the asymmetrical and hierarchical nature of the therapist-patient relationship can exacerbate rather than alleviate shame. As one therapist has noted, "By refusing to join his patient on the same level of discourse the therapist is guaranteeing that this patient will not lack for abundant shame experiences." BROUCEK, *supra* note 28, at

95. *See also* LEWIS, *supra* note 67, at 350 (noting that "[t]herapy itself provide[s] a ready source of humiliated fury resulting from the indignities of being a patient"). A shame-sensitive patient thus is difficult to treat by conventional methods: the patient tends to experience any unrequited interest, desire, or intimate disclosure as shameful and also will struggle mightily against any erotic transference in analysis, lest he or she "surrender[ ] to the power of archetypal insistencies, which [would bring] about an unacceptable loss of control . . . [which] is characteristically an entrapment, enslavement, or imprisonment." BROUCEK, *supra* note 28, at 95. Conventional psychotherapy and especially conventional psychoanalysis are inherently asymmetrical relationships and thus can *enhance* the shame of some patients, unless the therapist recognizes this peril and uses it as a therapeutic opportunity to confront the shame issues of the patient.

89. *See, e.g.*, Richard Weissbourd, *The Feel-Good Trap*, THE NEW REPUBLIC 12 (Aug. 19 & 26, 1996). *See also* RICHARD WEISSBOURD, THE VULNERABLE CHILD: WHAT REALLY HURTS AMERICA'S CHILDREN AND WHAT WE CAN DO ABOUT IT, 36–37, 86–88 (1996) (arguing that adolescents are a highly shame-prone population and that "psychological and sociological literature suggests that teenagers are disposed to violence when they suffer shame and helplessness in relation to basic life tasks"). *Cf.* John Elster, *Norms of Revenge*, 100 ETHICS 862 (1990) (noting that shame norms can support acts of revenge—like feuding—that are socially destructive).

90. *See* Tangney, Miller, Flicker, & Barlow, *Are Shame, Guilt and Embarrassment Distinct Emotions?, supra* note 52; June Price Tangney, Patricia Wagner, & Richard Gamzow, *Proneness to Shame, Proneness to Guilt, and Psycopathology*, 101 J. ABNORMAL PSYCH. 469, 470 (1992); Janice Lindsay-Hartz, Joseph deRivera, & Michael F. Mascolo, *Differentiating Guilt and Shame and Their Effects of Motivation*, in SELF-CONSCIOUS EMOTIONS: THE PSYCHOLOGY OF SHAME, GUILT, EMBARRASSMENT, AND PRIDE 274, 296 (June Price Tangney & Kurt W. Fischer, eds. 1995); June Price Tangney, Patricia Wagner, Carey Fletcher, & Richard Gramzow, *Shamed Into Anger? The Relation of Shame and Guilt to Anger and Self-Reported Aggression*, 62 J. PERSONALITY AND SOCIAL PSYCH. 669 (1992).

91. Lindsay-Hartz et al., *supra* note 90, at 296.

92. Kahan, *supra* note 11, at 3477.

93. If one simply seeks to describe some human responses in restaurants, under some circumstances, and some of their possible motivational explanations, then the tipping story is fairly useful. But if one seeks to predict specific individuals' behavior under changed circumstances, even in the same restaurants (or elsewhere), or to prescribe governmental interventions designed to *produce* these behaviors, or to determine what behaviors to produce, then the vignette offers little practical assistance. For example, if in the restaurant vignette, the waiter had been rude, would "we" still tip? (If some of us would not, why?) Or, what if we received a call on our cellular phone (which we mistakenly left on in the restaurant), during which we learned that a loved one is gravely ill? If we bolt from the restaurant without paying

a tip or the bill, would we be violating a social norm, or be in the grip of another one? Neither? What if we discovered only after eating that the bill in our wallet is a $10 bill, not a $20 bill, as we had believed, and the meal cost $9.89? If we leave only the $10 bill, will we have observed the applicable tipping social norm, given available means, or not? If we ourselves had once waited tables and always tip no matter how poor the service, what do we make of the past waitperson experience in assessing our tipping behavior? As Jon Elster has acknowledged, "At any given time we believe in many *different* norms, which may have *contradictory* implications for the situation at hand." ELSTER, CEMENT OF SOCIETY, *supra* note 1, at 129 (emphasis added).

94. Thus, it is very difficult to determine why a *particular* person might defy a norm. Consider the alternative explanations that "Aaron Green," a pseudonymous Freudian psychoanalyst, provides for why two prominent New York analysts slept with their patients, despite the very powerful professional taboo against such affairs and the risk of professional self-destruction. Their behavior can be seen, Green speculates, "as an instance of human frailty—the act of men in middle age tempted to grab at an opportunity for more joy from life . . . [*or*, as persons] intoxicated by their own renown and the idolatry directed at them . . . [*or*, as persons] who [have] an underlying sense of guilt . . . so strong that [they have] to do something self-destructive." JANET MALCOLM, PSYCHOANALYSIS: THE IMPOSSIBLE PROFESSION 104 (1980). These three constructions, moreover, hardly exhaust the ones that plausibly might explain these (or other) norm violations.

95. *See* Posner, *supra* note 3, at 13.

96. *See* STEVEN PINKER, HOW THE MIND WORKS, 365 (1997) (noting that although "[c]ultures surely differ in how often their members express, talk about, and act on various emotions . . . that says nothing about what their people feel. The evidence suggests that the emotions of all normal members of our species are played on the same keyboard.") Even if Pinker is correct about the common-keyboard metaphor, we're nevertheless capable of playing very different tunes.

97. *See* ELSTER, CEMENT OF SOCIETY, *supra* note 1, at 125 (emphasis added).

98. Kahan, *What Do Alternative Sanctions Mean?*, *supra* note 11.

99. *Id.*

100. I have elsewhere discussed in detail these potential problems with shaming penalties. *See* Massaro, *supra* note 27, at 691–703.

101. Kahan recognizes this risk. *See* Dan M. Kahan, *The Anatomy of Disgust in Criminal Law*, 96 Mich. L. Rev. 1621, 1623 (1998).

102. *Id.* This point—making emotions more explicit in law—has been made in different forms by others. *See, e.g.,* Lynne M. Henderson, *The Dialogue of Heart and Head*, 10 Cardozo L. Rev. 123, 125 (1988) (arguing that judges should acknowledge emotions rather than suppressing them); Samuel H. Pillsbury, *Emotional Justice: Moralizing the Passions of Criminal Punishment*, 74 Cornell L. Rev. 655 (1989) (arguing for a similar view); Martha L. Minow & Elizabeth V. Spelman, *Passion for Justice*, 10 Cardozo L. Rev. 37, 54–56 (1988) (same).

103. Kahan, *supra* note 101 at 42 (arguing that disgust may be essential to explain certain moral intuitions about punishment).

104. Kahan, Remarks at Emotion and Law Conference, May 23, 1998, University of Chicago.

105. Kahan, *supra* note 101, at 43.

106. *Id.* at 28.

107. *Id.*

108. Applying a similar, social-meaning chain of logic, other legal scholars now have joined Kahan in promoting penalties designed to withdraw status, communicate disgust, and evoke shame. Kathy Baker proposes that colleges should shame acquaintance rapists on college campuses by forcing each offender to wear "a bright orange armband or badge . . . unmistakably associated with his sanction." Katharine K. Baker, *Sex, Rape and Shame*, at 79 B.U. L. Rev. 663, 698 (1999). This would change the "social meaning" of sexual intercourse, Baker maintains, by depriving date rapists of the social esteem that they seek in demonstrating their masculinity through aggressive, nonconsensual intercourse. *Id.* at 676–77. Date rapists, according to this view, "do not see forced sex as really all that wrong," *id.* at 680–81, because the social meaning of the act as deviant is ambiguous. *Id.* at 689–90. This ambiguity robs the act of shameful meaning, and thus undermines deterrence of the crime. Her proposed solution, based on social norm and emotion-theory thinking, is to inscribe the proper social meaning of date rape through an unambiguous penalty: public shaming of the offender, on-campus, where the shaming is likely to have its most powerful effect on the offender and his peers. The social meaning ambition is to "change the definition of sex, so that it is understood to be not so much about intercourse, as about the communication involved in affirmative assent such that the failure to get affirmative assent is not a somewhat lesser fungible alternative, but is instead something completely other, like sex with a four year old." *Id.* at 697.

109. Lessig, *The Regulation of Social Meaning*, *supra* note 7, at 1009.

110. *Id.* at 1010.

111. *Id.* at 1013.

112. *Id.* at 1013–14.

113. *See* Baker, *supra* note 108.

114. Kahan recognizes this. Kahan, *supra* note 101, at 34 (noting that disgust furnishes "not only indispensable but also imperfect moral guidance").

115. Though even substances that might seem universally contaminating and thus disgusting to ingest, like urine, may not evoke disgust under (rare) circumstances where drinking it is essential to survival over a period of time. *See* James R. Averill, *The Acquisition of Emotions During Adulthood*, in THE SOCIAL CONSTRUCTION OF EMOTIONS, supra note 21, at 98–99 (discussing incident where this allegedly occurred). *See also* PINKER, *How the Mind Works, supra* note 96, at 368 (noting that "[t]o us, cow urine is a contaminant and cow mammary secretions are a

nutrient; in another culture, the categories may be reversed, but we all feel disgust for contaminants").

116. For an influential discussion of how these social norm "corrals" evolve, and the various ends they may serve, *see* ULLMANN-MARGALIT, *supra* note 1. *See generally* works cited in note 1 *supra*.

117. That much of this is cultural, Kahan also recognizes. Kahan, *supra* note 101, at 10–11.

118. Some literature suggests that some social norms may be both inefficient and normatively dubious. *See, e.g.,* ELSTER, CEMENT OF SOCIETY, *supra* note 1, at 139–47 (noting that "some norms make everybody *worse* off," and that "the social usefulness of social norms cannot be taken for granted").

119. Nor could they, given that other literature that analyzes the social interactions of humans suggests that criticism and negative gossip occupy very little conversation time in many important social interactions. *See* ROBIN DUNBAR, GROOMING, GOSSIP, AND THE EVOLUTION OF LANGUAGE 114 (1996).

120. Kahan, *supra* note 101, at 43.

121. DUNBAR, *supra* note 119, at 143.

122. This may be a matter of brain structure insofar as "pathways from the amygdala to the cortex overshadow the pathways from the cortex to the amygdala. Although thoughts can easily trigger emotions (by activating the amygdala), we are not very effective at willfully turning off emotions (by deactivating the amygdala)." LeDoux, *supra* note 23, at 303.

123. *See* DAVID GARLAND, PUNISHMENT AND MODERN SOCIETY: A STUDY IN SOCIAL THEORY 238 (1990). *Cf.* MARTHA GRACE DUNCAN, ROMANTIC OUTLAWS, BELOVED PRISONS: THE UNCONSCIOUS MEANINGS OF CRIME AND PUNISHMENT 185 (1996) (observing that the metaphor likening criminals to filth "has promoted an emphasis on various pollution-avoidance measures, such as segregation and banishment of the criminal" and that "has fostered a tendency to immerse criminals in dark, dirty, fetid places").

124. *See id.* GARLAND, *supra* note 123, at 238–39 (discussing link between Freud's theory of repression and the aggressiveness that often accompanies uttering of moral injunctions).

125. Given his enthusiasm for alternative sanctions that de-emphasize incarceration, this may well be Kahan's principal aim. *See* Kahan, *What Do Alternative Sanctions Mean?, supra* note 11.

126. *See* Claire Armon-Jones, *The Social Functions of Emotions,* in THE SOCIAL CONSTRUCTION OF EMOTIONS, *supra* note 21, at 59, where she observes: "'Anger' at someone who violates my rights . . . can have a special role in conveying the sincerity of my moral opinions. It can also be regarded as having a special role in criticizing the offender and in provoking repentance. In its critical role the 'anger,' as an emotional display, conveys to the offender with immediacy and force that his/her behavior is worthy of condemnation. Also 'anger,' in involving the desire to injure,

or seek revenge, poses an active threat to the offender, one which he/she could avert by repenting, but which I regard myself as entitled to convey."

127. On the difficulties of feigning emotions, *see* Robert Frank, *supra* note 1, at 166.

128. GARLAND, *supra* note 123, at 250.

129. *Id.* at 251. Garland elaborates on the communicative aspect of punishment as follows:

[P]enality communicates meaning not just about crime and punishment but also about power, authority, legitimacy, normality, morality, person-hood, social relations, and a host of other tangential matters. Penal signs and symbols are one part of an authoritative, institutional discourse which seeks to organize our moral and political understanding and to educate our senti-ments and sensibilities. They provide a continuous, repetitive set of instruc-tions as to how we should think about good and evil, normal and patholog-ical, legitimate and illegitimate, order and disorder. Through their judg-ments, condemnations, and classifications they teach us (and persuade us) how to judge, what to condemn, and how to classify, and they supply a set of languages, idioms, and vocabularies with which to do so. These signifying practices also tell us where to locate social authority, how to preserve order and community, where to look for social dangers, and how to feel about these matters, while the evocative effect of penal symbols sets off chains of refer-ence and association in our minds, linking the business of punishment into questions of politics, morality, and social order. In short, the practices, insti-tutions, and discourses of penality all *signify*, and the meanings which are conveyed thereby tend to outrun the immediacies of crime and punishment and "speak of" a broader cultural performance—which communicates with a variety of social audiences and conveys an extended range of meanings. No doubt it is "read" and understood in very different ways by different social groups—and the data we have on this crucial issue of "reception" (as the lit-erary critics call it) are woefully inadequate. But if we are to understand the social effects of punishment then we are obliged to trace this positive capac-ity to produce meaning and create "normality" as well as its more negative capacity to suppress and silence deviance. (*Id.* at 252–53; footnote deleted)

130. Consider the paroled sex offender who committed suicide, following dis-tribution of door-to-door notices in his rooming house that alerted neighbors that he was classified as a high-risk, violent sexual offender whose criminal record was subject to public dissemination under California's version of "Megan's law." Todd S. Purdum, Death of Sex Offender is Tied to Megan's Law, N.Y. Times, July 9, 1998, A13, col. 5.

131. GARLAND, *supra* note 123, at 274 (emphasis added).

132. *See* Rostain, *supra* note 3, at 25–26. Rostain describes the troubling norma-tive implications of social norm theory work as follows:

Translating social and normative phenomena into categories derived from a rational actor model has expressive implications. This analytic framework privileges self-interest and instrumental reasoning over other forms of thinking, which are relegated to the realm of the "irrational." Simply put, it encourages a "what's in it for me" attitude toward social relations. At the same time, it lends legitimacy to the view, implicit in much of the social norms scholarship, that law is primarily a tool for social control whose efficacy turns on the covert manipulation of people. An unintended effect of social norms theory may be that it undermines the very social structures and commitments it is seeking to shore up.

133. I have voiced similar reservations in connection with legal scholarship of the late 1980s about empathy and judicial decision making. *See* Toni M. Massaro, *Empathy, Legal Storytelling, and the Rule of Law: New Words, Old Wounds*, 87 Mich. L. Rev. 2099 (1989). But as I said there, the point is not that these emotions are irrelevant to law or that the work pursuing the connections is unimportant. Quite the contrary, I believe the work is extremely important and relevant, provided it is applied to law in a manner that is sufficiently sensitive to context and human complexities, and to the multiple ends to which all emotions may be directed. No emotion is categorically useful or useless.

I am very wary of potentially quite harsh criminal punishments that are defended on the basis of the need to teach particular *negative* emotional responses to criminal acts—such as shaming offenders. But I am no more sanguine about proposals based on the desire to teach *positive* emotional responses to acts or individuals, such as compassion or empathy. Misplaced empathy, like misplaced disgust, can produce normatively poor decisions—as in the tendency of some judges or juries to excuse offenders whose negative emotional response to homosexuality prompts them to engage in violent acts against gays and lesbians. Again, *no* emotion is normatively transfixed. Emotions are information, but not facts, in this respect.

Part II

Remorse and the Desire for Revenge

Chapter Four

Justice v. Vengeance
On Law and the Satisfaction of Emotion

Robert C. Solomon

> I think that the deterrent argument is simply a rationalization. The motive for punishment is revenge—not deterrence. . . . Punishment is hate.
>
> A. S. Neill

> Merciful God, do not have mercy on those who had no mercy.
>
> Eli Wiesel (on the 50th anniversary of the
liberation of Auschwitz)

In this essay, I am concerned with the expression and, more important, the satisfaction of emotion in law. In particular, I am interested in the desire for vengeance as expressed and satisfied by law or, more accurately, by the justice system. It is not an attempt to *justify* vengeance, nor do I intend to *reduce* punishment according to law to the expression of such emotions as hatred, vengeance, and resentment. Picasso's *Guernica* is an expression of outrage, indignation, and despair, and it would be a poorer painting (like a talented art student's rendition) if it were not for those emotions. But only an ideological hack would reduce the significance of *Guernica* to the emotions it expresses (like the bluenoses today who would ban Nabokov's *Lolita* as nothing but an expression of pedophilia). What I want to defend here is the ineliminable relevance of vengeance to considerations of justice and to law. I also want to examine the ways in which the often violent demands for vengeance may be sublimated and satisfied by law. My point is not to be outrageous. Like any normal person, I would argue that the purpose of punishment by law is deterrence constrained by considerations of justice. As an abnormal philosopher, however, I also want to argue that justice itself is (in part) a matter of emotion and that the desire for vengeance is basic to its concerns.[1]

Perhaps we should note right from the start that "vengeance" is not the name of an emotion as such, nor is there any single emotion name that corresponds to vengeance. The archaic *wrath* is perhaps the best we have. Its kin are anger and outrage, though pointed resentment is, perhaps, the emotion closest to vengeance. One might say (as Aristotle says of anger) that the desire for revenge is built into resentment, part of its motivational structure, but resentment is not yet vengeance, nor is anger. There is vengefulness, but this seems to refer to a general trait rather than a particular emotion, and there is the *desire* for revenge, of course, but desires in general lack the complex structure of emotions. "Vengeance" is typically used to refer to the desired outcome of certain intentional acts and strategies, not their motive or the emotion behind them. When I clumsily refer to vengeance as an emotion, therefore, I am only trying to avoid the intolerable awkwardness of always referring to "the complex of (various) emotions that gives shape to and motivates the desire for revenge and the demand for its satisfaction."[2]

How should we think about vengeance in the light of the law? How should we think about punishment and its relationship to revenge? To what extent is punishment in criminal law the expression of and the demand for satisfaction of revenge? What, then, is the role of mercy, forgiveness, and compassion in law? These are by no means comfortable questions and the answers, I think, are not comforting. As Arthur Lelyveld has written, "There is no denying the aesthetic satisfaction, the sense of poetic justice, that pleasures us when evil-doers get the comeuppance they deserve. The satisfaction is heightened when it becomes possible to measure out punishment in exact proportion to the size and shape of the wrong that has been done."[3] Try as we philosophers might, vengeance and its satisfaction will remain durable components of any realistic theory of human nature.

Jeffrey Murphy, in a previous, less kindly, less gentle incarnation, accepts such a thesis in the context of law and legal theory. "Speaking very generally, we may say that the criminal law (among other things that it does) institutionalizes certain feelings of anger, resentment, and even hatred that we typically (and *perhaps* properly) direct toward wrong-doers, especially if we are the victims of those wrong-doers."[4] I think that this is right even if it is also troubling, and even if Murphy himself has had a change of heart and mind about it.[5] I agree with him that we should be morally humble and epistemically skeptical in our felt need to punish. I agree too that self-deception plays a far larger and more dangerous role in resentment than is usually acknowledged. And I agree that "we should be very cautious about overdramatizing and overmoralizing what we must (regretfully) do . . . by portraying it as some righteous cosmic drama—as a holy war against ultimate sin and evil."[6]

But it is a nasty world, and we are part of it, body and soul. Philosophers may fantasize a "Kingdom of Ends" in which crimes and offenses and with them the urge and need to punish have all vanished. Or one might follow much-quoted Nietzsche in fantasizing an *übermensch* who lives "beyond good and evil," beyond *ressentiment* and so too without the need or desire to seek revenge. But we live in a world filled with crimes and offenses and so too with resentment and wrath. I thank Murphy for reminding me of the Walt Whitman quote, "beneath this face that appears so impassive hell's tides continually run . . . henceforth I will not deny them—for how can I deny myself?"[7] I do not put myself as a philosopher "above" the torrents and tides of feeling (nor did Nietzsche). Like it or not, I find that resentment and the desire for revenge are inextricably tangled up with the questions I ask about punishment and consequently questions about the law— and not only criminal law.

For the sake of my reputation both as maverick philosopher and decent human being, let me say, as bluntly as I can, that I will not be defending vengeance as such. Nor will I have anything encouraging to say to those who display unhealthy enthusiasm for vigilante justice and for the death penalty as the ultimate expression of vengefulness. But it seems to me that moral philosophy has for too long been suffocating from a bad case of "political correctness." Self-righteousness and professional peer pressure have converged to produce a literature that is utterly unrealistic. Praise of virtue and gentility have become de rigueur. To even consider the brutal opinions of hoi poloi is to place oneself out of bounds. And so we dismiss as beneath contempt and unworthy of discussion those powerful negative feelings that in fact move most people and help form their political views and opinions on social issues. Or, on such occasions as this, we consider them only to dismiss them with disgust.[8]

It is indeed easy to be disgusted by the small crowd of celebrants outside of Texas's Huntsville prison just before and during an execution, an occasion that is becoming wretchedly routine. But I find it much harder to be quite so self-righteous and superior when the father of the murdered girl bitterly says of her sadistic murderer, "I want him to fry."[9] One might agree with Nietzsche that vengeance follows from soul-squinting *ressentiment*.[10] Nevertheless, we need to acknowledge that we poor resentful creatures find ourselves living in a tit-for-tat world. We are all moral accountants, even if the bookkeeping varies considerably. Even Adam Smith writes, in his *Theory of the Moral Sentiments*, "The violation of justice is injury ... it is, therefore, the proper object of resentment, and of punishment, which is the natural consequence of resentment." The desire for vengeance seems to be an integral aspect of our recognition and reaction to wrong and being wronged. The popularity and pervasiveness of vengeance-plot movies is but one cheap symptom of a very general, very basic way of conceiving of justice, "wild justice" in the words of Francis Bacon. It is hard for me to imagine that criminal law can be understood without taking account of and to some extent satisfying such bitter sentiments.

I think that it would be foolish to ignore the role of vengeance in law even if our conclusion were to be that the law should sublimate rather than satisfy that powerful emotion. But as I said, I am not talking in terms of what most philosophers and legal scholars would call the *justification* of vengeance as punishment, nor do I want to reduce resentment and vengeance to mere *motives* for punishment, leading to the usual philosophical pronouncements about "genetic fallacies" and the separation of truth and justification from causal and genealogical accounts.[11] If we learn anything from Nietzsche, it is the deceptive nature and bad consequences of such dichotomous approaches. For far too long this century, philosophers used the ham-fisted distinction between the empirical (aka "nonphilosophical") and the a priori/conceptual (aka distinctively "philosophical") to dismiss out of hand any discussion of what was contemptuously considered to be "mere psychology" or simply "the facts of the matter." So, too, legal studies that draw a sharp line between the law and the rich cultural emotional life of a community cut the philosophical-jurisprudential phenomenon of punishment too "thin," devoid of the mess and fuss that in fact make up the human circus. What I seek is a more robust conception of legal punishment in which justice is not an abstract scheme but begins with our rich and complex nitty-gritty reactions to injustice, supplemented, elevated, articulated, and institutionalized by the law and philosophy.

In what follows, I would like to understand something about vengeance and how the law might be said to satisfy it. The first task is to get beyond the destructive antagonism between reason and the emotions. Vengeance is both an intense emotion and a cool, calculating strategy. I distinguish between vengeance, retribution, retaliation, and compensation, and then argue that vengeance does in fact have its "kernel of rationality." I examine some of the metaphorical structures of vengeance and suggest that the "satisfaction" of vengeance is far more complex and potentially civilized than is usually assumed.

Justice v. Vengeance, Reason, and Emotion

To say that the law is a vehicle for the expression and satisfaction of emotions, specifically revenge, is to take issue with a variety of views that construe the law in a strictly positivistic, utilitarian, or deontological way. I do not want to enter into this debate here, but I respectfully disagree with Judge Posner when he claims that "the internal perspective—the putting oneself in the other person's shoes—achieved by the empathetic imagination" has no normative significance in law.[12] I think and have argued that without that empathetic perspective, there can be no adequate conception of justice or law. I side, rather, with Robert Gerstein, who in defense of retributivism writes: "Vengefulness is an emotional response to injuries done to us by others: we feel a desire to injure those who have injured us. Retributivism is not the idea that it is good to have and satisfy this emotion. It is rather the view that there are good arguments for including the kernel of rationality to be found in the passion for vengeance as a part of any just system of laws."[13] I would go further and say that it is not a bad thing in itself to have that emotion and that it is usually a good thing to satisfy it if one does have it, although the notion of satisfaction does not require the directness that vengeance at its least imaginative often demands. The "kernel of rationality" that Gerstein refers to is usually denied, at least as a function of vengeance. Kant (and many other philosophers) deny any rationality to vengeance and attribute this particular kernel (which we will discuss shortly) to reason alone. But the argument I would like to put forward is that vengeance is not wholly irrational, does indeed contain a "kernel of rationality," and rightly demands satisfaction.

One standard way of understanding the relationship between law and emotion is as straightforward opposition. The law is by definition dispassionate. Emotions, obviously, tend to be passionate, or at any rate, not dispassionate. The law applies equally to everyone, playing no favorites. The emotions, by their nature, are partial and particular. This is not to say that there are no universal emotions (universal, that is, both in their occurrence and their scope), but the insistence on universality (however regional) that is built into the very notion of law does not usually apply to most emotions. Some emotions are directed toward universal objects (hating men, loving beauty) and a few contain universal claims (moral indignation can be understood this way), but emotions in general are defined by their perspectival or "biased" nature. Thinking schematically, the opposition view of law and emotion is classically captured by Immanuel Kant in his separation of reason (in its practical employment) and the "inclinations." The law (both internal/moral and external/"positive") is a product of reason. Emotion is the most obvious category (or family of categories) included among the inclinations. The precise interpretation of this opposition and how it works in Kant's ethics and political philosophy keeps a great many philosophers gainfully employed. I am more concerned here to break it down.

I have argued at some length and for many years that the opposition between reason and emotion is insidious.[14] Again, this is not to say that no such opposition is worthwhile or useful. Quite a few different distinctions serve a great many different purposes, for example, the distinction in law between "cold-blooded," calculated (and in that limited sense "rational") murder and "crimes of passion." So, too, there are legitimate distinctions to make between vengeance and retributive justice, for example, regarding a single-minded and stupid demand to "get even" without regard to fairness or due process. But, to set my course for the rest of this essay, there is no single distinction that would once and for all separate and oppose them, and any theory of retribution that ignores or denies the role of vengeance will be incomplete, at best. Emotion is not irrelevant to law, and any conception of law in purely dispassionate terms threatens to be inhuman. In his great novel *Crime and Punishment*, Dostoyevsky describes his character Raskolnikov as "fond of abstraction, and therefore cruel." So, too, some prominent conceptions of law and jurisprudence (not to mention philosophy and economics). Law is a human and cultural institution. It is therefore infused with and motivated by emotion, it expresses collective emotions (notably fear, respect, and indignation), and it is expected to satisfy emotions, and not necessarily just those that motivated it in the first place. Vengeance is shaped as well as institutionalized by whole cultures, their customs, stories, entertainments, and laws. In many cultures (let us not leap to label them "primitive"), vengeance and avenging wrongs are a matter of personal and family honor.[15] In civil society, vengeance and avenging wrongs become matters of common justice and law, but they are not thereby rendered irrelevant to the proceedings.

The idea that the law should satisfy vengeance, indeed, the idea that the law should satisfy anything at all apart from itself, apart from justice, apart from a very general intuition that the function of law is to serve the community that embraces it, is a topic of considerable debate. But vengeance is a special case, even within the often passionate debate about the role of passions in the law. Vengeance is thought to be especially dangerous and socially disruptive, typically violent, utterly unreasonable, and by its very nature *opposed* to law and its constraints. I would like to suggest, to the contrary, that vengeance need not be dangerous or disruptive, need not be violent, need not be unreasonable, and need not be opposed to law and constraint. According to this opposition view, one might say that the point of law is to make the passions more coherent, more consistent, more articulate, more perspicacious, more reasonable, more subject to scrutiny, more civilized. The law, like culture, shapes as well as expresses emotions. We should beware of the tendency to reinforce the opposition between reason and emotion by rendering emotion as primitive as possible—choosing the most irrational, destructive examples and then glorifying reason in an uncritical way (Aristotle's "spark of the divine," for instance).[16] To be sure, there are cases of "blind" rage that allow little to be said on their behalf, and no one would deny that there are often reasonable solutions to difficult emotional problems.[17] But to pack all of the reasonable solutions and their mode of deliberation into one set of categories ("reason, justice") and only the most unreasonable, vindictive, and ill-considered emotional responses into another ("emotion, vengeance") is to render reason insensitive and emotions devoid of sense.

Passions, I have argued, are constitutive value judgments, endowing and bestowing as well as recognizing the status and worth of their "objects."[18] But because judgments can be enhanced (as well as contradicted) by "higher level" judgments, i.e., reflection and self-criticism, they are by no means the "brute" mechanisms that they are often made out to be.[19] Vengeance in particular is both shaped and measured by way of reflection, albeit (as in most emotions) a rather biased and narrow-minded reflection. Justice requires long-term vision, but vengeance too is very different from simply "lashing out," and it is not at all "blind" (although it may well be myopic). (Remember which of the two female figures is typically depicted blindfolded, Lady Justice or the fierce-eyed furies.) John Belushi's oft-quoted advice "Don't get mad, get even" quite clearly suggests the deliberative, strategic, long-range scope of vengeance and its opposition to mere rage.

Quite the contrary of a state of rage, vengeance is typically quite "cool." It is thus worth noting that at least one feature of emotions as commonly (mis)understood is absent from vengeance: vengeance does not necessarily (and in any case does not continuously) display strong "feelings" in the immediate Jamesian sense. It is said that "revenge is a dish that is best served cold," suggesting the need for careful planning and, perhaps, the desirability of long-term suspense on the part of the victim.[20] But the absence of immediate affect does not mean that vengeance is dispassionate. Vengeance displays all of those traits of intensity, intractability, adamancy, and single-mindedness that are typical of powerful emotions. We might thus distinguish between rage as a short-term physiological response and outrage as an underlying motivational structure.[21] Thus, when authors define vengeance in terms of the most primitive responses and associations of ideas, as without "measure" or rationality, when they oppose vengeance to rational retribution, I would argue that they have already begged the question.[22] Yet vengeance rationalized is still vengeance, intensely passionate, but it now shares the virtues of objectivity and fairness that dispassionate law demands. The intensity of passion is not, contra a good deal of literature, necessarily proportionate to irrationality. There are emotions of increasingly sophisticated intelligence such that they deserve as well as require institutionalization in law.

In anger and outrage, one may well feel one's temperature rising, one's skin flushing, one's fists tightening and teeth gnashing, but vengeance is cool and calculating, devoid of the neurological fireworks that render these other emotions so often distracting and counterproductive. One displays a "burst" of anger, but one plots his or her revenge. Vengeance is a long-term investment. Indeed, one sometimes invests one's whole life in its successful completion and satisfaction. But this means that vengeance is also, whatever else it may be, reflective and rational in at least an instrumental sense (the only sense recognized by some philosophers and most economists). It requires thinking, planning, and perspective. The problem, of course, is that the perspective of vengefulness is limited. But one should not be too quick to insist that the perspective of vengeance excludes consideration of the public good. To the contrary, vengeful thinking is often empowered by the idea that "getting even" is in the interest of all. This is the view that was expressed (if overstated) in the majority opinion in the death penalty decision of *Gregg v. Georgia* (United States Supreme Court, 1976):

> The instinct for retribution is part of the nature of man, and channeling that instinct in the administration of criminal justice serves an important purpose in promoting the stability of a society governed by law. When people begin to believe that organized society is unwilling or unable to impose upon criminal offenders the punishment they "deserve," then there are sown the seeds of anarchy—of self-help, vigilante justice, and lynch law.[23]

If one purpose of law is to rationalize and satisfy the most powerful social passions, then vengeance must be considered first and foremost among them. It is not enough to say that such utilitarian concerns should simply be ignored and rejected, for, as Susan Jacoby argued many years ago, the denial of the desire for vengeance may well be analogous to the Victorian denial of sexual desire, and a similar psychological price must be paid for it.[24] Repressing the hunger for sex, one often finds that it reappears in new and more perverse manifestations. So, too, suppressing the thirst for revenge may well have devious manifestations that are much worse than its satisfaction.[25]

Vengeance, Retribution, and Retaliation: Some Distinctions

Before we go any further, I want to stake out the territory and make a few crucial points and distinctions. First of all, let us distinguish vengeance and retribution. Vengeance is a species of retribution, but not all forms of retribution are vengeful. Whether or not retribution can be justified solely by appeal to the dictates of practical reason, as Kant argued, surely there can be and are Benthamite formulas for the punishment of crimes that are devoid of passion and based simply on the coldly calculated utility of deterrence. So, too, what is usually called "rehabilitation" can be as cool and clinical as Anthony Burgess's treatment of #6655321 in *Clockwork Orange.*[26] But insofar as vengeance is an issue, the punishment it seeks is a form of retribution, and retribution, like vengeance, insists on some sort of "payback," not just deterrence or behavior modification. What I want to block is the too-easy distinction between vengeance and retribution in terms of law or legitimacy: that is, retribution is legitimate and is expressed in law; vengeance is illegitimate and is what the law is intended to block. That begs the question, whether vengeance can be legitimate and so whether vengeance can or should be expressed and satisfied in law. So, too, I want to block the definition of retribution in terms of rationality, exemplified in Kant, and the corresponding definition of vengeance in terms of its alleged irrationality. That too begs the question, in what sense(s) can vengeance be rational (and in what sense(s) does it tend to be irrational)?

Retribution is the general concept of "paying back" (its literal meaning). Strictly speaking, it applies to the exchange of goods and favors as well as the return of harm for harm. To describe it as the return of *evil for evil*, as Socrates does in the *Crito* and the *Republic*, and as many contemporary moralists do, is to beg any number of questions. Is harm necessarily evil, even if it is not inflicted for the sake of a greater good? Is punishment harm? Indeed, could refusing to punish be harmful to the offender? Bosanquet, following Kant, has suggested that the criminal offender has a *right* to be punished, and so it would be harming him not to do so. Plato suggests this (in the *Gorgias*, 525b). It has even been suggested that Christ's instruction to "turn the other cheek" could be counted as a harm, insofar as it shames and humiliates the offender.[27]

Kant can obviously be read as an advocate of legitimately doing harm in response to harm, but his conception of retribution is coupled with the curious idea that the criminal ultimately does the same harm to himself that he does to others. (The thief thus steals from himself by making property in general less secure, and so on.) I think that there are several deep insights here that lay hidden by the seeming absurdity of his suggestion. Nevertheless, we should suspend judgment, at least to begin with, about what is "evil" and what is not in the realm of punishment. At the very least, one would presume that most Christians would not consider God's punishment of the guilty to be evil. Even those who use "evil" rather promiscuously to refer to any harm are forced to distinguish between radically different degrees or kinds of harm. Surely the harm that is perpetrated by the criminal is different *in kind* from the harm that is involved in the punishment. Defenders of the rule of law will thus insist that legally sanctioned harm as punishment is not evil but just. On the other hand, those who are already suspicious or resentful of the power of government might argue to the contrary that legally sanctioned punishment is indeed radically different from personal vengeance in that it is *much worse*. It is premeditated and intolerably clinical in a way that personal vengeance is not. Thus Camus famously argues, "For there to be equivalence, the death penalty would have to punish a criminal who had warned his victim of the date at which he would inflict a horrible death on him and who, from that moment onward, had confined him at his mercy for months. Such a monster is not encountered in private life."[28]

But even those who condemn both crime and punishment are forced to admit that there is more evil produced in the absence of punishment than by its employment. Thus harm becomes good and necessary and our better sentiments are overwhelmed by nasty practicality. "Tit for tat" is the rule of reciprocity and retribution, and the description of "evil for evil" applies to only the most exceptional, regrettable, and hateful cases, not to punishment in general.[29]

Appealing back to the false distinction between (stupid) emotion and (rational) retribution, it is often suggested that retribution is thoughtful and vengeance is unthinking. But we have already pointed out that vengeance is by its nature time-consuming and thoughtful. It is surely rational on this account. Indeed, vengeance supplies a paradigm and a target for those who would criticize merely "instrumental" rationality, for vengeance is an excellent example of elaborate and often ingenious means-end thinking aimed at a dubious goal. The larger question, of course, is whether or not vengeance itself can be rational, or, more modestly, whether this or that particular desire for revenge is reasonable and justifiable. But before we get into these larger questions, let us simply note that whatever else vengeance may be, it is not merely a lashing out. And this, I believe, is the primary difference between revenge or vengeance and *retaliation*. The difference, one might say, is how much thought goes into them.

Retaliation is more or less immediate. It is a direct response. Accordingly, it may take very little thought or no thought at all. One "lashes out," possibly with a punch, more likely (in civilized company) with an insult or a verbal reply, "canned" and already prepared for any such occasion. In established practices with ready-made responses—for example, in the law—retaliation may nevertheless be a sophisticated matter, requiring considerable learning and practice and embodying extensive subtlety. In an Oscar Wilde, it can become extremely creative, indeed an art form. But what distinguishes retaliation from vengeance and makes the former much less philosophically problematic is the former's brevity. It is not thereby less violent or disruptive. It is by no means therefore more justified. (Where vengeance usually includes a well-rehearsed justification, retaliation usually proceeds without one, justifying its actions later and only if necessary.) But just because vengeance is so thoroughly thought out and self-justifying, it is therefore more problematic. As a long-term, calculated, instrumentally rational plan, seeking precise ends by way of well-planned means, it is therefore subject to the considerations of a larger rationality, albeit one that is, as Jeffrey Murphy rightly complains, all too prone to self-deception and self-aggrandizement.

Because retaliation tends to be quick and immediate, it is the sort of response that we recognize in even some of the less intelligent animals. Chickens and squirrels clearly display the tendency to return harm for harm, a peck for a peck, a bite for a bite, and while one may well argue that such reactions are instinctual—inborn, stereotyped, and more or less automatic—we also recognize a modicum of intelligence in them, in the (fallible) recognition of the offender, for instance. What is not so clear is whether the *measure* of the response is also a matter of recognition and control. An adult dog or cat will retaliate against an annoying puppy or a kitten in clearly measured responses. Most higher animals have some sense of "play" in which retaliatory responses are so measured, although down the phylogenetic ladder there is more of a tendency to all-or-nothing retaliation, which thus becomes mere reaction, with minimal rationality. Whatever else may be said against vengeance—that it is immoral, irrational, destructive—it has no such lowly analog.

Last but not least, I want to look briefly at the delicate distinction between vengeance and compensation. Vengeance is almost exclusively discussed with reference to the criminal law and in particular with reference to the most "heinous" crimes and the "ultimate" punishment for them, state-ordered execution, thus fulfilling an ancient ritual sometimes referred to as "bloodguilt." But it might be helpful to train the spotlight on a very different area of law, one in which talk of vengeance is deemed utterly inappropriate: civil law, and more specifically, tort law. The very notion of the "civil," insofar as it suggests more than a technical division within the legal system, suggests *civility*, the agreeable resolution of disputes. To be sure, there are offenders and victims—defendants and plaintiffs—but what is usually at stake is money or property, compensation rather than public humiliation, prison time or the possibility of execution. But we know, of course, that matters are by no means so clear and impersonal. The purpose of liability and tort law may be to compensate the victims and to encourage responsible behavior, but it is also to *punish* those who are responsible for the victims' plight.

The very existence of *punitive* damages makes clear that punishment is one aspect of civil law, but the revealing question is to what extent reparations and compensation are also to be construed as punitive. The notion of a *fine* for certain sorts of behavior is treated by many corporations simply as "a cost of doing business," as are parking fines for those with little time but substantial incomes. For the average citizen, fines clearly constitute punishments (although only the paranoid would construe these as anyone's "getting even" with them). Compensation is not supposed to be like this, but it too renders the line between deterrence and retributive punishment less clear. The simplistic idea that deterrence is forward-looking while retribution is backward-looking simply does not stand up to scrutiny. Even without introducing Heideggerian complexities about the nature of temporality, one can see that punishment is virtually always both forward- and backward-looking, even in that extreme case imagined by Kant in which a society is on the brink of dissolution.[30] And insofar as compensation not only is treated as "fair" but is personally motivated, there is at best a set of thin Chinese walls separating compensation as restoration, compensation as punishment, and compensation as the satisfaction of the desire for vengeance, re: the debt metaphor. One does not have to look and listen very hard to the plaintiffs in a great many liability suits to be convinced of the vindictiveness of their legal actions. ("Those bastards are going to pay!")

To be sure, civil punishment is virtually always defended in the name of "justice," whereas vengeance is simply dismissed as "inappropriate" or even "barbaric." To seek vengeance is simply unacceptable; whereas demanding justice is noble and unassailable. But in civil law, this well-worn distinction is hard to maintain in practice, indeed, difficult even to make out persuasively in theory. In criminal law, one can always retreat to the distinction between breaking the law and harming the victim, insisting that punishment must be understood in terms of the former, not the latter. But in tort law, especially, the question of laws being broken is not the focus of the complaint and of the demand for compensation. Whatever the function of such legal proceedings in terms of financial need and fairness, the presence of anger, resentment, and vindictiveness is the motivating force behind the persistence, the obstinacy, the economic irrationality, and the ruinousness of a great many lawsuits. To speak of justice in such cases is not so clearly as most philosophers seem to think to limit oneself to compensatory and distributive justice. That would render the proceedings in a great many cases clearly irrational, or it would reduce liability suits to the greedy gambling that is so often (and, sadly, accurately) depicted in such popular entertainments as *Seinfeld*.

In civil law, we use the word "justice" to refer to fair compensation, but throughout most of history the concept of justice has been far more concerned with the punishment of crimes and the balancing of wrongs than it has been with the fair (re)distribution of goods and services. "Getting even" is ambiguously located between vengeance and compensation, and where it is difficult to put an exact price on the extent of the damages, this ambiguity pervades the whole question of compensation too.[31] In criminal law, of course, the question of compensation becomes even more controversial. There is an ancient debate, which continues into the present century, about the relationship between retribution and compensation and their relative merits and barbarity. The ancient Greeks and many traditional cultures held compensation in relatively high esteem. In Papua New Guinea today, for example, the anger that readily gives rise to vengeance can be quite literally "bought off."[32] Not only is the destruction of property compensated for by the replacement of property (or its agreed-upon equivalent), the harming of a neighbor can also be compensated for by the payment of property. Marvin Henberg quotes the ancient laws of Eshnunna (ca. 2000 B.C.E.): "If a man bites the nose of another man and severs it, he shall pay 1 mina of silver. For an eye he shall pay 1 mina of silver; for a tooth 1/2 mina; for an ear 1/2 mina; for a slap in the face 10 shekels of silver."[33] Even in the case of killing, not retribution in kind but compensation was surely an advance on the endless and sometimes genocidal vendettas that plagued ancient tribal life. Henberg also quotes the ancient Hittite laws that specify that the life of a free person is to be compensated by four slaves, a slave by two slaves.[34] Thus even the crime of murder might be brought under the auspices of "civil" law (and taken out of the realm of revenge).

The ancient Hebrews adamantly opposed any such compensation, at least in the case of murder. The taking of a life, the ancient rabbis insisted, was not to be and could not be compensated by any payment whatever. Only blood could compensate for blood, a life for a life, a death for a death. We still tend to feel that serious crimes against a person should not be settled by mere compensation (although consider the two O. J. Simpson trials, one criminal, one civil). Even regarding crimes against property, the notion of compensation leaves out something essential, namely the "cost" of anxiety and humiliation (and other strong negative emotions) over and above the loss or temporary loss of the property in question.[35] Part of the problem (as many commentators have argued regarding questions not only of compensation and punishment but of comparative utility much more generally) is the incommensurability or at least the difficulty of finding "equivalences" that make some sense. Nevertheless, there is general agreement—

and it goes back millennia—that compensation is civilized in ways that vengeance is not.

What is most important, I think, is an obvious but overlooked aspect of the compensation process that distinguishes it from vengeful thinking, and that is that the very idea of compensation essentially involves *negotiation, discussion, and agreement* between the injured and the injuring parties. The desire for vengeance blocks any sincere negotiation.[36] I think that this is why many cultures consider compensation a significant advance over the older forms of retaliation and vengeance. Because compensation involves mutual action between the parties to an offense, this in itself helps heal wounds. It breeds mutual understanding, raises the discussion to a higher level, and introduces a broader perspective. This is what mediation—a still undervalued facet of American law—is supposed to do. Its virtues are not only the increased likelihood of more mutually satisfying settlements devoid of bloodshed but also the strengthening of bonds even between antagonists. Of course, the negotiated settlement in question may well be simply assumed as part of a long cultural tradition such that, in any given case, the actual negotiation may be negligible and the results ritualized, but the idea is that compensation, as opposed to retribution more generally, is very much a truly *civil* procedure. A tort system that dispenses with such mutually agreed-upon compensation in favor of protracted and mutually frustrating adversarial hostilities is, quite the contrary, typically most uncivil and differs from the harshest punishments—years of anxiety and lost opportunities, ruinous financial burdens, one's every waking moment spent dealing with the justice system—only in the technical details.

"An Eye for an Eye": Vengeance in Criminal Law

It is the heart of vengeance as well as the basis for criminal law, the idea that the punishment should "fit" the crime. One of the best-known precepts of retribution, which also serves as a structural model for vengeance, is the "eye for an eye" formulation of the Old Testament (Exodus 21, Deuteronomy 19, Leviticus 24). We have already rejected the "evil for evil" formulation as question begging, but the neutral equation of "like for like" will nevertheless serve us well.[37] It is the primitive prototype of all concepts and theories of retribution, including vengeance.[38] It has often been commented that this equivalence, which seems so irrefutably reasonable, is in practice almost impossible to instantiate. Even where it seems most plausible, a life for a life, an eye for an eye, there are devastating counterexamples and arguments. Lord Blackstone is said to have "exploded" the *lex taliones* in his *Commentaries on the Laws of England* (1765), insisting that one cannot requite fraud with fraud, forgery with forgery, even death with death. He gives the example of a decrepit, miserable assassin and honorable nobleman. How is the life of one in any sense the "equivalent" of the other? He also offers a notoriously cute legal counterexample: What if a two-eyed man knocks out the eye of a one-eyed man? This does indeed point to the literal deficiency of "like for like," but such charges of incommensurability again seem to miss the point.

What is that point? What it means for the punishment to "fit" the crime is not that there should be an exact equivalence or sameness. Reparation and compensation may make some claim to such exact equivalence, especially if there is only money involved (money is so easily quantified). But how does one compensate for "pain and suffering"? Indeed, how can there be compensation for a crime? A teller embezzles a thousand dollars from the bank. He can be made to pay back the money but that does not yet touch the crime. Punishment is always over and above any compensation, assuming (what we earlier disputed) that this distinction can be made with any reasonable clarity. Nevertheless, we still want to talk about "like for like." But in what way is a brief prison term "fit" punishment for any crime? In what way is unemployment or a ruined reputation "like for like," except in exceptional cases?[39] We may be clear that the draconian punishment demanded by the Qur'an (though rarely implemented), cutting off the hands of the thief, is not a fair punishment. Nevertheless, we can see in what brutal sense the punishment might be thought to "fit" the crime. But so, too, we see the proverbial "slap on the wrist" as unjust. The crime deserves a harsher punishment than *that*. What the "like for like" formula gives us is a demand for reasonableness, a demand for "measure" and fairness. Like the utilitarian formula with which it is sometimes compared, it should not be confused with an accountant's compulsiveness. It does not have analytic precision. Even if there were no convincing instances of equivalence, the formula is nevertheless profound and important.

The "like for like" formula is particularly important when it comes to vengeance because vengeance is often assumed to be "out of control," to have no limits. Unrestricted by law or social sanctions, it is thought to lead inexorably to escalating vendetta or total destruction. This ignores the force of cultural mores and local custom, of course, but cultural mores and local custom can themselves be subject to criticism. Several years ago, Afghan tribesmen summarily executed (by beheading) a hapless tourist involved in an automobile accident, one that (were the driver to have made an insurance claim) would have been proclaimed "faultless." But even in vendetta societies (contemporary Rumania is recently in the news as such), the culture and its custom set rather strict and sometimes bizarrely legalistic strictures on vengeance. These strictures and constraints in turn become part of every child's upbringing and education. It is part of the vengeance stories they hear. It informs their emotions, not only encouraging the emotions that drive toward revenge but also establishing internal limits. It is the very nature of vengeance, as a cultivated emotion, that it contains—or can be cultivated to contain—its own sense of measure, its own limits. This process can be furthered by law, not by prohibiting but by incorporating it.

When the Old Testament instructs us that revenge should be *limited* to "an eye for an eye, a tooth for a tooth, hand for hand, foot for foot, burning for burning, wound for wound, stripe for stripe"[40] it is prescribing just such limits. It is called the "*lex talionis*" just because it recommends "exact measure," whether exact measure is possible or not. It was such "equality" that Kant took to be an absolute rational principle in his *Philosophy of Law*, and, in more modern, jovial guise, there is Gilbert's musical *Mikado*: "an object all sublime / make the punishment fit the crime." The New Testament demands even more restraint, abstention from revenge oneself and patience to entrust it to God. Here, I suspect, even Jeff Murphy would suspend his doubts about epistemic competence and self-deception, if not his new reservations about retribution, God's reputation for epistemic competence and self-awareness being well established in Christian doctrine.

It is sometimes said that even if there were equivalence, the law cannot perform the role of avenger. Thus Blackstone insists that one can't requite fraud with fraud. But of course, individuals can. Requiting fraud with fraud is a popular theme, from Homer's *Odyssey* to Dumas's *Count of Monte Cristo* and contemporary elaborations like *The Sting*. The shocking truth is that many rapists are indeed requited with officially ignored if not sanctioned rape once they enter the obscene halls of our "correctional" institutions, and any number of everyday offenses that are no business of the law are nevertheless responded to in kind. There are punishments that the law cannot and should not impose, snubbing a neighbor because she snubbed you, for example. But the fact that the law is often not in a position to avenge wrongdoing and that vengeance sometimes provides a solution when the law cannot or does not does not mean that avenging wrongdoing is outside the proper scope of the law. It just means that some crimes, like fraud, are inappropriate for strictly "like for like" legal retribution. More important, what the law can clearly do is to impose "fit" and fair punishment for such offenses as fraud and rape that do not repeat the offense itself. "Like for like" thus becomes shorthand for retributive reasonableness.

The idea of "like for like," doing unto others as they have done unto you, is as old as civilization (and perhaps much older). It is, one might say, a nasty version of the Golden Rule. But "equality" ("like for like") is not the only formulation of the demand for rationality in vengeance and in retribution more generally. Several other metaphors pervade the vengeance and retribution literature and, more important, vengeance itself. This is an important point: These metaphors are not only picturesque ways of *talking about* vengeance, *they provide the structure of the desire and its accompanying emotions and define the sense of satisfaction.* The metaphors are by no means equivalent or even compatible, although something of the "like for like" formula—interpreted as a general canon of reasonability—lies behind all of them. Let me look at just three. There is, first of all, the "debt" metaphor, the idea of vengeance and retribution in general as "paying back." The word "guilt" comes from such an etymology in many languages, and the idea of "measure for measure" certainly bears out this quasi-economic metaphor.[41] The idea of debt is deeply embedded in law, and we still talk quite literally about a criminal's "paying his debt to society." Debts, however, can be repaid in many ways, not necessarily by a return of that which was taken.

Second, there are balance metaphors, portrayed by Lady Justice with her scales and advocated by Plato as "harmony," both within the individual psyche and in society as a whole. So, too, harmony was the social and psychic standard for Confucius and the Taoists at the other end of the ancient world. Every first-year biology student learns the importance of homeostasis and equilibrium in all of life. The idea is that crime, or serious offense, disturbs the balance or harmony of society as it certainly disturbs the equilibrium of the victim. Vengeance reduces or eliminates the disturbance, the imbalance, the disharmony. Insofar as one thinks of the rule of law as the great stabilizing force in society, one might say that the criminal justice system is the codification and implementation of just this primal need for not only social but cosmic stability. (I suspect that Murphy, like most modern philosophers, underestimates the extent to which these two dimensions are intermingled, and not just in Christian thought.)[42] Thus there is a good reason why all crimes are said to be "crimes against the state," not because of the government's commandeering of the law but because every crime causes a disturbance, an imbalance, a bit of trauma that goes far beyond the immediate victims. On a smaller scale, within the family or community, such trauma is even more pronounced. As with those traumas afflicting individuals, restoration cannot come just from the outside. The victim him- or herself must take an active role, if only (preferably) by getting in touch with the law. But on this model, vengeance becomes an aesthetic emotion, a felt need to put the world back into balance.

Third, there is the metaphor of "pollution," which one finds in the ancient notion of "blood guilt," which occurs throughout Greek tragedy and in many passages in the Old Testament and the Talmud. It is this metaphor, of course, that lies at the very heart of Christian theology, for how can one better explain what it means that "Christ died for our sins"? Pollution requires not balance or repayment but *cleansing*, and one of the oldest concepts of retribution involves the domestic metaphor of "blood washing away blood." Here "like for like" refers not so much to equivalence as to purifying effectiveness. The legal expression of vengeance as "putting away" criminals, sealing them off from society, if not exactly cleansing, nevertheless suits the pollution metaphor. The death penalty, needless to say, is the ultimate form of "putting away" and eliminating a criminal from society. But even lesser forms of punishment, notably prison, are clearly a form of quarantine, and vengeance is not so much "getting even" as it is "cleaning up the streets."

The pollution metaphor is harder to sell in today's literally polluted world. Victims of crimes do indeed complain that they feel "dirty" from the experience, and the language of "wiping out" crime bears some traces of the ancient metaphor. But if we broaden the notion of pollution to embrace the general social categories suggested, for example, by Mary Douglas in her *Purity and Danger*, the metaphor starts to feel more familiar.[43] What she calls "nontechnical pollution" and "pollution ideas" can be found quite easily in most people's political and social outlooks, whether the objects of their repulsion are minor criminals or members of opposing political parties, other races or the opposite sex. The sense in which a criminal is "branded" in our society is a clear sense of pollution thinking, and "rehabilitation," in one of its more civilized meanings, refers not so much to the alteration of a personality as to the reinstatement of a person to his precriminal status, the restoration of rights and privileges as a (no longer polluted) citizen.

The three metaphors yield three implications bearing on the expression and satisfaction of vengeance by the law. The first is that vengeance, *prop-*

erly construed, contains its own criteria for satisfaction and fairness. It is not a blind demand to do harm but a structured quasi-philosophical conception of a just world in the face of a grievous offense. It is said that vengeance knows no end, but this is not true. There is a very clear sense of satisfaction that is built into the idea of and the urge to revenge. What is unpredictable is the exercise of vengeance by novices, those with limited experience (or worse, experiences mainly informed by Hollywood and television) and little knowledge of the consequences of taking revenge. But that, of course, is an argument not against vengeance but in favor of experience, the deep experiences of a legal tradition and the collective wisdom of society and history. Vengeance is not always legitimate, of course, but only a moment's reflection is necessary to realize that we all recognize the difference between justified and unjustified revenge. Vengeance is not just the desire to harm but the desire to punish for good reason and to the right measure. The satisfaction of vengeance, accordingly, has not so much to do with the actual punishment as it does with reconciliation, which might not involve punishment at all.

Second, these basic metaphors indicate how deeply the felt need for vengeance pervades our thinking about ourselves, our relationships, and our society. Debt, balance, and cleaning up pollution are not merely metaphors but social structures, basic to being human whether or not part of "human nature." Without any posturing about the natural necessity of free markets, exchange and with it some conception of obligation and fairness is basic to our human sense of sociability. Debts are as essential to social life as culture and tradition, and to restrict the idea of debt to the exchange of *goods* is naive. Bads ("evils") are subject to fair exchange too. So, too, the idea of balance and harmony pervades almost all societies, with appropriate local variations, and so do both metaphors and real practical concerns about pollution and purity. But what begins to emerge here is our third implication, that what satisfies vengeance is not necessarily the harm of the offender, much less "like for like" literally construed. Here is where we should look for the sublimation of vengeance, not in terms of suppression by the more respectable forces of reason but in terms of its own growing awareness of its nature and its needs.

One can pay a debt in a variety of currencies, depending on the agreement between debtor and creditor. So, too, one can restore balance in a relationship, in a damaged family, in a community, or in a society by a number of means, the infliction of punishment being perhaps one of the least effective. One can clean up pollution and satisfy the desire for cleanliness without aggravating the pollution. (Blood for blood is additive, not cleansing.) But what is missing from the usual debates about vengeance is precisely this sense of the *relationship* between the victim, the offender, and the avenger. The offender is routinely treated as *other*, as "the criminal," as someone to whom something is to be *done*. But it seems to me that the sublimation and satisfaction of vengeance presents other possibilities in light of the three metaphors discussed above.

The notion of debt, in particular, involves the exchange of more than goods and evils; it involves the exchange of ideas and of demands, reciprocal feelings that might well be formulated in more abstract agreements or rules. So, too, the very nature of balance and harmony requires people "being tuned" to one another. "Putting the world back in order" (or cleaning up moral pollution) need not involve harm to the offender. Since ancient times, the urge to revenge has been confronted with Socrates' oft-repeated objection—that punishment is the return of evil for evil and so never legitimate, no matter how horrendous the crime. So, too, the harsh vengefulness of the Old Testament is mollified by the comparative kindliness of the New. But even Socrates allows punishment so long as the overriding result is moral improvement, and the kindly New Testament culminates in the harsh pronouncements of ultimate vengeance in Revelation. The language of vengeance has always been mixed, torn between the obvious need to punish and the powerful desire for vengeance and the inescapable awareness that, in fact, harm rarely undoes harm. Consequently, almost all thinkers struggle to find a way beyond vengeance or ways of satisfying vengeance without being vengeful.

It is generally agreed, aside from pie-in-the-sky fantasies, that vengefulness is "natural" and that punishment is necessary if society is to endure. Socrates and the New Testament as well as contemporary thinkers about vengeance insist that punishment, whatever else it may be, must be fair and conducive to good rather than further evil. Criminal law must be "correctional" rather than simply vengeful. It should put the world back in balance, not exacerbate the hatred and the violence that have already been caused. The mistake is to think that vengeance is opposed to these aims, or that vengeance does not already contain the "kernel of rationality" that requires measure and propriety.

Untutored and uncultivated, vengeance can be a dangerous social practice. "When you seek vengeance," says an old Chinese proverb, "dig two graves." But such arguments typically allude to the unpredictability or irrationality of the acts of individual agents (or families), not vengeance as embodied in law and established social custom. Retaliation has the virtue of quickness, but it lacks the virtue of reliability because it lacks adequate thought. Vengeance, by contrast, has the capacity for rationality, prudence, and cultural shaping. To be sure, vengeance is a powerful and therefore dangerous passion, but it is also a socially constructed emotion that can be cultivated to contain not only its own limits but a full appreciation of the general good and the law as well.

NOTES

Thanks to Brian Leiter, Susan Bandes, and Martha Minow, and special thanks to Marvin Henberg for his book, *Retribution* (Philadelphia: Temple University Press, 1990).

1. Robert C. Solomon, *Passion for Justice* (New York: Addison-Wesley, 1991; Lanham, Md.: Rowman and Littlefield, 1993).

2. Another terminological note, on "revenge" and "vengeance." I will treat these as synonyms, although their grammar is interestingly different. One *gets* or *has* revenge, but one *wreaks* vengeance. Then again, "I'll have my revenge" or even "I'll have my revenge on you." "Revenge" refers primarily to the person who gets even and is the more flexible, utilitarian word; vengeance refers rather stiffly to the whole complex of act, motive, and consequences. Nevertheless, the discussion and legitimation of one will unproblematically embrace the other, so I will use the terms interchangeably.

3. Arthur Lelyveld in *Punishment, For and Against*, H. Hart, ed. (New York: Hart, 1971), p. 57.

4. Jeffrey Murphy's essay in this volume and his excellent book (with Jean Hampton) *Mercy and Forgiveness* (Cambridge: Cambridge University Press, 1988), p. 2.

5. This volume, pp. 149–167.

6. Ibid., pp. 158–159.

7. Whitman, "You Felons on Trial in the Courts," quoted in Murphy's essay in this volume at p. 167.

8. This is the other side of disgust in the law, not disgust as a reason or excuse but disgust as an aspect of a hierarchical and contemptuous legal perspective.

9. On FOX News, July 15, 1998.

10. Nietzsche distinguishes, however, as I will, between ressentiment and vengeance and retaliation. Nietzsche makes quite clear that the "masters" he discusses (as opposed to the "slaves" who more or less resemble all of us) are healthier just because they take immediate action, smite those who offend them on the spot rather than suffer the poisonous simmering of the bitter juices of *ressentiment*. In-

sofar as vengeance follows from resentment and kindred emotions and so "simmers," Nietzsche is opposed to it. But if one considers retaliation as vengeance, then Nietzsche's views are more mixed. Ultimately, he argues against retaliation in favor of a much larger notion of justice, one in which one's soul is so large (cf. Aristotle's *megalopsychos*) that not even the gravest offenses are sufficient to distract from a life so enviable that most of us (including Nietzsche) cannot imagine it. (As Smiley Blanton once said, "Things that upset a terrier may pass virtually unnoticed by a great Dane.")

11. Murphy, this volume, pp. 150–51.

12. Richard Posner, *Overcoming Law* 381 (Cambridge: Harvard University Press, 1995), quoted in Susan Bandes, "Empathy, Narrative, and Victim Impact Statements," 63 *Univ. of Chicago Law Review*, 1996, p. 364.

13. R. S. Gerstein, "Capital Punishment: A Retributivist Response," *Ethics*, 85 (1985), pp. 75–79.

14. Solomon, *Passions* (New York: Doubleday, 1976; Indianapolis: Hackett, 1993).

15. See Andrew Sharp, *Justice and the Maori* (Auckland: Oxford University Press, 1990), and also G. Newman and P. Morongui, *Vengeance* (Lanham, Md.: Rowman and Littlefield, 1987). To be sure, one might insist that what rationality and "measure" are to be found in vengeance are ingrained in various social practices rather than in the emotion itself, but this, I think, is a fruitless distinction. The social practice is, among other things, the cultivation of the emotion, and the emotion is, in part, the internalization of the social practice. The more general thesis that hovers here is "the social construction of emotions," the thesis that an emotion is constituted by social norms and concepts. For good statements of the social constructionist position, see Rom Harré, ed., *The Social Construction of Emotions* (Oxford: Blackwell, 1986), and James Averill, "The Social Construction of Emotions" in K. J. Gergen and K. E. Davis, eds., *The Social Construction of the Person* (New York: Springer-Verlag. 1985).

16. Marvin Henberg, *Retribution: Evil for Evil in Ethics, Law, and Literature* (Philadelphia: Temple University Press, 1990), pp. 18, 79.

17. There is also a pathology of reason—it is sometimes called "ideology"—but I will not pursue this suggestion here. See my *Passion for Justice* (New York: Addison-Wesley, 1991), pp. 50ff.

18. A good discussion of appraisal and bestowal is in Irving Singer, *The Nature of Love*, Vol. I, revised edition (Chicago: University of Chicago Press, 1984), pp. 3ff. An excellent account of the recognition of value in emotions is Cheshire Calhoun, "Cognitive Emotions?" in Calhoun and Robert C. Solomon, eds., *What Is an Emotion? Classical Readings in Philosophical Psychology* (Oxford: Oxford University Press, 1984), pp. 327ff.

19. One should distinguish here between those more primitive and biologically based "basic emotions" or "affect programs" and "higher-level" cognitive and cul-

turally constructed emotions. See Paul Griffiths, *What Emotions Really Are* (Chicago: University of Chicago Press, 1997), for a good summary of these. Anger is generally recognized as one of the basic emotions (although resentment is usually not), and this leads quite naturally to the question whether some urge to retaliate is part of human nature. I will argue briefly later on that it is. But a considerable conceptual and cultural gap separates mere rage from retaliation and vengeance.

20. The drama of delay seems to be essential to revenge, as evidenced by so many movies and classic tales of revenge, from the Dumas classic *Count of Monte Cristo* to Fay Weldon's camp *Confessions of a She-Devil*. The excruciating process of imprisonment and appeals in death penalty cases might well be seen as additional punishment in just this sense. See the Camus quote from "Reflections on the Guillotine," pp. 132–33.

21. Rage as a short-term response is so obviously physiologically based that it can be induced by an electrode to the brain. Rage as an underlying motivational structure might much better be construed as great anger, where the intensity of anger is not to be understood as intensity of feeling or as extreme physiological upset but, rather, in terms of the depth and breadth of the concern and the motivation. On the physiological nature of rage, I am indebted to Patricia Churchland (author of *Neurophilosophy* (Cambridge, Ma.: MIT Press, 1986)) in conversation.

22. Two philosophers who explicitly oppose retribution to vengeance are Robert Nozick in *Philosophical Explanations* (Cambridge: Harvard University Press, 1981) and Henberg, *Retribution*.

23. *Gregg v. Georgia*, 428 U.S. 153 237–38 (1976) (Marshall, J., dissenting).

24. Susan Jacoby, *Wild Justice* (New York: Harper and Row, 1983).

25. Jeffrie Murphy quotes the esteemed Victorian judge and theorist James Fitzjames Stephen in this regard: "The forms in which deliberate anger and righteous disapprobation are expressed stand to the one set of passions in the same relation which marriage stands to [the sexual passions]." In *A History of the Criminal Law of England* (London, 1883), Vol. II, pp. 81–82, quoted in Murphy and Hampton, *Mercy and Forgiveness*, p. 3.

26. But while rehabilitation is on the face of it the very opposite of vengeance, an expression of empathy and caring, it too often turns out to be a cover for the most vicious punishments, as in the psychiatric wards for political prisoners in the now-defunct Soviet Union and as depicted fictitiously in Ken Kesey's *One Flew over the Cuckoo's Nest*.

27. Henberg, *Retribution*, p. 25.

28. Albert Camus, "Reflections on the Guillotine," in *Resistance, Rebellion and Death*, trans. J. O'Brien (New York: Knopf, 1960).

29. The "tit for tat" strategy for maintaining equilibrium has been famously defended by Robert Axelrod in his *Evolution of Cooperation* (New York: Basic Books, 1984) and has been suggested subsequently as an evolutionary product

that might properly be recognized as part of "human nature." One need not accept any such deterministic thesis, however, in order to recognize the plausibility of the hypothesis that unpunished transgressions tend to encourage further transgressions.

30. Immanuel Kant, *The Metaphysical Elements of Justice* (*Metaphysische Anfangsgrunde der Rechtslehre*), trans. John Ladd (New York: Macmillan, 1985), p. 102.

31. Recent much-publicized examples would be the class-action lawsuits against Dow Corning and Johns Manville, both of them ruinous to the companies, which filed for bankruptcy. In both cases, the complexity of the relationship between compensation and vengefulness can be indicated by the difficulty of the question, How can one *compensate* a person for years of pain and debilitation and a shortened life span? The difficulty is highlighted when—as in the case of ongoing suits against the tobacco industry—offers of compensation are institutionalized and taken up by the government in one form or another. The compensation is the same, but what is missing is the direct sense of punishing the defendants. Accordingly, there is widespread resistance among the plaintiffs regarding the adequacy of such an arrangement. In the Monsanto asbestos trial, the judge awarded a symbolic one dollar to each of the plaintiffs but then, in what Henry Fairlie calls a "burst of tortured reasoning," awarded sixteen million dollars in punitive damages. Henry Fairlie, "Fear of Living," *New Republic*, January 23, 1989, p. 16.)

32. From discussions with Steven Feld, now professor of anthropology at New York University. For a general discussion of the role of compensation and punishment, see Henberg, *Retribution*, pp. 61–68. Hubert J. Treston, *Poine: A Study in Ancient Greek Blood-Vengeance* (London: Longmans, 1923), discussed in Henberg, pp. 60ff.

33. Henberg, *Retribution*, p. 65.

34. Ibid., p. 66.

35. J. J. Finkelstein, "Ammisaduqa's Edict and the Babylonian 'Law Codes,'" *Journal of Cuneiform Studies* (1961), in A. S. Diamond, *Primitive Law* (London: Watts, 1950); quoted in Henberg, *Retribution*, pp. 65–68.

36. This is not to say, of course, that the desire for vengeance blocks any apparent negotiation or conversation. Quite to the contrary, the desire for vengeance inspires some of the most ingenious and disingenuous conversation, for instance, the conversations between Iago and Othello and between Edmond Dantes and his three tormenters.

37. An extensive and most helpful discussion and critique of this formula is by Henberg, who ultimately rejects it. See Henberg, *Retribution*, esp. Part II.

38. Ibid., p. 18.

39. When Al "Chainsaw" Dunlap was fired as CEO of Sunbeam Corporation after "downsizing" tens of thousands of hard-working employees and managers, there was a widespread sense of poetic justice, "like for like," throughout the corporate world. Even Dunlap's own son said to the press, "He got what he deserved."

"Commentary: At Least Chainsaw Knew How to Hire a Board," *Business Week*, June 29, 1998.

40. Exodus 21:24–25.

41. Nietzsche emphasizes this connection between "the major moral concept, Schuld" (guilt) and "the very material concept of Schulden [debt]." *On the Genealogy of Morals*, trans. W. Kaufmann (New York: Random House, 1967), Essay II, 4, pp. 62–63. One should not take at face value this connection between guilt as debt and economic exchange, quite apart from the fact that English does not display the same etymological similarity as German. Henberg interestingly wonders whether and how the guilt as debt metaphor varies between cultures with different economic systems, e.g., in barter versus market economies. *Retribution*, p. 67.

42. For example, Confucianism contains no such distinction. Roger Ames and David Hall, *Thinking Through Confucius* (Albany: SUNY Press, 1987).

43. Mary Douglas, *Purity and Danger: An Analysis of Concepts of Pollution and Taboo* (New York: Praeger, 1966). Judge Richard Posner has defended the pollution model in criminal law in "Retribution and Related Concepts of Punishment," *Journal of Legal Studies*, 9 (January 1980), pp. 71–92.

Chapter Five

Moral Epistemology, the Retributive Emotions, and the "Clumsy Moral Philosophy" of Jesus Christ

Jeffrie G. Murphy

> In her opinion the troubles in life were started by people who never looked into their own souls.
>
> Oscar Hijuelos, *Mr. Ives' Christmas*

Introduction

Nietzsche's writings have a remarkable capacity to trouble the soul, and I have recently found my own soul troubled by reflection on his remarks on retribution as a theory of punishment, a theory that I have long endorsed and defended.[1]

Nietzsche does not, of course, give intellectual arguments against the claims of retributivism—arguments that could perhaps be met by counterarguments. Rather, he offers a diagnosis of those who favor punishment on such grounds—speculating that, for all their high talk about justice and desert, they are actually driven by a variety of base and irrational passions—malice, spite, envy—passions for which Nietzsche uses the French noun *ressentiment*. At their best, retributivists—with their scorekeeping and their tit for tat—have the sensibilities of accountants: "their souls squint."[2] At their worst, retributivists are simply cruel.[3] Small wonder, then, that Nietzsche offers the following counsel: "Mistrust all in whom the impulse to punish is powerful."[4]

I see in myself, alas, a person whose impulse to punish has been—at least in some cases—very powerful, and Nietzsche has caused me to mistrust myself and the abstract theories I have been inclined to use to rationalize that impulse. In this essay I share with you the nature of my mistrust.[5]

In the main, I shall be focusing on Michael Moore's widely anthologized and justly admired essay "The Moral Worth of Retribution."[6] In that essay, Moore takes seriously the Nietzschean challenge to retributivism and argues that this challenge can be successfully defused if only we draw the proper distinctions.

In the course of his essay, Moore seeks to explore the use of emotions in moral epistemology, arguing that some emotions are epistemicly reliable—pointing us in what is morally the correct direction—whereas other emotions are epistemicly unreliable—pointing us toward moral error. He grants that if the retributive urge must be grounded in the family of base passions that Nietzsche labels *ressentiment,* then retribution is indeed undermined. He then argues that retribution does not have to be so basely grounded but should be seen as grounded instead in the rational and good emotion of guilt.

In what follows I shall argue that Moore's attempt to defuse the Nietzschean challenge fails. I think that many of his general points about emotions and moral epistemology are mistaken and shall argue that guilt fares just as badly as *ressentiment* as an honorable emotional basis for retribution.

I shall also argue that the main value of Nietzsche's challenge emerges if his claims are interpreted as what might be called lessons in moral humility—lessons that (ironically enough) are similar to those found in the famous New Testament report of Jesus stopping the stoning of an adulteress by saying, "He that is without sin among you, let him first cast a stone at her" (John 8:7).[7] Moore ridicules this remark and characterizes its use by Jesus, in the context of punishment, as "pretty clumsy moral philosophy."[8] Against Moore, I shall argue that the remark is not clumsy at all but is, rather, deeply insightful and deeply cautionary. I will also suggest (another irony) that a version of this same insight may be found in the ethical writings of that arch retributivist Immanuel Kant.

Moral Epistemology and the Emotions

In introductory logic we warn our students against committing the genetic fallacy—the fallacy of thinking that the falsity of a proposition can be demonstrated by a causal claim concerning the origins of the belief in that proposition. It might be tempting to dismiss Nietzsche's challenge to retributivism as an instance of that fallacy, and Moore is correct in seeing that this move would be too hasty.

It is, of course, logically possible for a proposition to be true even if the person believes that proposition for a variety of suspect reasons—e.g., retribution could be the correct theory of punishment, people could really in justice deserve the punishment they receive, even if those advocating their punishment on retributive grounds were motivated not by justice but by a variety of hateful passions.

However, as Moore rightly notes, this logical point should not blind us from realizing that the causation of a belief can be epistemicly relevant to the degree of confidence we place in that belief. Are we not properly skeptical, for example, of the testimony we receive from those who made their observations while drunk? It is logically possible, of course, that the beliefs that they formed in this state are true. However, given the high correlation between beliefs formed in this state and false beliefs, we are surely reasonable in our skepticism.

Moore claims that emotions, while not able logically to undermine truth or establish falsity, might still be used as what he calls *heuristic guides* to moral truth. By this, I interpret him to mean something like the following: We know that certain emotions are highly correlated with correct moral judgments, and other emotions are highly correlated with moral error— e.g., we know that *ressentiment*-based moral judgments are likely to be erroneous, whereas guilt-based moral judgments are likely to be correct. Thus he writes:

> [W]e should ask ourselves what [the criminal] deserves by asking what we would deserve had we done such an act. In answering this question we should listen to our guilt feelings, feelings whose epistemic import is not in question in the same way as are those of *ressentiment*. Such guilt feelings should tell us that to do an act like [that of a vicious murderer] is to forfeit forever any light-hearted idea of going on as before. One should feel so awful that the idea of again leading a life unchanged from before, with the same goals and hopes and happiness, should appear revoltingly incomprehensible.[9]

Thus, according to Moore, is Nietzsche answered. Insofar as we are guided by *ressentiment* in forming our punitive judgments, then—as Nietzsche rightly points out—our judgments are likely to be erroneous. When guided by guilt, however—a possibility Nietzsche did not consider—our retributive judgments are likely to be correct. Thus the way to avoid Nietzsche's problem is to make sure that our retributive judgments are grounded in guilt rather than in *ressentiment*.

Alas, all this simply will not work. It both concedes too much to Nietzsche and concedes too much to guilt. First of all, the concession to Nietzsche. Of course, *ressentiment* is going to be highly correlated with error since *ressentiment* is, by definition, an irrational and base passion. It means, roughly, "spiteful and malicious envy." It thus makes no sense to speak of rational or justified or honorable *ressentiment*—just as it makes no sense to speak of rational or justified or honorable malice.

But suppose instead we employ the English noun "resentment." It seems that we can speak of rational or justified resentment (just as we can speak of rational or justified indignation), and thus it would take more than a few Nietzschean sermons against *ressentiment* in order to make us reasonably doubt the epistemic reliability of resentment as a foundation for retributive judgments. I will below express some skepticism about regarding any emotion as the legitimate foundation of retributive judgments, but, if we are going to seek for such a foundation, I see no reason for thinking that resentment will be any less reliable than guilt.[10]

But is guilt epistemicly reliable? Does it merit the celebration that Moore conducts for it? I think not. Although guilt may not have its epistemic import challenged "in the same way" as *ressentiment*, it still faces some deep challenges. We all know (even without reading Freud) that our guilts are often neurotic—misplaced and irrational and destructive. Thus it is hard to see how any useful or fair idea of what others deserve can be generated merely by projecting from our own imagined feelings of guilt. Given a certain sort of upbringing and consequent neurotic or simply narrow personality, for example, a person might use his own imagined guilt feelings to demand very serious punishment for conduct that is (in my view) objectively trivial or entirely unobjectionable—e.g., masturbation or homosexuality or romance outside a particular religious or ethnic or racial group.

Should we then project only from guilt feelings that are rational? But what will these be—those that are based on a proper idea of wrongdoing and desert? If so, then the whole enterprise begins to look hopelessly circular: we are using prior concepts of evil and desert to decide which guilt feelings may be projected to yield an idea of what others deserve. But if we already know what level of suffering is deserved for certain evils, why not just give other people (and ourselves) that level of suffering and forget all this talk about guilt and projections from it?[11]

A Digression on Retribution

I would now like to explore the ways in which our personal shortcomings—including our emotional shortcomings—may legitimately serve to undermine our confidence in some of our retributive judgments. Prior to this exploration, however, I think it will be useful to distinguish several different senses of retribution, for only one of them is clearly vulnerable to the challenges I shall raise.

Retribution is, of course, punishment that involves giving wrongdoers what they deserve. There are at least five senses of desert, however, and thus at least five senses of retribution. The five are these: desert as legal guilt; desert as involving *mens rea* (e.g., intention, knowledge); desert as involving responsibility (capacity to conform one's conduct to the rules); desert as a debt owed to annul wrongful gains from unfair free-riding (the Herbert Morris theory)[12]; and, finally, desert as involving ultimate character—evil or wickedness in some deep sense.

I shall call this fifth kind of retributivism "character retributivism."[13] Although Kant defends different accounts of punishment at various places in his *The Metaphysics of Morals*, character retributivism is clearly his position in the famous passage where he argues that murderers must be punished, even if civil society disbands, so that these wrongdoers will receive what is properly proportional to their "inner wickedness" (*inneren Bösartigkeit*).[14] I have also on occasion defended this view—e.g., in *Forgiveness and Mercy*, where I reject Augustine's "hate the sin but not the sinner" counsel and advocate what I call retributive hatred toward certain unrepentant wrongdoers.[15]

Michael Moore, as I interpret him, embraces a particularly ambitious and robust version of character retributivism: state punishment as pursuing the same objective that older traditions assigned to God. Character retribution, the idea that evil people are to be punished in proper proportion to their inner wickedness, had its first and best home in the context of divine punishment—something that God might properly administer, on that final Day of Judgment, when He consults the ledger book of a whole human life and character. Whatever one might think of this as a theology, most writers on punishment—even most retributivists—would probably reject it as a legitimate objective of state punishment. But not Moore. Indeed, Moore claims that if he believed in God he probably would not favor this account of secular, state punishment. However, as an atheist, he claims that the state must take on the punitive task that older traditions reserved for

God. Otherwise the task of apportioning punishment to evil would be left undone, and that would be morally intolerable.[16]

I have, in several earlier essays, expressed skepticism that an account of state punishment based on this robust version of character retributivism is consistent with the idea of a liberal, secular state, and I do not propose to rehearse my arguments here.[17] In those same essays, however, I accepted (even celebrated) the moral legitimacy of character retributivism and expressed some regret that I might be forced to choose between it and liberalism. In the present essay I will explain why I have come to doubt even the moral legitimacy of character retributivism and will argue not simply that the liberal state should not pursue this goal but that virtuous individuals should not embrace or welcome it either—even as something to hope for from God. Here (ironically enough) I have an ally in Kant—at least when he is thinking not about state punishment but about punishment and personal virtue. In *The Metaphysics of Morals*, he writes:

> It is a duty of virtue not only to refrain from repaying another's enmity with hatred out of mere revenge but also *not even to call upon the judge of the world* for vengeance, partly because a man has enough guilt of his own to be greatly in need of pardon and partly, and indeed especially, because no punishment, no matter from whom it comes, may be inflicted out of hatred. It is therefore a duty of men to be *forgiving*.[18]

In some sense, the remainder of the present essay may be seen as simply an expansion—with the help of Jesus and Nietzsche—of this Kantian insight.

A Fresh Start: Retribution and Moral Humility

It is not a logical truth, of course, that character retributivists will be motivated by hatred, and indeed most (and surely Moore and my previous self) would claim that they are not so motivated. If Nietzsche is right, however, the possibilities for self-deception here are enormous.[19] Once we think we are in a position to make judgments about a person's deep character—about that person's ultimate worth or value as a human being—then it is almost certain that we shall be tempted, once we have labeled some people as evil or "rotten to the core," to come to think of them as so much scum and to respond to them contemptuously. And the road from contempt to cruelty strikes me as a short one. The transition from "you have a bad character" to "you are evil" to "you are scum" to "you deserve to be treated with contempt" to "you deserve whatever cruel indignity I choose to inflict on you" is not a logical transition. It is, however—and this is the insight I draw from Nietzsche—a rather compelling psychological transition, one that should make us very cautious about basing our justification of punishment on assessments of ultimate character.[20]

Those of us who are sophisticated philosophers may, of course, think that we can detach our intellectual retributivist views from the kind of self-deceptive cruelty against which Nietzsche warned. But self-deceiving people always think that they can do this; this is part of what it means to say that they are in a state of self-deception. Even if we could do it, however, do we want to put forth views that—given the psychological connections noted by Nietzsche—might well be used by others to feed the fires of social cruelty, fires that currently rage nearly out of control in the American public's current viciousness toward criminals? I hope not, and I think that Judge Richard Posner—hardly my idea of a soft on crime, bleeding heart sentimentalist—agrees with me. In a recent opinion, in language that is persuasive and eloquent, he warned against the irrationality and cruelty toward criminals that is increasingly driving our system of criminal justice in America:

> There are different ways to look upon the inmates of prisons and jails in the United States in 1995. One way is to look upon them as members of a different species, indeed as a type of vermin, devoid of human dignity and entitled to no respect.
>
> I do not myself consider the 1.5 million inmates of American prisons and jails in that light. We should have a realistic conception of the composition of the prison and jail population before deciding that they are scum entitled to nothing better than what a vengeful populace and a resource-starved penal system chooses to give them. We must not exaggerate the distance between "us," the lawful ones, the respectable ones, and the prison and jail population; for such exaggeration will make it too easy for us to deny that population the rudiments of humane consideration.[21]

I do not know if Judge Posner would welcome being located in the Nietzschean camp, but it is Nietzsche, I think, who provides the most plausible explanation of the psychological and social forces that Judge Posner rightly wishes to oppose.

In short: Realizing that we might be motivated not by justice but by cruelty should make us pause before we confidently march forward under the banner of character retributivism. This is Nietzsche's lesson in moral humility.

Nietzsche's lesson in moral humility is not the only such lesson relevant to an assessment of character retributivism, however. Two additional ones are provided by Kant as he seeks to mine his Christian background for moral nuggets of secular value. Let me quote at some length passages from his *Critique of Pure Reason* and his *Religion Within the Limits of Reason Alone*, the final passage rivaling Nietzsche in its passion and in the profundity of its psychological insight:

> The real morality of actions, their merit or guilt, even that of our own conduct, remains entirely hidden from us. Our imputations can refer only to the empirical character. How much of this character is ascribable to the pure effect of freedom, how much to mere nature, that is, to faults of temperament for which there is no responsibility, or to its happy constitution (*merito fortunae*), can never be determined; and upon it therefore no perfectly just judgments can be passed.[22]

> We call a man evil, however, not because he performs actions that are evil (contrary to law) but because these actions are of such a nature that we may infer from them the presence in him of evil maxims. In and through experience we can observe actions contrary to law, and we can observe (at least in ourselves) that they are performed in the consciousness that they are unlawful; but a man's maxims, sometimes even his own, are not thus observable; consequently the judgment that the agent is an evil man cannot be made with certainty if grounded on experience.[23]

> [People] may picture themselves as meritorious, feeling themselves guilty of no such offenses as they see others burdened with; nor do they ever inquire whether good luck should not have the credit, or whether by reason of the cast of mind which they could discover, if they only would, in their own inmost nature, they would not have practiced similar vices, had not inability, temperament, training, and circumstances of time and place which serve to tempt one (matters which are not imputable), kept them out of the way of these vices. This dishonesty, by which we humbug ourselves and which thwarts the establishing of a true moral disposition in us, extends itself outwardly also to falsehood and deception of others. If this is not to be termed wickedness, it at least deserves the name of worthlessness, and is an element in the radical evil of human nature, which (inasmuch as it puts out of tune the moral capacity to judge what a man is to be taken for, and renders wholly uncertain both internal and external attribution of responsibility) constitutes the foul taint of our race.[24]

In these passages Kant seems to be raising both cognitive and moral obstacles to the legitimacy of imputing deep character responsibility to others (and perhaps even to ourselves)—calling into question our capacity to judge such matters. The passages raise the question "Who are we to judge?" Do we know enough to occupy this role without gross negligence and error? Are we virtuous enough to occupy this role without hypocrisy?

Cognitive Obstacles to Character Retributivism

The deeper we probe in our retributive judgments, the more prone to error we are, and character retributivism requires the deepest probing of all.[25] For the inquiry here is not simply into wrongful acts (harm or free riding), or into voluntary control, or into such fairly surface parts of the mind as intention or knowledge *(mens rea)*, or even into episodic motive. It is, rather, a search into deep character—into such matters as whether the defendant possesses (to use the language of some capital sentencing guidelines) a "hardened, abandoned and malignant heart."[26] But are we in a position to know such deep character or to know the degree to which, if at all, people are responsible for the possession of such character? Kant suggests, in the first two of the three passages quoted, that the answer to these questions is no.

We face here the formidable epistemological problem that philosophers call "the problem of other minds" and perhaps even deep metaphysical worries about free will and determinism. It is hard enough—given human capacity for self-deception—to be very certain of one's own motives and fundamental desires, and there are staggering obstacles in the way of our making such judgments about others.[27]

Kant's own theory of imputation and desert, placing so much weight upon the radically free noumenal self that is unknowable through any empirical means (the only ones we have, alas), faces this problem in a particularly dramatic way.[28] Any theory that places weight on the inner life in determining desert, however, will face the problem to some degree. Even the attribution of such familiar (from the American *Model Penal Code*) *mens rea* conditions as purpose or recklessness faces nontrivial cognitive problems. And, of course, when we seek to target even deeper aspects of ultimate character and responsibility—to target "inner wickedness" or a "hardened, abandoned and malignant heart"—the cognitive problems become even more awesome.

It seems to me that these epistemological problems cannot, in justice, simply be ignored. If we really do not have the knowledge required to impute deep character depravity to others with any degree of reliability, then we act recklessly in inflicting misery on people as the suffering they deserve for their inner wickedness.[29]

What, then, are we to do? We could attempt a Thomas Nagel strategy and return to our strong retributive practices with a certain sense of irony and detachment.[30] This probably would not work, however, since the emotions required for strong retributivism are probably not consistent with irony and detachment. We could also adopt an essentially consequentialist theory of punishment, perhaps with some deontological side constraints—e.g., the negative retributive side constraint that we not punish anyone to a degree greater than he deserves. This will only work, of course, if we can analyze the concept of desert in such a way that it does not raise all the same problems noted above—e.g., "punish him no more than he deserves" had better not mean "punish him no more than demanded by his inner wickedness."

Perhaps the most promising prospect is to seek a weaker or more modest version of retributivism, one whose epistemological and metaphysical commitments are less deep. We could, for example, employ Herbert Morris's justification of criminal punishment: the claim that the criminal, as a free rider on a mutually beneficial scheme of social cooperation, must be punished in order to annul the unfair advantage his wrongful failure to exercise self-restraint has given him over those citizens who have been law-abiding.[31] Although this theory does not involve deep notions of inner wickedness, it may still properly be called retributive because it is a non-consequentialist theory of punishment that bases the justification of punishment on considerations of justice or fairness. (Free riders violate a duty of fair play to those who have given the law their voluntary compliance.) Some notion of desert is also captured—e.g., according to Morris, the criminal has a right to punishment and owes it as a debt to his fellow citizens. This theory would also require some consideration of states of mind and character (e.g., free riding is an intentional act), but ones that, given the less deeply retributive purpose of the practice in which the consideration will arise, will probably stretch our cognitive powers to a much less worrisome degree. Such a "moral balance" theory is, of course, not without its problems—and may even be open to the Nietzschean charge that some with the score-keeping souls of accountants will be drawn to it.[32] It does not, however, seem to flirt with cruelty.

To summarize: Even though the necessities of maintaining civilized life and schemes of just cooperation require that we sometimes make and act on our best judgments of wrongdoing and criminal responsibility (that we have trials and jails, in short), we should be very cautious about overdramatizing and overmoralizing what we must (regretfully) do here by portraying it as some righteous cosmic drama—as a holy war against ultimate sin and evil. Such a view would, among other things, tempt us to dangerous excesses—excesses that would harm others through our unjust treatment of them and harm us through our own corruption—as one is always corrupted when one would presume to occupy a role best reserved for the gods. As mere humans, with radically finite knowledge, it is perhaps better for us to admit that we are not totally clear about what we are up to here.

Moral Obstacles to Character Retributivism

There are at least two ways in which retributive judgments might seem inappropriate (unvirtuous and likely—but not necessarily—mistaken) because of moral failings in the person who makes them. First, they could involve the vice of hypocrisy: our demanding that others receive their just deserts when we ourselves are no better. (I take it that Jesus' "He that is without sin . . ." remark is an attempt to identify the hypocrisy in at least some acts of punishment.) Second—as noted by Nietzsche—retributive judgments could be seen as running a nontrivial risk of being motivated by such base passions as envy, malicious hatred, and spite, passions included by Nietzsche under the term *ressentiment*. I have already discussed the Nietzschean challenge, and I will close this essay by a discussion of the hypocrisy challenge.

Michael Moore, you will recall, attempts to make short work of Jesus' "He that is without sin . . ." remark, calling it "pretty clumsy moral philosophy." He writes:

> It is true that all of us are guilty of some immoralities, probably on a daily basis. Yet for most people reading this essay, the immoralities in question are things like manipulating others unfairly; not caring deeply enough about another's suffering; not being charitable for the limitations of others; convenient lies; and so forth. Few of us have raped and murdered a woman, drowned her three small children, and felt no remorse about it.[33]

Moore's point seems to be this: In the relevant sense most of us *are* without sin, and so we might as well feel free to pick up some stones and cast away.

Is this an adequate answer to Jesus and to the passage quoted earlier from Kant's *Religion*? I think not. The response is too shallow, for it fails to reflect the kind of serious moral introspection that Jesus and Kant are attempting to provoke. The point is not to deny that many people lead lives that are both legally and morally correct. The point is, rather, to force such people to face honestly the question of why they have lived in such a way. Is it (as they would no doubt like to think) because their inner characters manifest true integrity and are thus morally superior to those people whose behavior has been less exemplary? Or is it, at least in part, a matter of what John Rawls has called "luck on the natural and social lottery"?[34] Perhaps, as Kant suggests, their favored upbringing and social circumstances, or the fact that they have never been placed in situations where they have been similarly tempted, or their fear of being found out, has had considerably more to do with their compliance with the rules of law and morality than they would like to admit. Perhaps if they imagined themselves possessed of Gyges's ring (a ring that, in Plato's myth in Book 2 of *Republic*, makes its wearer invisible), they might—if honest with themselves—have to admit that they would probably use the ring, not to perform anonymous acts of charity, but to perform some acts of considerable evil—acts comparable, perhaps, to the acts for which they often seek the punishment of others.[35] If they follow through honestly on this process of self-examination, they (like Angelo in *Measure for Measure*) will have discovered the potential for evil within themselves and will have learned an important lesson in moral humility.[36]

Conclusion

This brings to a close my little sermonette on moral humility. I have suggested the following: (1) From Nietzsche we learn that our retributive judgments may be based not on justice but on cruelty and that we may be in a state of self-deception about this. (2) From Kant we learn that we may not be in a position to know that persons possess the responsible and evil character that we seek to target in the desert judgments of character retributivism. (3) From Jesus and Kant we learn that our own evil or our own potential for evil is such that, rather than seeking to give others the suffering they deserve for their evil, we should leave that task to God (or leave it undone) and seek to put our own personal moral house in order.

Does this mean that we should abandon institutions of punishment in some sentimental orgy of love and self-doubt? Of course not. What it does mean is that, in punishing, we should act with caution, regret, humility, and with a vivid realization that we are involved in a fallible and finite human institution—one that is necessary but regrettable. The danger arises when we forget—as some of us who are retributivists sometimes, I fear, do forget—that nothing but iniquity and madness awaits us if we let ourselves think that, in punishing, we are involved in some cosmic drama of good and evil—that, like the Blues Brothers, we are on a mission from God.

Let me then close, appropriately, with a final word from Nietzsche: "Whoever fights with monsters should take care that in the process he does not become a monster."[37]

NOTES

1. Nietzsche's reflections on punishment are spread throughout most of his major works. The best place to begin reading him on this and related issues is probably the Second Essay ("'Guilt,' 'Bad Conscience,' and the Like") of the 1887 *On the Genealogy of Morals*. (Friedrich Nietzsche, *On the Genealogy of Morals*, translated by Walter Kaufmann, New York: Vintage, 1989.) Nietzsche's remarks are about punishment in general, with no specific references to retributivism. I think it is obvious, however, that what he has in mind is punishment with a retributive justification—the idea that, in punishing, we are giving people what they in justice deserve. As will be noted later, he sometimes speaks favorably of punishment when the practice is defended with a nonretributive justification. My own defenses of the retributive theory of punishment may be found in my collection of essays *Retribution, Justice and Therapy* (Dordrecht: Reidel, 1979); my chapters in the book *Forgiveness and Mercy* by Jeffrie G. Murphy (Chapters 1, 3, and 5) and Jean Hampton (Chapters 2 and 4) (Cambridge: Cambridge University Press, 1988); and in my essay "Getting Even: The Role of the Victim," reprinted in my essay collection *Retribution Reconsidered* (Dordrecht: Kluwer, 1992).

2. "While the noble man lives in trust and openness with himself . . . , the man of *ressentiment* is neither upright nor naive nor honest and straightforward with himself. His soul squints." (Nietzsche, *Genealogy, supra* note 1, p. 38.)

3. "Almost everything we call 'higher culture' is based on the spiritualization of cruelty." (Friedrich Nietzsche, *Beyond Good and Evil,* translated by Walter Kaufmann, New York: Vintage, 1989, p. 158.) More cautiously expressed versions of similar thoughts may, of course, be found in other writers. See, for example, Chapter III of Thomas Hobbes's *De Cive,* and Karen Horney's marvelous essay "The Value of Vindictiveness" in *American Journal of Psychoanalysis* (Volume 8, 1948, pp. 3–12).

4. *Thus Spoke Zarathrustra,* Second Part, "On the Tarantulas," in *The Portable Nietzsche,* translated by Walter Kaufmann (New York: Viking, 1970), p. 212.

5. I have been assisted in reaching this not totally welcome self-perception not simply by Nietzsche but also by some essays by Marilyn Adams and Herbert Morris that are critical of my work on resentment, punishment, and forgiveness—essays that suggest, ever so politely and ever so indirectly, that views such as mine may grow out of excessive self-involvement, mistrust, and a lack of generosity of spirit. See Marilyn Adams's "Forgiveness: A Christian Model," in *Faith and Philosophy* (Volume 8, Number 3, 1991, pp. 277–304) and Herbert Morris's and Jeffrie G. Murphy's "Exchange on Forgiveness" in *Criminal Justice Ethics* (Volume 7, Number 2, 1988, pp. 3–22).

As I reflect on my own personal and philosophical struggles with retribution and related concepts over the years, I find myself increasingly making autobiographical references in the recent writings that reflect these struggles. I do this not (I hope!) merely as narcissistic self-indulgence but rather in the spirit of another insight by Nietzsche: "Gradually it has become clear to me what every philosophy so far has been: namely, the personal confession of its author and a kind of involuntary and unconscious memoir." (Nietzsche, *Beyond Good and Evil, supra* note 3, p. 13.) A similar thought has been expressed by Thomas Nagel: "Philosophical ideas are acutely sensitive to individual temperament, and to wishes." (Thomas Nagel, *The View from Nowhere*, New York: Oxford University Press, 1986, p. 10.) To the degree that Nietzsche and Nagel are correct about this, then, it might be useful if philosophers in general would "fess up" concerning the internal struggles that motivate some of their abstract speculations.

6. Michael Moore, "The Moral Worth of Retribution," in *Responsibility, Character, and the Emotions,* edited by Ferdinand Schoeman (Cambridge: Cambridge University Press, 1987), pp. 179–219. Although I am here selecting certain aspects of Moore's essay with which I want to quarrel, I want to make it clear to the reader how very much I admire the essay and how much I have learned from it.

7. I am well aware that I am using some of Nietzsche's insights for my own purposes and taking them in directions he would not welcome. Here, for example, is what he has to say about humility: "When stepped on, a worm doubles up. That is clever. In that way he lessens the probability of being stepped on again. In the language of morality: humility." (Friedrich Nietzsche, *Twilight of the Idols,* in *The Portable Nietzsche,* translated by Walter Kaufmann, New York: Viking, 1970, p. 471.)

8. Moore, *supra* note 6, p. 188. Moore is willing to concede (p. 193) that the passage may "charitably" be read as a counsel against falling victim to mob psychology, but he sees no deeper message in it.

9. *Ibid.,* p. 216.

10. In my chapters in *Forgiveness and Mercy* (*supra* note 1), I argue that some degree of resentment may be justified as an assertion of self-respect and may thus form part of a virtuous life. This is the good side of resentment, but perhaps (if Nietzsche is correct) it has a tendency to slide into *ressentiment* without our being aware of this. Guilt also, of course, has a good side insofar as it is a testament to the

fact that we care for others and our moral duties to them. But perhaps (as I shall suggest below) it has a tendency to slide into neurosis—everything from moral silliness to pathological self-loathing.

11. Moore (*supra* note 6, p. 183) suggests two ways in which one, using coherence to assess the adequacy of a moral theory, might attempt to defend a retributive theory of punishment. One strategy is to show that retributivism follows from some more general principle of justice that we think is true. The other strategy, favored by Moore, is to show that retributivism "best accounts for those of our more particular moral judgments that we also believe to be true." This strategy, called by John Rawls the methodology of "reflective equilibrium," selects as the best theory the theory that accounts for the largest set of our pretheoretical convictions. (John Rawls, *A Theory of Justice*, Cambridge: Harvard University Press, 1971, pp. 20ff.) But what if Nietzsche is correct about the origin and nature of our pretheoretical convictions concerning desert and punishment—that, whatever we may consciously think, these pretheoretical convictions are self-deceptive covers for *ressentiment*? Or what if we can tell a plausible story to plant comparable skepticism about pretheoretical convictions generated by guilt? What does this do to the use of reflective equilibrium methodology?

12. See Herbert Morris's "Persons and Punishment" in his *On Guilt and Innocence* (Berkeley: University of California Press, 1976), pp. 31–63.

13. I explore in greater detail the distinction between character retributivism (the view I am attributing to Moore) and grievance retributivism (the Morris view) in my "Repentance, Punishment and Mercy" in *Repentance: A Comparative Perspective*, edited by Amitai Etzioni and David Carney (Lanham, Md.: Rowman & Littlefield, 1997), pp. 143–70. In another essay, Moore rejects character (and favors choice) as a basis for criminal liability and excuse. ("Choice, Character, and Excuse," *Social Philosophy and Policy*, Volume 7, Issue 2, Spring 1990, pp. 29–58.) In "The Moral Worth of Retribution," *supra* note 6, however, his concern seems to be with punishment as deserved suffering as this value might be reflected not in judgments of liability but in sentencing; here issues of character move to center stage. Consider, for example, the weight that Moore gives (pp. 213ff.) to the murderer Richard Herrin's "shallowness"—his lack of guilt and remorse—in thinking about the punishment that Herrin deserves. For an instructive discussion of the very different roles that character might play in conviction and sentencing, see James Landon's "Character Evidence: Getting to the Root of the Problem Through Comparison," in *American Journal of Criminal Law* (Volume 24, Number 3, Summer 1997, pp. 581–615).

14. Immanuel Kant, *The Metaphysics of Morals*, translated by Mary Gregor (Cambridge: Cambridge University Press, 1991), p. 142.

15. *Supra* note 1, Chapter 3.

16. Moore, *supra* note 6, p. 217.

17. Jeffrie G. Murphy, "Retributivism, Moral Education, and the Liberal State"

(in *Retribution Reconsidered, supra* note 1, pp. 15–30), and "Legal Moralism and Liberalism," in *Arizona Law Review* (Volume 37, Number 1, Spring 1995, pp. 73–94).

18. *Supra* note 14, p. 253 (first italics mine). Kant does not always follow his own counsel on this matter. In his famous "moral proof" for the existence of God, for example, he argues that it is so vital (the *summum bonum*) that wrongdoers receive their just deserts (and good people their proper rewards) that—given that we cannot attain this goal in this world—we must postulate the existence of God as an agent who can bring this about in the next world. Of course we know that God will not be motivated by hate. How can we be so sure, however, that we are not so motivated when we believe in God in the hope that he will punish wrongdoers as they truly deserve? Are those who are charmed by Kant's moral proof subject to a Nietzschean diagnosis?

19. Moore, *supra* note 6, admits this (p. 216), but the admission strikes me as possibly perfunctory, for it seems in no degree to undermine Moore's own willingness to make supremely confident judgments about what suffering others—e.g., Richard Herrin—deserve. His response to Herrin and the other criminals he discusses could be read as superior and contemptuous. I think, alas, that such a response is also obviously present in some of my own previous work. It is possible, of course, that I misinterpret Moore here because I want company—desiring to draw another prominent retributivist into my tent so that I will not have to feel alone in my fear that I have perhaps fallen victim to some bad passions.

20. Recall again (*supra* note 13) that my concern here is mainly with criminal sentencing, not with criminal liability.

21. Johnson v. Phelan, No. 93-3753, United States Court of Appeals, Seventh Circuit, 1995 WL 621777 (7th Cir.[Ill.]).

22. Immanuel Kant, *Critique of Pure Reason,* translated by Norman Kemp Smith (London: Macmillan, 1933), p. 475.

23. Immanuel Kant, *Religion Within the Limits of Reason Alone,* translated by T. M. Greene and Hoyt H. Hudson (New York: Harper, 1960), p. 16.

24. *Ibid.,* pp. 33–34.

25. The cognitive and moral obstacles to character retribution that I present here were first developed with respect to the imputation of responsibility in my essay "Cognitive and Moral Obstacles to Imputation" (*Jahrbuch für Recht und Ethik,* Band 2, 1994, pp. 67–79).

26. In many American states, capital murder's *mens rea* requirement of "malice aforethought" may be inferred from recklessness if a killer is said to have the mental state or character defect variously characterized as "an abandoned and wicked heart," "a depraved heart," "a malignant heart," "a depraved mind," "wickedness of disposition, hardness of heart, cruelty, recklessness of consequences and a mind regardless of social duty," "wickedness of heart or cruelty," or (in the *Model Penal Code*) "extreme indifference to the value of human life." See generally Joshua Dressler's *Understanding Criminal Law* (New York: Matthew Bender, 1987), p. 461.

Even when a concern with inner wickedness does not find its way into the definition of the crime, it often arises dramatically when character is considered for purposes of criminal sentencing—particularly in capital sentencing. See generally Landon, *supra* note 13.

27. E. M. Cioran: "How to imagine other people's lives when our own seems scarcely conceivable?" (I copied this down years ago from one of Cioran's works, but I can no longer find the source.) For a careful and insightful exploration of the issues of this section of my paper—an exploration from which I learned a great deal—see Rebecca Dresser's "Culpability and Other Minds" in *Law &; Southern California Interdisciplinary Law Journal* (Volume 2, Number 1, Spring 1993, pp. 41–88).

28. If we claim that responsibility is a property of the noumenal self, we preserve a strong sense of desert because the noumenal self is (according to Kant) metaphysically free. The noumenal self, however, cannot be known through empirical means—e.g., observation of behavior. We can get around this cognitive problem by claiming that responsibility is a property of the empirical self. But the empirical self is (according to Kant) subject to causal determination, and this would seem to spell the end of any strong sense of desert. Any attempt to link up the two selves in a common theory would, of course, face the classic problem of interactionism familiar from the debates over Cartesian dualism. These problems might be overcome, but we are currently in no position to justify cheerful optimism that we really know what we are doing here.

Although I cannot pursue the matter here, it is possible (as my colleague Michael White has suggested) that attribution of desert in a deep sense might involve conceptual as well as cognitive obstacles. The concept of responsible inner wickedness might involve a notion of the self (or true self) that is incoherent.

29. In my view, there are two probably unanswerable questions that would need answers before we could confidently claim to be punishing people in proper proportion to their inner wickedness: (1) Have we in fact accurately determined the ultimate character of the individual? (2) Was the individual freely responsible for the development of that character? Not everyone, of course, thinks that the second question is relevant. John Kekes, for example, in his book *Facing Evil* (Princeton: Princeton University Press, 1990), thinks that the issues of free choice and responsibility are irrelevant to assessing a character as evil or wicked, and thus our failure to know about such matters must be irrelevant also. For Kekes, a person has an evil character if that person possesses (for whatever cause or reason) traits that tend to inflict harm on innocent people. I can see this as one possible analysis of evil and can also see it as a basis for a utilitarian response to evil—e.g., respond to people who are evil in this way by taking steps to neutralize the harm that they might cause. What I cannot see, however, is how any interesting concept of deserved suffering can be applied to persons who are evil only in this way.

30. See Thomas Nagel's "The Absurd" in his collection *Mortal Questions* (Oxford: Oxford University Press, 1979), pp. 11–23.

31. *Supra* note 12.

32. In *The Dawn*, Nietzsche speaks of "our abominable penal codes, with their shopkeeper's scales." (*The Portable Nietzsche, supra* note 4, p. 86.) Some of the problems faced by Morris's theory (a theory I once embraced wholeheartedly) are these: How are we to use this version of retributivism to grade criminal offenses on a scale of seriousness? It does not seem that murder (clearly a more serious crime than theft) is more unfair than theft. And if the criminal owes us a debt solely because we have exercised self-restraint and the criminal has not, then the criminal's punishment would have to be a function of how difficult it was for us to obey the law (i.e., how great a burden we found our own self-restraint). But this might produce a highly unpredictable and bizarre ranking of criminal offenses. Most of us who are normal and well brought up are probably not very tempted to murder or rape and are thus not aware of taking on much of a burden in refraining from these activities. The burden of self-restraint exercised here is, for most of us, far less than the burden we feel when paying our taxes. Do we then want to punish tax evasion as a more serious offense than murder or rape? Additional problems for Morris's view are generated by Robert Nozick's critique of the Principle of Fairness itself in *Anarchy, State and Utopia* (New York: Basic Books, 1974, pp. 90ff) and perhaps by my argument that given the radical inequality of benefits in actual societies, the Principle of Fairness will not impose upon all citizens equal obligations of obedience to law. On this issue, see my essay "Marxism and Retribution" in my collection *Retribution, Justice and Therapy, supra* note 1, pp. 93–115.

33. *Supra* note 6, p. 188. In the film "Dead Man Walking," Sister Helen Prejean cautions that no person should be judged solely on the basis of the worst thing that the person has done. Moore seems not to exercise such caution.

If one visualizes even this worst of criminals as the small child he once was, one might reach the moral wisdom expressed toward a serial killer by Felicia in William Trevor's novel *Felicia's Journey:* "Lost within the man who murdered, there was a soul like any other soul, purity itself it surely once had been" (London: Viking, 1994, p. 212).

34. John Rawls, *A Theory of Justice, supra* note 11, Chapter 2.

35. The Gyges's ring thought experiment could perhaps be used to help Morris's theory overcome one of the objections raised above in note 32—the objection that most of us are not aware of repressing impulses to murder and rape and thus do not demand that murderers and rapists be punished because they have failed to restrain impulses that we have restrained. But perhaps we are not aware of repressing impulses to murder and rape because these impulses have been so successfully repressed that they are generally unconscious. If we imagine ourselves possessed of Gyges's ring, however, we perhaps open a door that allows these impulses to become conscious.

36. See Walt Whitman's poem "You Felons on Trial in Courts." Saying of himself "beneath this face that appears so impassive hell's tides continually run," he concludes the poem thus: "And henceforth I will not deny them—for how can I deny myself?"

37. Nietzsche, *Beyond Good and Evil, supra* note 3, Epigram 146, p. 89. Nietzsche concludes the epigram with this observation: "When you look long into an abyss, the abyss also looks into you."

Nietzsche is best known, of course, for his suggestion that the idea of just or deserved punishment may be a mask for cruelty, may turn us into the very kind of monsters we seek to punish. He is also well aware, however, that sloppy sentimentality, an uncritical ethic of pity, and hasty tendencies to forgive can also infect punitive practices. In *Beyond Good and Evil* (*supra* note 3, p. 114) he writes: "There is a point in the history of society when it becomes so pathologically soft and tender that among other things it sides with even those who harm it, criminals, and does this quite seriously and honestly. Punishing somehow seems unfair to it, and it is certain that imagining 'punishment' and 'being obligated to punish' hurts it, arouses fear in it. 'Is it not enough to render him undangerous? Why still punish? Punishing itself is terrible.' With this question, herd morality, the morality of timidity, draws its ultimate consequence."

This is a very puzzling passage. In part, the passage seems to make the point that society must take steps to protect itself against criminals and that worries about *ressentiment* should not impede those steps. But the passage also seems to suggest that protection is not enough—that, in addition to neutralizing the criminal, we should also feel free to strike out against the criminal in some more robust way, that only timidity stands in our way of such a response. However, Nietzsche's own warnings about punishment's link to *ressentiment* seem to give powerful support to the very timidity and reluctance he here condemns. Perhaps there is some unescapable tension at the heart of punishment—a tension that will always generate anxiety in those who are aware of it—and perhaps this anxiety is a good thing. Perhaps it is good that, when we recommend punishment, we should always feel conflicted and slightly unclean about what we are doing. This might at least blunt our tendencies toward cruelty.

Chapter Six

Remorse, Responsibility, and Criminal Punishment:
An Analysis of Popular Culture

Austin Sarat

I. Introduction

Until relatively recently it might have been said with considerable confidence that at least one emotion is universally welcomed within, and by, the legal system, namely remorse in the face of wrongdoing.[1] The remorseful wrongdoer, it was generally thought, vindicated law's effort not only to control wrongdoing but to establish legal rules as norms that, as H. L. A. Hart noted, create moral obligations.[2] "Few ideas," Scott Sundby claims,

> reverberate at the core of the human psyche as strongly as that of atonement. Both as individuals and as a society, we expect those who commit wrongful acts to seek expiation. The value placed on atonement and the desire to cultivate it as a fundamental societal tenet can be seen everywhere.... Where the wrongful act is especially egregious ... those who refuse to seek absolution are viewed as outcasts who have forfeited their claim to live in society.[3]

Traditionally, law has encouraged remorse by rewarding it.[4] The law was as interested in the blameworthiness of the offender as in the harm his offense caused and, as a result, in his emotional reaction to his own wrongdoing.[5]

However, with the growth of guideline or mandatory sentencing, the position of remorse as a factor in criminal punishment has become considerably more controversial.[6] Some now believe that there is no place for assessments of remorse, that the focus of punishment should be on the acts committed by an offender, not the offender's emotional responses to those acts.[7] Others are skeptical of the capacity of legal decision makers to differentiate between the sincerely repentant and those whose remorse is prompted solely by the hope for reduced punishment.[8] Thus while the Federal Sentencing Guidelines specify "acceptance of responsibility" as a guideline and a factor relevant to a reduced sentence, they do not specify remorse or repentance as warranting similar consideration.[9] Acceptance of responsibility as so defined focuses on behaviors, e.g., pleas of guilty, rather than on the emotional lives of criminals.[10]

However, the controversy surrounding the 1998 execution of Karla Faye Tucker has fueled a revival of interest in remorse and renewed claims about its salience in determining punishment.[11] New voices have been raised seeking to rehabilitate remorse by insisting that the acceptance of responsibility and feelings of regret are important for what they tell us about the emotional disposition of the convicted offender.[12] Remorse, in these accounts, requires, first, an internalization of agency, a willingness to say that one could, and should, have done differently.[13] The initial step on the journey to remorse is a movement from being held responsible to accepting responsibility. Once the wrongdoer accepts responsibility, he is prepared to feel genuine sorrow for what he has done.

But remorse involves more than sorrow. It is a type of self-punishment. It "expresses itself as the exigency of a painful remembering. . . . [It] cuts deeply because we are obliged to retell, relive, and seek forgiveness for sorrowful events that have rendered our claims to membership in a moral community suspect or defeasible."[14] This includes, Harvey Cox contends, "a realistic awareness of the hurt and damage that has been caused to others by my misdeeds. Remorse . . . implies a degree of empathetic pain on the part of the one who has caused the fracture."[15]

The self-punishing, remorseful offender makes a complex moral claim on those harmed by his acts and those who judge him. The basis of this claim is that remorse demonstrates a change of heart on the part of the offender that should, in turn, engender a change of heart on the part of both victim and community.[16] In the name of equity and reintegration, so the argument goes, remorse blunts the edge of retribution; it engenders forgiveness, or at least sets the stage for forgiveness.[17] And, if not forgiveness, remorse at least seems to call for mitigation of punishment.

Moreover, remorse, unlike some other emotions, does not challenge reason but seems instead to be a reasonable/rational response to transgression.[18] Indeed we worry more about the wrongdoer who feels nothing or who responds through a careful cost/benefit calculus. Wrongdoers, as Et-zioni argues, "who are not remorseful are viewed as if they have offended the community twice: once in whatever offense they have committed and, second, in their refusal to acknowledge that mores were violated."[19]

Those who believe that the criminal law should welcome and reward re-morse typically rely, Jeffrie Murphy notes, on two different types of consid-erations.[20] The first is future-oriented and predictive; the genuinely re-morseful offender, so this argument goes, is simply less likely to offend again.[21] As a result, the community needs to be less worried about the of-fender and can afford to be more lenient. Second, remorse involves a change of heart, an alteration of character. Indeed, as Erving Goffman for-mulates it, remorse in the presence of wrongdoing represents a "splitting of the self into a blameworthy part and a part that stands back and sympa-thizes with the blame giving."[22]

The remorseful offender is, in an important sense, a changed, perhaps a different, person.[23] "The repentant person," as Murphy explains, "has a better character than the unrepentant person, and thus the repentant per-son . . . simply deserves less punishment than the unrepentant person."[24] Or as Morris notes, "The repentant person at the time of punishment is less blameworthy than an unrepentant one."[25]

Our society, I contend, both demands remorse and feels anxious in its presence. The demand for remorse is fueled by remorse's conservative, norm-affirming character. Whatever its consequence for the allocation of punishment, remorse is a retrospective embrace, and expression, of alle-giance to the existing normative order. Expressions of remorse "unequivo-cally enunciate the existence and force of shared assumptions that autho-rize existing social arrangements and demarcate moral boundaries."[26] Yet even in the face of such expressions, victims, judges, and citizens may feel anxious, troubled, and unsettled. Remorse, in one sense, always comes too late, after the damage is done, the hurt inflicted. It can help revisit the scene of the crime but never undo the damage done.[27] And, when remorse comes after the wrongdoer is apprehended or in the face of an impending pun-ishment, we worry that it is at best insincere or at worst fraudulent.[28]

In this essay I want to explore both the demand for and anxiety about re-morse in popular culture representations of crime and punishment. How does remorse fare in the popular imagination? What are the demands made on viewers when films about crime and punishment turn into stories of re-morse in which the wrongdoer sees the error of his ways, accepts responsi-bility, and expresses remorse? While the law may have become somewhat less attentive to remorse in allocating criminal punishment, popular culture, I contend, still gives a central role to accepting responsibility and expressing remorse in representations of crime and punishment. As Richard Weisman recently noted, "[R]emorse forms a central part of the crime narrative that is conveyed . . . to the public—the story of how and why the offender transgressed the criminal code. . . . By focusing on remorse, popular . . . discourse shows an interest not just in the act but in the offender's attitude towards his or her act."[29] This interest in remorse reaffirms the continuing role of emotion in calibrating our responses to wrongdoing.

My work builds on David Garland's suggestion that scholars should attend to the "cultural role" of legal practices, to their ability to "create social meaning and thus shape social worlds," and that among those practices none is more important than how we punish.[30] Punishment has traditionally been one of the great subjects of cultural production, suggesting the powerful allure of humankind's fall from grace and of our prospects for redemption. Punishment, Garland tells us, "helps shape the overarching culture and contribute to the generation and regeneration of its terms."[31] It is a set of signifying practices that "teaches, clarifies, dramatizes and authoritatively enacts some of the most basic moral-political categories and distinctions which help shape our symbolic universe."[32] But how we punish is itself shaped by cultural categories and responses to wrongdoing. While punishment lives in culture through its pedagogical effects and teaches us how to think about such basic social categories as intention, responsibility, and injury, it is also responsive to the normative dimensions of our cultural life.

The semiotics of punishment is all around us, not just in the architecture of the prison or the speech made by a judge as she sends someone to the penal colony but in both "high" and "popular" culture iconography, in novels, television, and film.[33] Popular culture representations of crime and punishment often are centrally tales of responsibility and remorse. They are tales that bracket larger questions about the etiology of crime or the appropriateness of particular types of punishment, and instead position their viewers as judges or jurors whose job it is to reflect on the justness of punishment for individual wrongdoers who may or may not accept responsibility or express remorse. In this paper I provide but one example of the way popular culture approaches these issues. The example I have chosen is *Dead Man Walking.*

Dead Man Walking, I argue, is preoccupied with the question of responsibility and remorse.[34] It demonstrates, and reinforces, the continuing hold of remorse on the popular imagination, even as it stirs our anxieties about it. To the extent the film contains an explanation of crime and a justification for punishment, both are located in the autonomous choices of particular agents. While building dramatic tension around the question of whether one person deserves the death penalty, this film conveys a powerful double message about responsibility and remorse: first, legal subjects can, and will, be held responsible for their acts; second, they can, and should, internalize and accept responsibility. This internalization is what makes remorse meaningful. *Dead Man Walking* is, in fact, a story of the evolution of remorse, of a coming to terms, and a sorrowful acknowledgment of a grievous wrong. Yet because the expression of remorse comes late in the film, and only in the face of an imminent execution, the film invites its viewers to ask whether the remorse that is expressed is sincere and meaningful. Nonetheless, the appeal of this narrative is, in the end, a reminder of the continuing significance of responsibility and remorse in the way in which we think about crime and punishment.[35]

II. Making the Punishment Fit the Crime: Moral Pedagogy and the Evolution of Remorse in Dead Man Walking

Every story about punishment is inevitably a story about crime, about its causes and the process of assigning responsibility for it. How we think about punishment is, in part, a function of what we know and think about the crimes that give rise to it. The prevailing common sense suggests that the severity of punishment should be proportional to the seriousness of the crime and that punishment should be deployed only against responsible agents,[36] against free and moral agents, persons capable of knowing right from wrong and choosing to do one or the other.[37] As former Supreme Court Justice Robert Jackson once explained, "The contention that injury can amount to crime only when inflicted by intention is no provincial or transient notion. It is as universal and persistent in mature systems of law as belief in freedom of the human will and a consequent ability and duty of the normal individual to choose between good and evil. . . ."[38]

This understanding of crime and punishment depends on what Stephen Carter calls "bilateral individualism."[39] As Carter explains,

> The dominant culture's understanding of victimhood awards the status of victim to someone who loses something . . . because of the predation of someone else. Victimization, then, is the result of concrete, individual acts by identifiable transgressors. . . . [The dominant understanding] invents a real-

ity in which the only victims are those who have suffered at the hands of transgressors, and in which any sanctions should be directed toward deterring or punishing those transgressors. . . . To one who accepts this vision, a world like ours, one in which so many violent crimes occur and go unpunished by the state, must seem a world in which the forces of order have lost control. . . . People are afraid of crime and are afraid of becoming victims. They want to strike back at someone to liberate themselves from fear. . . . [B]ilateral individualism can rationalize the need to strike back only by insisting that . . . transgressors are real, individual people, and other individuals have the right to turn their assaults aside.[40]

In this vision the legitimacy of punishment depends on a relatively precise moral calculus in which punishment is a measured and proportionate response to crime. Linking crime and punishment is the supposed reality of individual responsibility and moral blameworthiness.[41]

As exemplified by *Dead Man Walking*, Carter's bilateral individualism is a prevailing motif in popular culture. Stories of the lives and deeds of particular persons have much more dramatic appeal than stories in which causation is impersonal and diffuse and the source of crime is located in social structure.[42] Therefore, it is not surprising that popular films provide narratives of crime and punishment that focus on describing what a particular person did and on fixing responsibility on a blameworthy agent.[43] However, *Dead Man Walking* goes beyond fixing responsibility to the question of whether a murderer—Matthew Poncelet—will *accept* responsibility and, in turn, whether an acceptance of responsibility should be consequential in determining the justness of his punishment. The film invites its viewers to ask whether, everything else being equal, expressions of remorse should have any bite in structuring our responses to the wrongdoer.

This film focuses on someone already condemned to death, living on death row, about whose legal guilt there is little doubt, someone whose crime is graphically, and repeatedly, presented to us. It is a tale of a person coming to terms with his responsibility for a gruesome crime. Poncelet (played by Sean Penn) has been sentenced for his part in a double murder in which a classically clean-cut boy and girl are accosted while parking in the woods. They are led off into a clearing, where the girl is raped and repeatedly stabbed, and both ultimately are shot execution style.

Dead Man Walking inquires about the capacity of its viewers to recognize a shared humanity in, to empathize, and to care for or about someone who could commit such a heinous crime. It does so through the pairing of the condemned with a cinematic "buddy,"[44] a nun—Sister Helen Prejean—

who becomes the stand-in for the film's viewers. Can we have as much understanding and compassion as she does? Should we? Should it matter to us whether Matthew Poncelet accepts responsibility and feels remorse for crimes for which he has already been found legally responsible?

Images of the crime play a large role in suggesting how those questions should be answered. Poncelet's crime is presented in a variety of ways and reenacted repeatedly throughout the film in a duet with the impending execution. Visual equivalences are created, and the viewer alternately is positioned as crime-scene investigator, juror, omnipotent truth seeker, voyeur. Through its preoccupation with the scene of criminality, *Dead Man Walking* establishes the background conditions against which responsibility and blameworthiness can be fixed and punishment ultimately assessed.

While the use of the repeated reimagining of the crime puts us at the scene as both potential victim and killer, we see the crime most often from the perspective of the killer, first approaching the hapless victim and then acting out a murderous passion. What Young says about *Psycho* and *Silence of the Lambs* is also true for *Dead Man Walking*: "[W]hile offered temporarily the experience of identifying with the victim, the spectator is incorporated into the film much more significantly as an accomplice of the killer.... This ... identificatory relation is achieved through an association of the spectator's look with the gaze of the cinematic apparatus."[45] We are powerless to stop the violence that unfolds before us, and cinematically reminded of that powerlessness since we see crimes already committed for which the murderer is now in the custody of the state.

But we can, indeed must, judge the moral blameworthiness of the offender by becoming familiar with his emotional life. This imperative to judge in light of the emotions of the offender, with all their slipperiness and unknowability, is a reminder of the profound uncertainty that accompanies every act of judgment, every effort to do justice in individual cases. It stands, then, as an important reminder of the violence done when fidelity to rules—as in the use of guidelines in sentencing—purports to substitute for, or short-circuit, judgment.

In *Dead Man Walking* the drama of responsibility and remorse unfolds as a conversation, an accompaniment. Whereas accusation and trial leave Poncelet emotionally unmoved, it is Sister Helen who teaches him the value of accepting responsibility; it is her constant effort to get Poncelet to see his deed from the perspective of the victims and their families, as well as her love, that helps him come to feel remorse. In this sense *Dead Man Walking* is both a reminder of law's failure and of the inadequacy of its attitude toward emotions like remorse. Law takes remorse as an already established fact of someone's emotional life and weighs how to respond to it; it plays, and is prepared to play, no role in cultivating a particular disposition toward wrongdoing. The film reminds us that our emotional lives and the emotions with which law must deal, and to which it must respond, are neither fixed nor locked within each individual. It is an instruction in the power of moral pedagogy.

In this pedagogy, getting Poncelet to face the truth of the crime and his part in it is crucial. The crime is presented primarily through the imagination of the main character, Sister Helen. The scene of the crime provides a recurring dramatic frame within which the question of whether Poncelet deserves to die can be posed. The repeated reenactment of the crime in a series of flashbacks spread throughout the film is key to the construction of his subjectivity. It delineates the difference between *being* responsible and *taking* responsibility. It provides a baseline against which the significance of Poncelet's remorse can be judged.

Will Matthew Poncelet confess? Will he admit his true involvement and genuine culpability for the murders for which he was sentenced? Or will he go to his death still insisting that he was only an accessory swept up in the evil deeds of another? These questions, rather than any broader effort to understand the society of which his crime is a part, or the ongoing political and legal problems with the death penalty, provide the dramatic framing of the film. As Shapiro contends, "[T]he confession is, in fact, the pivot on which the movie balances. . . . It might also be said that without the confession, *Dead Man Walking* would give viewers little reason for opposing the execution since this sympathy is largely dependent upon the defendant's act of contrition."[46]

This film is more concerned with Sister Helen's ability to tame the savage beast in Poncelet, a heroic effort in the face of death, than about the question of whether state killing is compatible with our Constitution and our commitments as a political and legal community.[47] Insisting that legal responsibility is not enough to heal the wounds inflicted or to mark a soul that is saved is the work of Sister Helen. She becomes an advocate for accepting responsibility and feeling remorse. Thus she informs the parents of one of Poncelet's victims, "I want him to take responsibility for what he did." Sister Helen's insistence that Poncelet take responsibility does not serve as a gesture to allay doubts about his guilt, to nail down a legal judgment fraught with uncertainty.[48] She wants to reach and redeem him by connecting to his emotional life.

Throughout the film, Sister Helen works to constitute Poncelet as a fully responsible agent and to bring him to feel remorse. She does so, in part, by imaginatively reconstructing the crime and, in so doing, trying to figure out exactly what he did, if not why he did it. A chronology of such imaginative reconstructions provides the site at which responsibility and remorse gradually can be assessed as well as a continual reminder to the viewer of the salience of the "who did what to whom" problematic.

Dead Man Walking begins the visual reconstruction of the crime after Sister Helen has heard a verbal description of Poncelet's deeds[49] from the jaded prison chaplain, who warns her, "There is no romance here sister. This ain't no Jimmy Cagney 'I've been wrongly accused. If only I had someone who believed in me' nonsense. They [the men on death row] are all con men and they will take advantage of you every way they can."[50] This is a warning to the viewer as well. Be wary. Don't be taken in. Expressions of remorse may be easy to come by, but their sincerity is always hard to measure.[51] The chaplain's warning fuels our anxiety about remorse. It stands as a counterpoint, throughout the film, to Sister Helen's efforts to plumb Poncelet's emotions.

As Sister Helen leaves the chaplain and walks into the prison for her first meeting with Poncelet, the film moves back and forth between her observation of the strange world she is about to enter and scenes of the crime, set off in black and white. We approach a car parked in the woods; we see the barrel of a rifle; we see a shot fired, followed by the legs of someone lying face down, then a twisted and bruised arm, and finally a knife raised in slow motion in three repeated sequences and one dramatic, *Psycho*-like stabbing gesture. But in none of these scenes do we see the faces of the killers; we know something horrible has happened but we cannot yet fix responsibility. The anonymity of the criminals and the lack of narrative cohesion in this scene serve both to keep our gaze fixed on the horror of the act that is presented to us and to warn us that we, like Sister Helen herself, are not yet in a position to judge or to assign blame.

After each of the images of the unfolding crime in this scene, the camera cuts back to Sister Helen's increasingly disturbed facial expression, a kind of "What am I doing here, what have I got myself into?" look. What is left undecided is whether her distress is the register of her image of the crime, or the prospect of meeting the killer face-to-face, or both. But it is nonetheless important to note that at this point Sister Helen has not yet imagined the actual killing or the bloody bodies.

The camera's move to black and white and slow motion does the job of suggesting that it is a fantasy we are seeing. Yet it is an incomplete fantasy, though one already filled with dread even as it brackets the most visually horrible image of the crime. Without its most graphic detail, the scene of the crime is registered on Sister Helen's face as it would be on ours.

We see the crime sometimes only briefly as when, during a hearing of the pardon board, we look over the shoulders of its members as they listen to arguments about whether they should recommend clemency for Poncelet. The prosecutor arguing against clemency hands crime-scene photos to each of the board members. We see parts of several of the photos, shown in color to mark their status as representations of the real, as the camera moves behind the row of chairs on which the board members are seated. When the camera moves to the front, we see them going through the photos, but the wide angle of the shot makes it hard to discern their facial expressions. Finally, we return to a position behind the pardon board and get a close-up of a single photo of the naked body of a young woman bloodied by multiple stab wounds.

This is the very image that Sister Helen was unable or unwilling to conjure as she walked to her first encounter with Poncelet, and it provides a devastating moment in the film, a suggestion that only by refusing, at least initially, to contemplate the full horror of the crime can Sister Helen, or we, muster any compassion for someone who did what he did. The photo of the young, dead woman demands a response from the film's viewers, just as the prosecutor hoped it would demand a response from the pardon board. Who did this? More precisely, what kind of person could do such a thing? The photo works to narrow consideration, to keep the question of responsible agency at the center of our consideration. In its vividness and its horror it blots out almost everything else.[52]

III. Remorse as a Condition of Reconciliation

A similar effect occurs when, later in the film, the parents of one of the victims, Hope Percy, retell the story of the discovery of their daughter's body to Sister Helen. Their presence is a stand-in for those for whom blameworthiness and the emotional response of the offender are less significant than harm in fixing punishment. They insist that it is Poncelet's gruesome deed, not his subsequent repentance, that should be the object of Sister Helen's and, by extension, the viewers' attention. We see Hope's body with stab wounds clearly visible, again in color, suggesting that what we now see is an accurate recreation, not Sister Helen's incomplete imagining. "My daughter's body," Hope's mother recounts, "was found nude, spread eagled. . . . The police wouldn't let us go down to the morgue to identify the body. They said it would be too traumatic." Sister Helen listens intently, tears welling up in her eyes. This time the crime is viewed from the perspective of the surviving, grieving parents, their pain retold as if in a victim impact statement, recounting the way their daughter died and the consequences for their life.[53]

The Percys' characterization of Poncelet contains twin and somewhat contradictory elements. In order to believe that crime merits commensurate punishment, the Percys must hold Poncelet responsible, even if he doesn't take responsibility. He must be treated as a free agent who could have and should have made a different choice. At the same time, the anger that drives retributive punishment expresses itself in the view that Poncelet is unlike us, an animal, a monster.

Here *Dead Man Walking* captures something close to the heart of the desire that always fuels punishment. Punishment, as Connolly puts it, involves imagining the object of vengeance to be a responsible agent who deserves whatever he gets, and, at the same time, a dangerous monster with whom we must deal.[54] The work that remorse does in popular culture representations of crime and punishment is to humanize the criminal, to diminish, if not remove, the sense that he is *simply* a monster. As Hampton puts it, "If the wrongdoer does something to separate herself from the immoral principle or attitude which motivated her action, moral hatred of her no longer seems appropriate. . . ."[55]

"The desire to punish," Connolly notes, "crystallizes at that point where the shocking, vicious character of a case blocks inquiry into its conditions."[56] Gestures of responsibility and remorse, *Dead Man Walking* suggests, take on significance only in the face of that astonishment. They bring us to, and through, our shock not by fighting against it but by nurturing it, making it real.

The remorseful criminal joins us in our shock, coming to view his act as we view it and, in so doing, validating our response. As Goffman has noted, expressions of remorse are communications that (re)establish relations between a person who offends and a person who has been offended against.[57] Remorse builds a bridge between offender and the community astonished by his deed;[58] it establishes the basis for an imagined conversation in which the criminal hears and feels the full measure of the pain his crime caused and in which those aggrieved by it hear and feel the sorrow of the offender. Remorse, as Tavuchis claims, thus simultaneously represents and reenacts "consummated infractions and attempts to reclaim membership. . . ." Yet remorse does not diminish the gravity of the deed or the astonishment it engenders.

When we next are brought back to Sister Helen's imagining of the crime, the question of responsible agency begins to emerge ever more clearly. This is signaled through a return to black-and-white footage. Her revisiting of the crime is sparked as she is driven through the prison grounds to the special holding cell where inmates are kept in the days immediately before their execution. The crime is revealed as a series of scenes interspersed with her observations of the prison.

On this occasion her view is somewhat more detailed than in her first imagining. We see more than weapons and legs and arms; we are now able to identify the assailants and to see what they do. It is from this reconstruction of the crime that a tale of responsibility can be built. At this point, however, we must be wary because Sister Helen's reconstruction is based on replaying what she has heard from the Percys.

Yet she adds important details; she imagines Poncelet holding a rifle on Walter Delacroix, while his accomplice rapes Hope Percy. In her image Poncelet is surprised by his accomplice's brutality, scared and spooked when his accomplice comes over, grabs the rifle, and shoots Walter. This imagining is faithful to the story that, throughout the film, Poncelet has told to Sister Helen. It is a version of events that maintains some distance between him and the burden of full moral responsibility. That she believes it is testimony to her willingness to take things on the terms on which they present themselves, the very trait about which she was warned by the prison chaplain.

As Sister Helen later says to Poncelet, "You watched while two kids were murdered." Throughout, Poncelet insists that he is "innocent," having neither raped nor murdered anyone. While his claim of innocence is not legally tenable, if it were true it would diminish his moral responsibility and invite a reappraisal of the appropriateness of his impending punishment.

Late in the film, on the day of the execution, we finally get an apparently complete, authoritative, visual reconstruction of the crime. It is a reconstruction that serves to fix responsibility at the same time that it allays any doubt that we can know the truth of the crime. It is provided in response to Sister Helen's suggestion that Poncelet "talk about what happened. Let's talk about that night." The responding narrative is highlighted in its claim to truth because it is again accompanied by color photography of the crime scene. We follow Poncelet and his accomplice as they come upon Walter and Hope kissing in their car. The criminals force them out of the car by claiming that they are trespassing on private property.

Dead Man Walking fully reveals its commitment to the significance of Poncelet's emotional response and its belief that remorse is a step toward reconciliation when Sister Helen demands that Poncelet take responsibility for these acts. "What possessed you," she asks, "to be in the woods that night?" "I told you I was stoned," Poncelet responds. "Don't blame the drugs. You could have walked away," Sister Helen responds, fully embracing the language of agency, will, and bilateral individualism. Echoing themes in the classic individualist tradition,[59] Sister Helen insists that the responsible agent makes choices and must accept responsibility for those choices. "Don't blame [your accomplice]. You blame him. You blame drugs. You blame the government. You blame blacks. You blame the Percys. You blame the kids for being there. What about Matthew Poncelet? Is he just an innocent, a victim?" The language of responsibility directs attention away from the legal and political issues surrounding capital punishment just as it refuses to accept structure, accident, or conspiracy as justifications for actions. It insists that whatever the external factors that made an act possible, it is the choice to act that is crucial.[60]

It is this insistence that compels the viewers' attention; few, I think, find Sister Helen's efforts irrelevant. The imagined viewer finds the question of Poncelet's emotions, of his feelings about his crime, relevant not just to the question of his salvation but to the question of his status before the law. We are vitally interested in assessing his emotions in order that we can determine whether capital punishment fits the crime. At the same time, we worry that the ultimate unfolding of responsibility and expression of remorse comes late, too late, too close to the impending execution. As such, it may appear to be the desperate gesture of a frightened criminal, willing to say anything in the face of death.

The ultimate unfolding of responsibility for the crimes in *Dead Man Walking* comes in a telling just before we see the completion of this "truest," and most complete, reenactment of the crime. After his last call to his family, Poncelet says to Sister Helen, "It was something you said. I could have walked away. I didn't. I was a victim. I was a fucking chicken. He was older and tough as hell. I was boozing up trying to be as tough as him. I didn't have the guts to stand up to him. I told my momma I was yellow. She kept saying 'It wasn't you. It wasn't you, Matt' [pause]. The boy, Walter, I killed him." In this moment Poncelet takes responsibility in quite the way Sister Helen has been urging him to do. Ultimately, Sister Helen puts the question directly. "Do you take responsibility," she asks, "for both of their deaths [referring to Walter and Hope]?" "Yes ma'am," Poncelet, now sobbing, responds.[61] The construction of the legal subject as the responsible subject is completed as complex, uncertain causation is banished by a narrowly focused question and a simple response.

Sister Helen's question and Poncelet's response play out a "death-bed" confession that sets the stage for an act of contrition. His assumption of responsibility is enacted as religious ritual as well as a legally relevant fact.[62] The admission of guilt that law could not secure is finally obtained. Free will and responsibility are affirmed, and agency triumphs over structure. In spite of the anxiety that viewers may feel about his acceptance of responsibility and his expression of remorse, the former reassures us of the validity of bilateral individualism and suggests that behind every narrative of shared responsibility for crime, of structure overcoming agency, is a deep, authentic truth about choice and voluntary, if misguided, action.

It is only as Poncelet is himself being executed that the "complete truth" of the crime is presented visually, a truth he no longer contests. In this presentation we move from the scene of the execution back and forth to the scene of the crime. This quite literal effort to raise the question of whether execution is a just and proportionate response to murder shows Poncelet raping Hope and shooting Walter.

The question is further precipitated by the use of parallel images shot from above of Walter and Hope lying face down, arms and legs spread in the woods, and then of Poncelet lying face up, as if crucified. Are these the same acts, the film seems to ask? Or, as Justice Scalia recently argued, does "death-by-injection . . . look pretty desirable next to (the murder of a man ripped by a bullet suddenly and unexpectedly). . . . How enviable a quiet death by lethal injection compared with that."[63] Does *Dead Man Walking* condemn capital punishment, as Poncelet does when he says at the time of his execution, "I think killing is wrong no matter who does it, whether it is me, or y'all, or your government," or does it provide the strongest justification for it by refusing to let us forget both the nature and brutality of the crime to which it is a response and by suggesting that it is an indispensable predicate for the expression of remorse? The film is rigorously indeterminate in its answers to these questions.[64]

It is not, however, indeterminate in its attitude toward the significance of accepting responsibility and feeling remorse. Assuming responsibility is enacted in *Dead Man Walking* as a journey in which the responsible agent comes to acknowledge that he could have acted differently; he could have "walked away," but he chose not to. "Subjects, we say, are 'free.' They are not bound by the determined. They could always have done 'more' or done other than what they did. This is the basis on which we as legal subjects can be held legally responsible. . . ."[65] Yet while the discourse of responsibility insists on autonomy, the process through which Poncelet comes to take responsibility emphasizes his relationship to Sister Helen. "It was something you said," he tells her. It is this relationship with its promise that confession leads to forgiveness that enables Poncelet to do what law, with its promise of punishment, was unable to get him to do. However, as Peter Brooks has recently argued,

> The problem may be that the very act of confessing will so often be the product of a situation, a set of physical conditions, a psychological state that do not conduce to the fullest expression of human autonomy. . . . [T]he search for the true confession, the moment of the baring of the soul, may uncover that moment as one of human abjection. Telling the shameful truth may reap all sorts of psycho-social benefits . . . but it does not necessarily promote an image of human autonomy and dignity. On the contrary it reveals pathetic dependency and a kind of infantile groveling. . . . Even the most indisputable "voluntary" confession may arise from a state of dependency, shame, and the need for punishment, a condition that casts some doubt on the law's language of autonomy and free choice.[66]

The ultimate product of his confession is Poncelet's public acknowledgment of responsibility and expression of remorse in the ritual of the condemned's last words, uttered while strapped to an elevated gurney, with Poncelet in a Christ-like pose facing Walter's and Hope's families: "I ask your forgiveness. It was a terrible thing I did taking your son away from you. I hope my death gives you some relief." Here accepting responsibility is transformed into an expression of remorse. Poncelet presents no defense; he makes no excuses. What he did was just plain "terrible." In this acknowledgment he bridges the gap between himself and those whose lives he has shattered. He asks *their* forgiveness, and, in so doing, makes their pain his.[67] The significance of gestures like Poncelet's is captured by Goffman when he suggests that

> when an individual commits crimes deemed to be quite heinous, crimes for which his life is small compensation, he still may feel strongly obliged to ritually disavow his previous self and show that a person he now is sees his offenses from the perspective of the morally-minded man. No matter what is done to the individual by way of punishment for crime, he is likely to have a moment free before the punishment is inflicted to proclaim identity with the powers whose ire is about to be visited upon him and to express separateness from the self upon whom the justice will fall.[68]

While Poncelet's expression of remorse comes too late to affect the punishment that we see visited on him, it is at this point, and this point only, that the film invites its viewers to complete their deliberation on the question of whether Poncelet deserves to die. It is here in the presence of an expression of remorse that we are, so the film seems to say, now entitled to judge. It is here that both the relevance of remorse and the anxieties attendant to it seem most pressing. While the request for forgiveness is not directed to us, it is nonetheless crucial to the viewer's assessment of who Poncelet is at the moment when he is subject to legal punishment. And, that assessment is, in turn, crucial to our judgment of the justness of his punishment.

Even as it arouses our anxieties about remorse, *Dead Man Walking* provides cultural affirmation of the social indispensability of responsibility against those who would blur the distinction between criminals and victims. It refutes broad narratives of responsibility that would implicate us all in the contingencies that produce crime and would undermine the moral and legal scaffolding on which the apparatus of punishment is built. It calls for an assessment of both blameworthiness and harm in our reflections on punishment, and it suggests the centrality of accepting responsibility and feeling remorse in our judgment of the character of the wrongdoer.

IV. Conclusion: The Continuing Salience of Remorse

One might reasonably ask whether *Dead Man Walking's* tale about responsibility and remorse has any resonance with the American public. Here the best evidence is, I think, indirect. If I am right, the film seeks to position its viewers as jurors in the penalty phase of a capital trial. While viewers are positioned in several different ways—as investigators, truth seekers, voyeurs—the basic structure of viewing is juridical.[69] Though the film never takes us into a courtroom, it invites spectators to judge as if they were making a life and death judgment. As Carol Clover notes, "Anglo-American movies are already trial like to begin with.... [T]he plot structures and narrative procedures ... of a broad stripe of American popular culture are derived from the structure and procedures of the Anglo-American trial; ... [T]his structure and these procedures are so deeply embedded in our narrative tradition that they shape plots that never step into a courtroom."[70]

Through the film's extensive focus on the brutality of the crime and the suffering of those left behind, we are presented with aggravating factors. On the other side, we have the film's brief reconstructions of the life of the condemned and the reasons for his acts. Far more important as a mitigating factor, the film seems to suggest, is the fact that Poncelet ultimately takes responsibility and expresses remorse for his brutal acts. In the face of such a case, the film seems to ask, is he worthy of mercy? Or is the only mercy that can and should be provided God's mercy, not ours?

Some recent empirical work suggests the continuing salience of responsibility and remorse in answering these questions and in the way Americans think about crime and punishment. The research to which I am referring examined the decision making of jurors in capital cases in two states—California[71] and South Carolina.[72] It found those jurors to be deeply interested in the question of remorse. In trying to figure out whether a defendant is actually remorseful, they are attentive to the facts of the crime, the defendant's demeanor during trial, and what, if anything, the defendant says as a witness in his own defense.[73] Both studies show that remorseful defendants are significantly more likely to receive life sentences than to be sentenced to death.[74] Jurors identify the degree of defendant's remorse as "one of the most frequently discussed issues in the jury room at the penalty phase. . . ."[75] And, "when asked what might have swung their vote from death to life, one of the most frequent answers was some showing of remorse by the defendant."[76]

These findings, as well as the narrative of *Dead Man Walking*, remind us that whatever the current controversies surrounding the relevance and appropriateness of considering remorse as a factor in criminal punishment and whatever the anxiety provoked as we seek to assess the meaning and significance of remorse, it remains an important factor in popular culture. Both the film and the empirical research make clear the importance of the distinction between *being* legally responsible and *taking* responsibility. This distinction marks a space in which the modern legal subject can be said to reside, a space of individual autonomy, choice, and desert, a space in which the emotional responses of wrongdoers to their crimes are an important measure of their character and moral blameworthiness. It affirms bilateral individualism against more radical, structuralist accounts of crime.

Dead Man Walking is but one cultural artifact in which responsibility and remorse play a central role. But it tells, I have argued, a familiar and compelling story, a story in which the remorseful criminal relies neither on structural factors nor on a narrative of his own victimization. In this film, "the basic categories through which we judge murderers and assess penalties are themselves treated as stable and unshakable. The harsh childhood of the killer, for instance, is taken to 'mitigate' the crime or to provide 'extenuating' circumstances; but these experiences are not treated as elements that may enter into the very formation of the perpetrator's will itself."[77] Like all tales of responsibility and remorse, *Dead Man Walking* calls us to pay heed to the emotional life of the wrongdoer, to judge in the face of all our uncertainties about our ability to judge another's emotional life rather than trying to reduce anxiety by restructuring the logic of judgment. In the end, this film insists that emotion can, and should, play a crucial role in determining our responses to wrongdoers and our judgments about appropriate responses to wrongdoing.

NOTES

1. As Judge Shadur observed in *U.S. v. Torres*, 1987 U.S. Dist. Ct., N.D. ICC., Lexis 6968, 4, "Remorse is of course a factor to be taken into account in the sentencing process...." Also *U.S. v. Saunders*, 973 F2d, 1354, 1363 (1992), and H. L. A. Hart, *Punishment and Responsibility: Essays in the Philosophy of Law* (New York: Oxford University Press, 1968).

2. H. L. A. Hart, *The Concept of Law* (Oxford: Clarendon Press, 1961), 83–88.

3. Scott Sundby, "The Capital Jury and Absolution: The Intersection of Trial Strategy, Remorse and the Death Penalty," 83 *Cornell Law Review* 1557 (1998). Also Richard Weisman, "Detecting Remorse and Its Absence in the Criminal Justice System," unpublished essay, 1997, 14. "The remorseless offender," Weisman notes, "is divested of human qualities that all members of the community are presumed to share. Such a person is placed outside the social and moral order...."

4. For one example, see *U.S. v. Piper*, 918 F2d 839, 840 (1990).

5. "[I]t is striking how often judgments of the defendant's blameworthiness are based not on involvement in the crime itself but on assessments of character and behavior based on events occurring months and sometimes years after the offending behavior for which the defendant is convicted." See Stanton Wheeler, Kenneth Mann, and Austin Sarat, *Sitting in Judgment: The Sentencing of White-Collar Criminals* (New Haven: Yale University Press, 1988), 112.

6. See Michael O'Hear, "Remorse, Cooperation, and 'Acceptance of Responsibility': The Structure, Implementation, and Reform of Section 3E1.1 of the Federal Sentencing Guidelines," 91 *Northwestern University Law Review* (1997), 1507. Also John Winstead, "Nunez-Rodriquez and a Defendant's Acceptance of Responsibility: A Jailbreak from the Confinement of the Federal Sentencing Guidelines?" 85 *Kentucky Law Journal* (1996/1997), 1021, and Luke Dokla, "Section 3E1.1 Contrition and Fifth Amendment Incrimination: Is There an Iron Fist Beneath the Sentencing Guidelines' Velvet Glove?" 65 *St. John's Law Review* (1991), 1077.

7. Herbert Morris, "Persons and Punishment," in *Human Rights*, A. I. Melden,

ed. (Belmont, Calif.: Wadsworth Publishing, 1970). Also Andrew von Hirsch, *Past or Future Crimes: Deservedness and Dangerousness in the Sentencing of Criminals* (New Brunswick, N.J.: Rutgers University Press, 1985). For a discussion of this position and its relation to the history of criminal procedure, see Robert Wuthnow,"Repentance in Criminal Procedure: The Ritual Affirmation of Community," in *Repentance: A Comparative Perspective*, Amatai Etzioni and David Carney, eds. (Lanham, Md.: Rowman & Littlefield, 1997), 174.

8. As Judge Frankel put it, "The effort to appraise 'character' is, to be sure, a perilous one, and not necessarily an enterprise for which judges are notably equipped by prior training." *United States v. Hendrix*, 505 F2d 1233, 1236 (1974). Also, as Judge Shadur argues, [T]here is no way to know whether a defendant is truly remorseful for having committed the offense or whether his remorse is rather for his having been caught. . . . *U.S. v Torres*, 1987 U.S. Dist. Ct., N.D. ICC., Lexis 6968, 4.

9. See Herbert Morris, "Professor Murphy on Liberalism and Retributivism," 37 *Arizona Law Review* (1995), 95, 102. However, one commentator sees some ambiguity in the guidelines on this point. See O'Hear, "Remorse, Cooperation, and Acceptance of Responsibility." Also *U.S. v. Henry*, 883 F2d 1010, 1012. "To hold the acceptance of responsibility provision unconstitutional would be to say that defendants who express genuine remorse for their actions can never be rewarded at sentencing. This the Constitution does not require."

10. Ellen Bryant, "Section 3E1.1 of the Federal Sentencing Guidelines: Bargaining with the Guilty," 44 *Catholic University Law Review* (1995), 1269.

11. For one example, see Beverly Lowry, "The Good Bad Girl," *The New Yorker* (February 9, 1998), 60. The Tucker case also reminds us of the deep connection between remorse as a factor in our consideration of criminal punishment and Judeo-Christian beliefs. As Wuthnow notes in "Repentance in Criminal Procedure," "The modern connection between repentance and society's treatment of criminals is rooted historically in the Jewish understanding of *teshuvah* (or atonement) and in early Christian teachings about the redemption of individuals from sin" (174).

12. See Amatai Etzioni and David Carney, eds., *Repentance: A Comparative Perspective* (Lanham, Md.: Rowman & Littlefield, 1997).

13. Hiroshi Wagatsuma and Arthur Rosett, "The Implications of Apology: Law and Culture in Japan and the United States," 20 *Law & Society Review* (1986), 461.

14. Nicholas Tavuchis, *Mea Culpa: A Sociology of Apology and Reconciliation* (Stanford: Stanford University Press, 1991), 8.

15. Harvey Cox, "Repentance and Forgiveness: A Christian Perspective," in *Repentance: A Comparative Perspective*, 24

16. Jean Hampton, "The Retributive Idea," in *Forgiveness and Mercy*, by Jeffrie Murphy and Jean Hampton (Cambridge: Cambridge University Press, 1988), 154.

17. See Jean Hampton, "Forgiveness, Resentment and Hatred," in *Forgiveness and Mercy*, 41.

18. For one important discussion of the relationship between reason, emotion,

and criminal law, see Dan Kahan and Martha Nussbaum, "Two Conceptions of Emotion in Criminal Law," 96 *Columbia Law Review* (1996), 269.

19. Amatai Etzioni, "Introduction," *Repentance: A Comparative Perspective*, 9.

20. Jeffrie Murphy, "Repentance, Punishment, and Mercy," in *Repentance: A Comparative Perspective*, 157.

21. For one example of this argument, see *In re Rubinstein* 506 NYS2d 441 (1986).

22. Erving Goffman, *Relations in Public: Microstudies of the Public Order* (New York: Basic Books, 1971), 113.

23. For this understanding of the nature of remorse and the impact of expressions of remorse of the way wrongdoers are perceived, see Dawn Robinson, Lynn Smith-Lovin, and Olga Tsoudis, "Heinous Crime or Unfortunate Accident? The Effect of Remorse on Responses to Mock Criminal Confessions," 73 *Social Forces* (1994), 175, 182.

24. Murphy, "Repentance, Punishment," 157.

25. Morris, "Professor Murphy on Liberalism and Retributivism," 102.

26. Tavuchis, *Mea Culpa*,13.

27. "[A]n apology, no matter how sincere or effective, does not and cannot undo what has been done." Yet, as Tavuchis claims, "in a mysterious way and according to its own logic, this is precisely what it manages to do." See *Mea Culpa*, 5.

28. Etzioni, "Introduction," 9. As Etzioni rightly asks, "How can one determine that remorse is true? Many people, when faced with the apologies of politicians, criminals, and even friends and spouses, have doubts as to the motivation behind such expressions. . . . [R]emorse is doomed to be suspect in a world of public relations experts, spin doctors, and a jaded and cynical population."

29. Weisman, "Detecting Remorse and Its Absence in the Criminal Justice System," 1.

30. David Garland, "Punishment and Culture: The Symbolic Dimension of Criminal Justice," 11 *Studies in Law, Politics & Society* (1991), 191.

31. *Id.*, 193.

32. *Id.*, 195.

33. "[M]ass-mediated representations of prisoners function as a public display of the transgression of cultural norms; as such, they are a key site at which one may investigate the relationship of the individual to the culture in general, as well as the cultural articulation of 'proper behavior.'" See John Sloop, *The Cultural Prison: Discourse, Prisoners, and Punishment* (Tuscaloosa: University of Alabama Press, 1996), 3.

34. For a further analysis of these themes, see Austin Sarat, "The Cultural Life of Capital Punishment: Responsibility and Representation in *Dead Man Walking* and *Last Dance*." 11 *Yale Journal of Law & the Humanities* 101 (1998).

35. There are, of course, important differences between the laws regulating capital punishment and other kinds of sentencing. In capital cases there is less controversy over the status of remorse as a mitigating factor.

36. See *Robinson v California*, 370 U.S. 660 (1962).

37. Morris, "Persons and Punishment."

38. See *Morisette v. United States*, 342 U.S. 246, 250 (1952).

39. Stephen Carter, "When Victims Happen to Be Black," 97 *Yale Law Journal* (1988), 420–21. Robert Gordon calls this conception of responsibility "narrow-agency." It frames wrongs as "done by specific perpetrators to specific victims; the remedy is the limited and negative retributive sanction of the criminal process. . . ." See Robert Gordon, "Undoing Historical Injustice," in *Justice and Injustice in Law and Legal Theory*, Austin Sarat and Thomas R. Kearns, eds. (Ann Arbor: University of Michigan Press, 1996), 36.

40. Carter, "When Victims Happen to Be Black," 421–22

41. A second explanation for crime complicates the calculus of punishment, Carter notes, by altering the bilateral individualist's straightforward story of responsibility. It does so by pointing away from individual agency toward the sweep of history and the differential positions of the social groups from which criminals (and often their victims) come. *Id.*, 426. This "enterprise takes the form of a search for explanations rather than a search for villainous agents and attributions of blame; the remedial enterprise is directed to altering institutions, systems, and incentives rather than to exacting punishment. . . ." Gordon, "Undoing Historical Injustice," 38. A structuralist perspective is less intent on carefully reconstructing the crime and assigning personal responsibility; instead it uses the fact of crime to highlight the need to alter social structures.

42. Such stories are precisely the kind that defense lawyers in capital cases typically deploy in the penalty phase. See Austin Sarat, "Speaking of Death: Narratives of Violence in Capital Trials," 27 *Law & Society Review* (1993), 60. Also James Doyle, "The Lawyer's Art: 'Representation' in Capital Cases," 8 *Yale Journal of Law & the Humanities* (1996), 428–34.

43. At least in one sense, no matter whether one favors individualist or structuralist explanations, it is important to recognize that there is an asymmetry between the cultural life of crime and of punishment. While we are bombarded with representations of crime, punishment is almost invisible. See Alison Young, *Imaging Crime* (London: Sage, 1996). The scene of criminality is a familiar one, a common though not unproblematic sight for most citizens; the scene of punishment is neither familiar nor common. The result is that the bridge between crime and punishment works primarily at the rhetorical level, or the level of imagination. Seeing the scene of crime, confronted with its graphic depiction, we are left to identify a responsible agent and imagine a just punishment.

44. Many death penalty films are structured around a relationship of the condemned and another person who befriends her, or takes up her cause. In these films we are invited to see the condemned through that person. Harding contends that "these secondary characters are pivotal" in that they are often able to see the human face behind the monstrous deeds that bring someone to death row. If these secondary characters can see beyond the crime, then perhaps so can the viewers of the films. See Roberta Harding, "Celluloid Death: Cinematic Depictions of Capital Punishment," 30 *University of San Francisco Law Review* (1996), 1172.

45. See Alison Young, "Murder in the Eyes of the Law," 17 *Studies in Law, Politics, and Society* (1997), 44–45.

46. Carole Shapiro, "Do or Die: Does 'Dead Man Walking' Run?" 30 U. of San Francisco L. Rev. 1143 (1996).

47. *Id.* See also Harding "Celluloid Death," 1177.

48. At no point does the film invite its viewers to entertain such doubts.

49. The film presents a transposition from the verbal to the visual, where the verbal is at least initially given priority as an accurate rendition of events. On the significance of such transpositions, see Carol Emerson, *Boris Godunov: Transpositions of a Russian Theme* (Bloomington: Indiana University Press, 1986), chapter 1.

50. Jimmy Cagney plays the lead in *Angels With Dirty Faces*, one of the earliest death penalty films.

51. William Miller, one of the participants in the Emotion and Law Conference, argued that there is no such thing as remorse. Punishment, he suggested, is designed to get offenders to regret an action that, in the absence of punishment, they would not otherwise regret.

52. For a discussion of the powerful impact of such photos in capital trials, see Austin Sarat, "Violence, Representation, and Responsibility in Capital Trials: The View from the Jury," 70 *Indiana Law Journal* (1995), 1103.

53. On the significance of victim impact statements, see Austin Sarat, "Vengeance, Victims and the Identities of Law," 6 *Social and Legal Studies: An International Journal* (1997), 163.

54. William Connolly, *The Ethos of Pluralization* (Minneapolis: University of Minnesota Press, 1995), 45.

55. Jean Hampton, "The Retributive Idea," 154.

56. Connolly, *The Ethos of Pluralization*, 47.

57. Goffman, *Relations in Public*, 113.

58. See Tavuchis, *Mea Culpa*.

59. Morris, "Persons and Punishment."

60. My own view of this matter is that in any theory of punishment remorse is but one factor that may be taken into account, whether the punishment is death or something less severe. Moreover, were one to embrace a retributive rationale for the death penalty, remorse in itself would have no special claim in determining whether death was deserved.

61. As Weisman observes, "[F]eelings of remorse are painful— . . . they are unwanted and . . . involuntary. One is afflicted, burdened, or cursed with feelings of remorse. . . ." See "Detecting Remorse," 7.

62. On the connection between remorse in law and religion, see Cox, "Repentance and Forgiveness."

63. *Callins v. Collins*, 62 LW 3546 (1994), (Scalia J., concurring in denial of certiorari).

64. Harding suggests that "by alternating shots between the dying Matthew and

the victims the filmmaker poses many questions to the audience. The physical position of Matthew's body resembles that of his victims. Does that mean that Matthew is also a victim? Is it done to tell us that this penalty is acceptable by reminding us of the victims as their killer is dying? Or, does it mean that the death penalty is futile because all that has been accomplished is the taking of three lives instead of two?" See "Celluloid Death," 1176. In addition, Shapiro argues that "the movie indicates that Poncelet confesses and is redeemed only because of his death sentence." See "Do or Die," 1153.

65. Peter Fitzpatrick, "'Always More to Do':Capital Punishment and the (De)Composition of Law," in *The Killing State: Capital Punishment in Law, Politics, and Culture*, Austin Sarat, ed. (New York: Oxford University Press, 1998) 12.

66. Peter Brooks, "The Overborne Will," *Representations* (forthcoming) (typescript pp. 10, 12).

67. The film suggests that the link between remorse and forgiveness is contingent and uncertain. It does so by suggesting the varied reactions of the Percys and of Mr. Delacroix. The former seem unmoved by Poncelet's plea; the latter seems unsettled. He shows up at Poncelet's funeral and, in the film's last scene, is shown through a church window praying with Sister Helen.

68. Goffman, *Relations in Public*, 116.

69. The consequence of this juridical role is to bracket, or to derogate, broader questions about the legitimacy and meaning of capital punishment and to focus our attention on the particularities of a single case. This bracketing of these questions is recognizable in certain silences in both films, as well as in the way they portray the political and legal controversy surrounding capital punishment.

70. Carol Clover, "Law and the Order of Popular Culture," in *Law in the Domains of Culture*, Austin Sarat and Thomas Kearns, eds. (Ann Arbor: University of Michigan Press, 1998), 99.

71. See Sundby, "The Jury and Absolution."

72. Theodore Eisenberg, Stephen Garvey, and Martin Wells, "But Was He Sorry? The Role of Remorse in Capital Sentencing," 83 *Cornell Law Review* 1599 (1998).

73. *Id.*, 1–2. See also Mark Costanzo and Sally Costanzo, "Jury Decision-making in The Capital Penalty Phase: Legal Assumptions, Empirical Findings, and a Research Agenda," 16 *Law and Human Behavior* (1992), 185.

74. For findings that remorse plays a significant role in the way ordinary citizens think about punishment, see Robinson et al., "Heinous Crime or Unfortunate Accident?"

75. Sundby, "The Jury and Absolution," 5.

76. *Id.*, 11.

77. William Connolly, "The Will, Capital Punishment, and Culture War," in *The Killing State*, 16.

Chapter Seven

Democratic Dis-ease

Of Anger and the Troubling Nature of Punishment

Danielle S. Allen

Perhaps the most characteristic feature of twentieth century theories of punishment is a certain unease amongst theorists about how to answer the question "Why do we punish?" In the 1955 "Two Concepts of Rules"[1] John Rawls wrote:

> The subject of punishment has always been a *troubling* moral question. The *trouble* about it has not been that people disagree as to whether or not punishment is justifiable ... only a few have rejected punishment entirely.... The difficulty is with the justification of punishment: various arguments for it have been given by moral philosophers but so far none of them has won any sort of general acceptance; no justification is without those who detest it [emphasis added]. (37)

In 1968 the legal theorist H. L. A. Hart displayed a similar unease about how to justify punishment when he wrote in turn about the efforts of theorists to do so:

> [M]any are now *troubled* by the suspicion that the view that there is just one supreme value or objective (e.g. Deterrence, Retribution, Reform) in terms of which all questions about the justification of punishment are to be answered is somehow wrong: ... no clear account of what the different values or objectives are, or how they fit together in the justification of punishment can be extracted [emphasis added]. (*Punishment and Responsibility: Essays in the Philosophy of Law.* Oxford: Clarendon Press, p. 2 (1995)).

What Rawls wrote in the '50s and what Hart wrote in the '60s still applies: modern penal theory seems to be consistently characterized by an unease, a certain troubled-ness, about how to answer the question "Why do we punish?"[2] More specifically, this unease manifests itself in a conviction that no one of the standard justifications for punishment—reformative, deterrent, and retributive justifications—actually succeeds in justifying any sort of penal system that we would be willing to recognize as just. In this paper I will make an argument that the unease about justifications for why we punish stems from our failure to recognize the extent to which punishment has to do with failures in the relations between members of a community and with restoring a set of disturbed relationships. I will argue that recognizing the importance of thinking about such relationships in the context of penal theory would have an ameliorative effect on the ways that we think about punishment and on our ability to understand the process of justifying punishment.

The failures of the three standard justifications for punishment—reformative, deterrent, and retributive—are usually set out thus: The ideal of *reform* cannot explain why we use "hard treatment" (the imposition of suffering and pain) and not, say, a cushy Ivy League education in order to reeducate wrongdoers. The ideal of *deterrence* has a hard time explaining why we should limit the *extent* of punishments if ever-stricter punishments that are consistently enforced will, ostensibly, deter ever better. (As an example, we might say that speeding would probably be drastically decreased if the death penalty were imposed for exceeding speed limits and if every speeder were pulled over; a system of punishment based solely on deterrence would justify such extreme punishments.) The ideal of deterrence also has a hard time explaining why we should avoid making examples of the innocent; or why we cannot simply fake punishments provided that the public nonetheless believes that hard treatment follows on crime.

As for retribution—the idea that the wrongdoer should suffer his or her "just deserts" and deserves to suffer as much pain as he or she has inflicted—there is always in the first instance the worry that retribution is too close to revenge and its ugliness in tone, purpose, and effect. But critics also focus on the difficulties that retributivists have in their attempts to explain the idea of desert. To quote R. A. Duff:

> The central problem for any retributivist, whether negative or positive, is to explain the idea of desert. Punishment is supposed to be justified as an intrinsically appropriate response to crime; the notion of 'desert' is supposed to indicate that justificatory link between past crime and present punishment. But just what is that link? What is 'desert', which supposedly makes punishment the appropriate response to crime? (7)[3]

In "Two Concepts of Rules," Rawls tried to solve the problem of our un-ease over why we punish by arguing that punishment has to be justified on two fronts: as to punishment as a whole, and as to particular applications of punishment. Deterrent concerns, he argued, should justify having a penal system in general, while each individual case of punishment must be handled with a view to retributive guidelines. The argument is that the guidelines of retribution generate a set of cases in respect to which one may apply punishment as well as set limits on the level of punishment that can be applied. But justifications of deterrence must be invoked to explain why one punishes and the ends at which the penal system as a whole is directed. What matters about Rawls's idea—his marriage of deterrence to retribu-tion—is that Rawls found himself grudgingly having to accept, despite a distaste for it, a certain limited form of retribution as being at the heart of punishment on Kantian grounds. In general, most modern penal theories, including those of the reformative or deterrent stripe, follow Rawls in an unhappy acceptance of retribution as the basis of punishment. That accep-tance is unhappy because retribution is generally conceived of as being too closely linked to anger, an emotion that has been either ignored or vilified as irredeemably ugly and vengeful by most philosophers since Plato.

But a recognition that punishment is inevitably founded on some no-tion of retribution does not require that we accept that the idea that retri-bution necessarily has to do with tones of vengeance and with an uncon-ceptualized calculus of paybacks. Retribution itself can be otherwise con-ceived. In ancient Athens there was no unease about taking retribution as the justification for punishment, and so I wish to consider what retribution was in the Athenian context in order to shift our understanding of what ret-ribution is. I do this not in order to reclaim the Athenian approach to pun-ishment nor in order to propose a modern version thereof but simply to allow us to rethink the relationships among anger, retribution, and punish-ment. The particular approach to punishment that eventually came to be labeled "retribution" originally included not only a focus on anger and/or vengeance and not only an idea that the wrongdoer had something to pay back or give back but also a focus on the relation between the community and the wrongdoer. The Athenian recognition that wrongdoing and pun-ishment had to do with the relations between people arose from Athenians' willingness to take seriously the problematic nature of the presence of anger within the community and to see such anger as a problem that needed to be politically and ethically addressed and not philosophically swept into the corner. The ancient concern for the relationship between community and wrongdoer is the one element of the "retributive" approaches to punishment, as they existed before they became philosophically formulated as "retribution," that is not usually introduced in discussions of retribution and that would be worth some reflection.

The Athenians had no doubts about why they punished: it was simply because someone was *angry* at a wrong and wanted to have that anger dealt with. Specifically, the Athenians thought that it was primarily the anger of the *victim* that necessitated punishment. The Athenians revealed the strength of this idea in their penal practice. The city's institutions were structured so that it was possible for any citizen to prosecute on behalf of another or on behalf of the public, *but* despite this institutional possibility, the prosecutor was either the victim or was personally involved with the wrongdoer in 96 percent of the cases for which we have evidence (Allen, *The Politics of Punishing*, Princeton University Press, 1999). These personally involved prosecutors inevitably justified their prosecutions precisely on the grounds that they were seeking legitimate remedies for their anger. Any given case of punishment was thus always directed at resolving a problem that had arisen between two people, as well as at inflicting some sort of abstractly conceived "payback." Anger was so central to the Athenian experience of wrongdoing and punishment that courtroom litigants could describe laws as having been established for the purpose of establishing what levels of anger were appropriate for various acts of wrongdoing (e.g., Dem. 21.43; Aes. 1.176). Anger was assumed to be not only at the root of particular punishments but at the root of the whole structure of law itself. The phenomenon of anger was seen as an easy way to explain and justify punishment.

The Athenians, therefore, felt relatively little unease about *why* they punished, but they did nonetheless talk about wrongdoing and its punishment as events that involved the community in some sort of *disease*, even in some sort of *communal disease*. In Athenian tragedy, stories of wrongdoing and punishing are embedded in a language of illness, pollution, plague, and cure (e.g., *nosos, pharmakon, iasis, akos*). This is especially evident in the tellings and retellings of the myth of the House of Atreus, the story of how King Agamemnon wins the Trojan War and returns to his hometown of Argos only to be killed by his wife, Clytemnestra, in return for his having sacrificed their daughter Iphigeneia earlier and of how Clytemnestra, years later, is killed in turn by their son Orestes. As it turns out, Orestes has made his mother pay the price for having killed his father only to have the goddesses of vengeance/punishment, called the Erinyes, or—as they are better known to us—the Furies, set upon him and drive him out of Argos. The Furies' pursuit of Orestes eventually takes both the wrongdoer and his would-be punishers to Athens, where Athena sets up a court to try Orestes. This court, the Areopagus, acquits him.

The many different versions of the story of the House of Atreus use the trope of disease to describe the effect of wrongdoing on different members of the community. In one case, the victim, the murdered Agamemnon, is described as being a festering wound within the household (Euripides' *Electra*, 318). In another case, the wrongdoer, Orestes, is the person who is diseased and who is said to be a disease in the land (Euripides' *Orestes* 395, 831). And in yet other cases, it is the would-be punishers, the Furies, who are diseased and who bring disease to the land, dripping it from their eyes (Aeschylus's *Eumenides*, 480). In the story of the House of Atreus, all the parties to wrongdoings and the responses to it—victim, wrongdoer, punisher, and the community, or "land"—somehow share in a "disease." All parties to a wrongdoing are mutually implicated in the sickness of crime and punishment. The trope of disease symbolizes the idea that no party to the experience of wrongdoing is exempt from the trouble it introduces to the community.

The disease in which everyone was implicated was not just crime and punishment but even the disease of anger. The disease brought by the Furies emanates from their hearts or spirits, which are wrathful (*ek phronematon; mainadon, kotos, Eum.* 480; 499–506). As Apollo says, the avenging spirits that arrive as plagues and leprous ulcers may more generally be described as the wrath (*mhnᵒmata*) that arises from malignant powers underneath the earth (Aes. *Choe.* 278–84). Over and over again in Greek tragedy—in the Prometheus story, in the Medea story, in the Heracles myth[4]—the disease of anger is treated as being at the center of the problem of wrongdoing and the need for punishment. The victim and the would-be punisher suffer from a disease precisely insofar as they feel anger against the wrongdoer and feel a desire to respond to a wrongdoer in a violent fashion.[5]

It is noteworthy that the Furies, punishers whose anger is their disease, are said to drip disease from their eyes (Aeschylus *Eumenides*, 480). Greek conceptions of sight and vision characterized the sight as the transfer of physical properties from one person to another. "The eye was the source of a ray of light—of fire—that was necessary for vision. As eyes beamed, so they saw, hence the single act of beaming and seeing could not fail to affect the person who was the object of the illuminated/illuminating gaze" (MacLachlan, *The Age of Grace: Charis in Early Greek Poetry.* Princeton: Princeton University Press, 1993, p. 65). Aristotle provided a graphic example of the idea that vision could be understood as a physical transfer of properties from seer to seen when he wrote that mirrors end up covered with blood whenever a woman who is menstruating looks into them (*De insomnis* 2.495b.25-3).[6] Vision was conceived of as a process of two-way exchange between seer and seen, and an exchange of glances therefore typified intersubjective exchange. Anger, the stuff dripping from the Furies' eyes, was itself a form of disordered intersubjectivity; it marked out the fact that something had gone wrong in the relations between people.

The wrongdoer, in contrast to the victim and the would-be punisher, did not have an infection but rather was the infection. (e.g., Orestes in the *Eumenides* 470–80, 505; Orestes in *Orestes* 35, 570). It is not only the case that angry victims and would-be punishers were often said to display their anger in the eyes. That very anger was often said to arise upon a sighting of a wrongdoer or of some reminder of a wrong suffered (Allen, ch. 4).[7] Thus the nurse to Medea's children fears that the sight of them will trigger an act of rage in Medea (Eur. *Medea* 100) and Helen must move through Argos at night out of fear that she will be seen and stoned (Eur. *Or.* 57). The disease of anger was a direct response to the presence of a wrongdoer in the community. The wrongdoer was not diseased because he or she *felt* anger but because he or she inspired it.

For that matter, the "look" or "glance" of the murderer was said to spread pollution, a general form of defilement linked to disease.[8] The murderer's look was thought to have this power because the intersubjective exchange characterized by vision was thought to be a two-way exchange. To see was to be seen and to be seen was to see. To be subject to the murderer's look was also to see the murderer with one's own eyes. This in turn meant being inspired to anger and thereby infected by the murderer with the disease of anger. Interestingly, the Greek word for "glare" (*derkesthai*), to look angrily at someone, comes from the word for snake (*drakôn*), and the "glance" of snakes, like the glance of the "murderer," was said to spread poison. Wrongdoers and their acts of wrongdoing were poisonous and were like poisonous snakes because they introduced anger to the community; they introduced glares, glances, and poisonous looks, or, quite simply, negative forms of intersubjective exchange to the community.[9]

Punishment was understood as being a system that had to cure anger and that had to deal with the problem of disordered intersubjectivity. In

Euripides' play *Orestes*, one of the characters gives his city the following advice on how deal with Orestes:

> If the wife who shares his bed kills a man and the son of this one kills the
> mother in turn, and afterwards the one born of this one does away with mur-
> der by means of murder, where will a limit of these evils be reached? The an-
> cient fathers handled these matters nobly: whoever was stained with blood,
> they did not allow to come near to the sight of their eyes, nor to encounter
> them—but rather required such a person to make matters holy by exile and
> not to exchange blood for blood.   (Eur. *Ores.* 508)

Here the speaker recommends exile as a way to deal with anger. Exile is
useful precisely because it removes the wrongdoer from the *sight* of those
who are angry and thereby implicitly prevents an angry response of recip-
rocation.

For the Athenians, the problem of wrongdoing and punishment was expected to produce a communal unease or disease. It was in general the job
of punishment to remedy these negative forms of intersubjectivity. Punishment was assigned the task of curing not only the wrongdoer but everyone
in the community. There can be no doubt that in practice the Athenians
often used extremely violent methods of punishment in their attempts to
cure the community and to restore its peacefulness. But it is important that
a recognition of the idea that wrongdoing is a problem that touches on relationships within the community does not necessarily require a turn to violence as the way of dealing with that problem. Tragedy itself reflects an
awareness that the problem of anger can be addressed with words, with attempts to restore amity, and with exile instead of with violence (Allen, ch.
4). Even in tragedy where violence is so common, violence, as a way to resolve anger, was understood as a policy of last resort. An attention to the
role of anger in wrongdoing and punishment therefore does not necessitate
the satisfaction of anger but only that the community work to resolve the
anger and to restore the peace.

The form of "retribution" employed in the Athenian context thus turns
out not to be only about the "just deserts" of a wrongdoer, not to be typically about the "vengeance" of a victim but rather to be consistently about
recognizing a disruption to communal peace and the need to restore that
peace. Anger can be seen as a phenomenon that spotlights a problem, a
problem of disordered relationality within the community, and points to
the fact that wrongdoers, victims, and community all equally need to be
cured. All members of the community are in need of the restoration of

peaceful and friendly relations within the community. All members of the community are mutually implicated in the problem of wrongdoing and its punishment.

The Athenians dramatized this idea once a year at a festival called Thargelia, at which they administered a "cure" for themselves as a whole city.[10] The festival involved one particularly violent ritual. It was said that the Athenians had once killed a Cretan man named Androgeos and had afterward repented of their own act of wrongdoing. Every year, they drove two undesirable members of the community out of the city in rituals resembling stonings to deal with the problem of the city's guilt and implication in violence. Such a scapegoat was called a *pharmakos*. The word *pharmakos* is the human equivalent to the word *pharmakon*, which means both medicine and poison (we get words like "pharmacy" from this word). The ambiguity of the word *pharmakon* reveals, first of all, the problematical nature of punishment as viewed from the Athenian perspective: punishment forces a community into facing the paradoxical idea that acts of violence are expected to cure a community that otherwise disavows acts of violence.

The festival as a whole, however, revealed a second characteristic of the Athenian approach to punishing and to the idea of retribution. Thargelia marked the end of the year, and the day after saw a festival marking the beginning of the new. The Athenians moved through the year knowing that they would conclude it with a mock stoning, in which they would mimic a communal act of passion and admit to the communal desire to inflict harm. This they would do in order to cure themselves. The festival dramatized the certainty that the community's rules against violence would eventually break down; it dramatized that everyone was mutually implicated in the breakdown; and that everybody was mutually implicated in a system for restoring order that inevitably treated certain citizens as means to the ends of other citizens. The festival was an admission that a system of punishment founded on the principle of retribution requires explicit acknowledgment of the mutual implication of citizens with one another and of the implication of all citizens in a set of disordered relationships, which must be restored but that can be restored only by a process that imposes on different citizens in different ways and to different degrees. We can and should deplore the violent means that the Athenians used to make such an admission, but surely the admission itself is an important one: the admission that thinking about the problem of wrongdoing and punishment requires that we think about the community's desires and the problem of anger within the community and about how best to respond to those desires and that anger.

Responsibility for the fact that we are not inclined to think philosophically about the problem of anger in the context of punishment may be laid, in part, at Plato's door. Plato argued for reform in place of retribution, and his theory of punishment was a profound departure from the typical forms of thought that characterized his age. He repudiated a view that treated punishment as being an effort to respond to the problem of anger. Punishment should instead, he argued, deal with a wrongdoer's lack of virtue. Plato did not, it should be noted, reject violent punishments per se, only those that, rather than addressing virtue from a rationalist perspective, addressed anger.

In the *Protagoras*, Socrates and the sophist implicitly reject the Athenian approach to punishment during the course of a discussion of the question of whether or not virtue is teachable. When Protagoras makes the following argument, Socrates, for once, does not challenge him. Protagoras says:

> If you are willing to consider, Socrates, what punishment [*to kolazein*] does to wrong doers, the phenomenon itself [*auto*] will teach you that people think that it provides for virtue [*aretên*]. Those people who do not punish [*timôretai*] irrationally like beasts [*thêrion*] do not punish [*kolazei*] wrong doers with a view to or for the sake of whatever injustice has been done. No, the person who tries to punish (kolazein) according to reason [*meta logou*] does not punish [*timôretai*] for the sake of a past injustice [*tou parelêluthotos adikêmatos*]—for that which is done may not be undone—but rather for the sake of the future in order that the wrongdoer may not do wrong again and that another, seeing this one punished, may not do wrong. Since a person who punishes acts with this belief, that person also thinks that virtue is teachable; and punishes for the sake of averting [*apotropês*] evil.   (323d–324b)

Protagoras distinguishes two kinds of punishment: punishment that aims to deter and reform, and punishment that attempts to rectify the past. On Protagoras's account, people who punish with a view to the past (like the Athenians) rather than in an effort to reform may be considered akin both to wild animals and to irrational (*alogistoi*) creatures. As such, they, like the wrongdoer, need to be taught. Plato does deal with the victim's anger to some degree but by relegating consideration of such anger to a nonpenal part of the law effectively equivalent to modern civil law.[11] The realm of punishment is not expected to have to deal with anger. In the *Laws*, the Athenian stranger argues that victims and punishers are precisely not supposed to allow anger to enter into the experience of punishment, and victims and punishers ought to show pity and be gentle as long as the wrongdoer can be taught—or, rather, cured—says the stranger (Plato at *Laws* 731d).

Plato's shift away from the Athenian acknowledgment of the role of anger in punishment was accompanied by a reconceptualization of the nature of the "disease" involved in problems of wrongdoing and their punishment. For Plato, it was not the community that was diseased by wrongdoing but only the wrongdoer. He writes in the *Gorgias* (and this is something of a paraphrase):

> As the sick person goes to the doctor to be made well, so should the unjust person go to the judge to be made well. Just as medicine should be understood as "releasing us from disease [*apallattei nosou*]," justice (or punishment) should be understood as relieving us from licentiousness [*akolasias*] and injustice [*adikias*] [478a–b]. For justice/punishment "is a doctor [*iatrikê*] for baseness [*ponêrias*] and reforms us [*sôphronizei*] and makes people more just [478a–d]."

The Platonic Socrates co-opts the tragic trope of disease and in the process resignifies the trope and reconstitutes its "grammar" so as to designate a different problematic for wrongdoing. The disease involved in punishment is no longer anger, an attack from without that can touch any citizen. It is now baseness (*ponêria*), degeneration from within, touching only the wrongdoer.[12] The trope of disease no longer characterizes intersubjectivity in the community nor the problems of the mutual implication of citizens in the problem of a wrongdoing and wrongdoer. No reference to the community is needed in order for the punisher or the philosopher to understand the wrongdoer's disease of licentiousness and injustice. Those who have knowledge about virtue and vice can simply work on their own to reconstitute those who are diseased by baseness.

The limit to Plato's system for reforming wrongdoers (as described in the *Gorgias, Republic,* and *Laws*) shows itself when the dialogues' various interlocutors are asked to consider what to do with wrongdoers who simply cannot be reformed and cannot be taught virtue. The Athenian stranger characterizes such wrongdoers as "incurable" and argues for their full destruction with death and exile:[13]

> The best purge [*katharma*] is painful, as are all exceptional medicines [*hosa tôn pharmakôn toioutotropa*] and it is the purge that leads to punishment by means of a justice that uses retribution [*timôria*], when the goal of retribution is determined to be death or exile. This customarily releases the city from the greatest wrongdoers who, because they are incurable, do the greatest damage to the city.   (735e)

Plato's focus on curing the wrongdoer thus ultimately requires the complementary idea of "incurability," and this idea provides a justification for the total exclusion of the wrongdoer from the community. No longer is the person who must leave the city designated as a remedy for a community that is itself troubled or disordered. Plato makes the anger of the community irrelevant to discussion of punishment and simultaneously places the wrongdoer outside the community. Now the person who must leave the city is simply the incurable whole of the problem. Punishment need no longer be understood as involving the mutual implication of citizens in one another's lives and of the community with the wrongdoer.

Plato's repudiation of the Athenian emphasis on anger proved extremely influential, and the history of the philosophy of punishment is, amongst other things, a story of efforts to theorize punishment without addressing for or accounting for the problem of anger. Augustine, Hobbes, Beccaria, and Kant all repudiated the idea that a system of punishment should pay attention to anger or to the desire of the victim and other members of the community for punishment and to the evidence such desires provide of the disordered state of the community. They all shared a desire to put the problem of the anger to the side despite constructing otherwise quite varied theories of punishment. Augustine, like Plato, offered a reformative theory of punishment.[14] Their reformative theories eventually ceded to the deterrent theories of Hobbes[15] and Beccaria,[16] which in turn eventually gave way to Kant's theory of retribution.[17] (It is worth noting that Locke provides us with a retributive moment in the middle of the cycle,[18] and it is also worth noting that since the 1940s, there has been a similar cycle from reformative to deterrent to retributive theories of punishment in the criminological literature. More recently, theorists such as A. R. Duff and N. Lacey have articulated communitarian accounts of punishment that share with my approach an emphasis on the need to consider wrongdoing and punishment as events that affect not individuals but communities.[19] And Jeffrie Murphy has challenged penal theorists to reconsider the blanket repudiation of retributive emotions.[20]) From the perspective of the present investigation of the place of anger in thinking about punishment, the Kantian moment in the history of the philosophy of punishment is, other than the Platonic, the most important theoretical contribution, for Kant constructed a theory of retribution that was in no way founded on the problem of anger. The ideals of both reform and deterrence could easily be justified and explained without reference to anger and/or victims. The same was not true of retribution, which from its earliest conceptualization had been attached to anger. Kant, therefore, removed discussion of anger from the form of penal logic in which such discussion was most at home and finalized the exclusion of anger from the realm of philosophical speculation in the context of punishment.

Kant begins his theory of retribution by rejecting Platonic reform and Beccarian deterrence because, on his account, both forms of punishment treat the wrongdoer as a means to an end. Kant writes (describing both private and public cases, or civil and criminal cases):

> Punishment by a court can never be inflicted merely as a means to promote some good for the criminal himself or for civil society. It must always be inflicted upon him only *because he has committed a crime*. For a human being can never be treated merely as a means to the purposes of another. (Kant MM 104 [6:331])

According to Kant, the only form of punishment that does not treat the criminal as a means to an end is retributive punishment or, as he says, the *ius talionis*.[21] In order to keep retribution from being open to the same censure to which reformative and deterrent punishments are susceptible, i.e., that they treat the wrongdoer as means to an end, Kant argues that the victim's desires in regard to punishment must be ignored:

> *But punishment is not an act that the injured party can undertake on his private authority but rather an act of a court distinct from him*, which gives effect to the law of a *supreme authority* over all those subject to it; ... and when (as we must in ethics) we regard human beings as in a rightful condition but *in accordance only with laws of reason* (not civil laws), then no one is authorized to inflict punishment and to avenge the wrongs sustained by them except him who is also the supreme moral lawgiver; and he alone (namely God) can say "Vengeance is mine; I will repay." ... *It is therefore a duty of virtue not only to refrain from repaying another's enmity with hatred out of mere revenge but also not even to call upon the judge of the world for vengeance, partly because a human has enough guilt of his own to be greatly in need of pardon and partly and indeed especially, because no punishment, no matter from whom it comes, may be inflicted out of hatred.*   (6:460–61, emphasis added)

Furthermore, as the victim does not desire punishment, neither does the criminal. Kant writes:

> Accordingly, whatever undeserved evil you inflict upon another within the people, that you inflict upon yourself. If you insult him, you insult yourself; if you steal from him, you steal from yourself. ... But what does it mean to say, "If you steal from someone, you steal from yourself?" ... [6:332] *No one*

suffers punishment because he has willed it but because he has willed a punish-
able action; for it is no punishment if what is done to someone is what he wills,
and it is impossible to will to be punished.[22]   (6:335, empahsis added)

The secret of Kantian retribution is that no mortal wills or desires it, neither the criminal nor any other particular person.[23] Kant goes to such
lengths to separate punishment from any human passion or desire that
punishing becomes entirely a matter of the intellect. He writes: "Consequently, when I draw up a penal law against myself as criminal, it is pure
reason in me [*homo noumenon*], legislating with regard to rights, which
subjects me, as someone capable of crime and so as another person [*homo
phenomenon*], to the penal law, together with all others in a civil union"
(MM 6:331–36). This allows Kant not so much to justify punishment as to
remove it from the moral realm of choice, a point evidenced by the fact that
he uses the vocabulary of science and physical law to describe punishment.
In *The Metaphysics of Morals*, he describes reciprocal coercion as a concept
constructed by analogy with the physical "law of the equality of action and
reaction" (6:232–33). No mortal decrees or desires the reaction that necessarily follows on the action; instead, we must suffer it, as we generally suffer reactions to our actions, and punishment is evidence of the total impartiality, the scientific reaction, the blind eye, of law.[24] Kant's theory of
punishment effectively purified the concept of retribution of its historical
connection to anger, to citizens' wills, to passion and desire. He thereby finalized what Plato had begun: a transition away from an Athenian focus on
punishment as grounded in anger, where anger is understood as a phenomenon that marks not only the fact that something is wrong within the
community, between members of a community, between the community
and the wrongdoer but also the community's desire for peace.

As we saw in the case of Plato, the erasure of the human will and of the
problem of anger from theories of punishment ultimately motivated an
isolation of the wrongdoer from the community. In the *Laws*, the Athenian
stranger goes so far in setting up the incurables as a class apart that he permits the legislator to do away with the incurables in advance of their having done any wrong and even before legislation begins. Just as the shepherd
purifies his flock before he begins to train the animals, so the legislator
should purify his citizenry. "For in this way we commonly dispose of great
sinners who are incurable, and *are the greatest injury to the whole state*"
(*Laws* 735de). In social contract theory, there is a similar move to treat the
wrongdoer as the only person with a problem and as therefore existing outside society *by definition* and *ab initio*. In Hobbes' *Leviathan*, people who do

not accept the social contract's striving after moral perfection are the fools.[25] They are beasts in Locke.[26] And Rawls (1971, 575) writes in his Kantian *Theory of Justice*:

> Suppose that even in a well-ordered society there are some persons for whom the affirmation of their sense of justice is not a good. Given their aims and wants and the peculiarities of their nature, the thin account of the good does not define reasons sufficient for them to maintain this regulative sentiment. ... Now unhappily we are not yet in a position to answer this query properly, since it presupposes a theory of punishment and I have said very little about this part of the theory of justice. It is, of course, true that in their case just arrangements do not fully answer to their nature, and therefore, other things equal, they will be less happy than they would be if they could affirm their sense of justice. *But here one can only say: their nature is their misfortune.*
>
> (Emphasis added)

It seems that in the ideal society, citizens do not wish to be implicated in the use of violence on one another, or we might put it another way and say that they do not want to admit to their anger. We solve the problem of anger—of its ugliness and that of the violence of punishment—by defining those whom we have to punish as being outside society because of what they are—fools, beasts, cursed by nature—rather than because we have put them there. We do this rather than admitting that we punish because of what we need and that we are all implicated in this need. Once the problem of anger in the community is ignored, the wrongdoer is isolated and categorized as the only person with a problem. But such construction of the wrongdoer as, by definition, apart from and at odds with the community should give us pause. The pause should point to the need to rethink the relationship between the community and the wrongdoer, the need to rethink what it means to recognize retribution as the basis for punishment.

The philosophical tendency to ignore the mutual implication of victim, punishers, wrongdoers, and community in a set of disordered relationships that need to be rectified or restored by punishment has found historical embodiment in U.S. legal institutions. The near-total erasure of the victim from the process of punishment was accomplished with the invention, in the colonies, of a public prosecutor with sole right, to the exclusion of private prosecutors, to prosecute criminals.[27] This invention made all wrongdoing a matter of a contest between a depersonalized or abstract state and some individual wrongdoer. It is interesting that the colonial invention of the public prosecutor was not modeled on precedents from the British motherland (and still today does not apply de jure in the United Kingdom) and that it is an invention for which no modern historian is able to account. It is an invention that underlies modern definitions of punishment. Take Nozick: "*Yet though the victim occupies the unhappy special position of victim and is owed compensation, he is not owed punishment. (That is 'owed' to the person who deserves to be punished.)* The offender is not under an obligation to the victim to be punished; he doesn't deserve to be punished 'to the victim'" (*Anarchy, the State, and Utopia,* p. 138; emphasis added). Or take *Black's Law Dictionary*'s definition of punishment:

> Any fine, penalty, or confinement inflicted upon a person by the authority of the law and the judgment and sentence of a court, for some crime or offense committed by him, or for his omission of a duty enjoined by law. A deprivation of property or some right. But this does not include a civil penalty redounding to the benefit of an individual. People v. Vanderpool, 20 Cal.2d 746, 128 P.2d 513, 515.[28]

This theoretical erasure of victim, community, and mutual implication of citizens in wrongdoing and its punishment, exemplified by both institutions and theoretical definitions of punishment, depends on an obfuscation of the problem of anger, an obfuscation that justifies making the wrongdoer the only person with problems that are at issue in a situation of wrongdoing and punishment.[29] When we ignore the problem of anger, we end up defining the necessarily retributive basis of punishment in a Kantian fashion—in terms of having the wrongdoer pay something back in some abstract calculus—and we lose the Athenian insight: that wrongdoing poses us with the problem of having to restore peaceful relationships within the community.

To suggest that it would perhaps be worthwhile to think about the problem of anger when thinking about situations of wrongdoing and punishment is most emphatically not to condone indulging or "satisfying" anger but, rather, to point to four things that are revealed by an analytical attention to anger: (1) that wrongdoers are members of the community whose acts implicate the community, (2) that punishment arises from a need to deal with disordered relationships within the community, (3) that it is precisely anger that spotlights or signals the need to deal with those disordered relationships, and (4) that we need to make efforts not *to satisfy* anger but *to resolve* that anger and to restore peace in the community when anger arises. If retribution is of necessity the basis of punishment—and most theorists agree rather uneasily that it is—we should make the idea of retribution more ethically nourishing by returning to it the elements of the punitive situation that have been occluded by philosophical efforts to remove anger from the realm of theoretical speculation. The most important element is the importance of thinking about the relationship between the wrongdoer and the community rather than automatically and *ab initio* excluding the wrongdoer from the community. If we could redefine the idea of retribution so as to highlight its ability to signal our mutual implication in the problem of wrongdoing and anger, we could aim our punishments at restoring conditions of peace and friendship.[30] If we were to aim our punishments at peace, we might perhaps be less uneasy about why we punish.

NOTES

1. John Rawls, "Two Concepts of Rules," *The Philosophical Review* (1955), 3–13.

2. Theorists of punishment themselves argue that it is essentially impossible to justify punishment consistently. Take J. S. Mill: "All these opinions are extremely plausible; each is triumphant so long as he is not compelled to take into consideration any other maxims of justice than the one he has selected; but as soon as their maxims are brought face to face, each disputant seems to have exactly as much to say for himself as the others. . . . No one of them can carry out his own notion of justice without trampling upon another equally binding. These are difficulties; they have always been felt to be such" (*Utilitarianism*, 192).

A. Duff and D. Garland (1995) write: "To talk of 'the justification' of punishment might suggest that we need a unitary theory—one that founds the practice of punishment on some single value or on a set of non-conflicting values. Should we not rather accept Hart's argument that 'any morally tolerable account' of punishment 'must exhibit it as a compromise between distinct and partly conflicting principles' (Hart 1968, *Punishment and Responsibility: Essays in the Philosophy of Law*. Oxford: Clarendon Press, p. 1)." (*Oxford Readings in Punishment*. Oxford: Oxford University Press. p. 4.)

3. R. A. Duff and D. Garland, "Introduction: Thinking about Punishment," in Duff and Garland, eds., *A Reader on Punishment* (Oxford: Oxford University Press, 1995).

4. Similarly, in Sophocles' *Ajax* (40, 59, 232), Ajax's madness in his wrathful slaughter of the herds, his unwittingly unsuccessful attempt to avenge himself on Agamemnon and Menelaos out of anger (xÒlow), is also a disease (maniãsin nÒsoiw). In Euripides' *Medea* (520), what is said to be incurable when lovers meet in strife is anger (ÙrgØ dus¤atow). In the *Trachiniae*, lovelorn Deianira, slighted by her husband and considering how to respond, remarks that it is not noble for a woman to grow angry and accordingly she will apply a remedy (l fhma) that is more of a release (lutØrion) than is acting on her anger: a love-philter (552). The love-

philter Deianira uses turns out to be a poison that kills her husband. Just as the word for remedy *pharmakon* also means both poison and potion (as in the love-philter), punishment and remedy are intertwined. Deianira acts out, even if accidentally, the double-edged nature of punishment.

5. R. C. T. Parker (*Miasma: Pollution and Purification in Early Greek Religion*. Oxford: Clarendon Press. 1983, p. 106) has found the same thing: "Pollution appears not as a mess of blood, but as the anger of the victim, or of avenging spirits acting on his behalf, against the man who has robbed him of the life that is his right." R. Padel (*Whom Gods Destroy*. Princeton: Princeton University Press. 1995, pp. 148, 157–64) likewise connects *mêniai*, anger, and *lussa* with disease and pollution.

6. In the *Timaeus* (45bff), Plato describes the eyes as extending out of the body and therefore as being physically affected by the outer world. See also R. Padel. *In and Out of the Mind: Greek Images of the Tragic Self*. Princeton: Princeton University Press. 1992, p. 42.

7. J-P Vernant (*Myth and Society in Ancient Greece*, trs. by J. Lloyd. Sussex: Harvester Press. 1980, [1974], pp. 110–30) discusses the idea that the stain of pollution reaches mind as well as hands and involves a defilement associated with a dead man, his anger, and his dangerous thirst for vengeance.

8. See Soph. *OT* 100, 241, 310. Eur. *IT* 202.

9. E.g., Eur. *MoH* 1107, 1150, 1220, 1234; *IT* 202. *Or.* 480, where Orestes' eyes flash lightning. On snakes: Aes. *Pers.* 81; Eur. *Or.* 479–80. See also Padel 1992, 123–24.

10. Aris. *Kn.* 1405; Lys. 6.5; Lyc. 1.98f; Men. *Sam.* 481. See J. Bremmer, "Scapegoat Rituals in Ancient Greece," Harvard Studies in Classical Philology, 87, 299–320 (1983).

11. T. Saunders (*Plato's Penal Code*. Oxford: Clarendon Press. 1991) and M. Mckenzie (*Plato on Punishment*. Cambridge: Cambridge University Press, 1981) have pointed out that Plato divides wrongdoing into the doing of hurts (*blabai*) and the doing of injustices (*adikiai*); essentially, he gives the victim a role in relation to "hurts" rather than in relation to "injustices," and punishment is relevant only for the latter. The victim has two jobs: that of reconciliation and that of the reform of the wrongdoer. For instance: "The legislator must distinguish between injustice and hurt and must make the hurt good by law and save that which is ruined, raise up fallen, make dead or wounded whole. And when compensation has soothed the harm done, the law must always seek to win over the doers and sufferers of the several hurts from feelings of enmity to those of friendship" (Laws at 862b–c.). Plato does focus on the problem of disruptions within the community but not from the perspective of punishment.

12. Mackenzie 1981, Saunders 1991. Stalley ("Punishment in Plato's Laws." *History of Political Thought* 1995, vol. 16, pp. 476–96. "Punishment in Plato's *Protagoras*." *Phronesis*. 1995, vol. 40, pp. 1–19. "Punishment and the Physiology of the *Timaeus*." *CQ* 1996, vol. 46, 2, pp. 357–70) also discusses medical analogies in the *Timaeus* and in the *Laws*, citing for the latter 854c–55a, 862e–863c, 934c, 735e, 843d,

941d, 957e. All of these scholars have recognized the importance of the medical trope in this dialogue, but none has connected it to the trope of disease found in tragedy. The medical trope appears consistently throughout Plato: *Rep.* 444, 556 (not to be punished is to remain sick), 562 (sickness, physician, lawgiver), 567; *Tim.* 86 (disease of the soul, remedies), 106; *Sophist*: 220, 227; *Prot.* 322, 324; *Crat.* 405; *Crito* 48; *Statesman* 295, 296: "Gentle violence is used for their own good. What should it be called? In political art it is not disease but evil, disgrace, or injustice. And when the citizen contrary to law and custom is compelled to do what is juster, better, nobler than he did before, and this sort of violence is blamed, the last and most absurd thing he could say is that he has incurred disgrace or evil or injustice at the hands of the legislator who uses the violence"; 276–77, 297; *Laws*: 857a–864c9; 728b2–c5; 731b3–d5; 735d8–736a3; 793d7–794a2; 854c2–855a2; 864c10–e3; 866d5–868a1; 880d7–881b2; 907e6–909c4; 933e6–934c2; 938b5–6; 941c4–942a4; 944d2–3.

13. See Saunders (1991, ch. 13) on Plato's eschatology. A. Adkins (*Merit and Responsibility.* Oxford: Clarendon Press. 1960, pp. 304–12) on curability versus incurability.

14. Augustine makes the Christian God's punishment, like the legislator's, reformative and argues that mortal punishment should try to follow suit. For those who are trying to live in the city of God within the city of man, the goal of punishment is to approximate the divine justice of which we have but the faintest knowledge. "It is the duty of a blameless person not just to do no wrong, but to keep others from wrong doing and to punish it when done, so that the one punished may be improved by the experience and others warned by the example" (19.16). God knows how to reform, and God's retribution is just because it comes from God. Christ has taught us to turn the other cheek, however, so mortal punishment should seek only to reform and to correct. In fact, Augustine labels the law of retribution—Ill betide him who evil does—as a lust (14.15). As such, it should be fought against. The resemblance between Augustine's and Plato's prescriptions for punishment is close: We should attempt to punish the soul, and not the body, by aiming at reforming the soul in a fashion consistent with divine justice. This requires overcoming evils within ourselves since we all sin. (Passim.) Augustine, however, argues that ultimately mortal punishment is always inadequate to this task—even, Augustine makes a point to say, from a philosopher-judge.

15. Hobbes takes the line that punishment ought to be deterrent or reformative rather than retributive (*Leviathan*, ch. 28). Also, punishment is not owed to the victim, only compensation: "Law impose a summe of Mony to be payd, to him that has been Injured; this is but a satisfaction for the hurt done him; and extinguisheth the accusation of the party injured, not the crime of the offender" (*Leviathan*, ch. 28).

16. Beccaria introduces the utilitarian principle later made famous by Bentham that the aim of politics is the greatest happiness shared by the greatest number (*La*

massima felicità divisa nel maggior numero). Beccaria then asks the following questions (*Of Crimes and Penalties*):

> Is the death penalty really useful and necessary for the security and good-order of society? Are torture and torments just, and do they attain the end for which laws are instituted? What is the best way to prevent crimes? Are the same punishments equally effective for all times?

Beccaria answers his own questions thus:

> The purpose [of punishment] can only be to prevent the criminal from inflicting new injuries on its citizens and to deter others from similar acts. Always keeping due proportions, such punishments and such method of inflicting them ought to be chosen, therefore, which will make the strongest and most lasting impression on the minds of men, and inflict the least torment on the body of the criminal.... For a punishment to attain its end, the evil which it inflicts has only to exceed the advantage derivable from the crime. In this excess of evil one should include the certainty of punishment and the loss of the good which the crime might have produced.

Beccaria thus offers a theory of punishment that has three main features. First, on his account, the right of the sovereign to punish derives from the utilitarian necessity of punishment for the community rather than from any particular individual's right to punish. He says:

> Sometimes a man is freed from punishment for a lesser crime when the offended party chooses to forgive—an act in accord with beneficence and humanity, but contrary to the public good—as if a private citizen, by an act of remission, could eliminate the need for an example, in the same way that he can waive compensation for the injury. *The right to inflict punishment is a right not of an individual, but of all citizens, or of their sovereign.* An individual can renounce his portion of right, but cannot annul that of others.　(xx)

Beccaria thus argues that the individual does not hold any right to punish independent from the collective right. Any act of wrong-doing concerns all citizens and concerns them equally. It is not the victim's desires that should motivate a decision about what to do with a wrong-doer but rather the need to confirm that the sovereign power that inflicts punishment is constituted out of the participation of each and every citizen. For Beccaria, punishment itself is always a practice that comes to exist only when public sovereignty has arisen from citizens' cession to some central authority of their right to protect themselves.

He writes:

> The sum of all these portions of liberty sacrificed by each for his own good constitutes the sovereignty of a nation, and their legitimate depository and administrator is the sovereign. But merely to have established this deposit was not enough; it had to be defended against private usurpations by individuals each of whom always tries not only to withdraw his own share but also to usurp for himself that of others. Some tangible motives had to be in-

troduced, therefore, to prevent the despotic spirit, which is in every man, from plunging the laws of society into its original chaos. *It was thus necessity that forced men to give up part of their personal liberty, and it is certain, therefore, that each is willing to place in the public fund only the least possible portion, no more than suffices to induce others to defend it. The aggregate of these least possible portions constitutes the right to punish*; all that exceeds this is abuse and not justice; it is fact but by no means right.   (5)

The victim and the victim's desire for punishment no longer lie behind the idea of punishment.

Second, this refusal on Beccaria's part in any way to attribute to the individual or victim a right of punishment is described in terms of a rejection of passion. Beccaria has set out to reform systems of punishment of his day and age, which are, in his opinion "passions clothed with authority and power." Indeed, he desires a "body politic, which far from acting on passion, is the tranquil moderator of private passions" (xv).

Third, since individuals and their passions have no role to play in punishment, punishment must be wholly public, and the public and passionless nature of punishment prevents punishment from being an "act of violence." The public purpose of punishment requires that its execution be carried out by a wholly public agent. Beccaria assigns the role of punishing to the sovereign or legislator as maker of laws so that all punishments should follow simply and directly from the law with little intermediation from judges. "When a fixed code of laws, which must be observed to the letter, leaves no further care to the judge than to examine the acts of citizens and to decide whether or not they conform to the law as written; then only are citizens not subject to the petty tyrannies of the many—it enables them to calculate accurately the inconveniences of a misdeed" (iv). And judges receive laws from "the living society, or from the sovereign representing it" (iv). From what has thus far been demonstrated, one may deduce a general theorem of considerable utility, though hardly conformable with custom, the usual legislator of nations. It is this: *In order for punishment not to be, in every instance, an act of violence of one or of many against a private citizen, it must be essentially public, prompt, necessary, the least possible in the given circumstances, proportionate to the crimes, and dictated by the laws.*

17. Kant's theory does contain elements of deterrent thought, but it is his affirmation and positive acceptance of retribution that is philosophically significant because all other major theorists of punishment had found retribution incompatible with a utopian view of politics.

18. Locke, like the Athenians, is caught between the problem of passion and the problem of authority. He summarizes this conflict thus:

To this strange Doctrine, *viz*, That *in the State of Nature, every one has the Executive Power of the Law of Nature*, I doubt not but it will be objected, That it is unreasonable for Men to be Judges in their own Cases, that Self-love will make Men partial to themselves and their Friends. And on the other side, that Ill Nature, Passion and Revenge will carry them too far in punishing others. . . . But I shall desire those who make this Objection, to remember that Absolute Monarchs are but Men, and if Government is to be the Remedy of those Evils, . . . I desire to know what kind of Government that is, and how much better it is than the State of Nature where one Man commanding a multitude, has the Liberty to be Judge in his own Case, and may do to all his Subjects whatever he pleases, without the least liberty to any one to question or control those who Execute his Pleasure? And in whatsoever he doth, whether led by Reason, Mistake, or Passion, must be submitted to? Much better it is in the State of Nature wherein Men are not bound to submit to the unjust will of another: And if he that judges, judges amiss in his own, or any other Case, he is answerable for it to the rest of Mankind. (*Second Treatise*, sec. 13)

19. See N. Lacey, *State Punishment: Political Principles and Community Values*. London: Routledge, 1993; R. A. Duff, "Expression, Penance, and Reform," in J. G. Murphy, ed., *Punishment and Rehabilitation*, 3rd Edition. Belmont, Calif.: International Thomson Publishing, 1995.

20. See, *inter alia*, J. Murphy, "Getting Even: The Role of the Victim," in J. G. Murphy, ed., *Punishment and Rehabilitation*, 3rd Edition. Belmont, Calif.: International Thomson Publishing, 1995.

21. "But only the *law of retribution* (*ius talionis*)—it being understood, of course, that this is applied by a court (not by your private judgment)—can specify definitely the quality and the quantity of punishment ; all other principles are fluctuating and unsuited for a sentence of pure and strict justice because extraneous considerations are mixed into them . . ." (id.) [*MM* 104 (6:331)].

22. When Kant says, "[T]he law of punishment is a categorical imperative, and woe to him who crawls through the windings of eudaemonism in order to discover something that releases the criminal from punishment . . . ," he is making the point that categorical imperatives include not just injunctions to positive action but also injunctions against action; the law of punishment sets apart the injunctions to positive action so that we can understand the concept of right.

23. As Samuel Fleischacker writes, "The judge as judge thus appears to be a rather strange human being, and indeed it is not clear that he is, in his formal role, a human being at all. Kant goes to some lengths to separate the court from any human will" ("Kant's Theory of Punishment," *Kant-Studien* 79. 1988, p. 445). The desire to take revenge is a form of malice contrary to virtue (*MM, Doctrine of Virtue* 6:460).

24. It may perhaps be objected that Kant's stronger theory that punishment is an impartial act of the state rather than being the act of a victim or a response to a victim's desires results from the fact that he worked within a "civil law" or Roman-canon law framework rather than in a common law framework. In the former civil cases allowed the victim to sue for damages, but the state prosecuted in criminal

cases where punishment was at stake. This distinction was operative in France and Germany by the sixteenth century (R. M. Andrews, *Law, Magistracy, and Crime in Old Regime Paris, 1735–1789, vol. 1, The System of Criminal Justice.* Cambridge: Cambridge University Press. 1994, pp. 43–45, 417–21, 423; J. H. Langbein, *Prosecuting Crime in the Renaissance in England, Germany, and France.* Cambridge, MA.: Harvard University Press. 1974. pp. 129–131, 223; A. Esmein. *Histoire de la Procédure Criminelle.* Paris: Eduoard Duchemin [1887], 1978). In the English common law tradition the victim had (and in Britain still has) the power to prosecute a crime and therefore to initiate punishment. Thus it might be objected that Locke's theory that the right to punish inheres in each individual in the state of nature might be thought to reflect his position as a member of a society that institutionalized punishment in such a fashion. The same historical context, however, did not lead Hobbes to the same conclusions. Moreover, the British judicial system began using the Roman law distinction between civil and criminal cases, that is cases for which fines were imposed and cases for which punishments were capital, as early as the twelfth century (Pollock and Maitland, *The History of English Law*, 1895, 1968, bk. I, ch. 6). The distinction did not immediately impact the way in which prosecution was structured.

The distinction between civil and criminal cases was originally (in the Roman context) meant to distinguish between those crimes for which a wronged individual could receive only the lesser penalty of money and those crimes for which the injured party could indeed receive the greater penalty of capital punishment inflicted on the doer of the wrong. The distinction limited the extent of private vengeance and punishment that could be carried out in some cases but without making punishment any the less related to the private interests of victims. As we currently employ the distinction, however, the monetary penalties imposed in civil cases are no longer designated as "punishments." Instead they are referred to as "damages" (see Black's *Law Dictionary* as quoted in the text), and Foucault writes: "It is difficult to dissociate punishment from additional physical pain. What would a non-corporal punishment be?" M. Foucault, Discipline and Punish, trans. by A. Lane (London: Penguin Books, 1995, trans. 1977).

All of the philosophers discussed in this text except for Plato lived and wrote in a context where cases were divided into civil cases where monetary penalties were imposed and criminal cases where capital penalties were imposed. Plato, however, developed these categories for himself although the Athenians did not use them. Saunders has shown how Plato developed the categories of harm and injustice and defined the first as requiring compensation while the second requires punishment. The philosophers' general move away from retribution and their refusal to consider the problem of anger required that they draw a firm distinction between the two methods of dealing with wrongdoing: nonpunitive civil damages and criminal punishment. Punishment could be detached from anger by the relegation of the problems of anger to the realm of civil law.

25. "The Foole hath sayd in his heart, there is no such thing as Justice; and sometimes also with his tongue; He does not therein deny, that there be Covenants; and that they are sometimes broken, sometimes kept and that such breach of them may be called Injustice, and the observance Justice: but he questioneth, whether Injustice, taking away the feare of God, (for the same Foole hath said in his heart there is no God,) may not sometimes stand with that Reason, which dictateth every man his own good" (*Leviathan*, ch. 15).

26. "And one may destroy a Man who makes War upon him, or has discovered an Enmity to his being, for the same Reason, that he may kill a *Wolf* or a *Lyon*; because such Men are not under ties of the Common Law of Reason, have no other Rule, but that of Force and Violence, and so may be treated as Beasts of Prey" (*Second Treatise*, sec. 16).

27. Private citizens still prosecuted criminal trials in Britain on a regular basis into the eighteenth century. The American colonies adopted a system of exclusively public criminal prosecution in advance and, it would seem, independently of the mother country. N. V. Baker (*Conflicting Loyalties: Law and Politics in the Attorney General's Office, 1789–1990*. Lawrence: University Press of Kansas. 1992, pp. 38–40) writes that the invention of attorneys general at state and county levels taking over all criminal prosecution and removing prerogative from private citizens seems to have occurred de facto rather than de jure and without the express order to do so from the British Attorney General delegating the colonial attorneys. In fact, in Britain at this point the attorney general and solicitor general took on only cases that applied directly to the king, and justices of the peace took on only cases where there was no private prosecutor. This use of the private prosecutor in criminal cases in Britain continued until sometime after the colonial regimes had begun to use a public prosecutor. See T. A. Green, Verdict According to Conscience: Perspectives on the English Criminal Trial Jury, 1200–1800 (Chicago: University of Chicago Press) (1985), pp. 270–71; Langbein 1974, pp. 35–39, 44.

28. Likewise, in the 1994 *Oxford Readings in Socio-Legal Studies: A Reader on Punishment* (ed. by A. Duff and D. Garland), "a volume [that] brings together writings on the philosophy of punishment, penology, and the sociology of punishment" from some of the most significant theorists of punishment writing in the last fifty years, each of the fifteen essays treats punishment as something owed either to the criminal or to the state. Authors included in the reader are J. G. Murphy, J. Feinberg, A. von Hirsch, M. Tonry, J. Q. Wilson, and P. Hirst.

29. That modern philosophies of punishment have rather little to do with passion should come as no surprise. Recent work in moral and political philosophy, especially work with connections to the psychoanalytical tradition of Freud, Lacan, Kristeva, and Irigaray, and/or connections to feminist theory, has turned our attention to the predominant rationalism (setting Hume to the side) of the Anglo-American tradition of moral, ethical, and political philosophy. Martha Nussbaum, for instance, writes in *The Fragility of Goodness* (Cambridge, Cambridge University Press. 1985):

Our Anglo-American philosophical tradition has tended to assume that the ethical text should, in the process of inquiry, converse with the intellect alone; it should not make its appeal to the emotions, feelings, and sensory responses. Plato explicitly argues that ethical learning must proceed by separating the intellect from our other merely human parts; many other writers proceed on this assumption, with or without sharing Plato's intellectualistic ethical conception.   (15–16)

In a more recent book, *Poetic Justice* (New York: Basic Books. 1996), Nussbaum explicitly attempts to reintroduce the realm of passion, emotion, and poetry to the political world. Writers like Nussbaum, Carol Gilligan, and Annette Baier have tended to focus on "positive" emotions like pity, sympathy, trust, and compassion, or, like Kristeva and Irigaray, on the positive forces of the mother. Such emotions have previously been ruled out of philosophical and political court within the rationalist framework because they are said to lead to "mistakes" in decision making. Nonetheless, they are emotions that the rationalist tradition could forgive relatively easily because they are seen as expressions of goodness of heart. Negative emotions like anger, however, and emotions that entail a desire to harm, introduce rather different theoretical concerns than those that are occasioned by discussion of pity, fear, sympathy, empathy, compassion, and the like. It is not quite so clear that such emotions should be ruled back in or, if they should be, how they should be ruled back in.

30. There is no reason to think that concepts of responsibility, deterrence, and reform would have to be abandoned in such a project. Rather, we would recognize the role that all three concepts play in constituting and maintaining political orders in accord with norms of political friendship.

Part III

Love, Forgiveness, and Cowardice

Chapter Eight

Making Up Emotional People
The Case of Romantic Love

Cheshire Calhoun

> But one thing is certain: love was not made in heaven;
> rather, it was fashioned right here on earth, to meet spe-
> cific societal needs.
>
> James R. Averill[1]

The most common judicial argument for retaining the bar against same-sex marriage is that marriage, by definition, requires one man and one woman. Proponents of same-sex marriage find this definitional argument unsatisfying since it appears to beg the question "Why define marriage this way?" If the answer is that centuries of tradition support restricting marriage to heterosexuals, proponents can point to *Loving's* rejection of that same tradition as sufficient reason for preventing two people from marrying.[2] If the answer is that homosexuality is deeply immoral, proponents can point out that moral abhorrence is not sufficient justification either for depriving individuals of a fundamental right to marry or for engaging in sex discrimination.[3] What is puzzling about definitional arguments against same-sex marriage is that they look so weak. Where is the depth of the conviction that definitional arguments are good reasons coming from? Neither patriotic loyalty to tradition nor deep moral animus toward homosexuality sufficiently explains why opponents find same-sex marriage to be not just a violation of our traditions or deeply immoral but inconceivable as a real marriage. In what follows, I want to suggest an explanation. Both the moral condemnation of homosexuality and the definition of marriage as requiring one man and one woman are deeply bound up with the cultural construction of a particular emotion: romantic love.[4] Romantic love transforms sexual desire from a primitive, socially disruptive drive into an expression of the relational ideal of perfect unity. Romantic love also transforms the teleology of sex from mere bodily gratification to committed coupledom, parenting, and family life. It is thus romantic love that forges the connection between sexuality and family, marriage, and procreation. That Justice Byron White found "no connection between family, marriage, or procreation on the one hand and homosexual activity on the other" suggests that what he could not find in homosexuals was romantic love.[5] This is exactly what I want to suggest. The deep difference between homosexuality and heterosexuality is in part socially constructed by imputing to gays and lesbians a psychology that makes them incapable of romantic love and thus incapable of more than a simulacrum of marriage.

In pursuing this thesis, I have a number of aims. First, examining the link between same-sex marriage bars and the cultural construction of romantic love illustrates one interesting way that emotion enters into law: legal reasoning inevitably relies on assumptions about how people are emotionally constituted. The justification of alternative sanctions such as DUI bumper stickers or public apologies depends on the assumption that normal people will suffer shame from such penalties. Deciding what counts as duress or a mitigating passionate impulse requires making assumptions about which threats are sufficiently frightening to the average person that they constitute duress and which passions a normal person cannot be expected to resist absent a cooling-off period. And deciding whether or not to permit victim impact statements requires making assumptions about how juries will be emotionally affected by victim narratives.[6]

The assumptions that law has made about how people are emotionally constituted have not always been good ones. In Texas, for example, husbands who murdered their unfaithful wives formerly could expect to face manslaughter rather than murder charges.[7] Texas law assumed that wifely infidelity was such a deep affront to the honor of husbands that any man with a normal emotional constitution might react with deep and uncontrollable rage. Because legal reasoning can depend heavily on assumptions about how people are emotionally constituted, it is important for the law to be reflective about just what it is assuming about people's emotional lives and whether those assumptions are warranted. Doing so is especially critical whenever the law assumes that different kinds of people—men and women, whites and blacks, birth mothers and adoptive parents, adults and children, heterosexuals and homosexuals—are differently emotionally constituted and thus warrant different legal treatment.

A second aim in pursuing the link between same-sex marriage bars and the cultural construction of romantic love is to shift the way we think about the debate over gay and lesbian rights. Most often, this debate is taken to be a debate about sex. I want to suggest that the subtext of this debate about sex is a generally unstated debate about who is emotionally competent to experience romantic love and thus whose sex life is ennobled because it expresses an emotional ideal and has as its teleology marriage and family. If the deep issue is romantic love, not sex, then legal narratives that connect same-sex sexual coupling with same-sex romantic coupling may be important wherever gay and lesbian rights are at issue and not just in marriage rights suits.[8]

The third aim is cautionary. It is tempting to think that if one shows that an emotion, such as romantic love, or an emotional subjectivity, such as that of gays and lesbians, is socially constructed, then the argumentative work is done. A socially constructed emotion or emotional subjectivity, it might be thought, is an arbitrary one; and if arbitrary, that social construction is both unjustified and easily changed. Hence, it is tempting to think that all that is needed to reconstruct cultural understandings of gays' and lesbians' sexual-emotional lives are more and better counternarratives. Such narratives would include both cross-cultural narratives demonstrating that other cultures have not constructed gay and lesbian emotional subjectivity in a way that precludes romantic love and thus marriage. They would also include intracultural narratives countering stereotypes that impute promiscuity, sexual deviance, child molestation, relational instability, and the like to gays and lesbians.

This temptation is a mistake. It rests on a misunderstanding of what it means to say that an emotion or emotional subjectivity is socially constructed. Social constructionism does not entail that the ways in which cultures construct emotion must be completely arbitrary. On the contrary, social constructionism is the view that particular constructions of emotions are possible only on the backdrop of a set of social norms, social relations, and medical, psychological, biological, and religious beliefs. The worldview that made *amae* (a form of dependent love) possible for the Japanese, or that made *acedia* (a melancholy causing loss of faith in God) possible for medieval monks, is not a worldview available to us, and thus neither are these emotions.[9] The deconstruction of an emotion thus cannot be accomplished by merely observing the fact of its social origin. At most, attention to the cultural construction of emotions and emotional subjects opens a space for critical reflection on whether we ought to reconstruct them. The deconstructive work must instead be done by appeal to intracultural norms, practices, and conceptual schemes.

I begin in Part I by reviewing two social constructionist claims about emotions that are useful in articulating the thesis that gay and lesbian emotional subjectivity is socially constructed as one devoid of romantic love: the claim that all emotions are scripted, and the claim that outlawing some emotions is one mechanism for sustaining social hierarchies. In Part II, I turn to an examination of the way romantic love links sex to marriage. In Part III, I document the uncoupling of same-sex sex from romantic love in the psychoanalytic theories of the 1950s.

I

Emotional Scripts

Different theories of emotion give pride of place to different aspects of emotion—physiological disturbances, evaluative and factual beliefs, patterns of perceptual salience, and behavior. Social constructionist theories of emotions are distinguished by their emphasis on the scripting of emotions.[10] Emotional scripts specify the proper object of the emotion (such as the loss of a parent or an insult by an inferior), the physical symptoms (such as weeping or sighing), the goal-directed behavior (such as seeking revenge), and the fantasies or patterns of thought (such as imagining kisses or obsession with signs of betrayal) that typify an emotion. As one author describes them, emotional scripts are transitory social roles.[11] Like social roles, emotional scripts may be generic—as are the scripts for basic emotion types such as jealousy, happiness, pride, love, and discontent—or they may be highly specific, as are the scripts for the jealous husband, the ecstatic lottery winner, the proud parent of a newborn, the loving adult child of elderly parents, or the dissatisfied customer. We learn emotions by learning emotional scripts. We assess the genuineness of our own emotions by comparing our own experiences to those scripts ("Can I really be grieving if I can't cry about this loss?"). And we interpret our own and others' emotions by appealing to those scripts.

One implication of this view that emotions are socially scripted is that there is a sense in which emotions are performances, and in loving, hating, being jealous or furious we are always also impersonating someone who loves, hates, is jealous or furious. This claim is less paradoxical than it sounds. Learning what, for example, real love is and gauging just how real one's own love is requires having on hand examples of the real thing. One function of film, literature, theater—and even sitcoms, advertising, and comic strips—is to culturally circulate "paradigm scenarios" of the real thing.[12] Romeo and Juliet is a classic case in point. The story of Romeo and Juliet is a central script for real romantic love. The more like their story our own experience is, the greater our entitlement to claim that our own love is the genuine article. That is, our own love, to be genuine, needs to be like that of someone else (namely, the paradigm enactors); in this minimal sense emotions are impersonations.

Should our emotional experience fall short, there are a variety of ways of bringing it into greater conformity, and thus of intentionally performing an emotion. As Arlie Hochschild has argued, not only can we engage in what she calls "emotional labor," i.e., working ourselves up into an emotion, but we are often required to do so.[13] Spouses, for example, are expected to do the emotional labor that will either sustain or re-create the romantic passion that got them into the marriage in the first place. Relatives, friends, ministers, marriage counselors, and talk show hosts regularly remind couples of the importance of doing that emotional labor and offer advice on how to do it, including spending more quality time together, going on vacations, focusing on a spouse's better qualities, being more understanding of a spouse's faults, and spicing up sex.

That emotions are performances—something we do rather than merely suffer—is even more evident if one keeps in mind that emotions are not just internal feelings and cognitions, they are also partially constituted by patterns of intentional action.[14] Some emotions, especially species of love—parental love, love of country, romantic love—involve complex actions extending over a long range of time. The script for love of one's country, for example, includes signing up for military service, doing jury duty, attending Fourth of July parades, and purchasing, displaying, and properly caring for the flag. Scripts for romantic love are equally dominated by behavioral requirements; hence the many injunctions of the form "If you loved me, you would . . ." The more such complex and time-extended activities dominate an emotional script, the more obviously performative the emotion is.

When an emotion is strongly culturally prescribed, indeed idealized, the way romantic love is in our culture, individuals may find themselves more literally impersonating someone in love in order to live up to social expectations that a life well lived will contain romantic love. Averill and Boothroyd, for example, found that while 40 percent of subjects in their study of romantic love claimed to have had experiences resembling the paradigm scenario of love at first sight, only 5–10 percent were able to provide narratives of their own experiences that actually did conform to that paradigm scenario.[15] What this suggested to the researchers was that individuals (mis)interpret their own emotional experience in light of what they think it should look like.

What do these observations about the scripting of emotions suggest about the construction of heterosexual versus same-sex romantic love? First, our paradigm scenarios for romantic love exceptionlessly cast heterosexuals in the leading roles. Even in literature and film produced by gays and lesbians romantic love is more often upstaged by narratives of seduction or of coping with the realities of having a deviant sexuality, or a plot line that puts romantic love in an unseen past. Falling in love virtually never appears in any narrative.[16] Because same-sex romantic love violates the casting rules for romantic love, any same-sex performance of romantic love is vulnerable to being read as a drag performance.[17] Moreover, because our script for romantic love does not prepare us to see romantic love in gay and lesbian lives, same-sex romantic love is vulnerable to being interpreted as something else that is in the emotional scripts for gays and lesbians such as sexual obsession or displaced hatred of the opposite sex.

Second, given that a life containing romantic love is culturally prescribed for heterosexuals, vastly more cultural energy is spent on ensuring that heterosexuals do the emotional work necessary to produce and sustain romantic love. Gays and lesbians are simply not exhorted to fall in love, work at love, or stay in love. When they do fall in love, they face barriers to performing romantic love, barriers that include sodomy laws and the threat of reprisal for public displays of affection. Of particular importance are the barriers to completing the teleology of love in complex, time-extended activities like marriage and parenting. In short, not only is it harder to interpret gay and lesbian emotional performances as romantic love, it is harder to do a full-scale performance. A romantic lover is not a readily available kind of person for gays and lesbians to be, nor is our culture set up to produce same-sex romantic lovers as it is set up to produce enormous numbers of heterosexual lovers.

Outlaw Emotions

One advantage of a social constructionist approach to emotions is that it invites us to ask, "How are emotions implicated in social hierarchies?" Feminist work has been especially helpful in answering that question.[18] Hochschild, for example, points out that in hierarchical societies the underdog is expected to provide more emotional gifts, such as sympathy, cheerfulness, gratitude, love, and joy in others' good fortune.[19] Those higher in social hierarchies are not only exempted from showering those lower with emotional gifts but are permitted to indulge emotions that are unpleasant for the recipient, such as anger, contempt, and disgust.[20] Others have pointed out that members of disesteemed social groups are socially constructed as having more emotional (and less rational) subjectivities. And because emotion is itself socially constructed as biological (rather than cultural), irrational or arational, and passively experienced (rather than actively done), the association between emotion and disesteemed social groups works to sustain the cultural devaluation of both.[21]

Although both observations apply to sexual social hierarchies, it is a third connection between emotions and social hierarchies that I want to pursue. Alison Jaggar argues that social hierarchies are maintained by outlawing some emotional responses on the part of members of disesteemed groups.[22] Outlaw emotions, in her view, are a particular kind of inappropriate emotion. Inappropriate emotions violate emotional scripts for the proper object and context of particular emotions.[23] Outlaw emotions violate emotional scripts in ways that challenge social hierarchies. Welfare recipients who feel resentment rather than gratitude at welfare payments, racial minorities who feel anger rather than amusement at racist jokes, and women who feel discomfort or fear rather than feeling flattered at male sexual banter all experience outlaw emotions.[24] These instances of resentment, anger, and fear challenge dominant perceptions of what is going on (for example, that welfare payments are a generous gift to the undeserving) and dominant values (for example, the unequal worth of poor persons' lives or their lack of entitlement to basic necessities). What makes these emotions threatening—and thus outlaw rather than merely inappropriate—is that there are enough conceptual resources to make the case that in fact resentment, anger, and fear are more appropriate responses than gratitude, amusement, and feeling flattered, even if the dominant cultural view is that they are inappropriate responses. Outlaw emotions presuppose, as Jaggar points out, at least the beginning of a critical social theory.[25] And the experience of outlaw emotions may lead members of subordinate groups "to make subversive observations that challenge dominant conceptions of the status quo."[26]

Elizabeth Spelman's use of the concept of outlaw emotions suggests a second kind of outlaw emotion. An emotion may be considered outlaw not because, according to dominant social views, one should not be feeling it; it may be outlaw because, according to dominant social views, one cannot be feeling it. And one cannot be feeling it because that emotion is not within the range of one's presumed emotional competency. Since the emotion is taken to be outside one's emotional competency, the most one will be entitled to claim to feel is a close cousin to, or simulacrum, of that emotion. Spelman claims that women's anger has historically fit this bill:

> [W]hile members of subordinate groups are expected to be emotional, indeed to have their emotions run their lives, their anger will not be tolerated: the possibility of their being angry will be excluded by the dominant group's profile of them. Women are expected to be easily given to sadness, say, or to jealousy . . . but anger is not appropriate in women, and anything resembling anger is likely to be redescribed as hysteria or rage instead.[27]

To recognize women's anger would be to recognize that women take themselves to be authorized to judge wrongdoing.

Just as not all inappropriate emotions are outlaw emotions, so too, not all attributions of emotional incompetencies involve outlawing an emotion. Our cultural understanding of young children's emotional, sexual, and intellectual abilities suggests that children lack the emotional competency to experience romantic love. At best, young children can experience the developmental precursors that are cousins or simulacra of romantic love—infatuation, puppy love, crushes. Childhood romantic love is not conceivable as an outlaw emotion because we don't have the conceptual resources for making any case at all that children really do have the capacity for mature romantic love and that the attribution of incompetency is politically motivated. But when those conceptual resources are on hand, a case can be made that in producing theories about a particular group's emotional incompetencies, the culture aims not to describe the group's emotional subjectivity but to proscribe an emotion whose occurrence threatens the status quo. Because, as I will argue in the next section, romantic love endows sex with a meaning and value beyond mere sex, to recognize gay and lesbian romantic love would be to recognize that gay and lesbian sex is not mere sex. In a culture committed to denigrating homosexuality and lesbianism, one would thus expect to find attempts to uncouple same-sex sex from romantic love. This, as I will argue in the third section, is exactly what one finds in psychoanalytic literature of the 1950s and '60s that imputed to gays and lesbians an emotional incompetency for romantic love.[^28]

II

Love, sex, and marriage are objects of knowledge. Our knowing them socially constructs them. By this rather odd claim, I mean the following: Whatever we claim to know about, for example, love—its nature, its healthy and unhealthy forms, who can experience it, and so on—will have to be defended by appeal to some evidence. The strongest supporting evidence is not a brute experiential fact but the coherence of what we say about love with other knowledges, for example, evolutionary theory, theories of psychological development and personality disorders, the history of judicial opinions, what counts as great literature, and theories about what is humanly and morally valuable.[^28] Our knowledges, however, might have been other than they are; indeed, they were different in earlier periods of our own history. The medieval period, for example, could know that ideal love is courtly love—a love to which inequality, the unattainability of the beloved, nonrequitedness, and chastity were central. We know that ideal love is romantic love. Our knowledges socially construct love.

In this section, my aim is simply to review what we culturally know about love, sex, and marriage by drawing on snippets of authorizing discourse from a variety of disciplines. In the next section, I aim, less innocently, to review psychoanalytic theorizing of the 1950s and '60s that authorized "knowing" that gays and lesbians lack the competence for romantic love. If these psychoanalytic descriptions of gay and lesbian emotional subjectivity no longer ring true, no longer seem clearly supportable by other things we know, then the reconstruction of same-sex sex, the emotional subjectivity of gays and lesbians, and their competence for marriage is in order.

Romantic Love

She knew, and all too well, that what she loved and did not have was . . . a special perfectness, an exact, nonrepeatable thing that could not be found again. There was a value and a knowledge that were inseparable from this particular relation. To try to recapture or replace them would be as futile as to go hunting for a joke after it has gone by. (Martha C. Nussbaum, "Love and the Individual: Romantic Rightness and Platonic Aspiration")[29]

In the case of falling in love, which is only one of a variety of scripts relevant to mating, these roles are temporary—the young couple typically 'recovers.' However, if the love-script follows its conventional course within our own culture, it will result in marriage, and a more permanent set of roles, that of husband and wife will ensue. (James Averill, "The Emotions)"[30]

[A] happy marriage reflects the shared perception of a couple that they have achieved a special goodness of fit between their individual needs, wishes, and expectations—a fit that they regard as unique and probably irreplaceable, and that enables them both to feel cherished, respected, and, in many instances, passionately loved throughout their adult lives. (Judith S. Wallerstein, "The Psychological Tasks of Marriage: Part 2")[31]

Romantic love depends on a particular worldview. People are unique, nonfungible individuals. They are also, in some sense, incomplete by themselves. Luckily, it is possible for individuals to find among all the other individuals a perfect match, a soul mate, someone with the right chemistry. Romantic love also operates on a worldview of extreme scarcity: there is only one Mr. or Miss Right; true love happens only once in a lifetime. That it will happen is also part of the worldview supporting romantic love. Somewhere out there, there is someone who is right for me. Because we are made and destined for each other, because matches are made in heaven, romantic love is also destined to happen. In short, romantic love rests on the view that the world is set up for couples. The right people will find each other, love will happen, and their perfection of fit will link them forever together.

Although the plot line of romantic movies ends on the promissory note of a blissful future, the real plot line of romantic love extends through years of marriage and parenting. Those who fall repeatedly in and out of love and those who get into marriage but don't stay there may be suspected of not having really found true love or of suffering some psychological handicap to loving.

The plot line of love also extends through romantic love's transformation into marital love. The third quote above comes from an article titled "The Psychological Tasks of Marriage." The title is instructive; so is the comment that happy couples have achieved a special goodness of fit. Premarital romantic love may be effortless and irresistible; marital love is work. Commitment, sexual fidelity, loyalty, building a marriage, and working things out replace magnetic attraction. Absent a link to romantic love, marital love might well seem too grim and unattractive. Faith that marital love originated in genuine romantic love, that the best (if not perfect) person has been found, and that romance might be recaptured makes marital emotional work worth doing—indeed, provides a central justification for there being duties to a marriage.

Sex and Marriage

Closely bound up with the overarching supraidentity of the marriage is the crucial third task—that of creating a loving sexual relationship and protecting it so that the excitement that first drew the couple together will endure. A good sex life, however it is defined by the couple, is at the very heart of a good marriage. The bedroom is a privileged place for lighthearted play, erotic pleasure, laughter, adventure, passion, acceptable aggression, and achieving, at long last, freedom from childhood taboos. (Judith S. Wallerstein, "The Psychological Tasks of Marriage: Part 2")[32]

Would we allow the police to search the sacred precincts of marital bedrooms for telltale signs of the use of contraceptives? . . . Marriage is a coming together for better or for worse, hopefully enduring, and intimate to the degree of being sacred. (Justice William O. Douglas, Griswold v. Connecticut)[33]

The union of the reproductive organs of husband and wife really unites them biologically (and their biological reality is part of, not merely an instrument of, their *personal* reality); reproduction is one function and so, in respect of that function, the spouses are indeed one reality and their sexual union therefore can *actualize* and allow them to *experience* their *real common good—their marriage*. . . . (John M. Finnis, "Law, Morality, and 'Sexual Orientation'")[34]

At one level, psychologist Judith Wallerstein and natural law theorist John Finnis have radically different takes on marital sex. The childhood taboos that Wallerstein celebrates being liberated from are, one might imagine, exactly the taboos Finnis would insist stay in place. But what interests me is what Wallerstein, Justice Douglas, and Finnis all know about sex: that it is extraordinarily important to marriage. Among the nine psychological tasks of marriage, Wallerstein ranks creating a good sex life third (preceded only by emotionally separating from one's family of origin and building togetherness). That Justice Douglas considers the marital bedroom sacred suggests that whatever sexual activity occurs within those precincts has similarly high status. And Finnis is quite clear that marital sex is not merely instrumentally valuable as a source of pleasure but actualizes the "marital good" and realizes the marital ideal of two persons in one flesh. Although Finnis, unlike Wallerstein, studiously avoids celebrating sexual pleasure and insists on preserving the natural law link between sex and procreation, he is nevertheless a far cry from Augustine, who approved only sex whose specific intention was reproduction and preferred even then that one not enjoy it.

What both Wallerstein and Finnis know about sex is that in marriage it is not mere sex. The romantic image of perfect fit echoes in both Wallerstein's and Finnis's paeans to marital sex. A loving sexual relationship is, for Wallerstein, "bound up with" the sense that the "We" of the couple has its own identity separate from that of the individuals. For Finnis, sex expresses marital unity and a perfect fit that extends down to the perfect fit of penis and vagina and the happy coincidence of sexual pleasure with reproduction. Romantic love transforms one's individual, lusty urge for gratification into an act of "self-giving," the "realization of two-in-one flesh," and an expression of commitment to and "communion" with another person.[35] Romantic love ennobles sex by endowing sex with a meaning that transcends the body. Romantic sexual love expresses one's own personality and communes with the personality of another. Romantic sexual love points beyond sex to hope for a lifetime of couplehood, sharing, mutual respect, concern for another person's happiness, companionship and solace, the cooperative building of a life together, and the responsibilities of parenthood.

What Wallerstein and Finnis both know about heterosexuals is that they are made for this kind of sex. Finnis's conviction is grounded in the biological fact that male and female reproductive organs are made to fit together and result in procreation. Biology fits heterosexuals for "intercourse between spouses in a marital way."[36] Because this sex that is not mere sex is the only truly natural form of sex, and because only heterosexuals can do it, Finnis relegates same-sex sex to the same status as solitary masturbation and deems it unworthy of human beings.[37] Though not sharing Finnis's natural law assumptions, Wallerstein, too, clearly takes it for granted that heterosexuals are made for sex that is not mere sex. Nothing about heterosexuals themselves makes task number three—creating a loving sexual relationship—difficult. The obstacles to loving sex are all external ones, such as the demands of work and parenting that cause couples to postpone coupling.

If heterosexuals are naturally fitted for sex that is not mere sex, then none of their sex is really mere sex. Even the most unromantic sex will always point beyond itself to what it might have been or could yet be. Through its location in an emotional subjectivity that is ripe for romantic sexual love, all heterosexual desire is ennobled.

III

Although there has been a continuous production of knowledges that stigmatize gays and lesbians since the late Victorian period, the content of those knowledges has not been continuous. Sexologists like Havelock Ellis and Richard von Krafft-Ebing, whose views dominated from, roughly, the 1880s through the 1920s, were far more interested in what they took to be the inevitable gender ambiguity of gays and lesbians than in same-sex sexuality.[38] Although they recognized the possibility of situational factors, like same-sex schools, producing homosexuality and lesbianism, they believed that true "inverts" were born that way. Homosexuality was a congenital condition causing gays and lesbians to be neither clearly men nor clearly women in physical appearance, temperament, or inclination (for example, for sports). They were, instead, men-women.

With the popularization of Freud and the rise of schools of psychoanalysis, beginning in the 1930s and reaching their peak in the 1950s, knowledge about gays and lesbians shifted from gender to sex. Psychoanalysts rejected both the sexologists' claim that gays and lesbians are markedly gender deviant and their claim that homosexuality and lesbianism are rooted solely in constitutional factors. Most also rejected Freud's normalizing view that everyone is naturally bisexual and that a cure of homosexuality should not be attempted unless the patient has failed to adjust to his homosexuality and wishes treatment. As Irving Bieber observes, "All psychoanalytic theories assume that adult homosexuality is psychopathologic."[39] Homosexuality and lesbianism originate in pathological childhood relationships with both parents that produce a variety of neurotic anxieties and fears that infect the entire personality. The first diagnostic manual of mental disorders, DSM-I, published in 1952, categorized homosexuality and lesbianism among sociopathic personality disturbances.

In 1968, with the publication of DSM-II, homosexuality and lesbianism were reclassified more modestly as sexual deviations, in the same league with fetishism, voyeurism, sadism, masochism, and pedophilia. But by

1968, knowledge about homosexuality and lesbianism had undergone profound change. Published one year before the Stonewall riots, DSM-II was immediately controversial both within and beyond psychiatric quarters.[40] As a result, in 1973, homosexuality and lesbianism were declassified. The 1980s and 1990s have been marked by the production of yet a third set of knowledges about homosexuality and lesbianism. Coinciding with a period of general cultural anxiety about the American family, the dominant stigmatizing description of homosexuality and lesbianism is now expressed neither in terms of congenital mental defect nor psychopathological disorder. Instead, homosexuality and lesbianism have come to represent a chosen, deviant lifestyle that, in Finnis's words, is "deeply hostile to the self-understanding of those members of the community who are willing to commit themselves to real marriage" and that poses "an active threat to the stability of existing and future marriages."[41]

What I want now to suggest is that the psychoanalytic account of homosexuality and lesbianism authorized the uncoupling of same-sex sex from romantic love, and thus from marriage. Because that account has long since ceased to be authoritative and has not been replaced with new knowledge that sufficiently explains the uncoupling of same-sex sex from romantic love, contemporary moral condemnations of gay and lesbian "pretend" marriages and families are virtually foundationless. Natural law theorists, like John Finnis, have attempted to supply the missing "knowledge." But their views, harkening back to a natural law tradition that is no longer a vibrant part of our cultural knowledge and entailing a condemnation of most varieties of heterosexual sex that conflicts with cultural knowledge of the value of (hetero)sexual pleasure, are unlikely to be able to authorize the continued social construction of loveless homosexuality.

The Psychiatric Construction of a Loveless Homosexuality

In 1962, Irving Bieber and his colleagues published the results of a nine-year study, begun in 1952, of 106 male homosexuals and 100 male heterosexuals who were undergoing psychoanalysis.[42] Conducted by the Research Committee of the Society of Medical Psychoanalysts, the study was based on questionnaires about patients under the care of seventy-seven psychoanalysts.

This study occurred at a critical juncture in the history of knowledge about homosexuality. In 1948, Alfred Kinsey and his colleagues had published their study revealing that 37 percent of men had had orgasmic same-sex sex.[43] During the 1950s and into the 1960s, Thomas Szasz ruthlessly critiqued the psychiatric profession for engaging in social control of unacceptable behavior under the guise of treating illness.[44] In 1957, Evelyn Hooker published her pathbreaking comparative study of homosexuals' versus heterosexuals' psychological adjustment, concluding that there were no significant differences between the two groups.[45] In the same year, Britain's Wolfenden Committee concluded that homosexuality appears to be compatible with full mental health, that whatever psychological problems homosexuals suffer are likely the consequence of social attitudes, and that reorientation is not evidently possible (all views that Bieber and his team reject).[46] Bieber self-consciously positions psychoanalysts' pathologizing view in opposition to these normalizing ones.[47] Three years after the Bieber study, Judd Marmor published Sexual Inversion, a work that collected in one volume the major parties to the dispute over the psychological abnormality versus normality of homosexuality (and, to a much lesser extent, lesbianism).[48] Marmor's own view was that psychiatry reflects the mores of the time and that it is culture, not nature, that renders a sexuality normal or abnormal.

Speaking both for his research team and for psychoanalysts generally, Bieber concluded, "We consider homosexuality to be a pathologic bio-social, psychosexual adaptation consequent to pervasive fears surrounding the expression of heterosexual impulses."[49] Bieber, however, was well aware that psychoanalysts differed over the intrafamilial mechanisms that produce homosexuality.[50] Bieber's own view was that mothers of homosexuals typically are "close-binding-intimate," overly protective, and emotionally engulfing women who are prone to babying their sons, who discourage both masculinity and heterosexual contact in their sons and who at the same time often behave seductively to them, overstimulating them sexually. The fathers of homosexuals, by contrast, tend to be distant, detached, and hostile men who deprive their sons of paternal affection and create a deep childhood fear of injury. The combined effect of this doubly pathological parental relationship is the creation of a neurotic personality. Male homosexuals come to fear heterosexuality (in part because heterosexuality raises anxieties about incest that derive from their mothers' sexually seductive attitudes toward them). They also fear female genitalia, have underdeveloped masculine attitudes, fail to form boyhood friendships from which they might learn masculine attitudes, long for paternal affection, become pathologically dependent, and suffer general feelings of unacceptability and inadequacy that manifest themselves in social snobbery and (much more so, in Bieber's view) the desire for a large penis.

Romantic love enters the picture at three points in Bieber's theory. Not only do typical parents of homosexual sons relate pathologically to their sons, they also relate pathologically to each other. Theirs is a distinctly unromantic marriage. They spend less time with each other than do parents of heterosexual sons, less frequently share each other's interests, and lack a mutuality of sympathy, acceptance, concern, and respect for each other.[51] The wife is typically the dominant spouse and is minimizing, indeed openly contemptuous, toward her husband.

Romantic love enters at a second point precisely because the parents' own marriage is so loveless. Finding their husbands deficient, mothers of homosexual sons attempt "to fulfill frustrated marital gratifications with the homosexual son. A 'romantic' attachment, short of actual physical contact (specifically, genital contact), was often acted out."[52]

Given the absence of a marital model of romantic love and the incestuous character of the son's earliest experience of being romantically loved, it would be no surprise if same-sex sexuality ended up uncoupled from romantic love. Indeed, that uncoupling turns out to be overdetermined. The entire emotional subjectivity of homosexuality, on Bieber's account, wars against any true capacity for romantic love. "Homosexual patients were found to be compulsively preoccupied with sexuality in general and with sexual practices in particular. In addition to providing sexual release and gratification, the homosexual relationship served to fulfill a range of *irrational defensive and reparative needs*."[53] Not only are gay men fixated on sex, what they want out of sex is not a romantic relationship but escape from the anxieties produced by heterosexual contact, the affection never received from father, and, above all, a large penis.[54] As evidence for sexual desire's overshadowing place in gay men's emotional subjectivity, Bieber observes that "homosexuals were more often excessively preoccupied with sexuality in childhood"[55] and "[s]ignificantly more homosexuals start sexual activity before adolescence than do heterosexuals and more homosexuals are more frequently sexually active during pre-adolescence, early adolescence, and adulthood."[56]

The third and primary point at which romantic love enters Bieber's story, then, is in the conclusion that adult gay men lack the capacity for romantic love and stable relationships. I will here quote Bieber and other psychoanalysts at length, since I take the "knowledge" they produced to be what uncoupled same-sex sex from love and what helps to explain the definitional impossibility of same-sex marriage.[57]

On Bieber's view, the capacity for romantic love develops from non-pathological parenting, particularly mothering that encourages boys' masculinity and fathering that is warm and not sexually competitive.

> This type of parental behavior fosters heterosexual development which in adult life is characterized by the ability to sustain a gratifying love relationship. Parents who are capable of sexually constructive attitudes to a child usually are individuals who are capable of a love relationship with each other and provide a stable and affectionate atmosphere in the home.[58]

> Lacking such parenting, gay men's attempts to do more than sexually couple inevitably end in failure given the crippling anxieties that plague their emotional subjectivities. Such twosomes are usually based on unrealistic expectations, often accompanied by inordinate demands; in most instances, these pairs are caught up in a turbulent, abrasive attachment. These liaisons are characterized by initial excitement which may include exaltation and confidence in the discovery of a great love which soon alternates with anxiety, rage, and depression as magical expectations are inevitably frustrated. Gratification of magical wishes is symbolically sought in homosexual activity which is intense in the early phase of a new "affair." These relationships are generally disrupted after a period of several months to a year or so; they are generally sought anew with another partner and the cycle starts again.[59]

Elaborating the same point, Bieber observes that the "warmth, friendship, concern for the other's welfare and happiness" that occur in both heterosexual and homosexual relationships are, for gay men, unsustainable.

> [I]n the homosexual pairing, hostile and competitive trends (overt and covert) often intrude to prevent a stable relationship with a partner. We found many homosexuals to be fearful, isolated, and anxious about masculinity and personal acceptability. Ambivalence leads to impermanence or transiency in most homosexual contacts. The inability to sustain a relationship frequently arises from an inability to bring social and sexual relations into a unity. This problem is well illustrated by the superficial and evanescent quality of social activities often carried on at bars and in "cruising."[60]

Bieber's teammate, Cornelia Wilbur, issues the same judgment about lesbian relationships:

> Female homosexual relationships are characterized by great ambivalence, by great longing for love, by intense elements of hostility, and by the presence of chronic anxiety. They do not contribute to the individual's need for stability and love.[61]

They cannot do so because the frequency of hostile eruptions, verbal and physical fighting, and general destructiveness within the relationships renders those relationships impermanent.[62]

That same-sex relationships are destructive and impermanent was not a view peculiar to the Research Committee. It was what psychoanalysts, generally, of the 1950s into the 1960s knew about same-sex relationships. May E. Romm, one of the clinicians contributing to Marmor's Sexual Inversion, observes of lesbians: "Perhaps because homosexuals are, at all times more at odds with themselves than are most heterosexuals, their reactions to their love partners are frequently supercharged. Jealousy among homosexuals is frequently violent, with paranoid coloring."[63]

Writing in the late 1960s, Charles Socarides, a psychotherapist equally as influential as Bieber and even more unsympathetic, condemned same-sex relationships for their "destruction, mutual defeat, exploitation of the partner and self, oral-sadistic incorporation, aggressive onslaughts, attempt to alleviate anxiety and a pseudo solution to the aggressive and libidinal urges."[64] For him, they clearly lack what heterosexual relationships have: "cooperation, solace, stimulation, enrichment, healthy challenge and fulfillment."[65]

Conclusion

The inconceivability of same-sex marriage has surely had many sources, among them the inability of same-sex partners to biologically reproduce. Psychoanalytic literature of the 1950s and '60s is, so far as I can see, the last authoritative attempt to articulate just what it is about same-sex relationships that makes gay and lesbian marriages inconceivable. They are inconceivable because gays and lesbians, on that view, lack the emotional competence for romantic love. Indeed, their emotional subjectivity is dominated by emotions—anxiety, fear, hostility, rage, jealousy—that actively war against loving, concerned, and respectful attitudes toward any partners whom they might find. Their sexual desires, as a result, cannot rise above a mere quest for gratification, a fact that is compounded by the obsessiveness of their sexual desires. Sexual obsession combined with inevitable hostility to their own partners undermines any chance that gays and lesbians could achieve the teleology of romantic love: permanent, stable partnership. Among such individuals the romantic image of perfect fit has no place because they are too defective and too self-absorbed with their own neurotic anxieties to have or recognize a destined other. Same-sex marriages could at best have only the external form of marriage (for example, fidelity and permanence, though both are unlikely). They could not enact the substance of marriage, since the substance is supplied by romantic love.

From a standpoint nearly forty years after the Research Committee's study, the politics of Bieber's theory are more transparent. Our psychological knowledge is the post-1973 knowledge that homosexuality and lesbianism are neither sociopathic personality disorders nor sexual deviancies. Our knowledge of heterosexual marriages includes knowledge of their high level of impermanence, of the exploitation of women in gender-inegalitarian marital arrangements, of the recent history of marital rape exemptions, of the prevalence of domestic and child abuse, and of the anxieties, jealousies, and insecurities that routinely get acted out in marriages. In the 1990s, the conceptual resources are at hand for making the case that psychoanalysts of the 1950s were not describing gay and lesbian emotional subjectivity but were instead outlawing same-sex romantic love by attributing an emotional incompetence for love to gays and lesbians in order to maintain the sexual status quo.

This is not to say that psychoanalytic descriptions of gays and lesbians as sexually obsessive, promiscuous, deviant, and sick have entirely lost their hold. Those descriptions echo in 1990s condemnations of homosexuality and in the Defense of Marriage Act's (DOMA's) proponents' insistence that real marriages (as opposed to same-sex simulacra) must be defended. But those descriptions are now unmoored from the authoritative "knowledge" that once anchored them. Invoking those descriptions is thus risky business. Congressman Gerry E. Studds, for example, observed that during the course of the DOMA debates, the words "promiscuity," "hedonism," "narcissism," and "perversion" had all been "thrown around," but entirely off the record.[66]

This returns me to my original question: Where does the depth of the conviction that definitional arguments are good ones come from—especially if the psychoanalytic theories that uncoupled same-sex sex from romantic love and that underwrote the inconceivability of real same-sex marriages are no longer authoritative? The divorce of sex from romantic love persists in the scripting of love, in theory production, in everyday discourse, and in our social practices. Even if our theories no longer tell us that two men or two women cannot fall in love, our greeting cards, films, novels, wedding rituals, and the like assume that they do not. Even if our theories no longer tell us that two men or two women cannot complete the "psychological tasks of marriage," the production of theories based solely on an investigation of heterosexual partners tacitly assumes that they cannot. Even if our theories no longer attribute sexual obsession to gay and lesbian subjectivity, "promiscuity" and "sexual perversion" remain staples of everyday discourse about gays and lesbians. Even if our theories no longer tell us why same-sex marriages are inconceivable, the same-sex marriage bar and the legal litany that marriage by definition means one man and one woman tell us they are.

In short, psychoanalytic discourse's attribution of emotional incompetency for romantic love now survives in the absence of cultural images, practices, and theories about gays' and lesbians' competency for romantic love. Absent an affirmative social construction of gay and lesbian romantic love, same-sex sex remains vulnerable to being interpreted as mere sex and the narratives of coupledom to being interpreted as drag performances.

Even if few of us have read studies like Bieber's, adults in the baby boom and earlier generations should find his descriptions familiar. Congressional opponents of DOMA were, I suspect, not entirely genuine in their expressions of puzzlement over how anyone could think that a mere definition of marriage could defend the institution of marriage.[67] We are recent inheritors of a worldview that in fact does make sense of the claim that permitting same-sex marriages threatens the institution of marriage. On that view, to recognize same-sex marriages would be to deny that romantic love is a necessary foundation to the tasks of marriage and that the ideals of perfect fit and permanence are necessary to marriage; it would affirm instead that "marriage" need only be founded on sexual obsession.

But we are also even more recent inheritors of the depathologizing of homosexuality in psychiatric discourse. To recognize same-sex marriages thus also signifies a different threat, namely, the threat of undermining sexual hierarchies by acknowledging that gays and lesbians are emotionally competent to experience romantic love. DOMA invoked not the authority of medicine but the authority of the law to outlaw romantic love.

NOTES

This chapter's title is a play on Ian Hacking's title "Making Up People," in Reconstructing Individualism: Autonomy, Individuality, and the Self in Western Thought, edited by Thomas C. Heller et al. (Stanford: Stanford University Press, 1986).

I thank my students Paul McDermott and Mike Cuzzi for their thoughtful conversation, good cheer, and generosity in reading and discussing with me a large chunk of the law review literature on the emotions.

1. James R. Averill, "The Emotions." In Personality: Basic Aspects and Cur-

rent Research, edited by Ervin Staub (Englewood Cliffs, N.J.: Prentice-Hall, 1980), p. 171.

2. Loving v. Virginia 388 US 1 (1967).

3. Baehr v. Lewin 852 P2d 44 (Haw. 1993).

4. Condemnation of homosexuality and defining marriage heterosexually have multiple sources. In "Family's Outlaws: Rethinking the Connections between Feminism, Lesbianism, and the Family," in Feminism and Families, edited by Hilde Nelson (New York: Routledge, 1996), I examine the historical construction of gays and lesbians from the 1880s on as unfit for family life.

5. Bowers v. Hardwick 478 US 186,191 (1985).

6. See, for example, the work of authors in this volume: Dan M. Kahan, "What Do Alternative Sanctions Mean?" University of Chicago Law Review 63(1996); Dan M. Kahan and Martha C. Nussbaum, "Two Concepts of Emotion in Criminal Law," Columbia Law Review 96(1996): 269–374; Jeffrie G. Murphy, "Moral Death: A Kantian Essay on Psychopathy," in Ethics and Personality, edited by John Deigh (Chicago: University of Chicago Press, 1992); Susan Bandes, "Empathy, Narrative, and Victim Impact Statements," University of Chicago Law Review 63(1996): 361–412; Samuel H. Pillsbury, "Emotional Justice: Moralizing the Passions of Criminal Punishment," Cornell Law Review 74(1989): 655–710.

7. Kahan and Nussbaum ("Two Concepts of Emotion") analyze the evaluative beliefs that supported the different legal treatment of murderous husbands. My claim here is that the law imputed a different emotional psychology to men.

8. Mary Ann Case points out that the couple is precisely what tends to drop out in legal reasoning about homosexuality even where one would most expect to find it—in sodomy cases. Mary Ann Case, "Couples and Coupling in the Public Sphere: A Comment on the Legal History of Litigating for Lesbian and Gay Rights," Virginia Law Review 79(1993): 1643–94. I make use throughout of Case's use of the dual meaning of "coupling."

9. On *amae*, see Averill, "The Emotions." On *acedia*, see Robert Finlay-Jones, "Accidie and Melancholy in a Clinical Context," in The Social Construction of Emotions, edited by Rom Harré (New York: Basil Blackwell, 1986).

10. See for example, Averill, "The Emotions"; Ronald de Sousa, "The Rationality of Emotions," in Explaining Emotions, edited by Amelie Oksenberg Rorty (Berkeley: University of California Press, 1980); Arlie Russell Hochschild, The Managed Heart (Berkeley: University of California Press, 1983).

11. Averill, "The Emotions," p. 146.

12. "Paradigm scenarios" is de Sousa's term ("The Rationality of Emotions").

13. Hochschild develops the concept of feeling rules at length in The Managed Heart, chapter four.

14. For a sustained defense of the claim that emotions are things we do, see Robert C. Solomon, "Emotions and Choice," in Explaining Emotions, edited by Amelie Oksenberg Rorty (Berkeley: University of California Press, 1980).

15. Averill, "The Emotions," pp. 169–70.

16. The compelling depiction of romantic falling in love in the film The Incredibly True Story of Two Girls in Love is one of the few exceptions that proves the rule.

17. Case, "Couples and Coupling in the Public Sphere," p. 1664, including footnotes 87 and 89. This vulnerability to being read as drag is one of the reasons that legal counternarratives of same-sex "marital" relations are not guaranteed to have the desired effect of establishing the identity of same-sex and heterosexual loving relationships.

18. See, for example, Catherine Lutz, "Emotion, Thought, and Estrangement: Emotion as a Cultural Category," Cultural Anthropology 1(1986): 287–309; Elizabeth V. Spelman, "Anger and Insubordination," in Women, Knowledge and Reality, edited by Ann Garry and Marilyn Pearsall (Boston: Unwin Hyman, 1989); Alison Jaggar, "Love and Knowledge: Emotion in Feminist Epistemology," in Women, Knowledge, and Reality; and Hochschild, The Managed Heart.

19. Hochschild, The Managed Heart, pp. 84–85.

20. See William Ian Miller, "Upward Contempt," in his The Anatomy of Disgust (Cambridge: Harvard University Press, 1997).

21. See, for example, Lutz, "Emotion, Thought, and Estrangement."

22. Jaggar, "Love and Knowledge."

23. They can't, of course, violate the emotional script too thoroughly. An emotional experience that thoroughly violates the script for anger, say, would not be interpretable as anger at all.

24. Jaggar, "Love and Knowledge," p. 144.

25. Ibid. p. 145.

26. Ibid.

27. Spelman, "Anger and Insubordination," p. 264.

28. Lynn Hankinson Nelson explicates the sort of social constructionist account of knowledge on which I rely in "Epistemological Communities," in Feminist Epistemologies, edited by Linda Alcoff and Elizabeth Potter (New York: Routledge, 1993). Her example of the way that knowledge of the proton depends on a larger set of theories is especially helpful (pp. 135–38).

29. In Reconstructing Individualism, edited by Thomas C. Heller et al. (Stanford: Stanford University Press, 1986), p. 260.

30. In Reconstructing Individualism, edited by Thomas C. Heller et al. (Stanford: Stanford University Press, 1986), p. 153.

31. American Journal of Orthopsychiatry 66(1996): 217–27, p. 226.

32. Ibid., p. 223.

33. 381 US 479, 485–86 (1965).

34. Notre Dame Journal of Law, Ethics, and Public Policy 9(1995): 11–39, p. 28, italics in original.

35. Ibid., pp. 27, 30, 31.

36. Ibid., p. 29.

37. Ibid, p. 25.

38. Havelock Ellis, Studies in the Psychology of Sex, Vol. II: Sexual Inversion (1928). Richard von Krafft-Ebing, Psychopathia Sexualis: A Medico-Forensic Study (1947).

39. Irving Bieber et al., Homosexuality: A Psychoanalytic Study (New York: Basic Books, 1962), p. 18.

40. Ronald Bayer, Homosexuality and American Psychiatry: The Politics of Diagnosis (Princeton: Princeton University Press, 1987), pp. 39–40.

41. Finnis, "Law, Morality, and 'Sexual Orientation,'" p. 32.

42. Bieber, Homosexuality.

43. Alfred Kinsey, W. B. Pomeroy, and P. H. Gebhard, Sexual Behavior in the Human Male (Philadelphia: Saunders, 1948).

44. See, for example, Thomas Szasz, The Myth of Mental Illness (New York: Hoeber Harper, 1961), and "Legal and Moral Aspects of Homosexuality" in Sexual Inversion, edited by Judd Marmor (New York: Basic Books, 1965).

45. Evelyn Hooker, "The Adjustment of the Male Overt Homosexual," Journal of Projective Techniques 21(1957): 18–31.

46. This is Bieber's own description of the Wolfenden Report, Homosexuality, p. 15.

47. See especially Bieber's introduction to Homosexuality.

48. Judd Marmor, Sexual Inversion: The Multiple Roots of Homosexuality (New York: Basic Books, 1965).

49. Bieber, Homosexuality, p. 221.

50. See Bieber's introduction for a summary of then-current psychoanalytic explanations. For a summary of explanations of the origins of lesbianism, see Cornelia B. Wilbur's "Clinical Aspects of Female Homosexuality," in Marmor, Sexual Inversion.

51. Bieber, Homosexuality, p. 146.

52. Ibid., p. 313.

53. Ibid., p. 252, italics in original.

54. The previous quote continues with stunning passion: "It is irrational to seek feminine qualities in a male sexual partner; it is irrational to endow a large penis with special value; it is irrational for a person restricted by sexual inhibitions to believe that inhibitions can be ameliorated by contact with a large penis; it is pathologic to endow a large penis with magical, symbolic power."

55. Ibid., p. 193.

56. Ibid., p. 189.

57. This is not the only explanation, since there are multiple vectors that legitimate (or have in the past legitimated) the definitional impossibility of same-sex marriage. For a critical discussion of the natural law tradition, see Andrew Koppelman, "Is Marriage Inherently Heterosexual?" 42 American Journal of Jurisprudence 51 (1997).

58. Ibid., p. 313.

59. Ibid., p. 317.

60. Ibid., p. 253.

61. Wilbur, "Clinical Aspects of Female Homosexuality," in Sexual Inversion, p. 281.

62. Ibid, p. 279.

63. May E. Romm, "Sexuality and Homosexuality in Women," in Sexual Inversion, p. 297.

64. Quoted in Bayer, Homosexuality and American Psychiatry, p. 36.

65. Ibid.

66. Congressional Record, vol. 142, no. 103, July 12, 1996, p. H7491.

67. They suggested instead that reducing alcoholism and domestic abuse, raising the minimum wage, and providing health care benefits might be better strategies.

Chapter Nine

Fear, Weak Legs, and Running Away
A Soldier's Story

William Ian Miller

Statutes make for appallingly tedious reading unless primitively short and to the point as, for example, this provision in the early Kentish laws of Æthelberht (c. 600): "He who smashes a chin bone [of another] shall pay 20 shillings" or this one from King Alfred (c. 890): "If anyone utters a public slander, and it is proved against him, he shall make no lighter amends than the carving out of his tongue."[1] Yet on very rare occasion a modern statute can rivet our attention and when it does, it seems to do so by mimicking some of the look and feel of legislation enacted in less lawyer-ridden times. Consider the statute presently codified in the United States Code as part of the Uniform Code of Military Justice:

Misbehavior before the enemy
Any member of the armed forces who before or in the presence of the enemy—

(1) runs away;

(2) shamefully abandons, surrenders, or delivers up any command, unit, place, or military property which it is his duty to defend;

(3) through disobedience, neglect, or intentional misconduct endangers the safety of any such command, unit, place, or military property;

(4) casts away his arms or ammunition;

(5) is guilty of cowardly conduct;

(6) quits his place of duty to plunder or pillage;

(7) causes false alarms in any command, unit, or place under control of the armed forces;

(8) willfully fails to do his utmost to encounter, engage, capture, or destroy any enemy troops, combatants, vessels, aircraft, or any other thing, which it is his duty so to encounter, engage, capture, or destroy;

(9) does not afford all practicable relief and assistance to any troops, combatants, vessels or aircraft of the armed forces . . . when engaged in battle; shall be punished by death or such other punishment as a court-martial may direct.[2]

Making cowardice a capital offense strikes us as a kind of barbaric survival from a rougher age, a time, that is, when few doubted that courage ranked higher than pity or prudence in the scale of virtues. And if many of us today believe that capital punishment cannot be justified even for the sadistic torturer, what a shock to discover that, as an official matter at least, Congress reserves it for the person who cannot kill at all. Not to worry: although the state has the power and right to execute those who misbehave before the enemy, we are too unsure of ourselves, or maybe even too charitable, to enforce the statute maximally. We have done so but once since 1865 when Private Eddie Slovik was executed by firing squad "pour encourager les autres" in the bleak Hürtigen Forest of 1945.[3] Still, even if only by inertia, we have preserved the option.

Quite independent of the grimness of its sanctions, the statute prompts our attention because of its strangely absurdist quality. Most of its provisions seem merely to restate one another. What, for instance, is running away (1) that isn't also cowardly conduct (5)? And aren't paragraphs 2 and 8, the one covering the shamefulness of cowardice on defense, the other governing slacking off on offense, really special cases of cowardly conduct punished in 5? Paragraph 7 goes so far as to make jitteriness a capital offense to the extent one's nerves lead one to overinterpret causes for alarm, while paragraph 3, in contrast, authorizes putting the sleeping sentry before the firing squad apparently because he is not jittery enough even to stay awake.

There is also the statute's strange relation with fear. All law must pay homage to fear, for if the law does not succeed in nurturing the passions that will make it self-enforcing, such as a sense of duty or a special reverence for the law as law, it must have recourse to fear, the passion that underwrites all coercive law—fear of punishment or the fear of the shame of being execrated as a lawbreaker. But this statute places fear at its substantive core, for it is fear-impelled action that it mostly seeks to regulate.

Only paragraph 6—the stricture against looting—cares nothing about fear, not even the fear that you and your raping and pillaging comrades inspire in the enemies' civilian population as you quit your proper place to plunder. Like the other provisions, the antilooting provision is devoted to maintaining the delicate balance of forces that keep armies behaving as armies rather than as crowds. At times that balance is as susceptible to being undone by routing the enemy as by being routed by him. Success can be as disordering as failure.[4] The initial success of the German offensive on the western front in 1918 was stopped as much by the German soldiers stumbling upon stores of wine and cognac as by Allied resistance. But the weight of these strictures shows that loss of discipline and order bred by greed, cruelty, lust, and other manifestations of exultant riot is of significantly less concern than the loss of discipline bred by fear, slackness, and failure of nerve. Narrow self-interest in the exuberantly acquisitive style of the looter is just not as worrisome to an army as narrow self-interest in the life-preserving style of the coward. Fearfulness, not lust or gluttony, counts as a soldier's first sin.

There lurk in this strange statute various attempts at a theory of the moral and legal economy of courage, cowardice, duty, and fear in the context of the demands a polity, in this case the American polity, makes upon its combat soldiers. The exposition that follows, structured mostly as a gloss on the various provisions of the statute, seeks to reveal the features of that economy.

Running Away

Isn't running away, punished in paragraph 1, running like hell for the rear, precisely how we quintessentialize cowardice (punished in paragraph 5), just as casting away arms (punished in paragraph 4) so you could run away faster was how Plato and Aristotle quintessentialized it?[5] In fact, the very vividness of the image of running away has led some defendants to prefer being charged with the vaguer and more abstract cowardice under paragraph 5, considering it less prejudicial than an accusation of running away.[6] But statutory provisions that to the normal eye look duplicative will inspire interpreters to invent differentiating glosses, just as language itself, though needing all kinds of structural and particular redundancies, never quite allows a perfect synonym. So paragraph 5—cowardice—was read to require a showing of fear as a necessary element of the offense.[7] Cowardice had to be motivated by fear or it was not cowardice, but running away, it was decided, did not need to be so motivated. This strikes normal people, nonlawyers, that is, as somewhat perverse. Why else would anyone flee battle, run away, if not in panic, terror, or out of simpler fears of death and mayhem?

The military judges are often at a loss to give running away a meaning that can distinguish it from cowardice. One military court, which then became the final word on the subject, made this desperate attempt:

> This term [runs away] must connote some form of fleeing from an ensuing or impending battle. . . . [I]t appears that to limit the phrase to flight from fear or cowardice is too restricted. It would appear to be more in keeping with the offense, if an intent to avoid combat, with its attending hazards and dangers is considered as an essential part of running away.[8]

Running away is made a catchall for whatever motives other than fear might impel turning tail in battle. And what might these motives be? One could, I suppose, run away out of treachery, or out of love, or out of the most calculating thin-lipped prudence.[9] But the narrative suggested by each one of these motives seems incomplete without complementing them with fear. The most psychologically plausible motive for running away that dispenses with fear is fleeing in disgust, sick at being stuck in a situation where so much is asked of you and so little given you in return; not fear, but the feeling of being ripped off, revolted by unfairness and injustice. But one does not "run away" in this setting; the image is wrong, even the notion of "fleeing" misrepresents the insolence, even the fearlessness, with which one walks, sullenly saunters, or shuffles but manifestly does not run away, while muttering "f-k this."

But the court doesn't offer us a picture of sullen withdrawal. Still desperate, it turns to Winthrop's Military Law and Precedents, where Winthrop too evinces bafflement, and in good legal form provides authority for his bafflement by citing an older writer who was discussing something not precisely on point:

> RUNNING AWAY. This is merely a form of misbehavior before the enemy, and the words "runs away" might well be omitted from the Article as surplusage. Barker, an old writer cited by Samuel, says of this offense:—"But here it is to be noted that of fleeing there be two sorts; the one proceeding of a sudden and unlooked for terror, which is least blameable; the other is voluntary, and, as it were, a determinate intention to give place unto the enemy—a fault exceeding foule and not excusable."[10]

The court citing Winthrop citing Samuel citing Barker[11] hopes for some clarification in Barker's distinguishing between two types of fleeing, one in panic, which is excused as being so suddenly induced as to be largely involuntary,[12] whereas running away is calculated treachery, self-serving, and, by one view, a manifestation of narrowly construed interested prudence.

Panic, one suspects, is treated more generously because it is impractical to do otherwise. It usually involves large numbers in headlong flight and however harmful its consequences, it hardly makes sense to hand over the entire army to a firing squad. Barker's distinction between exceeding foule voluntary flight and less voluntary panicked flight follows immediately upon his discussion of Roman decimation. His association of ideas suggests that decimation might be suitable for generalized panic-propelled fleeing, but that fully individualized punishment, rated at 1.0 probability rather than at the 0.1 discounted group rate, be meted out to the voluntary calculator of his own immediate best interests.

No wonder prudence is such a suspect virtue in the extreme setting of combat, for in battle the prudence that qualifies as a virtue is not the prudence of each individual figuring out the wisest course for himself to pursue but the prudence of strategy and tactic at the level of the group. And what is prudence for the group often demands that the individuals that compose the group forgo more personalized prudence and opt instead for duty, heroism, honor, and glory, which provide them some kind of moral compensation for having the misfortune of being sacrificed for the greater good. Individualized prudence, we suspect, is too easily used to provide a serviceable gloss for cowardice. Cowardice, however, is not only about panic and no cases suggest that it is, the use to which Barker was put to notwithstanding.

A prosecution brought under paragraph 5, cowardly conduct, must show, as noted, that the conduct was motivated by fear. This is one of the few areas in the law where the decision maker is asked actually to find that the person was motivated by a particular passion, not just to find that the person was in the sway of some generalized powerful passion. How do we recognize that another was moved by fear? Do certain bodily clues give him away? Was he pale, did he tremble, sweat, shed tears, urinate or defecate in his pants? Few somatic indicators—facial expressions, blanchings, flushings, shakings—are unique to fear. We sweat from heat, shed tears in joy, grief, and merely from the cold. The most lethal saga hero of ancient Iceland grew pale in anger, not in fear. Montaigne observes that both "extreme cowardice and extreme bravery disturb the stomach and are laxative. The nickname 'The Trembler' given to King Sancho XII [he means actually his son Garcia V] of Navarre serves as a reminder that boldness can make your limbs shake just as much as fear."[13] Dysentery can cause us to befoul ourselves. And the fear of getting caught with one's pants down often leads the soldier, at least in the trenches of World War I, to become desperately constipated.[14] Fear does have a distinctive facial expression, but we can be in fear's desperate grip without looking like we are. Not only can the expression be suppressed when one is scared, but it can be faked when one is not scared.

This is not earth-shattering news. State of mind always ends up being inferred either by legal convention or by supplying the social knowledge necessary to make sense of whatever act or omission whose motivation we are searching for. If he trembles and runs away, or cries while curled up in a fetal position and hence cannot advance, then we judge that behavior to be a consequence of fear. And what about the specific feeling that we usually recognize to be fear? Do all fears have the same feeling? It is not clear that they do. Can we properly describe someone as motivated by fear if he runs away from obvious danger as if he were afraid, but who claims to have felt no inner surge, no grip in the gut, no sensation, that is, that most of us recognize as an accompanier of fear if not fear itself?

Gentle Offense versus Craven Defense

Fear has been read in as an element only in the specific charge of cowardice in paragraph 5. But it is also the psychological and social Éminence grise in other provisions. Paragraph 2 deals with the shameful abandonment or surrender of men, a position, or material; paragraph 8 deals with the willful failure to do one's utmost to encounter the enemy. Paragraph 8 can be seen as the failure to give cause to the enemy to violate their version of paragraph 2; that is, the most desired outcome of your aggressive moves is to cause the enemy to abandon shamefully what is its duty to defend. The "shamefully" explicitly makes this a moral issue, as well as a legal one. And that is quite fitting, for the goal of battle, as John Keegan has noted, is to bring about the moral collapse of your opponent, for battle is in the end always something of a moral contest, a matter of matching how character confronts demands of duty to perform dangerous action in the face of overwhelming desires to flee or quit, in the face of the instinct of self-preservation itself.[15]

Keegan's moral contest is bounded so as to make no distinction between the different moral and psychological claims made on the defender and the attacker. For him, this contest of character is, with due allowances for heroic failure, a matter of who, to borrow an image from Anglo-Saxon verse, controls the slaughter-place at the end of the day. Our statute, however, makes such a distinction. Paragraph 2 involves the kind of mettle needed to defend properly, paragraph 8 the kind needed to offend or attack. And although we understand failures under each provision to involve cowardice, it is not clear that these cowardices carry the same moral weight or are understood in quite the same way.

Courage on defense seems to demand a different mix of virtues and talents than courage on offense, and it may be that cowardice also varies with the different styles of courage demanded. We can, I think, imagine someone who is perfectly courageous when attacked, who will not flee, who will even die before abandoning the fight, who at the same time does not have the ability to initiate violence, who, if not quite a mass of quivering jelly, may tend to find too many reasons, with all the trappings of an admirable prudence, as to why it would not be in anyone's best interests to go over the top: a slacker. A person constituted like this would not strike us as a psychological impossibility. In fact U. S. Grant complained that such was exactly the problem with one of his generals—G. K. Warren: Warren was able to see "every danger at a glance," too many dangers apparently, and he delayed moving until he had made exacting preparations for each of them with the result that he never got to his appointed place in time to coordinate with others. But still "there was no officer more capable, nor one more prompt in acting, than Warren *when the enemy forced him to it*" (emphasis supplied).[16] Nor is the obverse unimaginable: someone brave in the attack but cowardly in defense. Some have suggested that this describes Mike Tyson's moral failure in his fights with Evander Holyfield, who, when his offensive ominous aggressiveness failed to cow the opponent, either folded sullenly or folded violently, but in such a way that announced he was quitting the field. Aristotle may have had such a type in mind in his rather implausible portrait of the rash man, who turns cowardly the moment he experiences any real resistance.[17]

Let me turn now to another matter. Consider this remarkable account from Abner Small, a Union officer, recalling the battle at Fredericksburg:

> I wondered then, and I wonder now equally, at the mystery of bravery. It seemed to me, as I saw men facing death at Fredericksburg, that they were heroes or cowards in spite of themselves. In the charge I saw one soldier falter repeatedly, bowing as if before a hurricane. He would gather himself together, gain his place in the ranks, and again drop behind. Once or twice he fell to his knees, and at last he sank to the ground, still gripping his musket and bowing his head. I lifted him to his feet and said, "Coward!" It was cruel, it was wicked; but I failed to notice his almost agonized effort to command

himself. I repeated the bitter word, "Coward!" His pale, distorted face flamed. He flung at me, "You lie!" Yet he didn't move; he couldn't; his legs would not obey him. I left him there in the mud. Soon after the battle he came to me with tears in his eyes and said, "Adjutant, pardon me, I couldn't go on; but I'm not a coward." Pardon him! I asked his forgiveness.[18]

Grand stuff this: the penitent self-understanding and the moral courage of the author, an officer, to beg forgiveness of one of his men. In another register this is an account of weak legs and the moral ambiguity of such cases. The spirit was willing, but the flesh was weak. The soldier's body just would not respond to the total dedication of his will to do the right thing, to go forward. If we decide the legs are blameworthy, but not the will, we, like Mr. Small, will be inclined to beg pardon of the soldier for calling him "Coward"; if we blame the will for not being able to overcome the fear that has turned his legs to jelly, then we too might call him "Coward."

By one account the soldier's body was completely overborne by fear, but his own perception was of having all the right feelings, the right motives, with his fear subdued or overcome if felt at all, only to be betrayed by a body that was an enemy to his good name, a rebel to his will. If we are likely to see him as fearful without the consciousness of his own fearfulness, he, instead, sees himself as fearless with a body mocking him by producing unmotivated fear symptoms. So he disowns his legs. How, though, are we to understand his weak legs?[19] Without a convincing account of mind and body, emotion and body, we do not know how to apportion blame as between body and soul. And we are not confident of how to make the call. Is this a peculiarly male form of hysteria? Do weak legs support a theory of unconscious emotions, or at least of unconscious fear?[20] Or are we talking about a much more primitive central nervous system ur-emotion? Do we see instead a conscious refusal of the soldier to recognize his true emotional state, whether we understand the refusal's mechanism to work by means of classic forms of self-deception or wishful thinking or by a process more akin to repression? And how do such tricks of consciousness fit in with William James's scheme in which the consciousness of one's emotional state is the awareness of changes in one's somatic state, that is, we are afraid because we tremble and our legs give way, rather than that we tremble and suffer weak legs because we are afraid? What if the refusal to admit fear is simply a refusal to take note of our body at all? Are we then fearing? Or fearing fear? Or simply falling apart at the seams? But then might not the soldier know he fears but what he means to indicate is that he does not ratify his fear; he means to move on in spite of it and is desperately ashamed that an undesired desire for safety is causing his body to defeat his desired desire to move forward? He does not, after all, will the various appraisals and beliefs that constitute fear; he need only look and listen and know where he is and what he is up to to have a more than reasonable serious apprehension for his safety.

Mr. Small's own psychological theory varies with the exigencies of the setting and no doubt ours would too. In the heat of battle Small was not as willing to be generously disposed toward the shaken soldier as he was upon reflection afterward and upon the soldier's poignant showing of his lack of shamelessness. Not only does the soldier shed tears of frustration, contrition, and shame, but he also responds to his officer's accusation as a man of honor would: he gives Small the lie, exactly the traditional manly challenge to a duel upon an accusation of cowardice. The poor man means well in the aftermath and our own and Small's lack of certainty as to the psychological and physiological components of weak legs make us incline toward lenity and thus believe he meant well on the field of battle too. And the statute follows Small and us in a small way.

If cowardice on offense runs into the moral and legal uncertainty of how to treat a case of weak legs, it at least gives us a hint that it was precisely this kind of case the statute had in its allegorical mind. Hence the demand of willful failure, not shameful failure, as in paragraph 2. The weak-legged attacker is given some small concession. He must will his legs' weakness to be culpable and so it seems our soldier may well be spared the firing squad. Nonetheless, cases of unwilled weak legs might still be shameful, as indeed our soldier desperately feared. Shame, unlike guilt, is felt not only for our voluntary failures but for what we happen to be, as the infirm, ugly, old, black, Jew, or weak-legged soldier can often attest. If he just can't help his weak legs, he may still be in the martial world a coward, but in the more nuanced judgment of one Civil War soldier, "a good coward," one at least who showed up for every battle and looked for no excuses to absent himself from it ahead of time.[21]

Cowardice on defense seems more craven than cowardice on offense. Our image is of begging not to be killed, turning tail and running, or simply despairing and not just not fighting, as on offense, but not fighting back. Failure under each provision, paragraph 2 or 8, is cowardly, and hence shameful, but only one offender, the miscreant defender, is branded shameful. Why the difference? There are several possible reasons. One involves the different stakes between losing as a defender and not measuring up as an aggressor. In the paradigm case we understand that the failure to defend means losing all; whereas the weakness on offense means you go home with your tail between your legs. But there is a home to return to. We are all expected to defend what is ours, our property and our loved ones. Consider too the almost ridiculous obviousness of this statement: the moral demand to defend to the utmost is greater than the moral demand to attack or aggress to the utmost. Even in aggressive honor-based cultures that is true. However fearful you are, you must defend, but no one expects everyone to volunteer to be the forlorn hope, the first through the breach in the wall. And as a psychological matter, we tend to find losses of what is already ours much more grievous than failures to acquire an equivalent amount of what is not ours.

The defender doesn't have the same kinds of choices the aggressor has or as many, for the latter is the moving party. It is aggressors who get to choose the timing, and even to determine that the battle will be on your turf rather than mine. The defender has no choice but to resist, even though he has some choices about how to carry this out: sometimes he must fight pitched battles, but other options are available, as long as they are understood to be forms of resistance. The Russians, for instance, have let the vastness of their land defeat its invaders until it was safe to assume an offensive posture; others have worn their attackers down with pesky gnatlike resistance, as Fabius did to Hannibal. But we should also note that Fabius had to muster great reserves of moral courage to persevere in the face of being thought cowardly by his countrymen for not engaging more aggressively.[22] Gnatlike resistance, though effective in the end, may in certain warrior cultures not look "manly" enough to preempt accusations of poltroonery. The prudent warrior must always endure suspect glances and innuendoes about his fearfulness and lack of nerve. The statute may capture some little bit of that mistrust of the good faith of justifications for retreat and surrender, holding the defender of hearth and home to a higher moral standard than the weak-legged attacker. The paradigm we see embedded in the statute—of invading aggressor versus the defenders of the homeland—grants the attacker other options; it even allows him to plead weak legs from time to time, but the defenders' legs must stand firm. And maybe too we seem to feel that we have more right to ask legs to stand still than to move forward, by which ruse we simply restate the differing moral stakes in not defending as opposed to not offending.

Throwing Away One's Weapons

The prescription against casting aside one's arms has a rich and long tradition. It is a triumph of a certain dunderheaded literalism that often characterizes law and the legal imagination that this provision, paragraph 4, wouldn't be understood to be implicit in paragraphs 1 (running away), 2 (shameful abandonment of a position), or 5 (cowardice), but especially 1. Running away, except as perversely understood by the military courts, and casting away one's weapons, as I noted earlier, are both meant to capture the quintessence of martial cowardice: headlong panicked, *sauve-qui-peut* flight:

> Well, what if some barbaric Thracian glories
> in the perfect shield I left under a bush?
> I was sorry to leave it—but I saved my skin.
> Does it matter? O hell, I'll buy a better one.[23]

The comic energy of Archilochus's little song is parasitical on the power of the norms he so gleefully confesses to violating. The wit of such self-mockery, at such brazen shamelessness, is possible only because the norm against running away and debarrassing oneself of one's burdensome weapons demands some kind of psychic homage even when not adhered to.[24] But there is another kind of heroic inversion that takes place here. To be this cheerfully a coward in a warrior culture may itself mimic courage: such unapologetic shamelessness requires a certain kind of fearlessness, as Aristotle recognized.[25] This is the fearlessness that informs what we might vulgarly call the "I-don't-give-a-shit-what-they-think" attitude in matters touching upon reputation, an attitude as unfathomable to most of us as is the berserk courage of the kind that we associate with Alexander the Great. In keeping with his perversely inverted courage Archilochus refuses even to allege fear as the reason for casting away his weapons. It is all a matter of rational choice. His weapons, as he observes, are completely replaceable, something that he is quite pleased to believe is not the case with himself. And although Archilochus knows he will have to fight again (that is one of the risks that running away does not completely resolve unless he is capitally punished for it), there is not the least hint he will do better next time.

Archilochus's wit also reveals that virtue funds a powerful comedic impulse dedicated to deflating virtue's own pretentiousness and goody-two-shoes piety. Archilochus's comedy celebrates a life-affirming world of very unrigorous virtue, what somber professors of virtue might even call vice. Life-affirming affability, as unrigorous a virtue as we might find, is not a trait we think of as likely to describe the hero as it does the amiable hedonist, who means well and even does well as long as life or limb are not at stake, who prefers to keep fear safely relegated to worries about whether the sauce is sufficiently piquant to satisfy his guest's palate. Yet unlike the other cardinal and theological virtues, courage thrives in certain restricted comedic veins. It is not just the butt of the comedic; in some cultural settings the heroic style means to be funny with the nasty in-your-face mordancy of gallows humor. Here the mockery is not directed against the virtue of courage at all but against all arguments that would undermine it, such as life itself.

With Archilochus compare the keen comedic eye of this Confederate soldier running away to beat hell at Sharpsburg:

> Oh, how I ran! Or tried to run through the high corn, for my heavy belt and cartridge box and musket kept me back to half my speed. I was afraid of being struck in the back, and I frequently turned half around in running, so as to avoid if possible so disgraceful a wound. It never entered my head to throw away gun or cartridge box; but, encumbered as I was, I endeavored to keep pace with my captain, who with his long legs and unencumbered would in a little while have far outstripped me but that he frequently turned towards the enemy, and, running backwards, managed not to come out ahead in this our anything but creditable race.[26]

John Dooley, our soldier, runs his anything but creditable race desperately aware of the comedy of trying to maintain the appearance of honor in headlong retreat: don't get shot in the back if you can help it and don't throw away your arms, although you realize that they have less than zero value to you now, pure dead weight. Dooley is a wit after a fashion. He is not unaware of a kind of double competition with his captain, one to see who can get away the fastest and the other to see who can get away the slowest. He envies his captain's benefits of rank: no pack, they are in a wagon somewhere, and no rifle. By this time the weapons of officers are becoming symbolic indicia of rank, like the pistols, whistles, and walking stick of the British officers who led their men into no-man's-land in the Great War. The ambivalence in the account and in the action itself gives the comedy multiple layers.

The heroic ideal of standing your ground at all costs turns out to give way before fear, and not an altogether irrational fear, though as in Archilochus the fear is not mentioned directly but supplied by the comic action. Both John Dooley and his captain are still giving respect to the norms they are not quite living up to by adhering to some of their forms: John will not throw away his gun or ammunition, though he is sorely tempted, and both he and his captain engage in the comedy of trying to prevent the ignominy of being shot in the back by running backwards every now and then. Comedy, we see, can be called to the rescue of heroic, even if it must mock it rather roundly while saving appearances.

It is the comic voice with its almost self-delighting self-mockery that indicates this is not culpable cowardice. The comedy is probably the surest sign that Dooley and Archilochus are not alone in flight. The whole army is in what might be generously called a retreat, a rather indecorous one at that. This is a pure case of running away to live to fight another day as long, that is, as they do not throw their weapons away. Dooley's attempts to maintain the forms of honor indicate quite well that he means to be back. Even Archilochus means to return with his new shield, but by throwing his old one away he committed an offense that Dooley may have wanted to commit, but his implicit contest with his captain to see who could minimize their mutual dishonor kept him honest. Archilochus, however, does more than just disarm himself, he arms the opposition.

From the military's point of view casting aside arms is a very serious matter. It renders the soldier useless; it arms the opposition, and in societies in which the work and material that was congealed into the weapon represented the most valuable objects in the culture, throwing away weapons was culpable waste, even sacrilege. But nonmilitary moralists take a kindlier view: Aquinas was willing to find the soldier who cast away his shield less sinful than the licentious man, because "grave fear and sorrow especially in dangers of death, stun the human mind, but not so pleasure which is the motive of intemperance."[27] But Thomas might also be underestimating the deliberative capacity of the weapon dropper. Dooley deliberately refrained from casting his aside; others might deliberately do so, for they might reason that an unarmed man might look like a noncombatant and thus fade by degrees into a general population.[28]

False Alarms

Paragraph 7 punishes capitally the person who causes false alarms and it must be seen as the companion of paragraph 3, which punishes the person who "through disobedience [or] neglect endangers the safety of command, unit, [or] place." One provision sets limits on jitteriness, the hyperalertness and excessive imagination that if not quite inventing danger overrates its imminence; the other seeks to limit the lack of jitteriness, the lack of imagination or insensibility that lets the sentry fall asleep on his watch. Falling asleep on the watch is a strict liability offense. It does not matter that you didn't mean to. And the same is the case for causing false alarms. There are no requirements in the provision that one causes them knowingly or intentionally, and no cases have read them in.[29] It is not only the prankster who set off the fire alarms in junior high (though he too) that the law can put before the firing squad but the nervous wreck, the poor, high-strung, anxious soul who suffers from being too alert to the prospect of danger and has not managed to develop the cool or the expertise that distinguishes the general danger of being in the presence of the enemy from the particular imminent danger that requires immediate and total mobilization. This poor soul does not feel the difference between the state of daily alertness to the possibility of alarm on the one hand and being alarmed on the other, between normal vigilance and the sense that something indeed is up. For we suspect that this is an imaginative soul and much too sensitive. Risk to him is not a probabilistic assessment but certain danger. His lot is constant insomnia and nausea.

My false alarmist, however, may also be the very man who is asleep at his post. Given that for him there is no distinguishing between the various levels of danger or its imminence, sleep, never easy to achieve under the best of circumstances, might just as well come at one anxiety-ridden time as another.[30] But we usually think of the sleeping sentry as utterly opposed to the false alarmist, as a study in insensibility, an anxietyless person for whom sleep has always been easy. And it is for this reason alone that he is simultaneously an object of the nervous insomniac's envy and his contempt.

The sleeping sentry and false alarmist contrast in other ways. As a purely Darwinian matter, the species needs an alarm system that engenders some false positives or it wouldn't be sensitive enough. A system that gave no false positives would have left us all in the viscera of our predators or slaves of our more sensitive enemies. But an alarm system too responsive would, as Goffman noted, have us spending all our time in dither and not in grazing, digesting, sleeping, playing, or whatever we need to do to survive.[31] This is why we divide the labor; the sentry is to be vigilant so that the rest can sleep. We want our sentry to be experienced and cool but not insensitive or dull. We need him alert or, if not alert, alertable by all those signs that, if we lived in a movie, would be accompanied by ominous music.

The false alarmist and sleeping sentry impose costs in different ways. The false alarmist runs up the bill each time he occasions a false alarm. To the obvious costs of wasted energy spent mobilizing, the physiological costs of misused adrenaline, mis-summoned fear, and loss of sleep should be added the disclosure of one's positions to the enemy by the mobilization or merely by the panicked firing into the threatening night. But the greatest cost is that false alarms lead to mistrusting the next true alarm. And although we may recoup some of these costs by the disbelief of future false alarms, that would be a penny-wise and pound-foolish accounting, for the alarm would not be disbelieved because false but disbelieved because of the belief that all alarms are more likely to be false than true. Such a belief leaves one effectively without a functioning alarm system. The jittery false alarmist, after all, does not mean to be false and in other settings his sensitivity may be a most valuable asset. True, its value suffers serious diminution if he is not right most of the time. And if he were right most of the time, we would consider him a man of experience and discernment, not a jittery pathetic wreck whom we can imagine putting up before the firing squad.

If the false alarmist imposes serious costs each time he blows it, that is not the case with the sleeping sentry. His sleep imposes harm if the attack occurs on his watch, otherwise his sleep, though negligent or even reckless, yields no great harm. But not quite. If others suspect he is asleep or know he is asleep, then they must increase their vigilance to compensate. Their anxiety levels rise and they begin to expend energy in dither that could have better been spent relaxing. The sentry functions in the way catastrophe insurance functions. Most days go by without our having gained much for carrying such insurance except the ease of mind having it confers. The sentry provides such insurance. He is meant to allow others to rest secure in the belief that his eyes and ears are just as serviceable at the moment as theirs would be.

To the extent that insensibility produces fearlessness, it may be very useful in the midst of combat either on attack or in defense. But in the myriad of soldiers' memoirs I have been plowing through fear is not the only psychically and morally destructive emotion that threatens soldierliness. Fear dominates in battle or in immediate anticipation of it, but soldiers do more than fight. They also stand and wait. Boredom defeats almost as many soldiers as fear. If fear defeats our false alarmist, boredom defeats our sleeping sentry, so bored he cannot generate the imagination to fear the consequences of his boredom.

Omnipotent Fear

The man of reasonable firmness who gives way to his fear has the basis for a successful claim of duress in the criminal law, but in the military the man of reasonable firmness can never give in to his fear unless a substantial number of others give in at the same time. If he is the only one or one of few who give way, we judge him to be of insufficient firmness. In cases of common duress the defendant is measured against a norm whose constraint on actual behavior can be hypothesized only by figuring what that hardly heroic "reasonable man" would do under like circumstances. But in war the norm is situated concretely: we know whether most hold firm or most don't. If most don't hold firm, they are all pretty much off the hook, for we do not, in the Roman style, cast lots and decimate the battalion.[32]

No one, however, doubts that soldiers are afraid.[33] There have been through time different views as to whether it was acceptable for them to admit openly that they were, but fear was clearly always a gloomy and tormenting omnipresence. Those few who qualify as genuine berserks aside, the dominant passion in battle, the one each party expects its comrades and its opponents to be intimately involved with, is fear. We might see all heroic literature as a desperate attempt to keep it at bay. One pays homage to it by working hard to deny it in oneself and to insult one's opponent with it. Agamemnon has images of Terror and Panic painted on the sides of his shield.[34] Before the battle of Gaugamala, Alexander sacrificed to Fear. Beowulf drinks and boasts the night before seeking out Grendel to raise the moral stakes of failure. Even Achilles, if not quite fearful, doesn't dare fight without armor as some of the Norse berserks would do. And Alexander again, who was surely a berserk in combat and feared no one in the host arrayed opposite him, nor the whole host for that matter, was still rather paranoid at times about suspected plots against his life from within his own ranks. (There is an interesting idea to pursue here: the different issues raised for the demands on our courage by our fear of enemies as opposed to our fear of friends. And this would hardly be solved by the fiat of declaring that our friends are those whom we do not fear.)

Commanders have always assumed the fearfulness of their soldiers. The subtlest observer of all, Thucydides, noticed the tendency of battle lines to extend by degrees to the right so that each army slowly flanked its opponent's left as it too moved to its right:

> This is because fear makes every man want to do his best to find protection for his unarmed side in the shield of the man next to him on the right, thinking that the more closely shields are locked together, the safer he will be.[35]

Exhortation speeches try to counter fear and reluctance with other pa-
sions: revenge, perhaps anger, confidence, bloodlust, and often, in extremis,
desperation. But no commander trusted to mere words. The Persians
whipped their men to battle; many a general used his cavalry to deter his
fleeing troops more than to engage the enemy. One military theoretician,
Raimondo Montecuccoli, a general on the Imperial side in the Thirty Years
War, spent the bulk of his treatise on how to prevent the natural cowardice
of one's own troops from taking hold to give enough time for the natural
cowardice of the troops on the other side to assert itself. He lists some of the
devices one may use to keep one's men on the field: let the enemy cut off
lines of retreat, forbid the inhabitants of nearby friendly cities from admitting any of the troops, dig trenches behind your troops, burn bridges and
ships, delegate certain men to shoot retreating soldiers.[36] When arraying
the troops and forming their lines, Raimondo advises embedding the cowards in the middle of the ranks behind the valorous ones whom they can
follow at less risk to themselves and hemmed in by the ranks behind them
so that their escape routes are clogged.[37]

One can also combat fear by instilling confidence, he notes. Nor does it
matter that that confidence is ultimately indistinguishable from those crude
self-deceptions that actually on occasion do succeed in bootstrapping us
into performing better than we have any right to expect. "One may conceal
or change the name of the enemy general if he happens to have a great reputation." Confidence can also be acquired by the indirection of stimulating
contempt for the enemy by presenting naked prisoners to the soldier. Once
they have viewed the captives' fragile, flabby, filthy, diseased, and infirm legs,
as well as their hardly valiant arms, then men will have no reason to be
afraid, for they will have had the chance to see the kind of people with whom
they must fight—namely, pusillanimous, humble, and tearful individuals.[38]

While cowards like me and a good portion of my readers may find in this
display additional reason to desert or flee rather than fight to the death,
Raimondo thinks otherwise:

> Indeed, the troops may come to fear the state of bondage themselves once
> they have perceived the wretched fate of such afflicted, shackled, castigated,
> and emaciated persons, and they may conclude that it will be better to fall in
> battle rather than, dragging on their lives unhappily, necessarily experience
> such contumely and calamity.[39]

Our statute joins Raimondo in adding to these *in terrorem* motivational
exercises. As we have seen, the statute authorizes the killing of cowards,

slackers, craven defenders, jittery false alarmists, and supposes to dissuade behaviors such as theirs by taking from them exactly what they sought to save: their lives. The statute testifies to the power of fear as a motivator: make them fear the court-martial as much as they fear the enemy. This is probably not the wisest strategy since it gives the soldier no reason, once the crunch is on, to prefer one outcome to the other; and it loses all its force should he fear the enemy more. Moreover, it is not uncommon that the coward in battle faces the firing squad with dignity and courage. Such was the case with Eddie Slovik, who spent his last moments trying to alleviate the anxiety of those who had to execute him. The fear that motivates cowardice may not just be the fear of death but the inability to suffer Death's malicious teasing. Certain death, whether by suicide or firing squad, may be a kind of relief, a good-bye to all that.

The statute also hints of another motivating fear; it is the fear of being disgraced as a coward, the fear of shame. This is hardly a startling revelation. It is a commonplace, the theme of honor itself, which demands that fear of losing on esteem and esteemability is worse than death. In this light the law can be seen not only as the scourge of those too shameless to be properly motivated by their sense of shame but also as a bit player in backing the norms that support the sense of shame. The law, then, though mostly negative in its means of motivating, also has a positive role to play in securing the behavior it desires.

To conclude, reconsider the statute. One may wonder at the impossible standard it sets. The soldier is to do his duty, but the duty demanded seems almost to be beyond the call of duty. It is as if the law asks not only that soldiers not be cowards but that they be courageous as a matter of routine. But then consider briefly paragraph 9, the one provision we have left unnoticed until now. It governs, among other things, the obligation to rescue. In contrast to the heroic demands of the other provisions not to run, not to fail willfully to advance, not to abandon shamefully a position, we move to the world of purest prudence: not to "afford all practicable relief." When it comes to rescuing your fellows, practicality and rationality are the standard, not courage, unless it be as Aquinas and others have argued, that courage is just the virtue reason and practicality need to keep functioning in fearful circumstances. Of course, it doesn't make sense to throw good bodies after bad unless it is rational to do so, that is, unless the likelihood of saving the endangered one is greater than the danger incurred by the rescuer to save him.

Yet it is precisely in the domain of rescue that twentieth-century battle has made its particular addition to the styles of the heroic. It is in the Great War that stretcher bearers get Victoria Crosses, and in Vietnam that medics get their Medals of Honor. In the Civil War the same medal was more likely to be awarded for rescuing the regiment's colors.[40] Is it that the antiglory, antihonor discourse has finally become sufficiently suspect that we prefer the heroism manifested in the greater love that lays down or risks its life for another as against those acts in which we suspect that the motive may be glory itself? Heroic culture would consider glory and honor as fine a motive as there could be; we mistrust it precisely because it seems, in spite of its frequent rashness and irrationality, self-regarding and even self-interested, even though it must risk self-sacrifice. By setting our heroic stories in narratives of rescue are we arguing for a kinder-styled heroic: selfless, fearless, and life-saving rather than life-destroying?[41] How do we fit this in with the suspicion that we may be as self-regarding now as ever it was possible to be? Or is it that we see the medic, the stretcher bearer as needing no special physical attributes, that they indeed are everyman or indeed everywoman, that they hold for all of us the possibility of grand action, even if we do not have the body of Ajax or the spirit of Alexander or the ability to kill other human beings even when it is in our best interests to do so?[42]

But for most of us I would guess that what is most salient in this statute is not its substantive commitments so much as its formal attributes. For surely the statute's most remarkable feature is its redundancy, which in a statute that seeks to punish capitally becomes a redundancy of both literal and figurative overkill. Yes, the statute excuses cases of weak legs as long as the mind did not willfully collude with the body to produce them and puts no extraordinary demands on the rescuer, but it otherwise is quite clear about reserving the firing squad for cowardice motivated by fear, and if that lets too many off the hook of culpability, it specifically includes the jittery alarmist, the person who turns tail for whatever motivation other than fear, the slack attacker, the person who casts away his weapons, the quiveringly craven defender, and the exuberant looter.

The statute received its present form in 1950 when it was cobbled together from the Articles of War and the Articles for the Governance of the Navy into a Uniform Code of Military Justice. Most of the clauses were already extant in the British Articles of War of 1769, which in turn were enacted virtually verbatim as the American Articles of War of 1776. In them are found the strictures against looting, shameful abandonment of a position, casting away arms, and causing false alarms, but not the clauses against cowardice and failure to engage, that is, the weak-legs provision. Those have their origin in the navy articles.[43] It is not, then, until 1950 when all these clauses were tossed together that military judges felt called upon to distinguish between cowardice and running away and we get, as a result, our explicit jurisprudence of fear; cowardice is motivated by fear and nothing else.

But this does raise one final matter for weak legs. Weak legs turn out to be a certain kind of sea legs. Not that the army couldn't always get the weak-legged advancer under various general orders,[44] but the navy was concerned less with the legs of its sailors, at least until they might have to board the enemy ship, than with the will of a captain to make his ship advance. The sailors could be standing on the deck with legs quivering and still be advancing because they were being borne by a higher will, willy-nilly. The provision that I have been dealing with as a weak-leg provision is historically not about legs at all but about a naval captain's weakness of will.

And one final observation about cobbling, statutory revision, and uniformity in this world of uniforms: it was the modern reform, the modern consolidation of the articles providing a uniform law for all the armed services that produced the archaic, casuistic, ad-hoc absurdist look of the present statute, not the remnants of pre-eighteenth-century diction still lingering about in shameful abandonments and the casting away of arms. It was the 1950 consolidators, that is the modernizers, who made this statute look more like a law of Æthelberht or Alfred than a law of the most advanced industrial power of the 1950 world.

NOTES

1. Æthelberht cap. 50; Alfred cap. 32. The provisions are most conveniently accessible in F. L. Attenborough, ed., The Laws of the Earliest English Kings (Cambridge: Cambridge University Press, 1922), 11, 77. I have altered the diction of Attenborough's translation.

2. 10 USCS at 899 (1997) Art. 99.

3. See William Bradford Huie, The Execution of Private Slovik (New York: Duell, Sloan and Pearce, 1954).

4. On crowds and armies, see John Keegan's discussion in The Face of Battle (New York: Penguin, 1976), 174–76.

5. See Aristotle's Ethics 5.2, 5.9; Rhetoric 2.6; Plato, Laws, xii.944e. See also Polybius on capital offenses in the Roman army, 333–34.

6. See United States v. Gross 17 (1968) USCMA 610; 38 CMR 408.

7. United States v. Smith (1953) 3 USCMA 25, 11 CMR 25; United States v. Brown (1953) 3 USCMA 98, 11 CMR 98; United States v. McCormick (1953) 3 USCMA 361, 12 CMR 117.

8. United States v. Sperland (1952) 5 CMR 89. The problem is not just to distinguish running away from cowardice within the confines of this statute but also to make sure running away is not expanded to eliminate the mercy implicit in the differently defined and lesser offenses of being absent without leave or some forms of desertion that did not take place in the presence of the enemy and were thus assumed to be motivated by something other than an intent to avoid combat. See 10 USCS ß885 (desertion); 10 USCS §886 (AWOL).

9. Running away is not always prudent. You are a much easier target to the enemy when you show your back because he need not worry about your firing back. And when whole armies turn and run, that is when they are butchered by the pursuing victors. Military strategists have often tried to impress their troops with the superior rationality of facing the enemy and fighting rather than fleeing in panic; see Keegan's discussion of Ardant du Picq, The Face of Battle, 70.

10. William Winthrop, Military Law and Precedents, 2nd ed. (Washington : G.P.O., 1920), at 624, cited in Sperland, at 92. Winthrop is discussing the provisions as they appear in the army's Articles of War, which provisions were later codified in the statute being glossed in the Sperland case and in this essay.

11. See E. Samuel, An Historical Account of the British Army and of the Law Military (London: William Clowes, 1816), 599–601; Robert Barker, Honor Military and Civill (London, 1602), 1.16.

12. Suddenness hardly precludes volition, but what Barker is after, it seems, is the difference between cold calculation and quick unreflective volition.

13. Essays I.54, trans. M. A. Screech, Michel de Montaigne: The Complete Essays (Harmondsworth: Penguin, 1991), 349.

14. See Richard Holmes, *Acts of War: The Behavior of Men in Battle* at 109 (New York: Free Press, 1985), on the problem of soldiers' relieving themselves. At stake is the misery of constipation versus the plague of diarrhea. Modesty produces former, fear latter, but that is not always the case either since bearing down under fire and artillery shelling can produce former. See Humphrey Cobb, Paths of Glory (1935; rpt. Athens: University of Georgia Press, 1987), 4: it is not diarrhea but constipation, contrary to popular opinion, that is the disease of the front. The Germans have the latrines zeroed in and so you hold it.

15. Keegan, The Face of Battle, 302.

16. Personal Memoirs of U.S. Grant (1885–86; New York: Library of America, 1990), 543, 580, 701–02. A refined ability to discern risk and difficulty may be in some respects necessary to a field general, but such a capacity also tends to prompt despair or indecisiveness in all but specially endowed sensibilities.

17. Nicomachean Ethics 3.7.

18. The Road to Richmond: The Civil War Memoirs of Major Abner R. Small, ed. Harold Adams Small (Berkeley: University of California Press, 1939), 70–71. Small, as the quoted passage readily reveals, possesses a literary gift.

19. For an ironic inversion of the weak-legs theme, see Tim O'Brien, Going After Cacciato (New York: Dell, 1979), 150, in which the legs of a soldier who resolves to fall down and opt out of the march toward battle refuse to give way: "the decision did not reach his legs."

20. To the extent that Freud's massive corpus allows for quotes that can back any number of propositions of varying consistency, note that in at least one place Freud, himself, spoke of the notion of unconscious emotions as incoherent: "It is surely of the essence of an emotion that we should be aware of it, i.e., that it should become known to consciousness. Thus the possibility of the attribute of unconsciousness would be completely excluded as far as emotions, feelings, and affects are concerned" ("The Unconscious," in the Standard Edition, ed. James Strachey [London: Hogarth Press, 1953–1974], 14: 177). Of course how we understand his statement depends not only on how we understand the notion of the unconscious but on what we mean by emotion too.

21. See the memoir of Robert J. Burdette, The Drums of the 47th (Indianapolis: Bobbs-Merrill, 1914), 101–8, quoted by Gerald F. Linderman, Embattled Courage (New York: Free Press, 1987), 166–67. Burdette's good coward in fact ran from every battle but he was distinguishable from bad cowards by not availing himself of the traditional means of avoiding taking any part in the initial attack: he did not feign illness or exhaustion, stop to tie shoes during the charge, or arrange hospital details, "he was beaten in every fight but he went in" every time.

22. See Polybius, Histories 3.89 in Polybius: The Rise of the Roman Empire, trans. Ian Scott-Kilvert (Harmondsworth: Penguin, 1979), 255.

23. http://cac.psu.edu/~ltv100/Classics/Poetry/archilochus.html

24. Tossing away the shield, rhipsaspia, was especially grievous in the phalanx style of fighting Archilochus was engaging in. Those accused of rhipsaspia "were assumed to have been among the first to have abandoned their friends in an effort to save their own lives during a general collapse of the phalanx; that is, they had endangered the men who kept their arms and were notable, or had no desire, to make good such an ignoble escape"; quoted from Victor Davis Hanson, The Western Way of War: Infantry Battle in Classical Greece (1989; New York: Oxford University Press, 1990), 63. Plutarch notes that, unlike helmet and breastplate, a man carried his shield "for the sake of whole line" because an unbroken shield wall was "virtually impregnable"; John Lazenby, "The Killing Zone," in Hoplites, ed. V. D. Hanson (London: Routledge, 1991), 95.

25. Nicomachean Ethics 3.6.

26. John Dooley, Confederate Soldier: His War Journal, ed. Joseph T. Durkin (Washington, D.C.: Georgetown University Press, 1945), 46–47.

27. Summa Theologiæ 2a2æ. Q. 142. Art. 3. Is Aquinas right? Is it harder to stand

and fight than to resist pleasureful indulgence? Don't we speak of the "courage" it requires to refrain from proffered pleasure? In any event, commanders and their men knew that the pleasures of alcoholic indulgence often served to stun the human mind in a way that worked to cabin fear.

28. This was a strategy that seemed more plausible up until the late seventeenth century, before the general appearance of distinctive military uniforms.

29. The Manual for Courts-Martial, 1984 IV.23. Art. 99, makes it an element of the offense only that "the alarm was caused without any reasonable or sufficient justification or excuse." Winthrop, Military Law and Precedents, 619, is explicit that knowledge of its falsity or the specific intention to occasion a false alarm need not be shown.

30. It is not rare to find reports of troops falling asleep under intense bombardment, not in nonchalance or even in exhaustion but as a kind of ostrich-like escape from intense horror. See the examples cited in Holmes, Acts of War 267.

31. Erving Goffman, Relations in Public (New York: Basic Books, 1971), 239.

32. Commanders in the French army, however, as late as the Great War, would still select a man by lot from each company when a regiment failed badly for execution; see Alistair Horne, The Price of Glory: Verdun 1916 (Harmondworth: Penguin, 1964), 64. Such an occasion forms the substance of Cobb's novel, Paths of Glory.

33. It is a deeply contested issue whether heroism is more properly pure berserk incapacity for fright, or whether it is fearlessness achieved by overcoming fear either through training or extraordinary assertions of will, or whether it is acting grandly in the continued presence of fear but in spite of it. We may also want to differentiate among heroism, bravery, and courage as to their relations to fear. These questions are obviously too large to take up here.

34. Iliad 11.35

35. Thucydides, The Peloponnesian War 5.71.

36. Raimondo Montecuccoli, Sulle battaglie, ed. and trans., Thomas M. Barker in The Military Intellectual and Battle: Raimondo Montecuccoli and the Thirty Years War (Albany: SUNY Press, 1975), 82.

37. Ibid., 92.

38. Ibid., 133–34.

39. Ibid., 134.

40. The most decorated British soldier in the Great War was a stretcher bearer; Holmes, Acts of War, 197.

41. On the intersection between the heroic and rationality, note that rescue narratives begin to become common only when medical care rises to a level at which the wounded and disabled are likely to survive if saved.

42. Horne writes (The Price of Glory, 181–83) that the most deserving of the title of hero at Verdun were those who occupied the humble categories of runners, ration parties, and stretcher bearers. Their jobs required them to be more exposed to

fire than even that endured by the front-line infantry, and the stretcher bearers were prevented by the demands of their task from hitting the deck when a shell whistled down upon them. Moreover, the last two categories were filled by the bad shots, the old, the musicians, that is, those who were known as miserably unmartial.

43. An Act for the better government of the navy, 1800. Sec. 1, Arts. 4–6.

44. See Winthrop, Military Law and Precedents, 623 n. 26.

Chapter Ten

Institutions and Emotions
Redressing Mass Violence

Martha Minow

If someone kills your child, tortures your lover, or brutalizes you, it is entirely understandable if you then feel a desire for revenge.[1] It is understandable if you wish that the same fate that person inflicted would befall him. The institution of criminal justice in liberal societies tries to tame or channel these understandable feelings. It transfers the authority and power to respond to private violence from the victim and the victim's loved ones to the state, and in so doing, cools the likely desire for inflicting comparable harm into a more general commitment to prosecute, and should sufficient evidence be adduced after a fair process, to punish.

But what if the violence was inflicted by state officials? Here the violation multiplies, for not only are the brutalities shocking and unacceptable, they also betray basic trust in those who govern and leave victims and their families and friends with no lawful or peaceful mode of redress.

One can hope that someday justice will be done. There will be a change in government (and one can work vigilantly for that). Then the past can be exhumed and redressed. Yet new emotions could understandably accompany such a course of events. Frustration and rage, resignation and anger, despair and impatience could each distinctly or in combination fill the hearts of those who survive governmental atrocities. If indeed the old regime is replaced, the temptation to use even lawful forms of criminal process to wreak vengeance can be great. Yet actions taken in that direction can unleash lawless bloodbaths or lay the ground for new cycles of revenge and revolution.

In many parts of the world, individuals and societies struggle with questions about how to respond to collective violence. The search for a response reflects a range of purposes, including a hope to deter future atrocities, a desire to overcome public denial, a hunger for reconciliation, and a thirst for punishing, shaming, or diminishing the wrongdoers. One additional potential goal behind responses to mass atrocities has become more explicit in recent years: the aim of helping victims and bystanders recover from trauma, to heal sufficiently to be able to turn to the rest of their lives with hope and vigor. It is not closure, in the sense of putting the past aside. Silence about or forgetting a regime of terror would only let its perpetrators succeed. Yet dwelling in the trauma, frozen in the past, would also let the offenders prevail. And carrying on with rage further deprives victims of the lives they otherwise could have led.

I am interested in whether, and how, the choice of societal responses can affect the ways individuals manage past experiences with horrific violence. In this preliminary set of speculations on the subject, I will briefly consider a range of societal responses and then consider the claims made in other contexts about the potential interaction between legal institutions and people's management of emotions. I will also explore theories of emotion that both can illuminate and be illuminated by these claims. I will close by considering the special problems raised by assessing people's judgments and emotions in response to violence. A question running throughout is whether there is an emotional response to the violation of the self produced by malicious violence that differs from vengeance without turning into denial or self-blame.[2]

Responses to Mass Violence

Some individuals, themselves victims and survivors, achieve a stance that is neither frozen in the past nor silent about it. Jadranka Cigelj, one of an estimated twenty thousand Muslim women and girls who were raped by Serb men between 1991 and 1995 in Bosnia, had been a lawyer before the war. Taken to the Omarska detention center, where torture, starvation, and rapes were daily features, she was released with others only when the international press came to investigate. She decided to collect testimony from other survivors and began to pursue prosecutions when the United Nations set up the International Tribunal for the former Yugoslavia.

Through a translator, she said, "When you come out of a place like Omarska, you're filled with negative emotions and it's natural to seek revenge. To seek revenge you must hate. But I remember the story of an 86-year-old woman whose 14 family members were murdered and she had to bury all of them with her bare hands. And she said to me, 'How can you hate those who are so repulsive?' I realized that the people I was directing my hatred toward were not worth that; they were only machines for murdering people.'"[3]

For Cigelj, a legal framework of accountability and punishment offered a path for redirecting her emotional responses. In her words, "When you think of a 15-year-old girl whose entire world was destroyed, who was supposed to have the experience of moving from childhood to womanhood under a moon somewhere in somebody's arms, when you think of how her youth was stolen and how she was turned into a wounded animal, you realize that what is important is to work toward a way to hold these people responsible and punish them. Then one day you wake up and the hatred has left you, and you feel relieved because hatred is exhausting, and you say to yourself, 'I am not like them.'"[4]

For this extraordinary woman, the focus on prosecuting and punishing the wrongdoers afforded a way past revenge. The existence of an institutional framework of international law providing for prosecutions helped, as did her own intellectual and emotional resources. For many others, as well, the public event of a trial and the process of establishing or reestablishing a rule of law, holding people to account for heinous acts, can restore a sense of fairness and afford a way to move beyond the past. The Nuremberg and Tokyo trials held after World War II have become symbols of and inspiration for the international movement for human rights.[5] After the recent arrest and plans for a trial of an individual allegedly involved in the abduction of children "of the disappeared" during the military junta in Argentina between 1976 and 1983, an Argentine newspaper ran the headline "God Exists."[6]

Yet the prosecutorial approach has its own limitations. First, there are never ideal circumstances affording enough economic and financial resources to investigate, prosecute fairly, and punish. As a result, prosecutions may seem selective or politicized, and thus unfair. In societies that remain sharply divided between groups that were in conflict during the period of violence or terror, trials for human rights violations may seem to create martyrs out of those who are pursued. The trials of border guards who shot people trying to escape over the Berlin Wall in East Germany had this quality, as well as the implication of scapegoating the front-line soldiers while letting off the "big shots."[7] Victims and bystanders may in response experience new waves of frustration, cynicism, disappointment, and anger.

In addition, trials conducted by a new regime to punish participants in the prior government can amount to a next phase of the conflict between groups, simply using other means. After the genocidal killings of some 800,000 people during 1994 in Rwanda, the reestablished domestic government arrested 115,000 people. By April 1998, the local courts had convicted 22 people and sentenced them to death. As tens of thousands of Rwandans came to witness the executions, reporters described a crowd apparently overtaken with bloodlust. International human rights leaders objected that the trials themselves failed to comport with international standards of fairness, often without defense lawyers or sufficient time to develop a defense. Rather than ending cycles of violence, the trials themselves seemed to observers another phase of revenge.[8] Precisely because the violence erupted as part of a political struggle, legal responses can be construed as simply another phase of civil war. Trials that fail to yield convictions, despite public perceptions that the defendants were to blame, can fuel even greater outrage than people might feel if no trials had been attempted.

A further limitation with trials involves a deeper question. Can a trial process contain the enormity of terror, genocide, mass violence? After the Holocaust, Hannah Arendt wrote, we "are unable to forgive what [we] cannot punish and [we] are unable to punish what has turned out to be unforgivable."[9] The sheer scope of collective violence, as well as the magnitude of the violations against individuals, may render the very mechanisms of individual trials trivial, irrelevant, or incommensurate. No punishment can fully express the proper level of outrage.

Alternative legal responses include removal or exclusion of prior governmental officials from office or from public benefits such as pensions, and commissions of inquiry to produce factual reports of the atrocities, their victims, and their perpetrators.[10] It could indeed relieve some fury, fear, and despair by victims to remove from their positions as judges, police, or administrators individuals who participated in ordering or enforcing acts of murder or torture. Certainly, to see such individuals still in positions of authority and privilege could well stoke a sense of injustice and frustration within survivors, and a governmental process of removal could both acknowledge those feelings and redirect desires for punishment into satisfaction with at least these measures of change and, perhaps, humiliation.

Of course, the removal process may go wrong. Incorrectly identified people or people who actually had little power may suffer.[11] Adam Michnick, an activist in the Polish Solidarity movement, opposed a proposal to purge communist collaborators from working in formerly state-run enterprises because of the dangers of unleashing vengeance that cannot be limited. He claimed that the logic of revenge "is implacable. First, there is a purge of yesterday's adversaries, the partisans of the old regime. Then comes the purge of yesterday's fellow oppositionists, who now oppose the idea of revenge. Finally, there is the purge of those who defend them. A psychology of vengeance and hatred develops. The mechanisms of retaliation become unappeasable."[12]

Another alternative, a commission of inquiry, could offer acknowledgment of the details and scope of atrocities that had been kept secret or subject to official denial. Commissions in Chile, El Salvador, East Germany, and elsewhere have tried to use the techniques of hearings, investigation, and public reports to gather and publicize facts about previously secret regimes of terror and repression. They seek to recognize the experiences of those victimized by the regimes and to trace lines of responsibility to the individuals, political practices, and ideologies that contributed to the harms. Because the violence and oppression reflected political divisions, the commissions aim for a kind of peacemaking. By inviting victims to speak to official, sympathetic listeners, the survivors may have a chance to restore their dignity and honor at least to some degree. Public hearings and reports can redress at least the secrecy and denial that so often surround terror and repression. The clandestine nature of torture and other human rights abuses by repressive powers doubles the pain of those experiences with the disbelief of the community and even jeopardy to the victim's own memory and sanity.[13]

The Truth and Reconciliation Commission (TRC) in South Africa additionally seeks to help the divided society move to a future committed to human rights, democracy, and peaceful coexistence among previously antagonistic groups. Its human rights committee focuses on rights violations committed by participants on all sides of the apartheid regime. It receives testimony from survivors and pursues independent investigations. By elevating the humanity of the survivors, the process seeks to model the values of respect for human dignity that the new government hopes to ensure for everyone. In giving survivors a chance to narrate their experiences before sympathetic witnesses, the TRC is designed not only to gather facts but also to reconnect individuals with a national community committed to establish and protect human rights and equality. In this respect, it is also devoted to establishing a moral baseline that does not equate abuses committed by the government with resistance efforts that also, wrongly, used violence.

The TRC also has an amnesty committee to consider applications for amnesty affording exemption from prosecution and civil liability for people who committed violations of human rights.[14] Individual applicants, whether they worked for the prior government or participated in oppositional movements, may receive amnesty only upon satisfying specified conditions. Applicants must convince the committee that they have disclosed fully the facts of misdeeds. They must demonstrate that their motives were political, not personal, and that the means they used where not disproportionate to the political objective. Without requiring either apologies by perpetrators or forgiveness from survivors, the TRC tries to establish a foundation of right and wrong while obtaining and broadcasting previously hidden information about atrocities. A reparations committee is authorized to recommend steps to compensate individuals and develop communal acts of symbolic and material rectification. Those recommendations in turn must be approved through the political process created and maintained under the new South African constitution.

Through these mechanisms, the TRC is intended to overcome ignorance and denial in the general community about the torture, murders, and other human rights violations committed by the old regime and by its opponents. It is supposed to express governmental acknowledgment of the past and to try to heal social wounds. The rhetoric of healing reveals the conception of trauma and health undergirding the process. Like therapy for individual survivors of trauma, the TRC is supposed to overcome repression and a sense of powerlessness for the entire society as well as for individuals. Two observers of similar investigatory commissions in Latin America explain, "[I]t is the process of compiling the commissions' report, as much as the final product, which is important . . . it is the involvement of broad sectors of society in providing information and in being listened to that is crucial."[15]

Looking forward as much as to the past, the commissioners hope to humanize everyone involved and help build bridges toward a shared future. Archbishop Desmond Tutu, who chairs the TRC, explains how its process expresses a view of restorative justice, "not so much to punish as to redress or restore a balance that has been knocked askew. The justice we hope for is restorative of the dignity of people."[16] Cynthia Ngewu, mother of an individual who was murdered, explained, "This thing called reconciliation . . . if I am understanding it correctly . . . if it means this perpetrator, this man who has killed Christopher Piet, if it means he becomes human again, this man, so that I, so that all of us, get our humanity back . . . then I agree, then I support it all."[17] While Ngewu might have come to this view on her own, the structure of a societal response framed in terms of accountability and reconciliation afforded a vocabulary and context supporting this response.

Yet, if used as a substitute for trials or mechanisms with direct negative consequences for perpetrators, a commission of inquiry may appear an insult to survivors or a theft of the forms of justice they would prefer. Even if the political dimensions of the underlying conflict seem to call for a response departing from criminal prosecution, efforts that stop short of determining guilt and ordering punishment imply that the acts of violence defy, elude, or escape society's mechanism for addressing crime. Put another way: even if the conflict can be viewed as a war, the victims may deserve or want public acknowledgment of the wrong done to their bodies and their lives. In addition, there are risks that a truth commission will fail to obtain crucial information, fail to attract a wide public audience, or fail to gain sufficient credibility across groups in a divided society to do anything other than confirm the preconceptions held by antagonistic groups. The amnesty and reparations features of the TRC are especially vulnerable to criticism. Timothy Garton Ash comments that as the committee work proceeds, "the amnestied killer immediately walks free" while the victim waits for decisions about reparations.[18]

The many criteria for evaluating potential successes and failures of political, legal, and institutional responses to mass atrocities could include their impact on the emotional states and well-being of members of the society. Especially the most recent response, the use of truth commissions, reflects a wager that emotions can be affected by the design of institutional response. Some theories of emotions support this view, but in turn those theories must be refined in light of reform debates over dispute processes, which I explore next.

How Are Disputing Institutions and Emotions Linked?

Legal responses to mass atrocity may seem sui generis, and yet they resemble other efforts to use dispute institutions to affect people's emotions. A public system of criminal laws and courts, it is commonly said, serves to channel emotional energy that otherwise would take a destructive form.[19] A system of legal rules and courts to handle divorces, in contrast, is often charged with exacerbating the bitterness and acrimony of family breakup.[20] In contrast, mediation, arbitration, and other alternatives to litigation are often advocated for use in family disputes and other contexts, because they reduce acrimony and promote harmonious relationships.[21]

Scholarship about the nature, causes, and features of emotions assists in unpacking these claims about the links between emotions and dispute processes. At the same time, looking at the elements of such claims could refine and enrich analysis of the emotions.

Chesire Calhoun and Robert Solomon offer a useful description of five approaches to understanding emotions.[22] Sensation theories emphasize the psychological feeling of emotions. Physiological approaches point to the physiological changes that mark emotions, whereas behavioral theories look to particular behaviors associated with distinct emotions.[23] As interesting or intuitively appealing as these approaches may be, they afford little insight into how legal processes do or could affect people's emotions.

The two remaining approaches suggest some clues. Evaluative theories connect emotions to their object and find logical connections between feelings and evaluations people have of others or of things. In this view, emotions are rational or else strong aids to the reasoning used in forging judgments.[24] Yet evaluative theories have to struggle with the acknowledged disjunction, often, between emotions and reliable perceptions and assessments. Building upon and refining evaluative theories are cognitive theories, which treat emotions as partly or wholly connected with beliefs. Emotions "presuppose factual beliefs about the emotional context."[25] Beliefs about the probability of an event, about responsibility, and about how patterns of social relationships affect whether someone comes to feel hope, shame, or jealousy. Asserted ties between legal institutions and the emotions of their users clearly connect emotions with beliefs. The beliefs are not themselves static but are potentially shaped and influenced by encounters with the legal process itself.

Thus, advocates of alternative dispute resolution (ADR) argue that courts not only are unduly expensive and slow but also deny parties a sense of control and autonomy, and therefore create frustration for the individuals involved. Melvin Eisenberg notes that the trial places the dispute in the hands of a "stranger-adjudicator" and makes each disputant "by posture a supplicant and by role an inferior. He must tacitly admit he cannot handle his own affairs. He must appear at times and places that may be decidedly and expensively inconvenient. He must bend his thought and perhaps his very body, in ways that will move the adjudicator. He must show various signs of obeisance—speak only when permitted, be orderly, and act respectfully if not deferentially."[26] Because the process gives the litigants no say in fashioning the result, which itself will be framed as a win-or-lose proposition, it "tends both to generate a state of tension and to drive the disputants irreconcilably apart, whatever the outcome."[27]

Here, emotions are linked in part to bodily experiences—such as the requirement that the litigant "bend his thought and perhaps his very body." More basically, emotions are connected to experiences of constraint, loss of control, and subordination. The inconveniences of lengthy waiting periods, directives to appear at particular places and at particular times, and the financial expenses triggered by the litigation are understood to generate negative emotional responses by litigants. At least as important to the negative emotions are the litigant's encounter with a win/lose alternative, which not only deprives the individual of a role in fashioning the result but also exposes the risk of arbitrariness and crude oversimplification in the trial's own construction of the truth. Because the litigants may well have contrary beliefs about both facts and fairness, the trial process is likely, in this view, to generate tension and distress.

Such negative emotions are triggered not only by conflicts with beliefs about the facts, the proper result, and the requirement of an all-or-nothing judgment; the triggers identified for negative emotions in litigation are the experiences induced by experience of litigation itself. As a system that demands obedience and causes experiences of powerlessness, the court process can generate frustration, embarrassment, and anger. It is not only beliefs about right and wrong or the underlying disputes that matter here but also direct encounters with frustrating and demeaning bureaucracies and practices. A cognitive theory of emotions is still relevant. Feeling frustrated or demeaned are senses connected with dashed expectations of order, control, and respect. But the direct encounter with irritating or frightening practices is an important feature of the asserted tie between litigation and emotions it can generate.

In addition, encounters with litigation can exacerbate or magnify negative emotions that exist because of the underlying conflict. Critics charge that litigation fuels animosities and conflict through the adversarial process. It enlarges the distance between the disputing parties. The adversarial structure of claims, defenses, and arguments presses the parties to emphasize their differences rather than any points of commonality or potential compromise. It fails to fix the breakdowns in communication or understanding that generate many disputes. In many instances, say critics, civil litigation complicates the parties' dispute with the intervention of lawyers who bring their own competing self-interest and concerns.[28]

Exacerbating negative emotions is especially likely in civil litigation involving divorce and child-custody matters. Before reforms that she helped to draft, Dean Herma Hill Kay argued that "divorce procedures themselves add to the bitterness and sense of personal failure . . . by requiring that at least one party be found guilty of marital fault."[29] Again, the idea of all-or-nothing, win-or-loss, guilt-or-innocence is the problem; it creates conflicts with the parties' own beliefs and invites heightened or extreme claims and charges by one party against the other. Kay's innovation—no-fault divorce—sought to alter the very concept behind marital breakup. Rather than requiring demonstration of blame attributable to one party, the reform calls for either mutual agreement to end the marriage or else one party's evidence of irreconcilable differences with the other party.[30]

Again, we can deepen a strand of the cognitive theory of the emotions. Beliefs about social relationships are among the sort that become the objects of emotions.[31] The dispute process organized by trials can not only affect the beliefs people have about their relationships but also direct experiences they have with people both in and beyond their social network. Critics argue that in litigation the relationships between the parties will be affected adversely by the conventional trial process. The adversarial framework, and lawyers working as adversaries, can produce hurtful statements, intrusive fact-finding, and a go-for-broke strategy that can push already strained relationships to a breaking point. This can happen in family disputes as divorcing spouses testify against each other and draw other family members, friends, ministers, and counselors into the dispute. It can also arise in commercial disputes between people and organizations that otherwise have ongoing relationships. For this very reason, scholars find that commercial actors involved in long-term relationships of mutual benefit very often forgo litigation and even the formalities of contract law, and solve their disputes some other way.[32] They know or fear that the disputing institution of courts will amplify the dispute and cause more jeopardy for the relationship.

Attention to existing or potential relationships—and the emotional states of participants—animates many who call for alternatives to court. Eisenberg, for example, maintains that alternatives like mediation[33] allow parties to share in controlling the process for managing their dispute, and "[a]s a consequence, the disputant must be treated with dignity, at the risk of a breaking-off; may participate freely and directly, unless he voluntarily chooses to negotiate through affiliates; and may have his full say, although some of what he says may seem rambling or irrelevant." Moreover, "it may suffice that the respondent admits either that he *might* have been wrong, or that the claimant's belief that he was wrong is held in good faith. Thus, participation in the process need not be overly threatening, and a reasonable degree of harmony between the parties can be maintained both during and after resolution of the dispute."[34]

Here, promoting a positive interaction between the legal process and the actual relationship between disputants during and after the process figures prominently in arguments for the alternative-dispute-resolution mechanism. Affording the parties more control over the process would improve their individual feelings of well-being as well as their incentives to cooperate and the likelihood of mutual satisfaction with both the process and the result. In addition, the possibility of a middle ground between blaming one or the other party appears to preserve chances for harmony between the parties during and after the dispute. Eliminating structures that push the parties into oppositional stances or competition for the scarce good of a positive result is intended to eliminate some of the negative emotions exacerbated by litigation. Devising a process that itself accords individuals respect and summons others to do the same helps to transform their negative experiences and encounters into more harmonious relations for the future.

The assumption, then, is that alternatives to conventional litigation can render palpable the importance of the relationships among disputants and perhaps broader patterns of social relationships. This, in turn, is especially important to reducing harm to the relationships during the disputing process and to promoting more constructive features of relationships in the future. Divorced parents who share the care of their children, business associates who continue to have transactional dealings, neighbors who still live near to one another, community groups and enterprises that need one another each could benefit from a focus on enhancing future relationships, as well as from minimized harm to whatever relationships already exist.

At least according to the claims of litigation watchers and reformers, negative emotions can be generated or exacerbated by encounters with the court process. The adversarial process can further fracture existing relationships in which disputes arise, with predictable increases in people's bitterness and unhappiness. In contrast, alternative procedures that give parties more control over both the process and result can encourage respect between disputants and improve their sense of comfort and satisfaction.

Some advocates of ADR maintain that this focus on relationships is itself an aspect or version of justice, not a departure from it.[35] Andrew McThenia and Thomas Shaffer describe ADR and settlement as a process of reconciliation in which the anger of broken relationships is to be confronted rather than avoided, and in which healing demands not a truce but confrontation. . . . Justice is not the will of the stronger; it is not efficiency in government; it is not the reduction of violence: "Justice is what we discover—you and I," Socrates said—"when we walk together, listen together, and even love one another, in our curiosity about what justice is and where justice comes from."[36]

If these claims are right, they suggest that students of the emotions should look at the roles that particular social practices, such as dispute processes, assign to individuals and the impact of those roles on human relationships. They should also consider not only the beliefs but also the actual experiences that generate and exacerbate negative emotions and that transform emotions by improving the prospects for harmonious relationships.

Prospects for Recasting Emotions after Violence

In contrast to the hopeful statement by ADR advocates, many critics doubt the prospects of mediation and other techniques. They do not reduce hostility except for parties already capable and willing to cooperate; they do not promote harmonious relationships where the ingredients are not already present. Or more peaceful disputing is purchased at the price of reinforcing preexisting power relationships, undermining rights, and sacrificing justice.[37] It is wrong to redefine justice, as would some mediation advocates, in terms of reduced conflict because conflict is what comes when people speak truth to power or resist unfairness or oppression. There may be no relationships of value to preserve, or their preservation may require countenancing subordination or violence in precise contravention of rights and justice. A framework of rights and justice can grant meaning even to victims of widespread civic justice in a way that peacemaking may not.

These issues are much debated in the context of conventional civil litigation. A special focus for debate concerns the appropriateness of ADR where one party has previously behaved violently toward the other party.[38] Is a woman simply mistaken if she does not feel fear or powerlessness when asked to mediate a dispute with her abusive husband? Or could she be in a good position to assess her own comparative advantages in using a trial process or an alternative process? Might she be thoughtfully assessing the risks to herself and her children from a litigation process where she loses even more control? These are in part empirical questions, but they are also questions about the relationship between emotions and the range of alternatives actually available in someone's life.[39]

A similar set of questions can be posed about alternatives to prosecutions for human rights atrocities. Many survivors of atrocity and the relatives of those who were tortured and murdered find the absence of prosecutions intolerable betrayals. Churchill Mxenge, the brother of Griffiths Mxenge, an antiapartheid lawyer murdered by the repressive regime, felt this very specifically in response to Archbishop Tutu's call for reconciliation and forgiveness through the truth commission process. Because Archbishop Tutu had promised at Griffiths's funeral that justice would be done, his brother found this call for reconciliation a direct affront.[40]

Do supporters of a truth commission, in contrast, have sound reasons to hope for improved relationships between torturers and the tortured, and feelings of reconciliation? Or do they simply reflect realistic assessments of the risks and failures that accompany prosecutions? These are important questions that should disturb any complacent assertions about the relationships between emotions and legal processes. It is problematic to forgo criminal prosecutions, with the clarity of blame and responsibility they represent.

That said, it does still seem worth investigating whether a commission of inquiry can enlarge the repertoire of emotions available to victims, perpetrators, and bystanders to include more than vengeance and denial. Individual human beings are just that, individual human beings, both before and after any one of them is victimized and then labeled as a victim. They are entitled to their own reactions, whether these take the form of anger, thirst for revenge, resignation, forgiveness, hope, stoicism, pride in survival.

Yet these feelings are not formed in a vacuum. They reflect existing and potential patterns of relationships and beliefs about what has been convention and what is possible. An alternative forum may assist members of a divided society in rebuilding, or building for the first time, relationships across their different communities. Affording an instrument for social response that focuses on restoring victims and acknowledging injustice may, at times, foster constructive emotions for people in a divided society who hope to live together in peace.

NOTES

This essay grows from my work on *Between Vengeance and Forgiveness: Facing History after Genocide and Mass Violence* (Beacon Press: 1998). Thanks to Susan Bandes and Samuel Pillsbury for helpful comments.

1. See Jeffrie G. Murphy, Introduction, in Jeffrie G. Murphy & Jean Hampton, Forgiveness and Mercy (Cambridge University Press: New York 1988), p. 16: "[A]

person who does not resent moral injuries done to him . . . is almost necessarily a person lacking in self-respect."

2. Also, is there a response that takes the form of demanding accountability without seeking either to punish the offender or to require the offender to participate in a process of confession and forgiveness? Although both of these alternatives can be important and valuable, they are limited and not suited for some people at certain times. So the question about an alternative emotional response is linked to alternative mechanisms for accountability. See infra (discussing truth commissions).

3. Gayle Kirschebaum, Women of the Year: Jadranka Cigelj and Nusreta Sivac, Ms. Magazine, 64, 67 (Jan./Feb. 1997).

4. Id., at 67–68.

5. See Theodor Meron, America and the World, National Public Radio (April 15, 1993), transcript #9315; Carlos Nino, Radical Evil on Trial 5 (Yale University Press, New Haven 1995).

6. Quoted in editorial, An Enemy of Argentina's People, Boston Sunday Globe, June 14 1998, F6, col.1.

7. See Tina Rosenberg, The Haunted Land: Facing Europe's Ghosts After Communism 261–305, 340–51 (Vintage: New York 1995).

8. James C. McKinley, Jr., As Crowds Vent Rage, Rwanda Executes 22 for '94 Massacres, New York Times, April 25, 1998, p. A1. Simultaneous prosecutorial efforts are under way through the International Criminal Tribunal for Rwanda, located in Arusha, Tanzania, which focuses on the relatively high-ranking government officials and reached no convictions during its first three years. Id.

9. Hannah Arendt, The Human Condition 241 (Chicago: University of Chicago Press 1958).

10. Other potential responses include the development of art, such as public monuments; the creation of days of mourning or days to honor resisters or struggles against oppression; grants of access to security or police files that had been secret; reparations; and public education. Public grants of amnesty or pardons are a form of response that a government may use because of pressure from still-powerful figures or because of hope, usually misguided, that this would offer a way to move past the past.

11. See Rosenberg, supra, at 67–121 (describing how Rudolf Zukal, noted dissident in Czechoslovak Socialist Republic, turned up on a purge list under the new regime).

12. Quoted in Lawrence Weschler, A Reporter at Large, New Yorker, Dec. 10, 1990, at 127.

13. One individual who was blinded by a police officer working for the South African apartheid government spoke before the South African Truth and Reconciliation Commission human rights committee and then was asked how he felt about coming there to tell his story. He replied: "I feel what has been making me sick all the time is the fact that I couldn't tell my story. But now I—and it feels like I got my

sight back by coming here and telling you the story." Testimony of Lucas Baba Sik-wepere, quoted in Antjie Krog, Country of My Skull (Random House: Johannes-burg 1998), 31.

14. The peaceful transition of power from the apartheid regime to democracy was crucially predicated upon a negotiated settlement that included a directive to the soon-to-be-elected parliament to adopt a law with mechanisms and criteria for granting amnesty for conduct "associated with political objectives and committed in the course of the conflicts of the past." Postamble, South African Interim Con-stitution 1993. Thus, as a matter of political reality, some form of amnesty was a condition for the peaceful creation of a democratic nation. In addition, a search for national unity stemmed from the combination of practical security sensed by the black majority, once it had voting rights, and economic necessity, given the contin-uing control by the white minority over vital economic resources.

15. Margaret Popkin and Naomi Roht-Arriaza, Truth as Justice: Investigatory Commissions in Latin America, 20 Law and Social Inquiry 99 (1995).

16. Quoted in Tina Rosenberg, Reporter at Large, Recovering From Apartheid, New Yorker, Nov. 18, 1996, pp. 86, 90. Tutu, and South Africa's Interim Constitution negotiated as part of the peaceful transition of power, refers to *ubuntu*, an African notion of community harmony and healing that includes the idea of human inter-dependence.

17. Quoted in Antji Krog, Country of My Skull (Random House: Johannesburg 1998), p. 109.

18. Timothy Garton Ash, True Confessions, New York Review of Books, July 17, 1997, pp. 33, 34.

19. See, e.g., 22 Am. J. Crim. L. 703, 710–11.

20. See, e.g., Harry D. Krause, Linda D. Elrod, Marsha Garrison, and J. Thomas Oldham, Family Law: Cases, Comments, and Questions 517, 925 (4th ed. West Publ. Co.: St. Paul, Minn. 1998).

21. See, e.g., Andrew W. McThenia and Thomas L. Shaffer, For Reconciliation, 94 Yale L.J. 1660 (1985); Leonard L. Riskin, Mediation and Lawyers, 43 Ohio St. L.J. 29 (1982). Public and scholarly debates also include fears that ADR will yield sec-ond-class justice, especially for women and people who historically held relatively little power. See Trina Grillo, The Mediation Alternative: Process Dangers for Women, 100 Yale L.J. 1545 (1991); Jana B. Singer, The Privatization of Family Law, 1992 Wis. L. Rev. 1443 (1992).

22. Chesire Calhoun and Robert C. Solomon, Introduction, in What Is an Emo-tion? Classic Readings in Philosophical Psychology 3, 7–22 (Chesire Calhoun and Robert C. Solomon, eds.; Oxford University Press: New York 1984). They acknowl-edge the dangers of oversimplification in any such summary.

23. Id., at 8.

24. Id., at 17–19, discussing works by David Hume, Franz Brentano, and others.

25. Id., at 22.

26. Melvin Aron Eisenberg, Private Ordering Through Negotiation, Dispute-Settlement and Rulemaking, 89 Harv. L. Rev. 637, 659–60 (1976).

27. Id. A distinct issue involves claims that access to courts helps to generate litigiousness, pettiness, and obsessiveness. See Marc Galanter, Reading the Landscape of Disputes: What We Know and Don't Know (and Think We Know) about Our Allegedly Contentious and Litigious Society, 31 UCLA L. Rev. 4, 10 (1983). That issue appears to involve competing views of regulation and the proper scope of freedom for the powerful to pursue self-interest regardless of community norms. See Owen M. Fiss, Out of Eden, 94 Yale L.J. 1669, 1671 (1985).

28. See, e.g., Harry T. Edwards, Alternative Dispute Resolution: Panacea or Anathema?, 99 Harv. L. Rev. 668 (1986); Jethro K. Lieberman & James F. Henry, Lessons from the Alternative Dispute Resolution Movement, 53 U. Chi. L. Rev. 424 (1986).

29. Herma Hill Kay, The California Background, written for the California Divorce Law Research Project, Center for the Study of Law and Society, University of California, Berkeley, Sept. 1977, quoted in Lenore Weitzman, The Divorce Revolution: The Unexpected Social and Economic Consequences for Women and Children in America (Free Press: New York 1985), pp. 16–17.

30. No-fault divorce can create a context for new negative experiences and emotions by allowing one party to walk out of a marriage and by impoverishing the party who retains custody of children. See Weitzman, supra.

31. See supra, n. 21 and accompanying text.

32. See Stewart Macaulay, Non-Contractual Relationships in Business: A Preliminary Study, 28 Am. Soc. Rev. 55 (1963); Ian MacNeil, The Many Futures of Contract, 47 S.Cal. L. Rev. 691 (1974).

33. Mediation involves a third party not as a decision maker to resolve the dispute but as a facilitator of communication and problem solving. The goal of mediation is to assist the parties in framing an agreement to which they each can subscribe.

34. Eisenberg, supra.

35. McThenia and Shaffer, supra.

36. Id., at 1665.

37. See Owen Fiss, Against Settlement, 93 Yale L.J. 1073 (1984); Penelope E. Bryan, Killing Us Softly: Divorce Mediation and the Politics of Power, 40 Buff. L. Rev. 441 (1992); Martha Fineman, Dominant Discourse, Professional Language, and Legal Change in Child Custody Decision Making, 101 Harv. L. Rev. 727 (1988); Judith L. Maute, Public Values and Private Justice: A Case for Mediator Accountability, 4 Geo. J. Leg. Ethics 503 (1991); Elizabeth M. Schneider, Gendering and Engendering Process, 61 U. Cinn. L. Rev. 1223, 1230 (1993); Eric K. Yamamoto, ADR: Where Have the Critics Gone, 36 Santa Clara L. Rev. 1055 (1996). Empirical research suggests that mediation is often disadvantageous to women, especially in contests over child custody. Junda Woo, Mediation Seen as Being Biased Against Women, Wall Street Journal (Aug. 4, 1992), B1, B5.

38. Scholars dispute whether mediation is problematic for intimate couples who also report domestic violence. Many observers argue that precisely that kind of case is unsuitable for the informal, collaborative decision making of mediation; see, e.g., Alison E. Gerencser, Family Mediation: Screening for Domestic Abuse, 23 Fla. St. U.L. Rev. 43 (1995). Others maintain that people who feel they lack power tend to end the mediation without reaching an agreement. See Jessica Pearson, Final Report to the State Justice Institute: An Evaluation of the Use of Mandatory Mediation (Oct. 1991). Some empirical studies report that many women who have been victimized by domestic violence nonetheless do not feel that impairs their ability to communicate or bargain during mediation. See Pearson, supra; Alaska Judicial Council, Alaska Child Visitation Mediation Pilot Project (1992). Voluntary election of mediation seems like the answer. See Colleen N. Kotyk, Note: Tearing Down the House: Weakening the Foundation of Divorce Mediation Brick by Brick, 6 Wm. & Mary Bill of Rts. J. 277 (1997).

39. Chesire Calhoun helpfully emphasizes that the cognitive dimension of an emotion does not ensure that the beliefs are accurate. She reasons, "What can we infer from a person's emotions? We can legitimately infer that the world must *appear* to them a certain way. To the acrophobic, heights appear dizzyingly treacherous. To the jealous, the beloved appears to have betrayed his love. But can we infer that the person must *believe* that the world is as it appears? No. The world often is not what it appears to be. And although we cannot prevent it from appearing the way it does, we can refrain from giving credence to the appearance. We can deny the real treacherousness of heights. We can deny the real betrayal of love *in spite of* appearances. Emotions are not beliefs, but we ordinarily believe that things are as they seem." Chesire Calhoun, Cognitive Emotions, 327, 342, in What Is an Emotion? Classic Readings in Philosophical Psychology (Chesire Calhoun and Robert C. Solomon eds.; Oxford University Press: New York 1984).

40. See Rosenberg, Reporter at Large, supra, at 88.

Part IV

The Passion for Justice

Chapter Eleven

Emotion and the Authority of Law
Variation on Themes in Bentham and Austin

John Deigh

Thinking about the authority of law can lead one to dizzying heights of wonder, like those reached in Ronald Dworkin's Law's Empire.[1] It can also lead to oppressive depths of despair, like those depicted in Franz Kafka's The Trial.[2] The stark contrast between the views of law found in these two works—one of fiction, the other of, well, legal fiction—illuminates old disputes over the nature of law and the grounds of its authority. Is law essentially anything more than a miscellany of imperatives and instructions issued by individuals or groups within a society who are specially designated to guide the society's members and by whom those members are disposed to be guided? And is its authority grounded in anything firmer or more certain than the existence of this general disposition in the membership? In particular, is its authority grounded in some moral property that law necessarily has?

Dworkin answers each of these questions with an unqualified yes. On his view, law is an enormously rich and complex intellectual object whose exposition requires a theoretical understanding of a very high order. The elements of positive law—statutes, judicial decisions, written constitutions, and the like—are on his view merely evidence of what the real law is, and the judge's task in any particular case is to discern from an assemblage of such evidence the true law that underpins these surface phenomena and yields the correct decision. To do this, the judge must have a theory that enables him or her to understand these disparate elements as forming a coherent system of normative political thought. On the best theory, Dworkin maintains, the disparate elements of positive law are unified through a set of underlying principles, which includes the abstract principles of justice and fairness at the core of the society's political morality. It is the best theory, moreover, not only in virtue of the coherence and unity it brings to our understanding of the law but also in virtue of the accuracy it achieves in its representation of the law. Hence, law, on Dworkin's view, is essentially more than a miscellany of imperatives and instructions. It is a coherent system of normative thought organized by fundamental principles of justice and fairness and perhaps by other principles of political morality and wisdom. It thus draws its authority from the authority of these principles, and since they are moral principles, the law's authority is a form of moral authority.

What is striking about the legal world that Kafka describes in The Trial, when compared with this grand vision of law that Dworkin presents, is how it turns Dworkin's vision upside down. One would never for a moment think that law in the world Kafka described was a coherent system of normative thought or that it rested on fundamental principles of justice and fairness. The arbitrary legal decisions and actions that define the protagonist's case are the essence of Kafka's characterization of law, and one would have to be a singularly obtuse reader to regard them, instead, as mere surface phenomena behind which existed a coherent and just legal order. This is, after all, a Kafkaesque world. At the same time, the law's authority in this world is compellingly evident throughout the novel. Indeed, its authority seems to be enhanced by the very incomprehensibility of the legal regime in which the protagonist finds himself enmeshed.

Not that there should be anything surprising in this. An institution's authority will appear increasingly imperious to those subject to its governance as it makes them feel increasingly small, and an institution can make those subject to its governance feel small by preventing them from understanding how the decisions applying to them were reached, what methods or reasons were followed in reaching them, and what their consequences are. The principle is the same as one we teachers know well. Few things if any, I submit, can make one seem a more profound teacher to one's credulous students than mystification. Students are dependent on their teacher for instruction; he or she is the authority under whose tutelage they have come; and by promoting their helplessness, a teacher can enlarge the authority he or she has in their eyes. Likewise with legal authority: it too will appear grander to those subject to it when it works to promote their helplessness.

To be sure, promoting the helplessness of those subject to one's authority is not the only way one can make one's authority appear grander. Another is to make the subjects feel more powerful, as we teachers do when we bring our students to a significantly deeper understanding and greater mastery of the material we're teaching and as governing authorities do when by the force of their decisions their subjects feel collectively empowered. The mechanism at work in this case is projection: the students or the governed feel more powerful as a result of successful teaching or popular governance, and they naturally project this feeling of greater power onto its source. Be this as it may, the point is the same in either case. The dynamic in the relation of authority to subject depends on an emotional bond between the bearer of authority and those subject to it, and insofar as this dynamic is essential to the relation, it follows that the relation itself entails this bond. Accordingly, the authority of law, being a specific case of this general phenomenon, is conditioned on an emotional bond between law and its subjects. The opposition, then, between Dworkin's view of law and that represented in The Trial is fundamental. For the idea implicit in Dworkin's view, that the law's authority derives from the authority of the basic principles of justice and fairness at its foundation, is directly contradicted by the possibility that the emotional bond between subjects and the law on which the dynamic of the relation between the two depends can form in a legal system, like the one imagined in Kafka's novel, that lacks such a foundation. My aim in this essay is to defend an idea of legal authority consistent with that depicted in Kafka's novel. Specifically, it is to defend the thesis that the authority of law is conditioned on an emotional bond between the law and its subjects.

I

The thesis needs to be clarified if not qualified. Baldly stated, it invites immediate criticism. For one thing, it is easy to imagine people who have no emotional tie to the law in their community but who are nonetheless subject to its authority. For another, one can also imagine the authority of law in the person of someone, a bullying sheriff, say, or a hanging judge, to whom none of those subject to his authority has an emotional bond. These cases may appear to refute the thesis. Yet once the character of the law's authority is understood, they will no longer seem incompatible with it. Two features, in particular, are important. First, the law's authority is authority with respect to a collective or community. Second, either the law's author-

ity is sovereign, which is to say, paramount in that collective, or the law represents the will of the individual or assembly of individuals who is the sovereign, and thus its authority comes directly from the paramount authority in that collective. By drawing the implications of these two features, one
can then see how, compatibly with both cases, the authority of law can be
conditioned on an emotional bond between the law and its subjects.

Consider the first case. Plainly, in any civil society there will be some
people who have no allegiance to the law. Outlaws, revolutionaries, and anarchists are examples that come immediately to mind. To explain their
being subject to the law's authority, despite their lacking allegiance to it, one
can point to the first feature, that legal authority is authority with respect
to a collective. As such, the law has authority over each and every member
of the collective. In this respect, the authority of law is like the authority a
coach has over a team. Such authority depends on the team's having allegiance to the coach, and it has such allegiance just in case the bulk of the
team's members have it. Accordingly, belonging to the team is sufficient for
being under its coach's authority, given that enough of the team's members
have an allegiance to her. Hence, even a rebellious member is subject to the
coach's authority. Similarly, then, outlaws, revolutionaries and anarchists
come under the authority of law by virtue of their belonging to a society in
which enough of the members have allegiance to law to secure its authority over the collective.

The second case is also common. Any legal system will have some officials who enforce the laws vigilantly, rigidly, and with a swagger, and officials of this sort invariably inspire fear and hatred among those subject to
their authority. Indeed, where the official is the chief and most visible en-
forcer of the law, the sheriff of a small, rural town, say, or the marshal of
some frontier territory, he may well be identified by those subject to his authority as "the law." In such cases especially, one might think, the fear and
hatred the official inspires in the subjects is incompatible with their having
allegiance to law, and therefore his authority could not be conditioned on
such allegiance. Yet attention to the second feature shows that the subjects'
fear and hatred of this official, even if universal, does not exclude their having allegiance to law. This is because the official's authority, like that of any
magistrate or administrator, is delegated. In other words, however domi-
nating he may be within his jurisdiction, he is not sovereign. His authority
is not paramount. The subjects' fear and hatred of him does not therefore
imply that they lack the emotional bond to law on which its authority is
conditioned. For the emotional bond between the law and its subjects on

which the law's authority is conditioned is a bond between the subjects and that which has paramount authority in the legal system. Consequently, the official's authority, being delegated, could be conditioned on such a bond despite the fear and hatred that the official inspires in those who fall within his jurisdiction.

II

These explanations, while they answer the initial criticisms of the thesis, that it cannot account for the law's authority over outlaws or its being administered by bullies, invite new ones, for it is evident that they echo ideas from the traditional positivist theory of law and consequently appear open to some of the same objections that showed that theory to be untenable. On the traditional theory, the theory developed by Jeremy Bentham and John Austin, law is a set of general commands that express the will of the sovereign, and the sovereign is that person or assembly of people whom the bulk of the subjects habitually obey and who habitually obeys no other person or assembly.[3] Accordingly, the law's authority is conditioned on a habit of obedience to the sovereign that those subject to the sovereign's authority have, and it represents the paramount authority in the legal system. The explanations of how it can be so conditioned compatibly with the law's having authority over outlaws and its being administered by bullies thus parallel the explanations of how it can be conditioned on an emotional bond between the law and its subjects compatibly with these two phenomena. And this parallel then suggests that some criticisms of the traditional positivist theory may well apply mutatis mutandis to the principal thesis of this paper.

Not all of these criticisms apply, however. Specifically, we can ignore those that fault the theory's doctrine that every legal system has a sovereign, a person or assembly of people whose general commands are the laws of that system.[4] These criticisms were perhaps the most damaging to the theory's credibility since, as is clear on reflection, many modern legal systems are ill conceived of as the issue of a supreme legislator or legislative body. But the thesis of this paper corresponds only to the traditional positivist idea that the law's authority is conditioned on the subjects' habit of obedience, and that idea, though incorporated into the theory's doctrine about sovereignty, is separable from it. Once separated, it escapes the criticisms that showed the doctrine to be untenable. So too, then, does the thesis that the law's authority is conditioned on an emotional bond between the law and its subjects.

A different line of criticism concerns the failure of the traditional positivist theory to capture the difference between valid exercises of legal authority and exercises of brute force.[5] The use of threats and violence to coerce others to act as one demands exemplifies the latter. The issuance of directives in accordance with the criteria of an authoritative performance of one's office exemplifies the former. Traditional positivism could, to be sure, distinguish between valid and invalid exercises of legal authority by officials whose authority was delegated. Valid exercises truly represented the will of the sovereign; invalid exercises did not. But the theory lacked the conceptual resources for explaining what determined in the first instance authoritative expressions of the sovereign's will. Consequently, it could not explain the difference between the authoritative directives of a sovereign and mere demands backed by threats from a person or group used to having their way with those to whom the demands were issued.

The problem goes to the root of the traditional positivist program. The program originated in Bentham's opposition to the theory of natural rights (and natural law) on which Blackstone rested his exposition of English law.[6] On this theory, what explains the difference between the authoritative directives of a sovereign and mere coercive demands by some individual or group used to having their way is the consent to be governed that the subjects are supposed to have given the sovereign, at least tacitly. Bentham, impressed by Hume's critique of the idea that political authority derives from such consent, rejected this explanation.[7] He maintained, instead, that the subjects' habit of paying obedience to the sovereign and their continued disposition to obey were all the conditions necessary for establishing the sovereign's authority over the subjects. On this point, however, he was seriously mistaken. For to distinguish the sovereign's authoritative directives from mere coercive demands by reference to the character of the subjects' responses to those directives, one must be able to explain the subjects' responses as rule-following behavior.[8] Otherwise, the relation of subjects to sovereign ceases to be political and becomes more like that of livestock to herdsman. Unfortunately for Bentham and the traditional positivist theory he developed, the concepts of habit and disposition are too thin to yield the needed explanation. One can use them to explain the subjects' responses as regular and predictable, but rule-following behavior is more than just regular and predictable behavior. It is conduct that flows from the reasons the rule being followed represents. It involves, then, the understanding of one's situation as calling, in virtue of the rule, for this conduct and thus making one liable to rebuke if one does not engage in it. Hence, to explain the subjects' responses as rule-following requires concepts whose import includes these cognitive states and liabilities. It requires concepts richer than those of habit and disposition.

The same line of criticism may then seem to apply to an account of the law's authority according to which it is conditioned on an emotional bond. It may seem to apply in this case because the concept of an emotional bond does not include, as part of its import, the cognitive states necessary to the production of rule-following behavior. Yet unlike the concept of habit, the concept of emotion, as is now widely recognized, includes cognition as part of its import. Emotions, that is, as is now widely recognized, are more than just inner sensations and pure feelings. Rather they are intentional states of mind and as such contain thoughts.[9] Consequently, while the general concept of an emotional bond does not entail concepts of the cognitive states necessary to the production of rule-following behavior, one can assume that there are types of emotional bond whose concepts do. For example, while the type of emotional bond newborns form to their mothers soon after birth plainly does not imply such cognitive states, the type that children develop to their parents with the internalization of parental authority does. This latter type was brought to prominence by Freud through his theory of how a child acquires a conscience or superego, and it is assumed as well in other theories of moral development, such as Piaget's and Rawls's.[10] Thus, by specifying this type of emotional bond as the type between the subjects and the law on which the latter's authority is conditioned, one can make the thesis more definite so that it is free of whatever problems traditional positivism has in understanding the subjects' obedience to the sovereign as rule-following behavior. On this more definite formulation, then, the thesis avoids the line of criticism concerning traditional positivism's failure to capture the difference between authoritative expressions of sovereign will and mere coercive demands by a person or group whose power dominates all others in the community.

III

This line of criticism will be familiar to readers of H. L. A. Hart's The Concept of Law.[11] Hart advanced it by drawing attention to the difference between being obliged to do something and being obligated to do it. The former, Hart pointed out, is an apt expression for circumstances in which one is compelled or coerced to do the action, whereas the latter is an apt expression for circumstances that fall under a social rule requiring one to do that action, a rule that one cannot disregard without risking censure. Because traditional positivism lacked the conceptual resources for explaining the subject's obedience to the sovereign as rule-following behavior, Hart argued, the theory could not account for the subjects' obligation to obey the sovereign. What it offered as an account of this obligation was better understood as an account of the subjects' being obliged to obey the sovereign. Correspondingly, then, what it offered as an account of the sovereign's authority over the subjects was better understood as an account of mere domination by one person or group over a whole population. In other words, traditional positivism could not distinguish authoritative expressions of the sovereign's will from mere coercive demands by a person or group whose power dominates all others in the community. It could not account for sovereign authority.

Hart then developed out of this criticism his own positivist theory of law.[12] On this theory, law is a complex system of social rules. At its foundation is a rule of recognition that officials in the system, particularly those who hold adjudicative office, use to determine the legal validity of the other rules. This rule of recognition is authoritative by virtue of its general acceptance by these officials. It defines their understanding of what in the system counts as law, and that they have this shared understanding is then sufficient, according to Hart, to give the rule its authority. Other rules are then authoritative by virtue of their meeting the criteria for validity specified in the rule of recognition at the foundation of the system. Thus Hart's idea, so it appears, is to replace the traditional positivist notion of a sovereign as the fount in any legal system of the law's authority with the notion of a rule of recognition as, in virtue of its general acceptance by the officials of a legal system, the fount of that authority. Whether or not this idea represents Hart's considered view is uncertain. The Concept of Law contains conflicting passages.[13] But even if this idea weren't Hart's considered view, his theory certainly encourages it, and other prominent legal philosophers have endorsed it.[14]

The idea that the authority of law springs from the general acceptance of a rule of recognition by the officials who administer and adjudicate the law, an idea I'll call the mandarin-centered conception of legal authority, clearly excludes the thesis that the law's authority is conditioned on an emotional bond between law and its subjects. To be sure, the mandarin-centered conception presupposes an understanding of the subjects' obedience to law as rule-following behavior. For the conception is part of a jurisprudential theory that identifies law with a complex system of social rules, and this system comprises rules that the subjects follow. But a person can follow rules without having an emotional bond to them. Playing checkers, for instance, does not require any emotional attachment to the game: alphabetizing one's address book does not require any emotional attachment to the practice. Similarly, one can administer rules or adjudicate the conflicts they generate without having an emotional bond to them. So the opposition between the mandarin-centered conception and the principal thesis of this paper is more than just a matter of whether the primary conditions of the law's authority in a legal system consist of the attitudes and conduct of its officials or those of its subjects. It is also a matter of whether these conditions consist merely of a shared understanding of and disposition to apply the criteria determining what rules and actions count as legally valid in that system or include as well or instead an emotional bond to the law. The mandarin-centered conception of legal authority therefore challenges the very idea that an emotional bond to the law is necessary to the law's having authority over its subjects.

This challenge, however, can be met. While the mandarin-centered conception does capture a kind of authority with which law is invested, it is not a kind that is specific to law as a political institution. Rather, it is the kind that any system of social rules has for those who participate in the activity the system defines and regulates. The rules of competitive games, for instance, have such authority, which is typically manifested in the officiation of the games by umpires, referees, timekeepers, scorekeepers, and the like. The authority of the rules springs from a shared understanding these officials and the game's participants have of what the rules are or how they can be determined (e.g., by consulting Hoyle or an official rule book), and it does not depend on the officials' or the participants' having an emotional attachment to the game. Similarly, the authority of law that the mandarin-centered conception captures springs from a general acceptance of a rule of recognition by the officials responsible for administering and adjudicating the law and does not depend on either the officials' or the subjects' having an emotional attachment to the law. But to conceive of the law's authority in this way is to lose sight of its authority as or as part of a system of government. It is to ignore its essentially governmental character. In other words, the mandarin-centered conception fails to capture the kind of authority at issue in the dispute between traditional positivism and the natural rights/natural law theory in opposition to which traditional positivism developed. Once this equivocation on the kind of authority in question is shown, it then becomes clear that the mandarin-centered conception poses no real challenge to the idea that an emotional bond to the law is necessary to the law's having authority over its subjects.

The mistake in the mandarin-centered conception lies in its implicit assumption that law is no more than a system of social rules under which a form of human activity is organized and in which there are officials on whose judgments the felicity of the activity depends. Law, being essentially a system of government, is more than a system of such rules. Governing is more than officiating. The mistake in the conception thus consists in its using generic features of law to define one of its essential characteristics. What is more, this mistake is traceable to Hart's program of putting at the foundation of a legal system, in place of the sovereign of traditional positivism, the notion of which he had skewered, a rule of recognition commonly accepted by the officials who administer and adjudicate the law.[15] For this replacement presupposes that Hart's notion of such a rule and the traditional positivist notion of a sovereign are at the same theoretical level, that they yield alternative theoretical explanations of the same legal phenomena, and this presupposition is false. The former notion is in fact decidedly more abstract than the latter. In particular, there is nothing distinctively political in Hart's notion of a rule of recognition, whereas the traditional positivist notion of a sovereign is a distinctively political one. As a result, whereas the traditional positivist notion contains elements necessary to explaining law as a system of government, Hart's notion does not.

On the traditional positivist notion, the sovereign is politically superior to the subjects in the sense that the sovereign's will, as it is expressed by the sovereign's general commands, dominates the will of each subject. Put differently, the sovereign's political superiority consists in the sovereign's setting ends for the subjects, through the laws the sovereign issues, that are superior to the ends the subjects set for themselves. In this way traditional positivism explains government of the subjects by the sovereign and so law as a system of government. By contrast, the notion of a rule of recognition commonly accepted by officials responsible for administering and adjudicating the law contains nothing that implies the superiority of the ends set by laws to the ends that those subject to the laws set for themselves and hence contains nothing to explain law as a system of government. To be sure, the traditional positivist explanation of law as a system of government rests on a doctrine about sovereignty that cannot survive criticism, as we noted in section II.[16] But the point holds nonetheless: to understand law as a system of government requires that one understand it as setting ends for the subjects that are superior to the ends that they set for themselves, and traditional positivism would afford such an understanding if its explanation were sound, whereas there is not even the possibility of arriving at such an understanding by conceiving of law as founded on a rule of recognition. The authority of law, then, entails the authority to set ends for the subjects that they do not set for themselves and that dominate many of those ends that they do set for themselves. The law's authority in this respect is the authority it has as a system of government. Such authority, it is important to keep in mind, is distinct from the power of government to coerce obedience, for the same arguments that bring out the difference between being obligated and being obliged apply as well to the difference between having authority and having power. Consequently, while the power of government to coerce obedience is conditioned on the subjects' vulnerabilities to harm and capacities for fear, the authority of law must be conditioned on something more. This additional factor, moreover, as the argument of this section has shown, cannot be the acceptance of a rule of recognition by the officials responsible for administering and adjudicating the law. Rather, it must be the subjects' allegiance to the law, their willingness to be governed by the law apart from their being vulnerable to the punitive sanctions by which it is enforced and capable of fearing those sanctions. It must, in short, be the subjects' willingness to subordinate their own ends to the ends the law sets for them. Hence, a defense of the principal thesis of this paper becomes a defense of the view that what explains the subjects' willingness to subordinate their own ends to the ends that the laws sets for them is an emotional bond between them and the law.

IV

Let us call this view the emotion-based account of the law's authority. Fully specified, it is the view that an emotional bond between the subjects and the law of the type exemplified by the bond children develop to their parents with the internalization of parental authority explains the subjects' willingness to subordinate their own ends to the ends the law sets for them. That such an emotional bond can explain this disposition is evident from the explanation its prototype supplies of a like disposition children acquire through socialization. For through socialization, specifically, the internal-

ization of parental authority during the child's early years, the child becomes sensitive to the wrongfulness of disobeying its parents and liable to
feelings of guilt and bad conscience over such disobedience, where before
the process occurred the child was merely cognizant of the dangers of disobedience and liable to anxieties about them and to fear of being found out
when it did disobey. And similarly, through the same process, respect comes
to characterize the child's attitude toward its parents and the rules and dictates they issue, where previously the principal motives of the child's obedience were wholly instrumental: a desire to receive praise and affection for
being "good" and a fear of the anger, unpleasantness, and loss of love that
come with being found "naughty."[17] These new motives of conscience and
respect that the child thus acquires constitute a disposition on the child's
part to do right even at the cost of forgoing pleasures it would otherwise
have happily consumed or experiencing discomforts it would otherwise
have instinctively avoided. This disposition is analogous to the disposition
to obey the law that legal subjects must have as a condition of the law's authority, and hence one can plausibly suppose that the same type of emotional bond that explains the former explains the latter.

In addition, it is plausible to suppose that the former is not only an ana-
logue of the latter but also its precursor. Socialization, after all, is a developmental process. Thus the disposition to subordinate one's own ends to
the ends the law sets for one arises out of precedent dispositions, the earliest of which is the disposition, acquired when very young, to respect the
rules and dictates of one's parents and to feel guilt and bad conscience over
disobeying them. In view of this plausible supposition, then, we can deepen
the emotion-based account of the law's authority by embedding it within
an overall account of this process that generalizes its chief idea. Accordingly, the process depends on the emotional bond one forms to one's parents with the internalization of their authority and on the subsequent
bonds one forms to various other people and institutions as one gets older.
These are, specifically, the people and institutions to whose authority one
becomes subject as one moves from the context of one's family to those of
school, church, work, and recreational and civic organizations. Hence, on
this account of the socialization process in question, the emotional bonds
one forms to one's parents and to the subsequent authorities and authoritative structures to which one becomes subject as one gets older explain the
successively more mature dispositions to submit to the rules and dictates of
these authorities and authoritative structures, including, in particular, the
disposition to subordinate one's own ends to the ends the law sets.

This account squares with the theories of moral development noted earlier, Freud's and Rawls's, in particular, that identify the initial acquisition of conscience with the internalization of parental authority.[18] On Freud's theory, the emotional bond one develops to one's parents with this internalization is at the root of the subsequent bonds one forms to other authorities and authoritative structures and is therefore the ultimate explanation of all the dispositions to submit to the rules and dictates of authority one acquires. For on Freud's theory the emotional bond to one's parents that develops in the formation of a conscience, a superego, survives intact in one's unconscious, and it then influences significantly, though unconsciously, the attitudes one takes and the feelings one experiences toward later authorities such as teachers, pastors, bosses, public officials, and the institutions they represent. By contrast, Rawls's theory does not explain these dispositions as products of unconscious material and mechanisms or as rooted in the emotional bond one forms to one's parents with the internalization of their authority. Instead, it assumes that the same factors that produced this bond are present as well in the wider social contexts into which one is introduced as one gets older, and consequently, similar emotional bonds to the people and institutions who bear comparable authority in those contexts are formed as one comes to understand and appreciate their role in one's life. Each of these bonds then explains the corresponding disposition one acquires to submit to the rules and dictates of the relevant authority. Either of these two contrasting theories of moral development thus represents a substantial elaboration of the emotion-based account. Either provides substantial theoretical support for it.

V

However substantial this theoretical support, the account may still fall short when compared with alternatives. We must consider, then, how well it stacks up against the competition. It is not possible, however, to examine all of the leading alternatives. I will, instead, consider two. One is due to H. L. A. Hart; the other to Joseph Raz. Hart's represents a volition-based account. Raz's represents a reason-based one. While there might, of course, be some other volition-based or reason-based account that offered stiffer competition, this possibility should seem remote once Hart's and Raz's are presented and examined. Theirs are representative of the two classes, and examination of them, though insufficient as a complete defense of the emotion-based account, should be sufficient as a presumptive one.

To determine how well the emotion-based account stacks up against Hart's and Raz's, let us consider whether either of theirs better fits the main features of the law's authority. Four have surfaced in the course of our clarifying and expounding the emotion-based account. First, the law's authority is authority with respect to a community. Second, either the law has paramount authority in that community or it represents the will of the individual or assembly who has paramount authority. Third, the authority of law presupposes that the subjects' compliance with the law is rule-following behavior. And fourth, the authority of law is the authority of government and, as such, depends on the willingness of the subjects to subordinate their own ends to the ends the law sets for them. The emotion-based account will then prove to be the superior account if it can be shown that neither Hart's nor Raz's fits these four features as well it does. And for this purpose it will suffice to consider how well they fit the first and the fourth.

On the account due to Hart, which he gave in The Concept of Law, legal authority is conditioned on voluntary compliance by those subject to it, or at least enough of them to solidify its force.[19] Thus he wrote in the penultimate chapter, "It is true, as we have already emphasized in discussing the need for and the possibility of sanctions, that if a system of rules is to be imposed by force on any, there must be a sufficient number who accept it voluntarily. Without their voluntary cooperation, thus creating authority, the coercive power of law and government cannot be established."[20] Clearly, the account fits the first of our test features well. Its explanation of the law's authority as authority with respect to a community is the same as the explanation an emotion-based account yields, except that it appeals to voluntary cooperation with law where the emotion-based account appeals to an emotional bond to law. If the bulk of the membership voluntarily cooperate with the law, then the law's authority over the community and so each of its members is secured.

Where Hart's account runs into trouble is in its explanation of the fourth feature. Because the voluntariness of an action does not depend on its motive, voluntary cooperation with the law by sufficiently many subjects can, on Hart's account, establish the law's authority regardless of the motives from which their cooperation springs, a point Hart himself makes a few paragraphs after the passage quoted above.[21] It follows then that, on his account, law would have authority over its subjects even if all those who cooperated voluntarily with it did so solely out of calculative self-interest, reckoning that the costs of noncooperation are not worth the benefits. But to act solely out of calculative self-interest means that one acts for one's own ends and does not subordinate them to ends that another or others have set for one. Hence, the fourth feature eludes Hart's account. This defect in the account is made apparent in a passing remark Hart makes, when he characterizes the voluntary cooperators on whose cooperation legal authority is conditioned as having allegiance to law and thus implies that their allegiance is the source of law's authority.[22] Purely calculative cooperators do not have allegiance to anyone or anything save themselves.

Of course, traditionally, political philosophers have maintained that the subjects' voluntary cooperation with the law establishes its authority on the grounds that such cooperation implies their consent to being governed by law and that such consent confers authority on the law. Hobbes, for instance, cited voluntary submission to the sovereign as a sign of such consent: in virtue of such submission one becomes a subject of the sovereign's authority, whereas refusal to submit would leave one essentially a captive or slave.[23] And Locke took voluntary enjoyment of the law's protection and its other benefits as signifying tacit consent to its governance.[24] On these accounts, the subjects' voluntary cooperation with the law establishes their allegiance to it, for the accounts take voluntary cooperation with the law to imply consent to its governance regardless of the motives from which that cooperation springs, and the consent then establishes the subjects' allegiance in virtue of implying a willingness to subordinate their own ends to the ends the law sets for them. Hence, these traditional accounts, unlike Hart's, fit the fourth feature. But for well-known reasons they are untenable. In particular, the thesis that voluntary cooperation with law implies consent to the law's governance has been thoroughly thrashed.[25] Hart's account avoids this thrashing, but at the cost of being disabled from explaining the subjects' allegiance.

Let us turn then to Raz's account.[26] This account is much more complex than Hart's. Its basic idea is that legal authority is conditioned on an understanding of law as a system of norms that purports to supply those it governs with reasons for action. Raz divides reasons for action into two kinds: interest-dependent and interest-independent.[27] An interest-dependent reason is a fact that weighs in favor of a person's taking a certain course of action because doing so would, on account of this fact, promote his or her interests. An interest-independent reason is a fact that weighs in favor of a person's taking a certain course of action because doing so is, on account of this fact, rationally required independently of his or her interests.

On Raz's view, all interest-independent reasons are moral reasons, and thus, in effect, he divides reasons for action into the prudential and the moral. We can ignore this thesis, however, the thesis that all interest-independent reasons are moral reasons. Its purpose is to show how legal authority makes a claim to moral authority and thus how Hart's famous thesis about the separability of law and morality can be challenged. We can thus regard it as a supplement to Raz's account of how the law's authority derives from its purporting to supply its subjects with certain interest-independent reasons for action. It is this account that we should examine.

Raz draws this account from his rather elaborate theory of reasons for action. An important element in this theory is the idea of second-order reasons for action. These fall into two types: reasons to act on certain reasons, and reasons to ignore certain reasons on which one has to act. Thus, if I offer to help you whenever you need it, as I might, say, if you were my neighbor and you or your wife had just given birth to triplets; then my offer is itself a reason for me to act on your requests for help, which is to say, a reason to act on the reasons your requests represent. And if I promise to drive you home right after a meeting, then I have reason to ignore the reasons I might come to have to do something else after the meeting—such as accepting a subsequent invitation to go to a movie—that would prevent me from doing what I promised. The promise, in fact, should be seen as generating both a first-order reason to drive you home and a second-order reason to ignore reasons to act in ways that would prevent me from driving you home. In this respect, it generates what Raz calls a protected reason for action. Raz then, with some additional complications, which need not concern us, explains having authority over someone as being in a position both to generate for that person protected reasons for action and to eliminate such reasons from the set of reasons that person has to act. Accordingly, the authority of law consists in law's being for its subjects both a generator of protected reasons for action and an eliminator of such reasons.

Raz's account clearly captures the fourth feature of the law's authority. To generate for someone a protected reason for some action Ø is to give that person both a first-order reason to Ø and a second-order reason to ignore reasons for doing things that would prevent him from Øing. In other words, it is to set a rationally required end for the person and to give him reason to subordinate his other ends to this end. Because the subjects are rational agents and therefore responsive to reasons, their recognition of the law as a generator of protected reasons for action amounts to a willingness to subordinate their ends to the ends the law sets for them. Thus, Raz's characterization of the law's authority as consisting in the law's generating for its subjects protected reasons for action fits the fourth feature well.

How well Raz's account fits the first feature, however, is another matter. Uncertainty lies in how it explains the law's authority over outlaws, revolutionaries, and anarchists. One possibility would be to follow the same pattern of explanation that the emotion-based account and Hart's account use. Accordingly, law would have authority over a community as a result of its generating protected reasons for the bulk of that community, and it would therefore have authority over outlaws, revolutionaries, and anarchists in virtue of their belonging to this community. Of course, the question would then arise, why does law generate protected reasons for most members of the community but not for these renegades? And a natural answer would be that the latter lacked the civic interests and public spiritedness that the former had and that disposed them to see the laws of their community as reasons for action. On this answer, however, facts about legislation—for example, that the legislature had banned private ownership of bazookas—would be protected reasons relative to the agent's interests, desires, and emotional dispositions. They would, that is, be interest-dependent reasons. Raz's reason-based account would, therefore, turn out to be merely an emotion-based account dressed up in an elaborate theory of reasons for action.

This, to be sure, is not what Raz intends. Rather, he sees these protected reasons as interest-independent and therefore as reasons for all subjects and not just for those who are civic-minded. His view rests on two assumptions. First, Raz assumes that if law has authority over its subjects, then that authority is legitimate. Second, he assumes that reasons generated by the law in any legal system in which the law's authority is legitimate are interest-independent. Accordingly, he can explain the law's authority over outlaws, revolutionaries, and anarchists, for given these assumptions, if the law has authority over any of its subjects, then it has authority over all of them in virtue of the interest-independent reasons it generates. The legitimacy of the authority ensures this result.

These two assumptions thus form the backbone of Raz's account. Since neither is self-evident, their defense becomes crucial to its cogency. Raz defends the first on the grounds that the relevant notion of authority is essentially normative. To say that x has authority over y in normative discourse implies that y has an obligation to obey x, and to attribute an obligation to someone in such discourse is to say in effect that, other things equal, the person ought to do the act or acts that fulfillment of the obligation requires. So attributing authority over y to x in a normative sense implies that, other things equal, y ought to obey x. Yet this implication would not follow, Raz argues, unless one assumed in attributing authority to x that the authority was legitimate. As Raz sometimes puts it, to make a claim to authority over someone is make a claim to legitimate authority. Thus, taking the notion of authority relevant to the philosophical question of the nature of the law's authority as normative, Raz concludes that the law's authority over its subjects is legitimate if it indeed has authority over them.

Raz defends the second assumption on the ground that what qualifies the authority of someone or some institution as legitimate is the person's or institution's fulfilling well the purposes for which they have authority. In the area of government, Raz maintains, the purpose for having authority is to generate for the governed certain kinds of reasons for action that in a population of rational agents would help significantly to reduce conflict among them and to facilitate their cooperation and thus bring about its benefits. These are interest-independent reasons, and consequently, Raz concludes, if the law's authority is legitimate, then the law is fulfilling well its purposes, which is to say, the reasons it generates for the subjects are interest-independent.

The question, then, of how well Raz's account fits the first feature comes down to whether these defenses are sound. Both, moreover, must be sound for the account to be cogent. Yet neither, in fact, is. Consider the first. Its pivotal thesis is that a claim to authority over someone is necessarily a claim to legitimate authority. If this thesis were true, then whenever a claim to authority over someone was made, it would make sense to ask whether the authority claimed was legitimate. Without doubt, it does make sense to ask this question when the authority claimed is delegated. Delegated authority is authority possessed by virtue of a right that has been conferred on the person or institution claiming to have that authority. Because one can always ask whether the conferral actually took place or whether the transaction it consisted in was valid or licit, it always makes sense to ask whether the authority claimed is legitimate. It also makes sense to ask this question when the authority, though not delegated, is conferred on the basis, say, of certain qualifications like being the eldest male child in a hereditary monarchy in which primogeniture is the rule of succession. In this case it makes sense because one can always ask whether the person claiming the authority truly has the qualifications. The problem, though, is that not every case of authority over someone is a case of delegated or conferred authority, and in cases in which it is neither delegated nor conferred it does not make sense to ask the question.

For instance, a believer who wondered whether God's authority over humankind was legitimate would be betraying some serious confusion about God, as if God ruled the universe by a right he had somehow acquired. God's claim to authority is not a claim to legitimate authority. Legitimacy is not something God needs to claim. Likewise, a parent who asserts her authority over her obstinate five-year-old with some such remark as "Because I'm your mother!" is not claiming legitimate authority over her child. What would be the point of that? It would, after all, have to be a very precocious five-year-old who could wonder whether its parents' authority was legitimate. In the small child's world, its parents have authority absolutely and not by virtue of custodial rights, say, that some state has granted them. The pivotal thesis, then, in Raz's defense of the first assumption is false.[28]

Raz's defense of the second assumption is no less defective. To hold, as he does, that the legitimacy of authority is a matter of how well the authority in question fulfills the purpose for which it exists is to treat the question of an authority's legitimacy as equivalent to the question of its rational justification. Specifically, given Raz's account of the purpose of governing authority, it is to treat the question of legitimacy as equivalent to the question of whether the subjects of this authority would be rationally justified in obeying it. Yet it is far from evident that a claim to legitimate authority over others is typically a claim to authority obedience to which would be rationally justified. It is not likely, for example, that when the House of York and the House of Lancaster were contesting which descendant of Edward III was the legitimate heir to the English throne, they were concerned with whose authority it would be more rational for the subjects to obey.[29] Sometimes questions of legitimacy turn on conformity to principles or rules that in themselves have no rational justification. Their normative force in a population consists in their having for generations been broadly accepted. Customs frequently have normative force in a society by virtue of broad acceptance by its members and a long history of being kept and followed, and where they concern the determination of governing authorities, as the customs on which hereditary monarchies are founded do, the question of legitimacy is not answered by considerations of whether obedience to the authority would be rationally justified. Raz's mistake thus consists in confusing the question of legitimacy with that of rational justification.

One can trace this mistake to Raz's view that normative discourse about authority and obligation is always resolvable into discourse about reasons for action. Raz holds this view because he thinks any practical judgment of the form x ought to $\varnothing$ implies a judgment of the form x has a reason to $\varnothing$.[30] Hence, once he sets out the logical relation noted above between attributing to x authority over y in the normative sense and holding that y ought to obey x, the view immediately follows.[31] And because Raz thinks the relation holds only if the attribution of authority in the normative sense implies the attribution of legitimate authority, he is led to think that establishing the legitimacy of x's authority over y amounts to determining that y has reason to obey x. Or in other words, the question of an authority's legitimacy is the same as the question of its rational justification. The ultimate source of this mistaken identification, then, is Raz's thesis that any practical judgment of the form x ought to $\varnothing$ implies a judgment of the form x has a reason to $\varnothing$.

To see why this thesis is at the root of his mistake, one must first recognize an important ambiguity in practical judgments of the form x ought to $\varnothing$. On the one hand, they may be hypothetical, in which case their validity depends on x's having a desire or interest whose satisfaction would result from x's $\varnothing$ing. On the other, they may be categorical, in which case their validity is independent of x's desires and interests. "You ought to take an umbrella," for instance, is typically asserted hypothetically, for it is typically offered as advice to someone who it is assumed wants to stay dry. "You ought to give more to charity" is typically asserted categorically, for typically one thinks charitable action is called for by the external circumstances of the person to whom this directive is addressed and without regard to that person's desires or interests.[32] There is no question that one can always interpret a practical judgment of the form x ought to $\varnothing$ as x has a reason to $\varnothing$ when the judgment is understood to be a hypothetical one. Because the judgment in this case is made on the assumption that x has a desire or interest that would be satisfied by x's $\varnothing$ing, the interpretation is uncontroversial. But Raz cannot take the practical judgments the attribution of authority to the law implies as hypothetical, for then their validity will depend on the subjects' having certain desires or interests, and some outlaws may not have them. In other words, he cannot take these judgments as hypothetical without making the first feature of the law's authority inexplicable on his account. Hence, he must take them as categorical. And at this point his mistake in identifying the question of an authority's legitimacy with that of its rational justification becomes obvious.

After all, it is not uncontroversial whether one can always interpret a practical judgment of the form x ought to $\varnothing$ as x has a reason to $\varnothing$ when the judgment is understood to be a categorical one. Quite the contrary. Such an interpretation is tantamount to saying that x cannot be fully aware of his circumstances and also utterly indifferent to Øing unless x is to some degree irrational, and opinion sharply and deeply divides on whether mere failure to take a positive attitude toward doing an action when one lacks the desire for or interest in any end the action would achieve can ever be irrational.[33] The question has been hotly debated since Hume's famous denial in his *Treatise*.[34] Nor does one need to take sides on this question to see Raz's mistake. Plainly, whether some person's or institution's authority over others is legitimate is not always a controversial question, and even when it is, the controversy does not typically concern philosophical uncertainties about the reason-giving force of categorical "ought's." On Raz's account, by contrast, the question is always controversial and always controversial in this way.

Hart explained normative discourse about authority, obligation, rights, and other features of law by distinguishing between internal and external statements.[35] When one makes the former, Hart declared, one makes them from an internal point of view. It is the view of someone who accepts the rules and standards the law comprises as guides to conduct. When one makes the latter, Hart continued, one makes them from an external point of view. This is the view of an outside observer, someone who notes facts about the legal system of the group he is observing but who does not accept its rules and standards as guides to conduct. It makes sense therefore to construe Raz's view that normative discourse about authority and obligation is always resolvable into discourse about reasons for action as intended as either a replacement for or a supplement to Hart's explanation. That is, it makes sense to take Raz to have advanced this view either on the assumption that the subjects' responsiveness to interest-independent reasons, rather than some internal point of view, is the key to explaining normative discourse about authority and obligation in the law or on the assumption that such responsiveness explains what Hart meant by an internal point of view. On either interpretation, however, the view would fail. It falls short, as we've seen, of explaining the normative force that attributions of authority to law carry.

An emotion-based account of the law's authority does better. Because the internal point of view on Hart's explanation is the view of people committed to the law as a guide to their conduct, one can plausibly assume that some emotional bond to the law lies behind this commitment. Hart's internal point of view, in other words, can plausibly be understood as the product of an emotional bond to the law. On an emotion-based account, then, for those who have such a bond to the law, that the law has authority is a reason for obeying it, whereas for those—like outlaws, revolutionaries, and anarchists—who do not, it need not be a reason for obedience. This understanding of the normative force that attributions of authority to law carry is surely more plausible than one on which either outlaws, revolutionaries, and anarchists suffer from some cognitive defect, some ignorance of their circumstances or deficiency in their reasoning, or the authority of the law they oppose is illegitimate. Here too, then, in the matter of explaining normative discourse about the law's authority and the subjects' correlative obligations, the emotion-based account appears more cogent than a reason-based account such as Raz's.

VI

When the laws of Athens in Plato's Crito address Socrates and assert their authority over him, an emotional bond between Socrates and the law becomes evident.[36] The laws, in reproving Socrates for contemplating disobedience, remind him that they are his parents and that the disobedience he is contemplating would be a worse wrong than dishonoring his parents. Their metaphors and comparisons unmistakably show the strength and type of bond that exists between the laws and Socrates. This great work on the authority of law, with its passionate speech in favor of fealty to law, no less than Kafka's novel, testifies dramatically to the thesis I have defended in this paper.

NOTES

I am grateful for the helpful comments I received from the participants at the conference on emotions and the law at which I presented an earlier draft of this chapter. I wish to thank, in particular, Susan Bandes, Daniel Brudney, Jeffrie Murphy, Connie Rosati, and Martha Nussbaum for their perceptive remarks.

1. (Cambridge: Harvard University Press, 1985).

2. Trans. by Willa and Edwin Muir (New York: Random House, 1956).

3. Jeremy Bentham, "Of Laws in General" (H. L. A. Hart, ed. (London: Athlone, 1970), pp. 1, 10–13, 18–21) and A Fragment on Government (Cambridge: Cambridge University Press, 1988), pp. 39–43; and Austin, The Province of Jurisprudence Determined and the Uses of the Study of Jurisprudence (London: Weidenfeld and Nicolson, 1955), pp. 133–36, 193–96. For a comparative discussion of Bentham and

Austin, see H. L. A. Hart, "Bentham's Of Laws in General" in his Essays on Bentham: Jurisprudence and Political Theory (Oxford: Oxford University Press, 1982), pp. 105–26.

4. See H. L. A. Hart, The Concept of Law (Oxford: Oxford University Press, 1961), pp. 70–76.

5. The criticism is due to Hart; vide n. 11.

6. A Fragment on Government, pp. 93–95.

7. Ibid., p. 51. For Hume's critique, see A Treatise of Human Nature, bk. III, pt. 2, sec. 8.

8. This point is due to Hart; vide n. 11.

9. Among the many works that have made and elaborated this point, see Anthony Kenny, Action, Emotion and Will (London: Routledge & Kegan Paul, 1963); Robert C. Solomon, The Passions (Garden City, N.Y.: Anchor/Doubleday, 1976); Jerome Neu, Emotion, Thought and Therapy (Berkeley: University of California Press, 1977); William Lyons, Emotion (Cambridge: Cambridge University Press, 1980); Ronald de Sousa, The Rationality of Emotion (Cambridge: MIT Press, 1987); Patricia Greenspan, Emotions and Reasons: An Inquiry into Emotional Justification (London: Routledge, 1988); and O. H. Green The Emotions: A Philosophical Theory (Dordrecht: Kluwer Academic Publishers, 1992). For a discussion of these and other cognitivist accounts of emotion, see my "Cognitivism in the Theory of Emotions," Ethics 104 (1994): 824–54.

10. See Sigmund Freud, The Ego and the Id, chs. 3 and 5, and Civilization and Its Discontents, chs. 7 and 8 in The Standard Edition of the Complete Psychological Works of Sigmund Freud, James Strachey, gen. ed. (London: Hogarth Press, 1969), v. 19, pp. 28–39, 48–59, and v. 21, pp. 123–45; Jean Piaget, The Moral Judgment of the Child, trans. by Marjorie Gabain (New York: Free Press, 1965); and John Rawls, A Theory of Justice (Cambridge, Mass.: Belknap Press, 1971), ch. 8.

11. See especially The Concept of Law, pp. 79–88.

12. See ibid., esp. pp. 97–120.

13. Ibid., p. 95; cf. p. 196.

14. See, e.g., Neil MacCormick, "The Concept of Law and The Concept of Law" in The Autonomy of Law: Essays on Legal Positivism, Robert P. George, ed. (Oxford: Clarendon Press, 1996), pp. 163–194; and Jules Coleman, "Authority and Reason" in The Autonomy of Law: Essays on Legal Positivism, Robert P. George, ed. (Oxford: Clarendon Press, 1996), pp. 287–319.

15. The Concept of Law, pp. 97–107.

16. Supra, pp. 289–291.

17. For further discussion of these aspects of moral development see my "Love, Guilt, and the Sense of Justice" and "Remarks on some Difficulties in Freud's Theory of Moral Development," both of which are reprinted in my The Sources of Moral Agency: Essays in Moral Psychology and Freudian Theory (Cambridge: Cambridge University Press, 1996), pp. 39–93.

18. Supra, n. 4. See also the essays cited in n. 17.

19. See The Concept of Law, pp. 196–97. Hart may have subsequently abandoned this account in view of Raz's criticisms. See "Commands and Authoritative Legal Reasons" in his Essays on Bentham, pp. 241–68.

20. The Concept of Law, p. 196; italics in original.

21. Ibid., pp. 198–99.

22. Ibid., p. 196.

23. Leviathan, ch. 22, pars. 10 and 14.

24. The Second Treatise of Government, §119.

25. For a clear and thorough statement of the case against taking the subjects' consent to be the basis for political authority, see A. John Simmons, Moral Principles and Political Obligation (Princeton: Princeton University Press, 1979), pp. 57–100.

26. The Authority of Law: Essays on Law and Morality (Oxford: Clarendon Press, 1979), pp. 3–33; and The Morality of Freedom (Oxford: Clarendon Press, 1986), pp. 23–69.

27. Practical Reason and Norms (Princeton: Princeton University Press, 1990; reprint from 1975), pp. 28–35.

28. Of course, Raz could remake the defense by withdrawing this thesis and asserting instead that the law's authority was conferred or delegated authority, for if its authority were conferred or delegated, then its claim to authority over its subjects would be a claim to legitimate authority. But to make this assertion would be to deny the second feature of the law's authority. Moreover, it would require stretching the concepts of conferral and delegation far beyond the normal limits of their use. It is not, for these reasons, a plausible fallback.

29. Philip Soper, in "Legal Theory and the Claim of Authority," Philosophy & Public Affairs 18 (1989): 209–39, gives a similar example in criticism of Raz's account: "Second, it would seem to be one consequence of [Raz's] justification thesis that authority loses its legitimacy whenever a particular legislature is found to fall below the average in practical reasoning ability—a situation that, at least in the United States, cannot be ruled out in advance even in high levels of government let alone local city councils" (p. 226).

30. The Authority of Law, p. 12; see also Practical Reason and Norms, pp. 15–33.

31. Supra, p. 303.

32. On this distinction, see Philippa Foot, "Morality as a System of Hypothetical Imperatives" in her Virtues and Vices (Berkeley: University of California Press, 1978), pp. 157–73.

33. See Bernard Williams, "Internal and External Reasons" in his Moral Luck (Cambridge: Cambridge University Press, 1981), pp. 101–13.

34. A Treatise of Human Nature, bk. II, pt. 3, sec. 3.

35. See The Concept of Law, p. 99.

36. Crito, 50a–54d.

Chapter Twelve

Emotion versus Emotionalism in Law

Richard A. Posner

I. Introduction

Much of the behavior that law regulates is emotional—think of the murder of an adulterous spouse, the kidnapping of a child by a parent denied custody, or the daubing of paint on a fur coat by an animal-rights activist. Or it is shockingly devoid of emotion (the "cold-blooded" murder). Or it arouses the emotions—often sympathy for the victim of a crime or a tort and indignation at the injurer, but sometimes sympathy for the injurer, as in killings by "battered wives"—of people who hear or read about the incident. The law itself is conventionally regarded as a bastion of "reason" conceived of as the antithesis of emotion, as operating to rein in the emotionality of the behavior that gives rise to legal disputes. The emotionality of acts that are regulated by the law, and the law's emotional or nonemotional response to that emotionality, raise a number of issues for the legal system. I address four. The first is how the fact that a wrongful act is precipitated by an emotion should affect the law's evaluation of the act. Should emotionality make the law come down more or less hard on the violator? I discuss this question with particular reference to "hate crime" laws and to provocation as a mitigating factor in criminal punishment. The second question is whether and how the law should use emotion. The third is what the emotional state of the law's administrators, whether judges, jurors, prosecutors, or police, should be. Should they be emotionless, like computers? If not, how precisely should emotion enter into their judgments? And fourth, what screens or filters first should be used to assure that the administrators are in the correct emotional state (whatever exactly that is) when carrying out their legal duties?

Some help in answering these questions comes from the cognitive theory of emotion, which originated with Aristotle and has been greatly elaborated in recent years by philosophers and psychologists.[1] Challenging what despite Aristotle had become (not only in law) a thoroughly conventional antithesis between rationality and emotion, these theorists argue that emotion is a form of cognition, not just in the obvious sense that emotional reactions are usually triggered by information but also in the sense that an emotion expresses an evaluation of the information and so may operate as a substitute for more conventional forms of reason. For example, when we react with anger to being informed of some outrage, the reaction expresses disapproval, and we might have arrived at the same place as the end point of a step-by-step reasoning process. The evaluative function of emotion implies that a failure to react to a particular situation with a particular emotion might demonstrate not a superior capacity to reason but instead a failure of understanding or, in the case of moralistic emotions such as compassion and indignation, a rejection (not necessarily reasoned) of the society's moral code. Particular emotional reactions in particular situations can, thus, often be praised as appropriate to the situation or criticized as inappropriate either because they are evoked by misinformation or because they are based on an incorrect evaluation of the situation.

Another thing that is misleading about dichotomizing reason and emotion is that it confusingly envisages a struggle between motivational and nonmotivational elements of personality. Reason is not (*pace* Kant) motivational; knowing what is the right thing to do must be conjoined with a desire to do the right thing for action to result. When we say that a person did not allow himself to give way to his emotions (for example, he resisted that piece of chocolate), we mean that an aversive emotion ("self-control"—the aversion to being weak-willed) was stronger than the attractive emotion. There is no action without emotion.

Nevertheless, it would be a mistake to think that the cognitive approach to emotion abolishes traditional concerns about emotionalism. The dichotomy of reason and emotion, misleading though it is, captures an important truth. We all have the experience of making mistakes because of pride, anger, or other emotions. Emotion is an efficient method of cognition in some cases but an inefficient one in others. One might put it this way: emotion short-circuits reason conceived of as a conscious, articulate process of deliberation, calculation, analysis, or reflection. Sometimes this is all to the good; emotion focuses attention, crystallizes evaluation, and prompts action in circumstances in which reflection would be interminable, unfocused, and indecisive.[2] But in situations in which making an intelligent decision requires careful, sequential analysis or reflection, emotion may, by supplanting that process, generate an inferior decision. Or perhaps it would be better to say that too much emotion or the wrong kind of emotion may generate the inferior decision, for as I shall argue in discussing emotion in judges, emotion is necessary to precipitate any decision that is not merely the conclusion of syllogistic or other purely formal reasoning—the kind of reasoning a computer can do better than a human being. Decision is a form of action, and as I said earlier, there is no action without emotion.

It is possible to be a little more precise about what is meant when we say that a person is "emotional" or that a person's judgment is distorted by "emotionalism." We mean that that person has given undue salience to one feature of the situation and its associated emotional stimulus, neglecting other important features. So we might call a judge "emotional" who was so consumingly affected by the ghastly injuries of a tort plaintiff that his perception of the other legally relevant features of the case was completely occluded.

We expect the appellate judge to be less emotional in this sense than the trial judge because the appellate judge is more removed from the emotionally most salient features of the case. The appellate judge does not deal in person with the parties and witnesses, only with the lawyers and the trial transcript and other documents (with only the occasional photograph).[3] The configuration of the appellate process can thus be seen as an institutional response to the danger of emotionalism viewed as the giving of too much weight to a salient feature of a complex situation. In everyday life we respond to this danger by various personal strategies such as trying to "control" our anger so that it will not cause hasty, ill-considered, soon-regretted actions.

The idea of emotion as a kind of cognitive shortcut explains why jurors, like children, are more likely to make emotional judgments than judges. The less experienced a person is at reasoning through a particular kind of problem, the more likely that person is to "react emotionally," that is, to fall back on a more primitive mode of reaching a conclusion, the emotional. It is primitive in a quite literal sense. Emotions, like sex, are something that we have in common with animals, who, having smaller cortexes than humans, rely more heavily than humans do on emotions to guide their actions. The fact that emotions are discernible in the youngest infants is a further clue that we are dealing with an innate characteristic. Like other parts t from our cultural—en- ell adapted to the condi- olutionary biologists use beings evolved to essen- well adapted to the con- r concern that the emo- pitating a decision that complexity that may not onment), have benefited

description of emotion have done, that every "correct" emotional reaction can be translated into an analytical judgment. Such a view would reflect an excess of rationalism. Many of our thoroughly approved emotional reactions are prior to any rational reconstruction, the latter being in these cases pure rationalization. Try giving a good "reason" for becoming upset at seeing someone mistreat an animal. I return to this important point in Section VI.

II. Law: Pro or Con Emotion?

The introductory discussion suggests (I turn now to the first question that I said I would be addressing) that the legal system could have no uniform policy toward emotion any more than it could have a uniform policy toward information or belief. The significance of the emotional component of behavior regulated by law is bound to depend, rather, on the purpose of the particular law. Take criminal law. If one assumes that its basic purpose is to limit dangerous activity, the question of how the criminal law should treat emotion requires relating emotion to dangerousness; it is immediately apparent that the relation varies not only across but within crimes. Consider the case of murder. Often but not always the presence of strong emotion tends to mitigate the dangerousness of the criminal and the absence of strong emotion tends to aggravate it. The "cold-blooded killer" (psychopathic, affectless)—a murderer for hire, for example—is particularly dangerous. His propensity to kill is not confined to those rare situations in which a natural aversion to killing breaks down, as in the case of most crimes of passion, and his coolness will make it easier for him to maneuver to avoid being caught.

It could be argued, however, in contradiction to what I just said, that the more "emotional" the crime, the more rather than the less severe the punishment should be because a greater threat of punishment may be necessary to deter in those circumstances. But not only do the greater ease of catching the emotional criminal and the lesser risk that he will repeat the crime (because it is situation-specific and the situation is unlikely to recur) tend to offset the need to ratchet up the punishment to assure deterrence; in addition, most crimes of passion involve an element of provocation on the part of the victim, and provocation may provide a reason for lighter punishment.[4] Although the lighter punishment increases the likelihood of crimes against provokers by reducing the expected punishment cost of such crimes, it reduces that likelihood by increasing the expected cost of provocation (the provoker is more likely to be attacked, since the expected punishment cost of the attacker is less, and knowing this will be less likely to provoke). If the latter effect predominates, a reduction in the severity of punishment in cases of provocation will reduce the amount of crime.

At the other extreme, the "serial" killer and certain types of sex criminal (and many serial killers are sex criminals) are particularly dangerous because they are driven by powerful emotions to commit the same crime over and over again. Their emotion makes them more rather than less dangerous.

These two examples show that the law cannot be pro or con emotion as such. The law recognizes that emotionality is a dimension of human behavior, but its reaction to that fact is shaped by the purposes of particular laws applied to particular situations rather than by any overarching position on the goodness or badness of emotion.[5] Both the least and the most emotional criminals may be, as in the case of murder, the most dangerous and therefore the most deserving of harsh punishment. Granted, this conclusion assumes that the purpose of criminal law is to deter or otherwise prevent crime, and not everyone will accept that this is its purpose. But my general point holds regardless: the law cannot be expected to be flatly for or flatly against emotion or emotionality.

III. Hate Crimes

The discussion in the preceding section leads me to question whether there should be a separate category of "hate crimes" that are punished more harshly than the same offenses not motivated by hatred.[6] Like most emotions, hatred is morally neutral; the moral evaluation of an emotion depends on the object of the emotion. Unless you are the kind of Christian rigorist who takes the Sermon on the Mount literally, as a guide to living in this world rather than (as it was intended) preparing for living in a next world believed to be imminent, you will not think it immoral to hate Hitler or Stalin. And I would add (so far am I from being a moral rigorist) that I do not consider it immoral to hate criminals, philanderers, braggarts, or even beggars (who in today's America are mainly a species of con man), though I shall argue later that it is wrong for officials, and in particular judges, when in the exercise of their office, to hate anyone. Crimes of passion are frequently motivated by hatred for the victim, and yet the emotionality of the act is properly regarded as a mitigating factor if it indicates that the act is unlikely to be repeated because it was triggered by a confluence of circumstances that is unlikely to recur.

When we speak of "hate crimes" we mean something quite specific: that the object of the criminal's hatred is a particular kind of group rather than an individual and that the members of the group are not outlaws (if they were, it would not be a crime to prey on them). There may be merit to enhanced punishment in these circumstances even if the sole concern of the criminal law is with dangerousness. First and least, if the criminal's target is a group rather than an individual, this particular criminal may be more dangerous than the average criminal because he has more people in his sights, as it were. This point seems rather dubious, however, because it does not distinguish the hate criminal from the burglar, say, for whom every owner or occupant of residential or commercial premises is a potential victim. A better point is that if members of particular groups (for example, blacks in the South in the Jim Crow era, and homosexuals today in some areas of the country) are less likely than other crime victims to report a crime against them or to receive effective protection from police and other law enforcement authorities, the expected benefits to criminals (wholly apart from the emotional state of the criminal) of preying on members of the group will rise, warranting heavier punishment.[7] Heavier punishment is also warranted if the psychological harm to the victim of such a crime is greater when the victim knows that the criminal is motivated in part or whole by hatred of the group to which the victim belongs, or if the crime imposes an emotional cost (greater than a differently motivated but otherwise similar crime would impose) on people who are fearful of becoming victims of crime, or if the perpetrator derives an added benefit from the crime in the form of enhanced status among his fellow bigots.

We should distinguish among three types of hate-crime perpetrator: cold-blooded bigots; impulsive juveniles, who are in fact responsible for the majority of hate crimes;[8] and the deeply emotional hate criminal, symbolized by the "homophobe," who, deeply concerned about his own sexual identity, kills a homosexual who propositions him. The last category of hate crime overlaps with the crime of passion and raises the issue whether provocation should not result in a lighter punishment for many hate crimes. Homophobic murder *is* a crime of passion, and like other crimes of passion is situation-specific. But it also resembles the murder of prostitutes in not being confined to persons with whom the murderer has a direct relation (like the adulterous spouse).

What about the impulsive juveniles? They might be thought more deterrable than the homophobe because their emotions are less deeply engaged, but less deterrable because of the emotionality of youth: the imbalance that I noted earlier between emotion and reason in the judgments of the young.

To summarize the discussion to this point, hate crimes may indeed be on average somewhat more dangerous than otherwise similar crimes that are not motivated by hatred for a group. But the advocates of punishing hate crimes more heavily than other crimes do not insist on a tight linking of greater punishment to greater dangerousness. The classic hate crime is the murder of prostitutes, as by Jack the Ripper and his many emulators. Punishing it more heavily than the average murder could be defended by reference to relative dangerousness. Yet it is not what advocates of enhanced punishment for "hate crimes" mean by the term. They mean crimes against members of groups for which they have a particular solicitude, such as blacks, Jews, and homosexuals.[9] By defining hate crimes by reference to favored groups, and by thus severing the relation between group-hate crimes and dangerousness, these advocates inject politics into the criminal law, much as the Soviets did with their concept of "class enemies." If the proper criterion for grading criminal punishment is dangerousness, the presence and the object of hatred are relevant only insofar as they bear on the criminal's dangerousness. A person who kills homosexuals because he hates homosexuals is more dangerous than a person who kills the man who has cuckolded him, but not more dangerous than a person who kills prostitutes because he hates prostitutes. As long as criminal sentencing takes full account of the bearing of the criminal's object on his dangerousness, the nonpolitical concerns that motivate advocacy of the "hate crime" classification are taken care of automatically, and there is no need for the classification.

Not only no need; in such a case the use of the classification to increase (or decrease) punishment is inconsistent with freedom of belief and conscience. If two crimes differ not at all in dangerousness but only in the fact that one is motivated by a belief that the judicial authorities reprobate (a belief, for example, that homosexuals are evil or dangerous), then to punish that crime more heavily is to punish belief, not action. Compare two criminals. Both blackmail homosexuals. They differ only in that one does it purely for money, and the other partially out of hatred of homosexuals. Blackmail by the first blackmailer is not a hate crime; blackmail by the second is. To punish the second more heavily is to punish (to an extent measured by the increment of punishment of the second blackmailer over the first) an opinion about homosexuality. I do not think we should punish opinions, however repugnant we may find them.

This conclusion owes much to the cognitive theory of emotion. The cognitive element in emotion shows that when a criminal is punished more heavily because of the emotional state in which he committed the crime, we may be punishing cognition, and therefore opinion or belief, and not merely raw emotion.

The Supreme Court has rejected the First Amendment challenge to hate-crime laws that I have just sketched on the ground that hate crimes do more harm than other crimes because they are "more likely to provoke retaliatory crimes, inflict distinct emotional harms on their victims, and incite community unrest."[10] This is judicial sophistry. The point about retaliation actually implies that the weaker the group targeted is, the less likely it is to retaliate, and hence under the Court's analysis the *less* harmful the crimes against it are![11] The point about community unrest seems just to repeat the first or the second point in different words. The point about "distinct emotional harms" may be correct[12] but probably is not;[13] and in any event it is the sort of vague and coarse-grained justification for punishing opinions that the Supreme Court usually rejects in First Amendment settings. Is it really more distressing to be assaulted because you're a member of a group whom your assailant hates than because he hates you as an individual? If you're black, is it worse to learn that a white has tried to kill you because he hates blacks, or that your son has tried to kill you to inherit your money? The answers will vary from case to case, and this casts doubt on the adequacy of the hate-crime categories to pick out the more serous crimes, even apart from the arbitrariness of the categories and the lack of any *need* for them since the issue can readily be handled either case by case or by a rule or standard that is based on a nonideological criterion, such as the provision in the federal sentencing guidelines requiring enhanced punishment of crimes against "vulnerable victims."[14] And notice the paradox that enhanced punishment for hate crimes has less going for it when the crime is murder, since often the victim will not know the motivation of the murderer—indeed, often he will have no foreknowledge of the murder and hence incur no emotional distress (though other members of the group may). But the hate-crime statutes do not recognize this paradox.

The objection, in short, is not to varying the punishment for crime according to the harm suffered by the victim or the deterrability of the criminal but to varying it in order to make a political or ideological statement, or (what is often the same thing) to accommodate the pressures of politically influential groups. Ideology and interest-group politics have no proper place in a criminal justice system. In rejecting this precept, the supporters of hate-crime laws, some of whom are deficient in historical memory, are playing with fire. It was not long ago that a political or ideological conception of the role of criminal law would have justified less, rather than more, protection of that law for blacks, homosexuals, and other minorities. Proponents of hate-crime law may respond that in those bad old days the enforcement of the criminal law on behalf of these groups was often unenthusiastic, and this is true. But there is a difference between failing to protect people adequately against private hostility and making that hostility a basis for punishment. The first practice is wrong; the second is wrong and dangerous.

IV. Hating the Criminal

It would be a mistake to infer from the discussion in the preceding section that hatred and cognate emotions such as disgust and revulsion have no place in criminal punishment. It would be a particularly serious mistake to confuse hatred *by* the criminal with hatred *of* (or disgust for) the criminal. The latter is an ineliminable feature of criminal justice in at least three respects. First, disgust underlies the criminalizing of "immoral" conduct that cannot be shown to cause temporal harm, such as intercourse with animals, cruelty toward animals, desecration of corpses, and public nudity. Second, hatred informs the decision to impose capital punishment under the essentially standardless capital-sentencing regime created by the Supreme Court. And, third, even when sentencing guidelines are used to curtail judicial discretion in sentencing and to do so in part by banishing many "emotional" factors, either the drafters of the guidelines or the judges in their diminished area of discretion are bound to consider emotional factors, such as remorse, that either increase or decrease the hatefulness of the criminal.

Disgust when sufficiently widespread is as solid a basis for legal regulation as tangible harm. To deny this—to contend that the only proper basis for criminal (or perhaps any) law is utilitarianism or some other moral theory—is to exaggerate the proper as well as the actual role of moral reasoning in the moral and criminal codes.[15] Not when it lacks a "rational" basis, but only when there is no consensus, does moral regulation become political or ideological in a disreputable sense; it is the disintegration of the moral consensus concerning the evil of homosexuality that has made the laws against sodomy so questionable a feature of criminal justice.

In making this argument, I am making a sympathetic bow toward the expressive theory of morality, fittingly in a work on the role of emotion in law. In this theory a moral judgment is an expression of a strong attraction to or repulsion by the behavior being evaluated. The cause of the emotional arousal need have nothing to do with any "reason" that might be offered by a moralist. Reasons can always be offered, but they have the air of rationalization. To offer an argument addressing why parents should not be allowed to kill their infant children seems to miss the point; it would be like arguing to someone who finds sex disgusting that there is no reason for his disgust. To place the entire criminal code on a "rational" basis would wreak havoc with our moral code.

The second and third points with which I began this section have to do with sentencing. The Supreme Court in the name of the Constitution's cruel and unusual punishments clause has forbidden the states and the federal government to make capital punishment the automatic or even presumptive punishment for specific classes of act. Government can specify the classes of act that make a defendant "ineligible" for the death penalty, but the jury must be allowed to consider the eligible defendant's character in deciding whether to impose the penalty. The consequence is that the issue in capital sentencing hearings tends to be how hateful the defendant is. The defendant's lawyer tries to portray him as sick, deprived, or penitent, and the prosecutor tries to portray him as evil and remorseless. Since the moral category of evil, the medical category of crazy, and the social-psychological category of deprived all overlap and many murderers are found in the area of overlap, juries in capital cases are often left entirely to their own devices in deciding whether to decree death.

As emphasized in Austin Sarat's contribution to this anthology, judges and jurors want defendants to exhibit remorse,[16] that is, recognition of having done wrong and regret for the wrong and its consequences for the victims. But remorse is such an interior state of mind that the judicial system can never have much confidence that the defendant is remorseful rather than merely forensically resourceful. Moreover, the more the defendant accepts responsibility for his act, thus demonstrating remorse, the more evil he makes the act and therefore the actor (himself) seem by depicting it as the product of his own depraved will rather than of evil companions, a deprived upbringing, an addiction, or a psychiatric illness.[17] In a capital case, with its elaborate sentencing hearings, the defendant can pursue a "two-track" strategy, where he takes full responsibility for his crime in his own testimony but his "mitigation expert" presents evidence that the defendant is being too hard on himself, that really his crime was the product of circumstances rather than of a depraved will. Those who do not believe in free will as a metaphysical reality think that the only significance of the defendant's proclaiming his remorse is to show that he is not an open rebel against the legal system—something that would make him more dangerous both by example and as evidence of his propensity to commit further crimes when and if released from prison.

The discussion in the preceding section of this paper provided ammunition for an oblique defense of basing the criminal law on a policy of deterring or (normally through imprisonment) preventing the unjustified infliction of temporal harm. Such a policy is politically neutral and reasonably objective, and this is preferable to using the criminal law to enforce current ideas of politically correct behavior or to randomize the imposition of capital punishment. But as I just explained, you cannot push this view of the proper scope of the criminal law too far, given the lack of functional justifications for some of our deepest moral intuitions that we want to embody in law. I return to this important point later.

V. Shaming Penalties

Recent interest in the use of shaming penalties (mostly publicity of various sorts, such as requiring a convicted sex offender to display a poster in his front yard that reads, "I am a convicted sex offender," or requiring vandals to clean sidewalks while wearing prison garb) puts in focus the question when if ever the law should try to induce an emotional state as a component of punishment. The shaming penalties recall a long history of public punishments designed to humiliate and degrade the convict and awe or frighten the spectators. This history had seemed to end, for the most part, with the rise of the prison in the nineteenth century, as a result of which criminal punishments are now normally carried out in secret.[18] Because imprisonment has become very costly, however, there is renewed interest today in alternative punishments, including shaming.[19]

Once it is acknowledged, as it must be, that people are capable of suffering "emotional distress" (the intentional infliction of which—except by the state when it is punishing criminals!—is a tort), the shaming penalties are seen as just another way of inflicting disutility on convicted criminals. Instead of depriving them of their liberty, the state subjects them to humiliation. It may inflict the same disutility, and thus achieve the same deterrent effect, as imprisonment, but at lower cost.

Yet even when the cost saving is substantial, there are three objections to the public humiliation of criminals. The first is that while the threat of imprisonment deters crime, imprisonment itself prevents crime so long as the offender remains in prison, and this preventive effect is lost when public humiliation is substituted for all or part of a prison term. If there is no substitution—if the shaming penalty is tacked on at the end of the prison term, to increase the severity of the sentence—there is no cost saving, although there may be a gain in deterrence.

Now it is true that with or without substitution, a shaming penalty may have a preventive effect after all, though here the form of the shaming penalty is critical. The sign outside the sex offender's house serves not only to humiliate the offender but also to warn potential victims to keep away from him. But the preventive effect will be less than that of imprisonment unless the period in which the warning is required to be in effect is considerably longer than the term of imprisonment for which it is a substitute would be, for not all potential victims will learn of the warning or take effective precautions in response to it. This implies that the most effective shaming penalty is the one that is tacked on at the end of the normal prison sentence. But, to repeat, in that case there is no economizing on the cost of imprisonment except insofar as the publicity effect of the shaming penalty reduces recidivism (by alerting potential victims) or increases deterrence, that is, except insofar as by making criminal punishment more severe, the shaming penalty reduces the amount of crime and so the aggregate cost of imprisoning criminals. But lengthening prison terms could have the same effect. If a 1 percent increase in the length of prison sentences led to a 2 percent decrease in the incidence of crime, the prison population would be smaller by roughly 1 percent.[20]

Second, if there is greater variance across persons in the disutility from humiliating punishments than in the disutility from loss of liberty, it will be more difficult to calibrate the humiliation punishment schedule—especially if more than one form of such punishment is employed. And third, public punishment tends to rob the criminal of his dignity; the public is fairly invited to execrate, shun, and ridicule him. This may engender a socially unhealthy "we-they" or "enemy within" public attitude toward criminal punishment.

VI. Judicial Emotion

The third question that I said I would address is the proper emotional state of the judicial officer, whether judge or juror. To what extent if any should the judicial officer's emotions be engaged by the case? A formalist, that is, one who thinks of legal analysis on the model of solving logical puzzles or mathematical problems, would probably answer, "Not at all." This would not be quite correct. Solving the most difficult logical and mathematical problems, the kind computers still can't solve, may require such emotions as wonder, delight, and pride; recall what I said earlier about the role of emotion in decision making. Nevertheless, a number of the strongest emotions, such as anger, disgust, indignation, and love, would be out of place because they would interfere with the problem-solving process rather than provide an efficient shortcut.

Is the answer different when, as is true in the most interesting legal cases, by which I mean cases that present difficult and important questions of law (as distinct from fact), a dispute cannot be resolved by a purely algorithmic procedure but requires recourse to intuition, moral feelings, the balancing of opposed interests, and political preferences? It is somewhat different. In some ways the danger of emotionality is greater the more uncertain the decision-making task, since the resistance put up by "objective" (in the sense of affectless) considerations will be weaker. Most people can add two and two correctly whatever their emotional state, but when the intellectual challenge is greater, the danger that the response will be "swayed" by emotion is greater too. This is one reason for the many rules designed to limit a judge's emotional involvement in a case, such as the rule that forbids him to sit in a case in which a relative is a party or a lawyer, or in which he has a financial interest.

At the same time, sound judicial decision making may require more emotions than just those that you need for performing any nonalgorithmic task. In particular, it may require indignation and empathy. Indignation is the normal reaction to a violation of the moral code of one's society. More important, it is often the mode by which a violation is identified. As I suggested in discussing the emotional basis of morals offenses, it is often difficult to give a persuasive *rational* account of a moral rule, including a moral rule to which the law has annexed a sanction for violation. This is true whether the rule is against urinating or masturbating in public, against public nudity, against pederasty, against polygamy, against infanticide, for or against abortion, against involuntary euthanasia, against intercourse with beasts or human corpses, against mistreating animals, against gladiatorial combat, against adult nonprocreative incest, against prostitution and obscenity, against gambling, against self-slavery, against public executions, against mutilation as a form of criminal punishment, or against some forms of discrimination (but not others). We "know" that urinating in public is bad only because we have a revulsion against the idea of it. Many of our other moral convictions as well resist reflection or reexamination because they are embodied in deeply rooted, inarticulable emotions. And many of these arational convictions are embodied in the law and imposed on people who do not share them, or (more commonly) do not act in conformity with them because they derive utility from the conduct that the rule forbids.

I thus take the cognitive significance of emotion even more seriously than Martha Nussbaum, a leading philosopher of the emotions, who in her contribution to this anthology argues that disgust is a "bad" emotion that should not influence the law. She makes reason the tribunal that reviews the emotions and decides which the law should encourage. I claim that the bedrock of many of our moral rules is emotion, not emotion-evaluating reason.

Suppose that a legal rule intended, as many legal rules are, to attach sanctions to the violation of a moral rule that has no plausible social-functional justification were challenged before an emotionless judge. This judge would have difficulty rejecting the challenge because he would not have and could not be given rationally convincing reasons for the rule. The rule (say, against a mother's killing her infant) would strike him as arbitrary, whereas a person with a normal emotional endowment would reject the challenge out of hand because his emotions told him to do so. And this is the right response if you think as I do that it is not the proper business of judges to dismantle the moral code of their society or, what would come to much the same thing, to insist that it be rationalized convincingly.

The other emotion that is important for the judge to feel when faced with a case that cannot be decided by purely formalistic reasoning is empathy or fellow feeling.[21] This point is easily misunderstood as inviting the judge to show partiality to whichever party to the case tugs harder on his heartstrings. My point is virtually the opposite. The importance of judicial empathy is to bring home to the judge the interests of the absent parties,[22] or in other words (the words of cognitive psychology) to combat the "availability heuristic." This is the tendency to give too much weight to vivid immediate impressions, such as sight over narrative, and hence to pay too much attention to the feelings, the interests, and the humanity of the parties in the courtroom and too little to absent persons likely to be affected by the decision. The operation of the availability heuristic is illustrated by the debate over abortion. Before ultrasound images of early fetuses became common, the heuristic favored the proponents of abortion rights, because they could tell vivid stories and even show photographs of women killed by botched illegal abortions, whereas the abortion "victim," the fetus, was hidden from view. Ultrasound, by making the fetus visible, canceled the rhetorical advantage that the proponents of abortion rights had enjoyed by virtue of the heuristic.

The availability heuristic is one of a long list of distortions in reasoning that have been identified by cognitive psychologists. Not all of them involve the emotions. The crooked appearance of a straight stick in water is an example of a perceptual distortion that owes nothing to emotion or emotionality. The availability heuristic crosses the line that separates the emotional from the "purely" cognitive; it is responsible for a number of tricks of memory that owe nothing to the emotionality of the events recalled (or not recalled). But when the heuristic is triggered by the emotional charge of a particular feature of a situation it is appropriately regarded as an example of a clash between emotion and reason.

The availability heuristic (so understood) leads to shortsighted adjudication—whether excessive lenity for the murderer who makes an eloquent plea for mercy, the victim being unable to enter a counterplea by reason of being dead; or an excessive tilt in favor of the rights of tenants, oblivious of the effect on the rental rates to other tenants when landlords factor the court-created higher cost of rental housing into their other costs and pass a fraction, possibly a large fraction, of them on to tenants in the form of higher rentals; or a tax break for a struggling corporation, ignoring the fact that other firms will pay higher taxes as a result and will pass on a part of the additional cost to consumers. You don't need much in the way of empathy to be moved by a well-represented litigant pleading before you. The challenge to the empathetic imagination is to be moved by thinking or reading about the consequences of the litigation for absent—often completely unknown or even unborn—others who will be affected by your decision. Thus, contrary to the claims of its detractors, the economic approach to law is profoundly empathetic because, although it does not wear its heart on its sleeve, it brings into the decisional process the remote but cumulatively substantial interests of persons not before the court—such as future seekers of rental housing, future victims of murderers, future taxpayers, and future consumers. As Shakespeare has Angelo (in his role as judge) say in *Measure for Measure* in response to Isabelle's plea that he show pity for her brother, "I show it most of all when I show justice; / For then I pity those I do not know, / Which a dismissed offense would after gall."[23]

There is thus no tension, as is commonly assumed, between judicial detachment and judicial empathy. Detachment is not "cold" when it involves creating an emotional distance between the judge and the parties (and witnesses and others in the judge's presence) in order to create space for an imaginative reconstruction of the feelings and interests of absent persons potentially affected by the judge's decision. The name that the legal system gives to this "detachment empathy" is "judicial temperament." The judge who gets so emotionally involved in the immediacies of the case that he is blinded to the interests of the absent parties is said to lack judicial temperament; the most prominent contemporary example is the late Justice Harry Blackmun.[24] We don't have an official name for the judge who displays the opposite form of emotionalism—a weird pride in maintaining a complete, inhuman indifference to the parties before him. But such judges are not admired.

Excess of pity is not the only type of emotionalism that is to be reprobated in a judge. Excess of rage is similarly deplorable. It fosters an unhealthy "we-they" mentality in which criminals are regarded as outcasts and vermin rather than as errant members of the community.

But it would be misleading to conclude that good judges are less "emotional" than other people. It is just that they deploy a different suite of emotions in their work from what is appropriate both in personal life and in other vocational settings. Self-control is not only an emotion but a strong emotion because it is a check on strong emotions, and empathy is an emotion and of course indignation is as well. Thus it is by no means clear that judges are less emotional than the average person unless "emotional" carries its (usual) connotation of situationally inappropriate emotionality.

VII. Emotion Filters in the Law of Evidence

The last question I take up is how the rules of evidence should be configured to help the judicial officer attain the proper emotional state sketched in the preceding section. The question can be focused by considering the issue of "victim impact" statements in death cases. The issue arose after the Supreme Court had held that the defendant in such cases could present evidence designed to appeal to the jury's sense of mercy. Had the Court stopped there and not allowed similar evidence to be presented by the victim's family and friends—evidence designed to engender the same sympathy for the victim as the defendant was trying to engender for himself—the Court would have been distorting the process of empathetic consideration. The defendant, pitiably pleading for his life, would have been standing before the judge and jury in all his palpable humanity, while his victim, dead and gone, would have been invisible. Think of Antony in *Julius Caesar* exhibiting the body of Caesar at Caesar's funeral and bidding Caesar's wounds to plead for him. This was an early as well as fictional example of a victim impact statement, but it illustrates the point well enough. The living occludes the dead and absent; the victim impact statement seeks to redress the balance; it is like my earlier example of the ultrasound picture of the fetus. Anyone genuinely concerned about the distorting effect on judgment of the availability heuristic, rather than merely concerned to reduce the number of executions, should applaud the Court's decision to allow victim impact statements.[25]

It has been argued that since the jury will have learned a lot about the victim during the guilt phase of the trial, evidence about the victim at the sentencing phase is redundant.[26] But that is also true about the murderer, whom defense counsel will have sought to present in a sympathetic light during the guilt phase. Moreover, much victim impact evidence concerns the effect of the victim's death on the victim's survivors, and such evidence will not have figured in the guilt phase. And to the extent that the evidence is redundant, its emotional force—the focus of the objection—will be blunted.

Also unconvincing is the argument that the victim is more likely than the murderer to come from the same social class as the jurors and so the jury will require additional help in understanding the potentially mitigating circumstances of poverty or deprivation or discrimination that may have impelled the murderer to his crime. Taken to its extreme, the argument implies that when the murder victim is rich, and the jurors and murderer of average income, victim impact evidence should be allowed, but not mitigating evidence. More generally, it implies complicating the litigation process with considerations of class alien to American ideology. In any event, most murders are between members of the same social class, namely, what used to be called the "lower" class. This implies that most murder victims have the same background of deprivation as the murderers, so that the banning of victim impact statements would actually penalize the law-abiding poor. What is true is that allowing victim impact statements "discriminates" against murder victims who do not have loving relatives, and so could be thought to cheapen the lives of the poor and friendless and to magnify the effect of social class on punishment. But this is really an argument not for excluding victim impact statements but for appointing a victim's representative to be Antony to the murderer's Julius Caesar and bid his dumb wounds to speak. To exclude victim impact statements might save a few murderers of the rich and popular, but it would further cheapen the lives of the poor and marginal by reducing the likelihood that their murderers would be executed.

It is also not a good objection to the victim impact statement that it appeals to the jury's sense of vengeance rather than to the "nobler" emotion of mercy. Mercy is nobler than vengeance only in the sense of being less natural[27] and less practical. On both counts it is more appealing to our modern rigorists (many found in the academy), who, like the early Christians, seek to set themselves apart from the herd by living (nowadays they are much more likely simply to advocate) a life that is repugnant to most people and that if adhered to steadily by enough people would bring society grinding to a halt. Vengeance is undoubtedly problematic; it is a prime example of an emotion that was functional in the ancestral environment, when there was no state to enforce a criminal law, and is much less functional under modern conditions.[28] Yet it is still indispensable, for without it few crimes would be reported and deterrence would often fail as a method of social control. Excess of mercy is as socially destructive as excess of vengefulness. (This is my earlier point that the Sermon on the Mount, with its turn-the-other-cheek morality, is not a practical formula for living.) Mercy in sentencing means lighter sentencing; lighter sentencing means more crime; more crime means more victims of crime. So mercy for victims implies severity for criminals, and mercy for criminals implies more victims of crime. Mercy is thus on both sides of the balance. And in one of the pans is also justice, while in the other side is the availability heuristic, pushing for one-sided, shortsighted, sentimental penal practices.

In defending victim impact statements I do not mean to suggest that the law should open the door all the way to emotional appeals in litigation. Indeed, an argument could be made for banning both victim impact statements and pleas of mercy by defendants in order both to minimize the operation of hatred in the sentencing process without distorting the balance between victim and murderer and to reduce the length and cost of criminal proceedings. And certainly there are emotional appeals that hurt rather than help the cognitive process, such as gruesome photographs of a murder victim that the prosecution wants to put in evidence not in order to establish victim impact but in order to establish guilt, an issue to which the photographs will often be irrelevant. Cognitive theorists of emotion, while right to complain about the excessive dichotomization of reason and emotion, should also be the first to admit that emotion can get in the way of rational processes and engender avoidable mistakes.

The law has an elaborate set of doctrines for fending off dangerous intrusions of emotion into the judicial process, especially when a case is tried before a jury; as inexperienced legal decision makers, jurors are particularly susceptible to the distorting effects of emotion. Evidence of a witness's bad character is therefore carefully circumscribed in a trial, and the presiding judge is empowered to exclude evidence more likely to inflame than to inform the jury and to set aside a jury's verdict if it seems to have been the product of passion rather than of reason. A proper understanding and critique of these rules might profit greatly from a careful examination of them in the light cast by the systematic study of the role of emotions in law. But I shall not attempt that formidable analytical task here.

NOTES

I thank Dimitri Karcazes and Christopher Ottele for research assistance, and Susan Bandes, Richard Cooke, Martha Nussbaum, Charlene Posner, Eric Posner, Cass Sunstein, and participants in the Conference on Emotions and the Law sponsored by the University of Chicago and DePaul University and held on May 23, 1998, for comments on an earlier draft.

1. See, for example, John Deigh, "Cognitivism in the Theory of Emotions," 104

Ethics 824 (1994); Jon Elster, "Emotions and Economic Theory," 36 *Journal of Economic Literature* 47 (1998); Robert H. Frank, "The Strategic Role of the Emotions: Reconciling Over—and Undersocialized Accounts of Behavior," 5 *Rationality and Society* 160 (1993); William Lyon, *Emotion* (1980); Martha C. Nussbaum, *Upheavals of Thought: A Theory of the Emotions* (University of Cambridge Press, forthcoming), esp. chs. 1 and 3; Keith Oatley, *Best Laid Schemes: The Psychology of Emotions* (1992); Ronald de Sousa, *The Rationality of Emotion* (1987); Robert C. Solomon, *The Passions* (1976); Michael Stocker with Elizabeth Hegeman, *Valuing Emotions* (1996); R. B. Zajonc, "Feeling and Thinking: Preferences Need No Inferences," 35 *American Psychologist* 151 (1980).

2. Cf. Elster, note 1 above, at 61–62, discussing studies that show that persons rendered emotionally flat by brain damage have difficulty making decisions.

3. See generally John C. Shepherd and Jordan B. Cherrick, "Advocacy and Emotion," 138 *Federal Rules Decisions* 619 (1991).

4. See Alon Harel, "Efficiency and Fairness in Criminal Law: The Case for a Criminal Law Principle of Comparative Fault," 82 *California Law Review* 1181 (1994).

5. Hence I do not agree that the criminal law takes "an ambivalent stance toward emotions." Dan M. Kahan and Martha C. Nussbaum, "Two Conceptions of Emotion in Criminal Law," 96 *Columbia Law Review* 269, 325 (1996). That implies that the law ought to make up its mind whether it is for or against the emotions. The proper stance is a nuanced one rather than either-or.

6. For an excellent discussion, see James R. Jacobs and Kimberly Potter, *Hate Crimes: Criminal Law and Identity Politics* (1998).

7. See Lu-in Wang, "The Transforming Power of 'Hate': Social Cognition Theory and the Harms of Bias-Related Crime," 71 *Southern California Law Review* 47, 57–58 (1997).

8. Jacobs and Potter, note 6 above, at 89.

9. See, for example, Kahan and Nussbaum, note 5 above, at 269, 313–14, 350–55 (1996). See also Jacobs and Potter, note 6 above, at 77: "Hate crime laws . . . demonstrate the impact of identity politics on criminal law."

10. Wisconsin v. Mitchell, 508 U.S. 476, 487–88 (1993).

11. See Jacobs and Potter, note 6 above, at 88.

12. As argued in Wang's article, note 7 above.

13. Jacobs and Potter, note 6 above, at 83–84.

14. See, for example, United States v. Lallemand, 989 F.2d 936 (7th Cir. 1993), upholding the enhancement where the victim of blackmail was a homosexual—but upholding it not because the defendant was motivated by hatred of homosexuals (it seems that his motivation was purely financial) but because the homosexual was deeply "closeted" and therefore highly unlikely to complain, which reduced the expected punishment cost of the blackmailer.

15. This is a theme of my book *The Problematics of Moral and Legal Theory* (1999), esp. chs. 1 and 2.

16. See, for example, Todd E. Hague and Jason Peebles, "The Influence of Remorse, Intent and Attitudes toward Sex Offenders on Judgments of a Rapist," 3 *Psychology, Crime and Law* 249 (1997).

17. This is a real problem in administering the "acceptance-of-responsibility" punishment discount in the federal sentencing guidelines. See United States v. Beserra, 967 F.2d 254 (7th Cir. 1992).

18. The story is told with great vividness in Michel Foucault, *Discipline and Punish: The Birth of the Prison* (1977).

19. See, for example, Dan M. Kahan, "What Do Alternative Sanctions Mean?" 63 *University of Chicago Law Review* 591 (1996); and for criticism, Toni M. Massaro, "The Meanings of Shame: Implications for Legal Reform," 3 *Psychology, Public Policy, and Law* 645 (1997).

20. Suppose that at time *t*, before the increase in prison sentences, the number of convicted criminals is 100 and the average prison term 100 months, so that the aggregate prisoner-months for which the prison system must budget is 10,000. If at time t+1, because of the deterrent effect of the longer prison sentences, there are only 98 criminals, each to serve 101 months, the aggregate prisoner-months will fall from 10,000 to 9,898.

21. Empathy is one of the best examples of the cognitive character of emotion. The cognitive element of empathy is imagining the situation of another person; the affective element, which marks it as an emotion and not merely a dimension of rationality, is *feeling* the emotional state engendered in that person by his situation.

22. As emphasized in Richard Cooke, "The Hazards and Virtues of Judicial Sympathy" (c/o Judge Robert Cowen, U.S. Ct. App. 3d Cir., unpublished, August 1997). See also Richard A. Posner, *The Problems of Jurisprudence* 412–13 (1990).

23. *Measure for Measure*, act 2, scene 3, lines 127–29.

24. See Richard A. Posner, *Law and Literature* 292–93 (rev. and enlarged ed. 1998) for an extended discussion of Justice Blackmun's judicial temperament.

25. Payne v. Tennessee, 501 U.S. 808 (1991).

26. These and other arguments against victim impact statements are summarized in Note, "Thou Shall Not Kill Any Nice People: The Problem of Victim Impact Statements in Capital Sentencing," 35 *American Criminal Law Review* 93 (1997). See also Susan Bandes, "Empathy, Narrative, and Victim Impact Statements," 63 *University of Chicago Law Review* 361 (1996); Martha C. Nussbaum, "Equity and Mercy," 22 *Philosophy and Public Affairs* 83 (1993).

27. Not *un*natural; it is closely related to altruism, and we know that some situations will generate altruistic impulses even toward strangers. The word "mercy" is often used, however, to denote the extreme of altruism that is associated with Christian ethical teachings.

28. See Posner, note 24 above, ch. 2 and references cited there.

Chapter Thirteen

Harlan, Holmes, and the Passions of Justice

Samuel H. Pillsbury

Unlike politics, religion, or the arts—other fields that regulate, critique, or analyze human behavior—the law is uncomfortable with feelings. Anglo-American legal culture has long held that law is good to the extent that it comes from detached, principled—and dispassionate—decision makers. Thus that quintessential figure of American justice, the judge, dresses in a somber black robe, sits at a high bench, and employs universal principles of reason to surmount the self-interested passions of the litigants. Legal culture demands that judges of all kinds and in nearly all legal settings display "judicial temperament," meaning that they remain above the emotional turmoil of the parties and their lawyers.[1]

But emotion's place in legal culture is not so simply captured. It turns out we have mixed feelings about feelings, even in law. For example, how do we reconcile law's formal commitment to dispassion with the common words of praise for a lawyer or judge that she—or he—displays a passion for justice?[2] How can passion, a word signifying strong emotion, be linked with justice, our ideal for law? Does this mean that emotion can play a legitimate role in judging? These are some of the questions pursued in this essay on emotion in judicial decision making.

The essay centers on the lives and work of two of our legendary Supreme Court justices, Oliver Wendell Holmes Jr. and John Marshall Harlan. Both men left permanent and positive marks on legal doctrine and analysis; as a result, both have significant claims to legal greatness. Yet it would be hard to find two individuals with more different emotional personalities than these men whose long careers on the Court overlapped for some nine years at the beginning of the twentieth century. Equally intriguing, each justice has suffered his severest attacks from those who found fault with the judge's emotional personality. Critics of Holmes have argued that his jurisprudence lacks moral content, a deficiency they trace to the man's lack of feeling for his fellow man. Meanwhile Harlan has been criticized as a judge who distorted legal doctrine to reach the conclusions his heart desired.[3]

Assuming, as I will, that Harlan and Holmes achieved greatness in at least some of their legal writings, their examples provide an excellent introduction to the complexities of emotive influence on appellate decision making. A look at a small sample of their work—Harlan's dissent in *Plessy v. Ferguson* and Holmes's dissent in *Lochner v. New York*—reveals a host of possibilities for emotive analysis in law. We see that emotions, especially emotions concerning ideas, play an important role in good judging. We see the possibilities of a new kind of legal analysis that joins biography to doctrine, allowing for an integration of personality and emotion with the formal reasoning of law. Interestingly, emotive analysis also reinforces traditional legal reasoning, by showing how the variety of emotive influence and its subtle effects make critical a discourse in which public reasons can be articulated and discussed. Emotive influence may tell us where a judge comes from but, by itself, cannot tell us whether the judge's position is justified either in morals or law.

The emotive analysis introduced here also reveals the conceptual and terminologic inadequacy of most current discussions of emotion in law. The nearly universal tendency in legal argument to treat emotion terms as self-defined and as normatively obvious constitutes an enormous obstacle to analysis and understanding. At a minimum we will need a new vocabulary of emotion to realize the possibilities of emotive analysis in law.[4]

Defining Emotion: Feelings about Persons and Ideas

A natural starting point for any examination of emotion's effects on the law would be a definition of emotion. This proves more difficult than it sounds, however. Defining what should and should not count as emotion—for example, whether an emotion must be accompanied by an urge to action or may comprise a mood, whether emotion must involve a cognitive assessment of a person or situation—these and other conceptual issues have occupied the time and efforts of a number of modern philosophers of emotion. Meanwhile some have argued that the term *emotion* covers such a wide range of phenomena that no single definition is possible.[5] Fortunately, a complete conceptualization of emotion is not necessary to explore emotive influence on judicial decision making. In evaluating emotion's impact on judges, it will be enough to concentrate on the feelings of individual judges, what mental health scientists call affect. By feelings I mean, at a minimum, a person's reaction to another person, creature, thing, situation, or idea, which reaction includes some degree of psychological (and probably physical) arousal. Because in law we are concerned with those feelings that create a motivation for a particular kind of action, we can restrict our analysis to those emotions that involve a positive or negative view of the person, creature, thing, situation, or idea, thus providing a normative direction to the individual's reaction.

This definition encompasses the strong emotions such as fear, anger, and sympathy that are usually directed toward other persons and that provide much of the high drama in human life. In experiencing such emotions, the individual takes a strong pro or con view of another individual or group, a view that usually comes directly out of the emotion-holder's sense of his own place in the world. Such emotions present major problems in judges because of the possibility—probability in many cases—that emotive norms will vary from legal norms. For example: a judge rules against a motion because the lawyer arguing it reminds the judge of his former wife; a judge imposes a harsh sentence less because of the defendant's crime than because it reminds the judge of a crime suffered by a relative, a crime committed by someone of the same age, class, and race as the defendant. In each case the judge's person-directed emotion distorts legal judgment by introducing legally irrelevant factors to the decision.

The definition of emotion offered here goes beyond person-directed emotions to include emotions about ideas. We commonly recognize that individuals have emotional attachments to abstract concepts; indeed, we often hold such attachments in great esteem. When we say that a friend is deeply committed to his nation, to God, or to the principles of free speech, for example, we refer not just to an intellectual state but to an emotional commitment that will translate idea into action. We mean that the individual cares so much about these concepts that she will sacrifice time, energy, and perhaps much more for them. Such commitments are inextricably emotional. Not that emotional commitments to ideas are always positive. Stalin, Hitler, and Pol Pot are but a few of history's evil doers whose work was guided by an impassioned ideology. My only point is that humans are frequently emotional about ideas, just as they are about individuals, and any serious look at emotive influence on judging must consider both sorts of feelings.

This broad definition of emotion helps reveal the complexity of emotive influence on judges. We cannot simply inveigh against all emotion in judging; instead we must make critical distinctions between different contexts and kinds of emotions. To be a good judge may *require* certain emotional commitments. For example, consider the qualities needed for a judge to make a legally correct but very unpopular decision. A good judge will make such a decision because she feels strongly about obeying the constitution and the laws of her jurisdiction, so strongly that she will follow the law's dictate even when the decision will bring her professional and personal obloquy.

Setting the Question

Before we examine the background and work of Harlan and Holmes, I need to set the basic parameters of our inquiry. I assume for purposes of this essay that Justices Harlan and Holmes have major claims to greatness based, in part, on the opinions examined here. Likewise, I assume that the emotional dynamics revealed by the opinions analyzed say something important about the connection between emotion and judicial achievement. Each of these assumptions may be questioned. Some have certainly questioned the achievements of these judges. Others may argue that the particular opinions studied here do not reflect their best efforts. It may also be true that the opinions, or the emotional dynamics behind them, are uncharacteristic of their authors, or of other great appellate decisions. Certainly two opinions constitute too limited a sampling for any firm conclusions about the relationship between emotion and law in the work of either justice, let alone appellate judges generally.

The decision to concentrate on widely praised opinions also means that we can devote little or no attention to the shortcomings of each justices's emotional personality. Any full-scale consideration of emotive influence on appellate decision making would look hard at the judge's failures as well as successes. In the case of Harlan and Holmes, examples of the downsides of each justice's emotional personality will readily come to mind for those who know the justices' work, and I will allude to some here. The main point, though, is to consider the variety of emotions that may contribute to just decision making.

My question is: How did the judge's feelings about the parties or issues— or lack of such feeling—influence his opinion? To what extent did judicial emotion inspire judicial greatness? While the answers to these questions must remain suggestive based on the limitations of the inquiry, they prove intriguing enough to warrant further work. We see that understanding emotive influence may significantly enhance our understanding of law.

We begin with biography, for learning about the dynamics of emotive influence on judging involves learning about the unique individual beneath the uniform black robe.

Harlan: The Force of Outrage

John Marshal Harlan presents such a colorful figure that the historian's challenge is less to bring him alive for the reader than to prevent his becoming a dramatic caricature. A large, athletic, handsome man, he lived a long public life with great conviction and engagement, despite some astonishing reversals in philosophy. As a Supreme Court justice, he displayed the manner, though not always the views, of the southern politician he had been in his pre-Court career. He was passionate, loud, moralistic, self-confident, bold, and overtly patriotic. His judicial writing still resounds with his emotional personality, his words booming with his oversize presence and passionate commitments.

Harlan was born in rural Kentucky in 1833. He grew up in a house full of law and politics—Harlan's father was a lawyer who was prominent in the state's Whig party. Harlan Sr. won election to Congress and later won statewide office as the attorney general of Kentucky. In addition to law and politics, the other guiding force in the Harlan household was religion. Harlan's parents were devout Presbyterians, and their son was a firm believer in the same religious tenets throughout his life.

Harlan followed his father's professional path, becoming a lawyer whose first interest was politics. A large, striking figure on the stump, with a booming voice, he was a tireless political campaigner who won elections to positions as city attorney, county judge and later attorney general of Kentucky. His political career was also studded with defeats: he lost campaigns for the House of Representatives, and the state governorship—twice.

Harlan's political views were always strongly held, but even in an age of great political change, his reversals of philosophy and allegiance were remarkable. The great issues of his day were slavery and states' rights. Harlan came from a slave-holding family, himself owned slaves, and in his early political career, following the demise of the Whig party, became a vigorous supporter of the avowedly racist and anti-immigrant American or Know-Nothing party. Nevertheless, when the Civil War broke out, Harlan's Whiggish loyalty to the Union prompted him to enlist in the Union army as a colonel. He served the Union cause as an officer until 1863, when the death of his father caused him to resign his commission to assume financial responsibility for the extended Harlan family. At this point Harlan's enthusiasm for the Northern cause remained limited. In the 1864 presidential contest, Harlan campaigned for Democrat George McClellan, who urged a negotiated settlement with the South, and against the Republican incumbent, Abraham Lincoln, who was committed to a military resolution. Following the war, Harlan strongly opposed the proposed Thirteenth Amendment to abolish slavery, arguing it would infringe states' rights. By 1868, however, Harlan had converted to the Republican cause. After joining the newly dominant national party, Harlan became its most effective proponent in Kentucky, helping build a Republican party structure in the state. Meanwhile, in his postwar law practice, Harlan became an effective and well-known advocate of civil rights for blacks. Later Harlan proved the most vigorous advocate for the use of the Reconstruction amendments to curb racial discrimination to sit on the Supreme Court in the nineteenth century.[6]

As a justice, Harlan cut a distinctive figure both in personal manner and legal philosophy. Holmes described him—apparently literally—as the last of the Supreme Court's "tobacco spitting judges."[7] For his unorthodox views on the Reconstruction amendments and other legal matters, Harlan became known as the Great Dissenter, dissenting in more than three hundred cases during his long tenure on the Court.[8] Nor did he dissent quietly. When he disagreed with the majority, Harlan frequently wrote long and vigorous dissenting opinions, and on many occasions delivered portions of these dissents orally from the bench. Late in his career he disturbed the other justices and prompted public criticism for his bench-thumping, high-volume reading of dissents apparently designed to shame opposing justices.[9]

Harlan's personal life appears to have been stable and happy, revolving around his wife and family. At twenty-three, Harlan married Malvina French Shanklin of Indiana. It was a happy marriage, and to all appearances Harlan was a devoted, loving husband for the rest of his life. He fathered six children in whom he took great pride and who went on to their own successes. (A grandchild became the second Justice John Marshall Harlan.) Harlan took considerable pleasure in the physical side of life, including athletic contests and eating.[10] In his later years he became an avid golfer, taking to the course in a striking outfit consisting of a bright cap, scarlet coat, Scotch-plaid trousers, and hosiery that one observer likened to "a rainbow winding around his well-shaped calves."[11]

Holmes: Yankee Dispassion

Just as Harlan personified many of the classic traits of southern populist leaders—hot-blooded, personal, engaged, and boldly moralistic—so Holmes personified many of the characteristics of a regional elite, in Holmes's case, the Boston Brahmin. Holmes was dispassionate, detached, intellectual, and culturally sophisticated.[12] But Holmes's detachment went beyond any regional or class style. For a man who was professionally and intellectually engaged in many of the critical issues in public law in the United States in the late nineteenth and early twentieth centuries, Holmes kept a surprising emotional distance from current events; although he had many social and professional friends, he had no intimates in his life, with the possible exception of his wife. From childhood until death, in his private and his public life, he always stood apart from others, and it is this aspect of his personality that has always attracted the most notice.[13]

Holmes grew up in Boston's social and intellectual elite, attending its schools until graduation from Harvard College in 1861. Holmes's father was a Boston doctor who, after a brief career in medical research, became a nationally known magazine columnist. In his school years, the younger Holmes also demonstrated some literary ambition. Then came the Civil War.

After college, Holmes enlisted in the Union cause with the enthusiasm that many Northerners of his class had for the adventure of war and the righteousness of the conflict. Like many other soldiers, he found his ideals severely tested by the horrors of mortal conflict. Three times during his three-year army stint, Holmes was seriously wounded and sent back from the front to recover. Twice he returned to his unit and to battle. After his third recovery in 1864, Holmes resigned his commission. Holmes came out of the war expressing ambivalence about the Union's claims to justice in the conflict. Though he supported the abolition of slavery, throughout his life he never displayed much sympathy for black Americans or their civil rights.[14] He seemed to feel that the South had as legitimate reasons for fighting as did the North.[15]

Following his military service, Holmes went to law school and became a practicing business lawyer. The work does not seem to have captured his spirit. He developed neither an interest in business nor a taste for the personal dramas that often lie at the heart of legal disputes. Nor did he become involved in politics. Although he worked as a lawyer and then judge in major centers of American political life—Boston and Washington, D.C.—Holmes never showed much interest in the partisan dramas that swirled around him. His most important formative experience in law appears to have been his work as a scholar. He wrote law review articles, coedited a legal journal, and, in conjunction with lectures given at Harvard Law School, produced a monograph about the development of common law.[16]

During his judicial career, first on the Massachusetts high court and then the United States Supreme Court, Holmes lived a life carefully isolated from many aspects of his social surroundings. He did not socialize outside his class, did not read newspapers, and made no other effort to ascertain the "facts" of the lives of those different from him in intellect, education, class, geography, or race.[17] Yet in his decisions, Holmes displayed considerable independence from standard class allegiance. His rulings could not be predicted based on his personal views of the litigants or social policy; indeed, he often seemed to rule against those with whom he would have agreed in another context.

In his personal life, Holmes displayed a similar detachment. His father had worried about the extent of his removal from ordinary human connections. Writing of a fictional figure called the Astronomer, believed to be modeled on his son, Holmes Sr. described a "strange unearthly being: lonely, dwelling far apart from the thoughts and cares of the planet on which he lives ... I fear that he is too much given ... to looking at life as at a solemn show at which he is only a spectator."[18] In his adult life, Holmes had many friends with whom he amiably corresponded, often about work, culture, and matters of the mind. He was not close to other members of his family; his marriage produced no children; and his relationship with his wife appears to have been amiable but not especially romantic, at least on his side. Even for a nineteenth century white male New Englander with a Puritan heritage, he was considered by many to be cold and distant.[19]

Holmes's voluminous writings in many respects support this portrait of the dispassionate man. The most striking quality of his written thought is its skepticism: his willingness to question all claims to ultimate validity, whether in law, psychology, or any other field. Similarly, religion played no apparent role in his adult life. While in his early life he expressed some religious leanings, as an adult, he neither displayed religious affiliation nor showed any sign of religious belief. In his writings, both public and private, Holmes refused to commit himself to any substantive principles of right and wrong.

Still a puzzle remains. How could an entirely dispassionate man accomplish so much? What could inspire the extraordinary efforts Holmes made to further the law throughout his long life? On closer examination, we find another side to Holmes. He did have his passions, but they did not concern individuals or substantive principles. He was passionate about intellectual pursuit and personal achievement. He may not have formed the usual attachments to the men and women around him and clearly remained skeptical of many of the faiths they held dear, but he was deeply passionate about legal insight and intellectual achievement.[20]

Consider again Holmes's attitude toward the Civil War. Although Holmes questioned the larger aims of the Union effort, he found meaning in military honor, in the sacrifice of the soldier for fellow men and nation— concepts about which he was passionate. An excerpt from a Memorial Day speech entitled "The Soldier's Faith" illustrates:

> I do not know what is true, I do not know the meaning of the universe. But in the midst of doubt, in the collapse of creeds, there is one thing I do not doubt, that no man who lives in the same world with most of us can doubt, and that is that the faith is true and adorable which leads a soldier to throw away his life in obedience to a blindly accepted duty, in a cause which he little understands, in a plan of campaign of which he has no notion, under tactics of which he does not see the use.[21]

Holmes understood the importance of passionate, principled commitments in understanding human affairs. Responding to those who ascribed ideals to mere self-interest, he stated: "Nonetheless they are there. They are categorical imperatives. They hold their own against hunger and thirst; they scorn to be classified as mere indirect supports of our bodily needs, which rather they defy; and our friends the economists would do well to take account of them."[22]

Holmes saw his judicial work as a kind of intellectual combat—a courageous and lonely contest for ends that were ultimately unknowable, made worthy by the fierceness of the struggle:

> Only when you have worked alone—when you have felt around you a black gulf of solitude more isolating than that which surrounds the dying man, and in hope and in despair have trusted to your own unshaken will—then

only will you have achieved. Thus only can you gain the secret isolated joy of the thinker, who knows that, a hundred years after he is dead and forgotten, men who never heard of him will be moving to the measure of his thought—the subtle rapture of a postponed power, which the world knows not because it has no external trappings, but which to his prophetic vision is more real than that which commands an army.[23]

Holmes's drive for intellectual achievement inspired him to look harder, or at least differently, at legal problems than other judges or lawyers. He would not be satisfied with legal truisms and reached for something more basic, and often uglier, beneath doctrine's surface sheen. In an age when many judges labored especially hard to create the impression of law's infallibility, Holmes's quest for timeless achievement drove him to speak plainly of power's dictates and, to a lesser extent, logic's demands. His extraordinary appetite for legal work and his genius for aphorism may be traced to a similar source. This was a man driven by a passion to leave a lasting mark on every area of law he could touch.

A New Analytic Method—Reading for Emotion

Having met our judges, we are nearly ready to examine their legal work. We will consider one opinion by each man: Harlan's dissenting opinion in the 1896 case of *Plessy v. Ferguson*, and Holmes's opinion in the 1905 case of *Lochner v. New York*.[24] We will look at each in hopes of answering this question: To what extent do these documents reflect their authors' emotional personalities? How did each judge's emotions influence his formal reasoning? Before we can address these questions, though, we must answer one about methodology. How do we find emotion in the cold record of an appellate judicial opinion?

The appellate opinion is a formal document, carefully drafted and revised to persuade according to the norms of legal discourse. The appellate opinion aims for a magisterial, dispassionate voice in which personal experiences and commitments are eschewed in favor of general principles. In this context, overt emotionality is normally taken as a sign of too much personal involvement. As a result, judges (and in recent times their law clerks) work hard to excise signs of personal feeling from their work. And yet emotion's influence is not so easily erased. In most cases, emotion remains an important motivator of the judge's conclusions, and a careful reader may find its traces even in a published opinion.[25]

Reading a legal opinion for emotion is different from reading for logic or doctrine. The reader becomes a hunter of feeling, looking for signs based on knowledge of the author and humanity generally. The search is based on a truism about human nature: that persons have feelings about anything of significance to them. Indeed, it may be tautological to link feeling with personal significance; our emotions signify an event's or a person's significance to us; in some sense emotions may constitute significance. Thus we can surmise that a judge engaged in deciding a case of great significance to others, and therefore of importance to the judge's career, will probably experience some emotions concerning the decision. We can presume that if the judge devotes the time and energy to write a dissent and thereby risks the loss of goodwill of colleagues and general criticism from the legal community, the judge's emotions are involved in the decision.

The judge's text of decision will supply many signs of emotion. Sometimes these are obvious, as where the judge uses overtly emotional language. More often emotion's traces appear in subtler ways. Beginnings and endings often give important clues to salience, both logical and emotional. The judge's presentation of basic facts may reveal the author's emotional outlook. We look to see if the factual account suggests active consideration of an individual or group's perspective, a sign of sympathy, or whether the fact presentation is pro forma or hostile, suggesting indifference or distaste. The same technique may be applied to the account of the parties' rival arguments. Does the presentation cast an individual or group in an especially negative light, perhaps signifying hostility, or an especially positive light, suggesting the opposite?

The emotion-hunter looks for literary qualities as well. Particularly lively prose may signal the author's personal engagement in the subject addressed. Where the prose takes on a recognizable, individual voice, breaking out of the dull legalese of judicial-speak, we may surmise that here the judge speaks personally, and perhaps emotionally. Such passages are not necessarily those where the argument's logic is most compelling but where the prose has greatest personal force, where, as the cliche goes, the author speaks from the heart. We also look for gaps and silences. What is missing that might appear if the emotional perspective were different? From what the judge does not say that he might have said, we can sometimes ascertain the feelings he did not wish to reveal.

In searching out emotion, the reader works like an archeologist or historian, constantly moving between the tangible text and background knowledge of the author, the case, and humanity generally. From the perspective expressed in the opinion, the reader tries to extrapolate back to the emotions that may have inspired it. It is as if we were given a photograph and asked to reconstruct the camera and its placement at the time the picture was taken. From a basic knowledge of human nature and a particular knowledge of the individuals and situation involved, we can often draw a rough picture of the emotional relationship between author and subject.

There are of course hazards in this enterprise. We may get it wrong. The usual reason we get it wrong is that we are fooled by the author about his or her emotional state. The author may intentionally deceive us in order to conform to the norms of the profession or the emotional expectations of his readers. Or the deception may be unconscious; the author may not recognize his own emotional state. In either case, the wary reader has some means of detecting emotive deception.

We are perhaps most familiar with deliberate deception. The judge may pretend to have sympathy for persons or ideas that she in fact lacks. The judge may seem to wring her hands in anguish at the harshness of a result that in fact causes her great satisfaction. As in other contexts, the emotion-hunter must be on guard for signs of insincerity. Does the judge protest too much, perhaps revealing a suspicious concern for image? Does the judge emphasize the inevitability of a legal outcome where in fact the law appears unsettled, leaving the decision maker more discretion than the judge admits? The reader may indulge in thought and emotion experiments. If the judge really felt the anguish that she reports, does it seem likely that she would declare the law as clear as she claims it is? Using these and other techniques, the emotion-hunter may, at least some of the time, uncover deliberate emotional deception.

We are less familiar with unconscious emotional deception, but in appellate judging it may be more common than the deliberate variety. We know well enough that humans often fool themselves about their own feelings. Sometimes it takes another to point out our own emotional state—that we are acting angry, or sad, or happy, when we believe that we feel otherwise. Thus the judge who proclaims dispassion, or even a particular kind of feeling, may be deceiving himself as well as the unwary reader. The emotion-hunter's main technique here is largely the same as with self-conscious deception: to look for a conflict between overt stance, reasoning, and holding. If the judge's formal expression suggests one emotional stance while the actual path of legal analysis suggests another, we have to consider the possibility of self-deceptive emotion.

Plessy v. Ferguson

In the modern history of constitutional law, *Plessy v. Ferguson* has gained a particularly notorious status. Like a handful of other infamous decisions, the Court's holding that Louisiana could, consistent with the equal protection clause of the Fourteenth Amendment, require railroads to segregate passengers by race, now stands as a landmark of injustice. Justice Brown's opinion for the Court in *Plessy* signaled the constitutional approval of a wide variety of Jim Crow laws that enforced racial segregation throughout the South. *Plessy*'s permissive stance toward race segregation remained the law of the land until changed by judicial decisions and legislation in the 1950s and '60s. The lone dissenter to the *Plessy* decision was John Marshall Harlan.

Harlan's dissent in *Plessy v. Ferguson* is discursive, lacking a clear overarching structure; Harlan builds the force of his argument less by logic than by repetition and overt appeals to emotion. In these respects, the dissent reads more like a political speech than a legal brief or judicial opinion.

The opinion opens with a flat description of the Louisiana statute challenged in the suit. The first hint of feeling emerges in the third paragraph:

> While there may be in Louisiana persons of different races who are not citizens of the United States, the words in the act "white and colored races" necessarily include all citizens of the United States of both races residing in that state. So that we have before us a state enactment that compels, under penalties, the separation of the two races in railroad passenger coaches, and makes it a crime for a citizen of either race to enter a coach that has been assigned to citizens of the other race.[26]

The juxtaposition of broad racial citizenship with the state law's requirement of racial separation, enforced by criminal penalties, suggests a fundamental wrong, a cause for anger. In this passage Harlan provides a preliminary version of his later, more impassioned, plea for equal rights of all United States citizens.

In the succeeding paragraph Harlan's tone again becomes legalistic, as he details the public trust status of railroads. Then once more the judge's voice becomes personal and takes on the cadences of the stump speaker:

> In respect of civil rights, common to all citizens, the constitution of the United States does not, I think, permit any public authority to know the race of those entitled to be protected in the enjoyment of such rights. Every true man has pride of race, and under appropriate circumstances, when the rights

of others, his equals before the law, are not to be affected, it is his privilege to express such pride and to take such action based upon it as to him seems proper. But I deny that any legislative body or judicial tribunal may have regard to the race of citizens when the civil rights of those citizens are involved. Indeed, such legislation as that here in question is inconsistent not only with that equality of rights which pertains to citizenship, national and state, but with the personal liberty enjoyed by every one within the United States.[27]

In this passage Harlan has established his primary themes: that pride of race does not support legal discrimination, and that fundamental American principles of liberty and citizenship require equal rights for white and black races.

Throughout the opinion Harlan expresses and appeals to patriotic sentiment about the fundamental law of the land, especially the Reconstruction amendments. For example, Harlan writes that the Thirteenth Amendment, abolishing slavery, was "followed by the fourteenth amendment, which added greatly to the dignity and glory of American citizenship, and to the security of personal liberty" by its privileges and immunities, due process, and equal protection clauses. "These notable additions to the fundamental law were welcomed by friends of liberty throughout the world. They removed the race line from our governmental systems."[28]

The further Harlan proceeds in his dissent, the stronger the feeling in his writing becomes. A clear note of anger emerges when he considers Justice Brown's claim that the Louisiana statute was not designed to indicate black inferiority. Brown had written that any stigma from segregation was "solely because the colored race chooses to put that construction upon it."[29] Harlan treats this argument as an insult to his readers' intelligence:

> Every one knows that the statute in question had its origin in the purpose, not so much to exclude white persons from railroad cars occupied by blacks, as to exclude colored people from coaches occupied or assigned to white persons. . . . The thing to accomplish was, under the guise of giving equal accommodation for whites and blacks, to compel the latter to keep to themselves while traveling in railroad passenger coaches. No one would be so wanting in candor as to assert the contrary.[30]

As a southerner Harlan knew too well why the Louisiana legislature required segregation, and he could not stomach the bland deceptions of Brown's majority opinion.[31]

As Harlan continues, he turns to his traditional constituency, the moderate whites of the South. He appeals to racial pride, to white supremacy, but only as the opening for a broad appeal for legal equality:

The white race deems itself to be the dominant race in this country. And so it is, in prestige, in achievements, in education, in wealth, and in power. So, I doubt not, it will continue to be for all time, if it holds fast to the principles of constitutional liberty. But in view of the constitution, in the eye of the law, there is in this country no superior, dominant, ruling class of citizens. . . . In respect of civil rights, all citizens are equal before the law. The humblest is the peer of the most powerful. The law regards man as man, and takes no account of his surroundings or of his color when his civil rights as guarantied by the supreme law of the land are involved. It is therefore to be regretted that this high tribunal, the final expositor of the fundamental law of the land, has reached the conclusion that it is competent for a state to regulate the enjoyment by citizens of their civil rights solely upon the basis of race.[32]

Harlan then blasts the majority with a single-sentence paragraph that sets the tone for the remainder of the dissent: "In my opinion, the judgment this day rendered will, in time, prove to be quite as pernicious as the decision made by this tribunal in the Dred Scott Case."

Harlan now becomes a kind of biblical prophet, predicting dire conflict as a result of the majority's decision:

What can more certainly arouse race hate, what more certainly create and perpetuate a feeling of distrust between these races, than state enactments which, in fact, proceed on the ground that the colored citizens are so inferior and degraded that they cannot be allowed to sit in public coaches occupied by white citizens? . . . State enactments regulating the enjoyment of civil rights upon the basis of race, and cunningly devised to defeat legitimate results of the war, under the pretense of recognizing equality of rights, can have no other result than to render permanent peace impossible, and to keep alive a conflict of races, the continuance of which must do harm to all concerned.[33]

Finally, Harlan expresses sympathy for blacks victimized by segregation laws: "We boast of the freedom enjoyed by our people above all other peoples. But it is difficult to reconcile that boast with a state of the law which, practically, puts the brand of servitude and degradation upon a large class of our fellow citizens,—our equals before the law."[34]

Obviously, Harlan's dissent presents no great challenge for the emotion-reader. In his *Plessy* dissent he expressed loathing for at least some forms of race discrimination; he displayed anger at white dissembling about racial motivations; and he sympathized with the suffering of black Americans. He declared his passions for certain national ideals—for racial peace and, most especially, for a particular view of freedom protected by the Constitution, one that guaranteed equality in public-law treatment for all classes and races. Taken together, these emotions form Harlan's passion for justice in matters of race discrimination.

Harlan's passion for justice was embodied, in the sense that it appears to have come out of Harlan's experience with flesh-and-blood individuals, both white and black. Even though the opinion mentions no individuals, it is suffused with concern for the individual human experience. Harlan writes about the experience of race discrimination from the white perspective—the desire to exclude a perceived inferior class. He also suggests something of the black experience—the hatred and resentment that must flow from the experience of exclusion from public accommodations on the basis of race.

Harlan's passion for justice was substantive in the sense that he expressed firm ideas about right and wrong in human interaction. These ideas of right and wrong were expressed in legal terms, but compared with those of other justices, rested less on prior case precedent and the Framers' intent than on Harlan's own vision of the meaning of American history. In Harlan's view the Anglo-American history of the struggle for freedom was a struggle to make "the humblest . . . the peer of the most powerful."[35] Following the Civil War, Harlan saw the nation extending this commitment to its former slaves, to African Americans. They should be free from public discriminations like any other citizens. To believe this, he urged, was nothing less than to believe in America. It was Harlan's version of patriotism.

Lochner v. New York

We now consider another landmark "bad" decision of the Supreme Court, its ruling in *Lochner v. New York*. For most American lawyers today, the majority's opinion stands as a classic example of bad constitutional law, symbolizing the excesses of the substantive due process doctrine that it espoused. The case's enduring fame comes largely from the dissent of Holmes, whose attack on substantive due process became a rallying cry for critics of the Court and later won over the Court itself.[36]

Prior to 1937, the United States Supreme Court used substantive due process to scrutinize a variety of federal and state economic and social reform laws. The Court selectively overturned laws on minimum wages, hours of work, work conditions, and other reform legislation on the grounds that these laws exceeded the government's police powers and violated the constitutional right to contract. In *Lochner* the question presented the Court was whether the State of New York had violated substantive due process by passing a law prohibiting employers from asking bakers to work more than sixty hours a week.

Joseph Lochner had been convicted of the misdemeanor of requiring a baker in his employ in Utica, New York, to work more than the statutory maximum hours. On appeal to the Supreme Court, a five-justice majority ruled that New York's maximum-hours law was unconstitutional as an impermissible infringement on Lochner's right to contract.

Writing for the majority, Justice Peckham found the health concerns of bakers unremarkable; he declared them typical of the industrial workplace. For Peckham, this presented a dangerous possibility: if the state could limit hours for bakers, it could limit hours for nearly any industrial workers. Peckham saw such widespread legislative regulation of the labor marketplace as a serious infringement of the liberties of both employers and employees to contract for themselves. Four justices disagreed with this conclusion; Harlan penned a dissenting opinion for himself and two other justices; Holmes wrote a dissent for himself alone.

From the beginning to the end of his concise dissent, Holmes focuses on the abstract principles of economics, government, and constitutional powers that the appeal involved. After expressing regret at the obligation of dissenting, he states: "This case is decided upon an economic theory which a large part of the country does not entertain."[37] In this way he establishes a characteristically Olympian viewpoint, encompassing the entire nation, the Court, and economic theory.

The reader for emotion is immediately struck by what Holmes leaves out of his opinion. Nowhere in his dissent does Holmes discuss the actual working conditions of bakers. This is in contrast both to Justice Peckham's derogation of health concerns and fellow dissenter Harlan, who relies heavily on social science evidence to show the special health problems of bakers. Nor does Holmes consider the individual interests of the defendant, Lochner. Lochner makes no appearance by name or proxy in the opinion; his business and liberty interests are addressed by only the most sweeping of abstractions. From this highly detached treatment of the facts, we may infer that Holmes cared little for the people involved in the case. He was neither sympathetic nor hostile to bakers or to their employers. In the usual sense of emotion—feelings about the individuals involved—Holmes was indeed dispassionate.

Considering emotion in the broader sense, however, we see Holmes's unique passions expressed in the dissent. What engages Holmes's interest here is not individuals but ideas. He is concerned with constitutional theory, particularly the relative powers of court and legislature under the federal Constitution. Holmes opens his discussion of the constitutional issues by noting the many laws imposed on businesses, from Sunday-closing laws to prohibition of lotteries, which prior courts permitted despite their effects on liberty to contract. Holmes then moves from legal doctrine to economic theory, observing that Americans have many different ideas about the proper structure and organization of the nation's economy—and that the Constitution takes no stand on economic theory. It is this latter point that seems to engage Holmes the most, for it is here that his individual voice rings out most clearly. In the middle of a listing of traditionally accepted forms of business regulation, Holmes declares: "The 14th Amendment does not enact Mr. Herbert Spencer's Social Statistics. . . ." Later in the same paragraph he writes:

> [A] Constitution is not intended to embody a particular economic theory, whether of paternalism and the organic relation of the citizen to the state or of laissez faire. It is made for people of fundamentally different views, and the accident of our finding certain opinions natural and familiar, or novel, and even shocking, ought not to conclude our judgment upon the question whether statutes embodying them conflict with the Constitution of the United States.

The short opinion closes with a long paragraph of classic Holmesian jurisprudence—aphoristic, dry, subtle, and provocative:

> General propositions do not decide concrete cases. The decision will depend on a judgment or intuition more subtle than any articulate major premise. But I think that the proposition just stated, if it is accepted, will carry us far toward the end. Every opinion tends to become a law. I think that the word 'liberty' in the 14th Amendment, is perverted when it is held to prevent the natural outcome of a dominant opinion, unless it can be said that a rational and fair man necessarily would admit that the statute proposed would infringe fundamental principles as they have been understood by the traditions of our people and our law. It does not need research to show that no such sweeping condemnation can be passed upon the statute before us. A reasonable man might think it a proper measure on the score of health. Men whom I certainly could not pronounce unreasonable would uphold it as a first installment of a general regulation of the hours of work. Whether in the latter aspect it would be open to the charge of inequality I think it unnecessary to discuss.[38]

Especially as compared with Harlan's dissent in *Plessy*, Holmes's *Lochner* dissent seems to lack feeling. We find here no personal appeals, no rhetorical flourishes, no calls to patriotic fervor, national identity, or the moral lessons of history. We find no colorful adjectives or adverbs, let alone stirring nouns or verbs. This does not prove as much as it may seem, however.

Consider for a moment how we would expect this opinion to read if Holmes were truly dispassionate about the case. Assuming that Holmes took the same position on the law, we would expect him to author a dissent concentrating on the similarity between the New York law on bakers' hours and other state business regulations that had previously passed constitutional muster. From a dispassionate author—one emotionally uninvolved in either the persons or the ideas presented—that is all we would expect. We would not expect the dispassionate judge to make grand generalizations about economic theory and constitutional jurisprudence. If he did not care about the case—either the individuals or the issues—why would he bother? We would not expect aphorisms on social Darwinians, popular opinion and lawmaking, and legal syllogisms. We would expect these only from a jurist who *cares* about the case in some way. Now it is true that Holmes's opinion may reveal someone who did *not* care about the particular dispute between Lochner and the State of New York or about the plight of bakers or their employers generally. But this does not mean Holmes was dispassionate about the issues the case raised, the resolution of which was, after all, his main task as a justice.

In his dissent Holmes demonstrated a great deal of care for the legal issues involved, enough so that he mounted a frontal assault on one of the most important principles of federal constitutional law of the day. Holmes used his opinion to expose the logical and constitutional deficiencies of the majority's reasoning, to yank the cloak of legalism from substantive due process and expose the economic theory that lay beneath. Here we see Holmes willing, even eager (notwithstanding his initial protest about the unfortunate obligation of dissent), to puncture the comfortable legal mythology of his Court colleagues. Holmes flatly rejected the claim that substantive due process provided a politically neutral and historically sanctioned means of overseeing government's efforts to regulate the economy. The prose may be abstract and spare, but that does not mean Holmes's heart was not beating a little faster, or that he might not imagine the playing of a trumpet (or perhaps a French horn) in the background to signal his reaching for timeless truth.

In Holmes's *Lochner* dissent we see a judge whose emotional and intellectual commitment to a deeper truth and to making himself a place in legal history led him to a relatively radical vision of constitutional law. These twin passions inspired him to reject the dominant constitutional paradigm of his day.[39] Note that Holmes's legendary detachment from other persons, while clearly displayed in this case, proves neither necessary nor sufficient for his decision. Holmes may not have cared about bakers or their employers but because he did care about finding a logical and historically sanctioned principle to guide constitutional review of economic regulation, he pushed the bounds of accepted legal analysis. The principles and the process involved in deciding the case engaged Holmes emotionally as well as intellectually; without that engagement the dissent he wrote is unimaginable.

Faith in Justice

What do the examples of Harlan and Holmes suggest about emotion's contribution to judicial decision making? Can we discern in the limited sampling of the work of these quite different judges a quality or qualities that might be called a passion for justice? I suggest—and given the limited nature of this exercise I can do no more than suggest—that Harlan and Holmes each had a passion for justice that built on their individual, and quite different, beliefs in the justice ideal. To use a religious term, both had faith in justice. By this I mean each had a deeply held belief, generated from personal experience, that there exist norms to guide legal decision making beyond those of doctrinal tradition and the preferences of the powerful.

Harlan's faith in justice may be the simplest to explain because it comes in the most familiar form: a belief in certain substantive principles of right and wrong. A man of few doubts, his view of justice was shaped by a set of core religious, moral, and political beliefs about the nature of the American ideal. These beliefs translated directly into positions on equal protection and other constitutional doctrines. Harlan was a true believer in constitutional law as a source of definite moral norms. He believed that there were right answers to the legal questions put to him and that he had those answers, regardless of the views of the rest of the legal community.

Holmes's faith in justice was both more procedural and more metaphysical than Harlan's. Holmes doubted the existence of clear principles of right or wrong, at least in the sense that Harlan believed. Holmes saw justice as a process, a struggle toward ultimate insight sometimes partially glimpsed but never fully gained. Holmes sought particular and often contingent truths, not all-encompassing, ever-lasting Truth. The possibility of establishing more honest and more logical principles on which to base legal decision making was enough to inspire his challenging analysis and his legal creativity. Yet for all his hard-nosed skepticism and procedural focus, Holmes understood that at bottom he also was inspired by faith, not empirical proofs. He stated:

> We all, the most unbelieving of us, walk by faith. We do our work and live our lives not merely to vent and realize our inner force, but with a blind and trembling hope that somehow the world will be a little better for our striving. Our faith must not be limited to our personal task; to the present, or even to the future. It must include the past and bring all, past, present and future, into the unity of a single continuous life.[40]

Significance

Assuming that Harlan and Holmes shared a faith in justice, albeit in quite different forms, what does this signify? Or, to put it more bluntly, so what? Does this exercise in legal and biographical analysis really teach us anything we did not know before? Initially the results may seem meager. We hardly needed extended analysis to realize that great judges, like great achievers in any field, require faith in values and in their own possibilities to inspire their work. We are left with the truism that great accomplishments require great drive. Nor is a passion for justice sufficient for great judicial achievement. The judge's personal values, analytic ability, breadth of mind, patience, and determination are but a few of the other prerequisites of judicial achievement. In fact, having a passion for justice can be a negative characteristic. A passion for justice can inspire extraordinarily bad decisions that more dispassionate judges would avoid.[41]

When we look to the further implications of identifying various passions for justice, however, we see some important potential benefits. We begin with the most obvious. The examples of Harlan and Holmes teach us—or perhaps remind us—of something easily missed in the highly deliberative, rationalistic culture of modern law: that emotional character matters in law. Judges may fail in their work due to emotional shortcomings, just as they may fail from deficiencies in reasoning. The examples of Harlan and Holmes illustrate some particular emotional hazards with respect to ideas.

By nature and function, the law is a conservative enterprise; it seeks to establish and maintain order by fixed rules. This conservative function often inspires rigid thinking. It becomes hard for the legally trained to imagine legal structures different from those of the status quo. Harlan and Holmes show how a passion for justice may inspire the lawyer or judge to see new landscapes on the present terrain. Without that vision, the other justices in *Plessy* complacently accepted the states' power to require racial segregation; the majority in *Lochner* assumed that the Constitution gave it authority to restrict political regulation of the economy.[42]

The examples of Harlan and Holmes teach that, even when practiced at its highest level of abstraction and sophistication, law involves both intellect and feeling. In judging, as in all other human endeavors, there can be no easy separation of emotion and rationality. In most instances rationality is inspired by, infused with, and in turn affects emotions. The law's standard imprecation against all judicial emotion simply will not work because we need some kinds of passion for good decision making. For example, in recent years judging has become more bureaucratic, with judges required to process ever-increasing numbers of cases. In this work environment the most serious emotional hazard may be that of becoming jaded. Judges may come to view their work as mundane, requiring the mechanical application of traditional principles to new facts, without any larger normative dimension. Judges may easily lose faith in the possibility of justice, or to put it differently, forget that miscarriages of justice may occur even when the bureaucratic rules of law are followed.

This preliminary analysis raises a number of provocative questions about the qualities of a good judge. What are we to make of the enormous emotional differences between Harlan and Holmes? What do these differences say about the personal qualities we should look for in a judge? We often assume that there is an ideal judicial type, some perfect blend of intellect and heart, courage and discretion, empathy and detachment that describes the perfect judge. Yet here are two of our legendary justices who appear at opposite ends of the emotional continuum. For all his extraordinary ability, the idea of a Supreme Court composed of nine Oliver Wendell Holmeses sends chills up the spine. Yet would we rest any easier with a bench composed of Harlan clones? Perhaps the problem is this notion of an ideal judge. Perhaps there is no perfect judge for all cases, no single individual with the ideal blend of qualities to resolve all cases. While we may imagine the perfect judge for a particular case, no living, breathing human being will be well qualified to decide all potential legal controversies. To use

Harlan and Holmes as examples, Harlan's tendency to grand moralistic judgment made him relatively ill equipped to do the close, doctrinal work often critical to the interstitial development of case law.[43] Similarly, Holmes's lack of empathy for individuals clearly did lead him astray on occasion.[44] We are left with a sobering reminder of the humanity of law and the importance of emotive diversity in judicial ranks.

An appreciation for emotive diversity takes us only so far, however. In an interesting twist, the more we understand about emotive influence on judicial decision making, the more we should appreciate the importance of doctrinal discourse. In part because each individual's view of a case will be influenced by individual experiences and personalities—by emotive dispositions—that may not be shared by others, we need a discourse that we do share. The principles of precedent, logic, and other traditional legal norms provide that shared discourse. Indeed, those norms provide our legal bottom line. Emotive analysis may foster better understanding of a judge's work, but legal evaluation of that work depends finally on legal norms, not emotion.

This perspective on emotion and doctrine may give us another way of conceptualizing law. The twentieth century in America has seen a long-running academic debate about the nature of law. Inspired in part by Holmes, the Legal Realists early in this century argued that the formal ideals of law—determinacy, precedent, logic, and the like—were at worst a sham and at best an incomplete explanation for psychological, economic, and sociologic influences on the legal decision maker. The Realists emphasized the importance of the personal experiences and foibles of the judge—what he had for breakfast was the oft-used phrase—in determining the outcome of a particular decision. In more recent years, Critical scholars have built on the Realist critique, emphasizing gender, race, and class influences on legal decision making. While these attacks on legal objectivity and certainty have had considerable impact, especially in our view of law's past, contemporary courts continue to swear allegiance to the most formal understandings of doctrine and legal reasoning. There remains an apparently unbridgeable gulf between the ideals of law espoused by those with legal power and the realities of decision making put forward by critics.

I do not want to claim too much for emotive analysis—the conflict between Realist critique and formalist ideals goes far beyond concerns with emotional influence—but the technique does promise an intriguing way of reconciling rival views of law's nature. Using emotive analysis, we can still grant the power of precedent and logic in the formal discourse of law even as we recognize the ordinary humanity of the decision maker, an individual susceptible to emotive influence. We can do this because emotive analysis shows us how the judge came to a decision, without necessarily speaking to its moral or legal validity.

To sum up: emotive analysis should permit us to understand better how personal experience shapes intellectual reasoning and influences the law.[45] It should help decision makers better understand and regulate their own decision processes. In this way it will help reconcile the formal discourse of legal decision making with the psychological dynamics of decision making. None of the possibilities of emotive analysis will be realized unless we develop a more precise vocabulary of emotion, however.

Just as sound legal analysis often begins with a redefinition of normative terms used in everyday conversation, so emotive analysis must begin with a redefinition of emotion terms. First year law students learn that in legal discourse, words like *intentional, knowing, reckless,* and *negligent* have particular meanings, narrower and more precise than the definitions of the same words in ordinary, nonlegal discourse. Students learn that the quality of legal reasoning often depends on the precision of word usage. Similarly, to undertake useful emotive analysis, we need a redefined emotive language. For example, in ordinary language the word *sympathy* covers a wide variety of benevolent feelings toward a person or situation. Sympathy may be based on the subject's morally relevant suffering or morally irrelevant suffering. It may be based on conduct or status. It may be weak or strong, conscious or unconscious. Distinctions such as these may well determine the relevance of sympathy in the particular legal context. But ordinary language makes no such distinctions.

With a new vocabulary of emotion we can do the substantive work of building moral and legal philosophies about the appropriateness of particular kinds of emotional reactions to particular human situations and to particular ideas. We need to develop such philosophies to guide decision makers on how to integrate their own emotional reactions to controversies with applicable legal principles. We need philosophies of emotion on which to base legal judgments concerning the emotional experiences of the parties during the events in controversy.

To illustrate more concretely how much work and of what kind we have to do to realize the possibilities of emotive analysis in law, I have attached as an addendum a brief critique of judicial treatment of emotion in a recent, high-profile criminal case.

Final Thoughts on the Court's Odd Couple

In emotional terms Holmes and Harlan were the judicial odd couple, the Felix and Oscar, the Mr. Spock and Dr. McCoy of the turn-of-the century Court.[46] Where Harlan shouted, Holmes dryly declared; where Harlan plunged into the midst of political and legal disputes, Holmes stood apart, interested but also disengaged. And yet compared with many other judges, we see that Harlan and Holmes shared a basic characteristic: an emotional commitment to, a faith in, norms beyond those of settled doctrine. They were committed to the justice ideal.

Holmes's notion that even "the most unbelieving of us" strive for something more in our lives, for some level of coherence not readily apparent in ordinary discourse, points to what may be the most promising result of this inquiry, the possibility of joining heart and mind in our understanding of law. The legal academy has spent much of this century in deconstruction and dissection, in pulling apart the formal apparatus of law to reveal and critique the actual dynamics of decision making. That has proven important work, but it represents only half the task of legal reform. Perhaps now we can concentrate on putting the pieces back together, albeit in different ways. Perhaps now we can integrate biography with doctrine, and emotion with reason, creating a conceptual whole that does justice to the many dimensions of law.

Addendum: The Au Pair Case and Contemporary Legal Discourse on Emotion

Most of the issues raised in this essay may seem far removed from contemporary courtrooms, but they are not. Especially at the trial level, judges must daily resolve important issues about emotion. Unfortunately, the legal state of the art with regard to emotive analysis is not highly developed. An opinion in a recent high-profile case illustrates.

In the fall of 1997, after a jury returned a second-degree murder verdict against Louise Woodward for causing the death of an infant in her care, Massachusetts Superior Court Judge Hiller B. Zobel exercised his statutory power to substitute a verdict of manslaughter.[47] In his written memorandum of decision, Judge Zobel relied heavily on emotive judgments.

Zobel opened with a quote from John Adams's defense of British soldiers for the so-called Boston Massacre, expressing the law's traditional hostility to emotion. Lawyer Adams told an eighteenth century Boston jury that the law must be "deaf as an adder to the clamours of the populace."[48] Applying Adams's imprecation to the current case, Judge Zobel declared that "the Court may not . . . take into account the feelings of those the death has affected." He stated that the law under which he operated "requires a judge to view the entire case with a clear and steady eye" and that he reached his decision "[a]fter intensive, cool, calm reflection. . . ."

Yet later in the opinion, the judge indicated that he believed emotion could have great normative importance for legal decision making. The judge used an emotional reference to question the prosecution's decision to bring a first-degree murder charge. Zobel observed that there were—barely—sufficient factual grounds to support the charge, then added, "[w]hether obtaining the indictment in that form was wise or *compassionate* is not for the Court to say at this time" (emphasis added).[49] More significant for the judge's ultimate decision was his conclusion that the defendant's emotional state was inconsistent with the malice aforethought necessary for murder. The judge found that "the circumstances in which the Defendant acted were characterized by confusion, inexperience, frustration, immaturity and some anger, but not malice (in the legal sense) supporting conviction for second degree murder. . . . I view the evidence as disclosing confusion, fright, a bad judgment, rather than rage or malice. . . ."[50]

Without considering the legal or moral merits of Judge Zobel's decision, we can question the adequacy of his emotive analysis. Like most judges, Zobel made arguments about emotion without sufficient definition of terms or articulation and justification of concepts. To be fair, some of his emotional arguments were obvious enough not to require further articulation or defense. Obviously, neither sympathy for the victim's family nor the sensationalized, talk show dramaturgy that constituted a good deal of the media discussion of the case should affect legal decision making about the defendant's legal culpability. Other emotive points required much more discussion to be persuasive, however.

Why should the prosecution be compassionate in its charging decisions? If compassion is an important quality in a prosecutor who files charges, what sort of compassion is needed? Should the prosecutor feel compassion for the victim, the defendant, or others? How much should he or she feel and on what basis?

Judge Zobel indicated that the verdict should be manslaughter rather than murder if the defendant acted out of fright and confusion and some anger but not rage. Why? Do these emotional distinctions have universal normative content—can they be made into general legal principles—or do they relate only to the circumstances of this case? Are fright and confusion always mitigating emotions? What of fright and confusion that turn to anger? How do we distinguish "some anger" from "rage"? What legal or moral difference does this emotive distinction make? More generally, was the judge primarily concerned with the feelings that the defendant actually experienced in her care of the infant or was he concerned with the reasons she acted as she did?[51]

Judge Zobel's treatment of emotion is typical of contemporary legal discourse in that emotions are described in general terms without specific definition and treated as normative concepts without analysis or explanation. The judge makes broad generalizations about emotion, assuming its danger, or worth, without sufficient attention to the nature of the particular emotion involved and its context. He assumes that standard emotion terms stand for normative concepts, when the most basic analysis of emotion reveals that they do not. In a manner all too typical of contemporary legal discourse, the judge's account of emotion leaves some of the most important issues unarticulated and, perhaps, unconsidered. We can do better than this.

NOTES

For their comments and support, I would like to thank the participants in the symposium on emotion and law held at the University of Chicago Law School in May 1998, and especially Susan Bandes and Richard Posner, who offered particularly useful critiques. Thanks should also go to my research assistant, Suzy Snyder, for her help in gathering material for the essay.

1. On the requirements of judicial dispassion, see generally Jeffrey M. Shaman, The Impartial Judge: Detachment or Passion? 45 DePaul L. Rev. 605 (1996). For an interesting recent exploration of the normative value of emotion in the political realm—where appeals to emotion are endemic but nevertheless controversial—see D. Don Welch, Ruling with the Heart: Emotion-Based Public Policy, 6 So.Cal. Interdisc. L. J. 555 (1997).

2. E.g., Morris S. Dees, Jr., A Passion for Justice, 12 T.M. Cooley L. Rev. 547 (1995); Harold Hongju Koh, A Tribute to Justice Harry A. Blackmun, 108 Harv. L. Rev. 20, 21 (1994).

3. On Holmes, one of the most insightful and critical accounts of his detachment remains that of Yosal Rogat, Mr. Justice Holmes: Some Modern Views, 31 U. Chi. L. Rev. 213 (1964). See also Grant Gilmore, *The Ages of American Law* 48–51

(1977); Shaman, The Impartial Judge, *supra* note 1. On Harlan, see, e.g., G. Edward White, John Marshall Harlan I: The Precursor, in *The American Judicial Tradition* 128, 133–34, 144–45 (1976). Meanwhile defenders of Harlan have always noted and commended the passion of his legal work. "His affection for the Constitution and the institutions existing under it amounted to a religious fervor." Edward F. Waite, How "Eccentric" Was Mr. Justice Harlan? 37 Minn. L. Rev. 173, 187 (1953). Probably the most famous quote about Harlan is one attributed to Justice David J. Brewer, who stated that Harlan "goes to bed every night with one hand on the Constitution and the other on the Bible, and so sleeps the sweet sleep of justice and righteousness." Quoted in Tinsley E. Yarbrough, *Judicial Enigma: The First Justice Harlan* viii (1995).

4. In so doing, I draw on a long tradition, dating back to the Legal Realists, of commentators who have insisted on the importance of emotion to legal decision making. For recent accounts of the value of certain kinds of emotion to legal decision making, see Martha C. Nussbaum & Dan M. Kahan, Two Conceptions of Emotion in Criminal Law, 96 Col. L. Rev. 269 (1996); Samuel H. Pillsbury, Emotional Justice: Moralizing the Passions of Criminal Punishment, 74 Cornell L. Rev. 655 (1989); Lynne Henderson, Legality and Empathy, 85 Mich. L. Rev. 1574 (1987). For emotion's relation to judicial decision making specifically, see Nussbaum, Emotion in the Language of Judging, 70 St. John's L. Rev. 23 (1996); Susan Bandes, Empathy, Narrative and Victim Impact Statements, 63 U. Chi. L. Rev. 361 (1996); Cheryl L. Wade, When Judges Are Gatekeepers: Democracy, Morality, Status and Empathy in Duty Decisions (Help From Ordinary Citizens), 80 Marq. L. Rev. 1 (1996); Shaman, The Impartial Judge, *supra* note 1. For a recent philosophic account arguing for the importance of emotion to moral reasoning, see Michael Stocker with Elizabeth Hegeman, *Valuing Emotions* (1996); see also Jeffrie G. Murphy & Jean Hampton, *Forgiveness and Mercy* (1988); Ronald DeSousa, *The Rationality of Emotion* (1987); Robert C. Solomon, *The Passions* (1976).

5. See Amelie Oskenberg Rorty, Introduction, *Explaining Emotions* 1–4 (A. Rorty ed. 1980).

6. Indeed, few justices prior to the second half of the twentieth century could claim a stronger record on the constitutional protection of civil rights.

Some have argued that Harlan's commitment to racial equality stemmed from his personal history. Harlan may have had a half brother who was part black and who grew up to be the financial success of the family. See Yarbrough, *Judicial Enigma, supra* note 3 at 10–20. In his adult life he met and showed respect for one of the leading black advocates for civil rights, Frederick Douglass. *Id.* at 83–84, 142.

7. Quoted in Yarbrough, *supra* note 3 at viii. Harlan was a tobacco chewer. Loren P. Beth, *John Marshall Harlan: The Last Whig Justice* 174–75 (1992). In general, Holmes took a dim view of Harlan's intellect but admired his heart. Holmes said Harlan's mind was "like a great vise, the two jaws of which cannot be closed closer

than two inches of each other." *Id.* On Harlan's death, Holmes wrote a friend: "[T]his morning Harlan the Senior Justice died and everything is put off. The old boy had outlived his usefulness—but he was a figure of the like of which I shall not see again. He had some of the faults of the savage, but he was a personality, and in his own home and sometimes out of it was charming. On my 70th birthday who but he bethought himself to put a little bunch of violets on my desk in the Court? He dissented alone in the Standard Oil and Tobacco cases and showed most improper violence towards his brethren, but I regarded it as partly senile. Peace to his ashes." Letter to Alice Stopford Green, October 14, 1911, *The Essential Holmes* 3 (R. Posner ed. 1992).

8. See Waite, *supra* note 3 at 182.

9. See Yarbrough, *Judicial Enigma*, *supra* note 3 at 172–75; Beth, *John Marshal Harlan*, *supra* note 7 at 200. See also Holmes's comments on Harlan, note 7 *supra*. Harlan himself wrote the following concerning his public reading of his dissent in the Income Tax Cases:

As this case was one of vast importance, I determined that I should be heard. So I read my opinion in a clear, distinct, audible tone of voice, which, I am told, rang through the courtroom so that everyone present heard each word of the opinion and took it for what it was worth. My voice and manner undoubtedly indicated a good deal of earnestness, and I am quite willing that it should have been so interpreted. I feel deeply about the case, and naturally the extent of my feeling was shown by my voice and manner.

Quoted in Yarbrough, *supra* note 3 at 174.

10. This thumbnail sketch and the biographical details that follow are drawn from the following sources: Yarbrough, *supra* note 3; Beth, *supra* note 7; David G. Farrelly, A Sketch of John Marshall Harlan's Pre-Court Career, 10 Vanderbilt L. Rev. 209 (1957).

11. From an unidentified newspaper account, quoted in Yarbrough, *supra* note 3 at 208.

12. The term *Boston Brahmin* was coined by Holmes's father, the columnist, to refer to the intellectual and upper-class elite of Boston. G. Edward White, *Justice Oliver Wendell Holmes: Law and the Inner Self* 11 (1993). The Brahmin designation refers to the Indian caste system in which the Brahmins occupy the top social rank.

13. The biographical literature on Holmes is extensive. Recent full-length biographies include White, *Justice Oliver Wendell Holmes*, *supra* note 12; Sheldon M. Novick, *Honorable Justice: The Life of Oliver Wendell Holmes* (1989); Gary J. Aichele, *Oliver Wendell Holmes, Jr.: Soldier, Scholar, Judge* (1989). The classic work on Holmes's early years is Mark DeWolfe Howe's two-volume *Justice Oliver Wendell Holmes: The Shaping Years, 1841–1870* (1957) and *Justice Oliver Wendell Holmes: The Proving Years, 1870–1882* (1963). There is also a rich and illuminating biographical literature in law review articles. Among the articles I have found particularly useful are Adam J. Hirsch, Book Review, Searching Inside Justice Holmes, 82 Virginia L.

Rev. 385 (1996); Thomas C. Grey, Holmes and Legal Pragmatism, 41 Stan. L. Rev. 787 (1989), and Rogat, Mr. Justice Holmes, *supra* note 3.

14. See White, *Justice Oliver Wendell Holmes, supra* note 12 at 341–43.

15. He stated in a Memorial Day speech: "I think the feeling was right—in the South as in the North." He continued: "I think that, as life is action and passion, it is required of a man that he should share the passion and action of his time at peril of being judged not to have lived." An Address Delivered May 30, 1884, at Keene, N.H., before John Sedgwick Post No. 4, Grand Army of the Republic (Memorial Day speech), *The Essential Holmes, supra* note 7 at 82.

16. The Common Law (1880).

17. On his distaste for facts, see Rogat, *supra* note 3 at 244–48. See *id.* at 244 for Holmes's disinterest in partisan politics.

18. Quoted in Rogat, *supra* note 3 at 243. For more on Holmes Sr.'s concern about the detachment of his son, especially with regard to his engagement and then marriage to Fannie Dixwell, see Howe, *Justice Oliver Wendell Holmes: The Proving Years, supra* note 13 at 5–9.

19. Holmes seemed to recognize his own lack of fellow feeling, writing that when he heard of men "whose dominant motive is love of their kind," it made him feel "like a worm," but observed that "most of the great work done in the world comes from a different type." *Holmes-Einstein Letters* 106 (J. Peabody ed. 1964), quoted in Aichele, *supra* note 13 at 108. For his lack of feeling for his brother who suffered and died in early middle age of asthma, see *id.* at 107.

20. See White, *Justice Oliver Wendell Holmes, supra* note 12 at 476–78.

21. An Address Delivered on Memorial Day, May 30, 1895, at a Meeting Called by the Graduating Class of Harvard University, *The Essential Holmes, supra* note 7 at 89.

22. Address of Chief Justice Holmes At the Declaration of the Northwestern University Law School Building, Chicago, October 20, 1902, *The Essential Holmes, supra* note 7 at 99. In a lighter vein, but to similar effect, he wrote a friend concerning the real grounds of social discontent:

> For a quarter of a century I have said that the real foundations of discontent were emotional not economic, and that if all the socialists would face the facts and put the case on that ground I should listen to them with respect. I used to tell my wife or she used to tell me, it was a joint opinion, that the manner of the Beacon Street women toward their servants and employees did more than the women were worth to upset the existing order.

Letter To Harold Laski, May 24, 1919, *id.* at 142. Similarly, in the sentence that precedes the portion quoted in the text from The Soldier's Faith, Holmes asked:

> But who of us could endure a world, although cut up into five-acre lots and having no man upon it who was not well fed and well housed, without the divine folly of honor, without the senseless passion for knowledge out-

reaching the flaming bounds of the possible, without ideals the essence of which is that they can never be achieved?

23. Conclusion of a Lecture Delivered to Undergraduates of Harvard University, February 17, 1886, *The Essential Holmes, supra* note 7 at 220. To similar effect is an excerpt from a letter he wrote to Benjamin Cardozo:

> I always have thought, that not place or power or popularity makes the success that one desires, but the trembling hope that one has come near an ideal. The only ground that warrants a man for thinking that he is not living the fool's paradise if he ventures such a hope is the voice of a few masters. . . . I feel it so much that I don't want to talk about it.

Quoted in Mr. Justice Holmes, in *Selected Writings of Benjamin Nathan Cardozo* 86 (M. Hall ed. 1947).

24. These cases are found in the United States Reports at 163 U.S. 537 and 198 U.S. 45.

25. This assumes the opinion is the personal product of the judge—that the judge who signs the opinion penned its words. When the opinion has been drafted by law clerks and only edited by the judge, as is often the case today, emotional influence is much harder to trace.

26. 163 U.S. at 553.

27. *Id.* at 555.

28. *Id.* at 555.

29. *Id.* at 551.

30. *Id.* at 557.

31. The Court at this time was dominated by northerners. Brown was born in Massachusetts and practiced law in Michigan. See *The Supreme Court Justices* 256–60 (C. Cushman ed. 1995). Brown began his autobiography this way: "I was born of a New England Puritan family in which there has been no admixture of alien blood for two hundred and fifty years." Quoted in *id.* at 256.

32. *Id.* at 559.

33. *Id.* at 559.

34. *Id.* at 562.

35. *Id* at 557.

36. For a somewhat revisionist view of the case, the Supreme Court, and substantive due process in general, see Howard Gillman, *The Constitution Besieged: The Rise and Demise of Lochner Era Police Powers Jurisprudence* (1993).

37. *Id.* at 75.

38. *Id.* at 76.

39. Holmes suggested only the negative half of what became the new constitutional paradigm for the Court: that it would not constitutionally scrutinize economic legislation but would reserve its oversight powers for laws affecting "discrete and insular minorities." See U.S. v. Carolene Products, 304 U.S. 144, 152–53 n. 4 (1938).

40. Address at Ipswich, At the Unveiling of Memorial Tablets, July 31, 1902, *The Essential Holmes, supra* note 7 at 74.

41. One example may be Chief Justice Roger Taney's ambitious effort to solve the slavery question once and for all in Scott v. Sandford, 60 U.S. 393 (1856). The opinion, which among other things declared the Missouri Compromise unconstitutional, seems inspired by an extraordinary faith of the author in his own vision of constitutional justice, a vision quite different from that of most legal and political leaders of the antebellum period.

42. We can easily miss this aspect of Holmes's and Harlan's achievements because modern law and culture have converted their dissents into accepted wisdom. At the time they wrote, however, each justice's ideas seemed radical to the status quo. Because of this we may praise their foresight. In emotional terms what we should value most are their passions for justice, which drove them, in different ways, to see legal issues differently than their colleagues. Without their particular faiths in justice, neither of these historic dissents would have been written. And we cannot be sure what path the law would have taken without their prophetic words to guide it.

43. See White, *supra* note 3.

44. See Buck v. Bell, 274 U.S. 200 (1927) (supporting forced sterilization of mental "defectives" based on the science of eugenics).

45. An interesting example comes from Morton J. Horwitz's *The Transformation of American Law, 1870–1960* (1992), a work of intellectual legal history. Horwitz spends a considerable portion of the book discussing Holmes's contribution to legal philosophy in the nineteenth century. Horwitz is careful to situate Holmes's thought within the ongoing intellectual controversies of his age, something rarely done by legal commentators, who usually emphasize Holmes's prescience concerning later developments in the law. Horwitz's discussion of Holmes's thought in *The Common Law* (1881) and how it evolved to that expressed in *The Path of the Law* (1897) is focused almost entirely on ideas, on the formal ideology of law. Then in an asterisked note at the close of the chapter, Horwitz writes that he recently came across letters from Holmes to Lady Claire Castleton, an Irish aristocrat whom he met in the summer of 1896 and whom he appears to have fallen in love with. *Id.* at 142–43. Horwitz quotes from what appear to be love letters from Holmes to Lady Castleton and then states:

> Before I had read any of this, I had felt strongly that the "The Path of the Law" represented an astonishing intellectual leap for Holmes. I supposed that the best way to understand it was "only" as intellectual history. Now one must ask whether and to what extent it was the discovery of some deep—and previously unfulfilled—love that produced in Holmes what Freud called an "oceanic" feeling, inducing him to transcend the prior categories of his thought.

Id. at 143. If Horwitz is correct, that the experience of a deep romantic love had an important effect on Holmes's legal philosophy, this should not in any way diminish the intellectual achievement involved. Holmes's romantic inspiration neither proves nor disproves the merit of *The Path of the Law*. But it does reinforce the interconnection between heart and mind, demonstrating that even if our primary interest in a judge is intellectual and rationalistic, the judge's emotions cannot be ignored if we wish a full understanding of the judge's work.

46. The references here are to, first, Neil Simon's play and then movie, *The Odd Couple*, concerning two mismatched middle-aged roommates, the fastidious Felix and the slob Oscar, and, second, to the Paramount television series and later movie series *Star Trek*, in which the twin emotional poles of the starship *Enterprise*'s crew were marked by the half-human, half-Vulcan Spock, allegedly devoid of emotion (though always displaying some hidden emotional influence in moments of crisis), and Dr. McCoy, also known as "Bones," who was constantly fulminating against Spock's coldness in the midst of great human drama.

47. CNN On-Line Service, Judge Zobel's Decision on Massachusetts v. Woodward, Nov. 10, 1997.

48. *Id.* at 1. Also a legal historian, Zobel is the coeditor of John Adams's legal papers and author of *The Boston Massacre* (1970).

49. *Id.* at 7.

50. *Id.* at 10.

51. For example, in the criminal law of provocation there is an ongoing debate about whether murder should be mitigated to manslaughter because the defendant experienced overwhelming emotion, thus reducing his ability to respond nonviolently, or because the defendant had particularly good reasons for anger at the victim. For the former view, see, e.g., Richard Singer, The Resurgence of Mens Rea: I—Provocation, Emotional Disturbance, and the Model Penal Code, 27 B.C. L. Rev. 243 (1986); Joshua Dressler, Rethinking Heat of Passion: A Defense in Search of a Rationale, 73 J. Crim. L. & Criminol. 421 (1982). For the latter view, see, e.g., Dan M. Kahan & Martha C. Nussbaum, Two Conceptions of Emotion in Criminal Law, 96 Col. L. Rev. 269, 305–23; Andrew Von Hirsch & Nils Jareborg, Provocation and Culpability in *Responsibility, Character, and the Emotions* (F. Schoeman ed. 1987) and Pillsbury, *Judging Evil: Rethinking the Law of Murder and Manslaughter* 125–60 (1998). Under the former approach, the subjective experience of emotionality takes precedence; under the latter, we are most concerned with whether the victim did, or appeared to do, a significant wrong to the defendant. Emotion plays an important role in the doctrine either way, but a quite different role depending on whether we emphasize its sensational or cognitive aspects.

Index

Action: as a manifestation of emotion, 12, 247–49

Alternative Dispute Resolution: as a response to mass atrocity, 272–75, 276, 280–81

Amnesty, 269–71

Anger: as a basis for punishment, 194–206; compared to vengeance, 129–34. *See also* Vengeance

Anti-semitism: role of disgust in, 29–30. *See also* Disgust

Appalachian Trail murders, 36–38. *See also* Homosexual provocation defense; Provocation defense

Appellate opinions: reading for emotional content, 339–41

Archilochus: his account of cowardice, 250–53, 262. *See also* Cowardice

Arendt, Hannah: writings on genocide, 268. *See also* Mass atrocities, genocide, and terrorism

Aristotle, 196, 310; view of indignation, 26. *See also* Indignation

Athenian attitudes toward punishment, 194–204. *See also* Exile; Plato; Scapegoating rituals in ancient Greece; Thargelia Festival

Augustine: on punishment, 201, 208, 228

Availability heuristic, 323–25

Beccaria: on punishment, 201, 208–10

Beldotti homicide case, 52–54, 66–69, 75–76. *See also* Disgust

Bentham, Jeremy: account of obedience to law, 78, 290–91. *See also* Obedience to law

Bieber, Irving: views on homosexuality of, 230–34, 235, 236

Biography: role in learning about emotion, 331, 334

Bosnia: rape of Muslim women in, 266–67. *See*
also Collective (governmental) violence; Mass atrocities, genocide, and terrorism

Carter, Stephen: on "bilateral individualism," 172–73, 188

Cognition: role in emotion, 6–7, 128–31, 150–52, 291, 310–12; in relation to disgust, 322; in relation to hate crimes, 316–17; in relation to retribution, 157–59; in relation to romantic love, 227–34; in relation to shame, 87–89. *See also* Disgust; Hate crimes; Retribution; Romantic love; Shame

Collective (governmental) violence, 266–71, 277; amnesty for, 269–71; institutional responses to, 266–71, 277, 278; prosecution as a response to, 267–68. *See also* Alternative Dispute Resolution; Amnesty; Bosnia; Mass atrocities, genocide, and terrorism; Nazism; Reconciliation; Truth and Reconciliation Commission in South Africa; Truth commissions

Communitarian theories of punishment, 201. *See also* Etzioni, Amatai

Compensation, 134–37, 142–43; ancient Hebrew attitude toward, 136

Contamination: as an element of disgust, 23–25

Courage: as a requirement of the Uniform Code of Military Justice, 247, 258, 262–63. *See also* Uniform Code of Military Justice

Cowardice, 242–60. *See also* Uniform Code of Military Justice

Critical legal studies, 352

Dead Man Walking, 3, 160, 166, 171–83. *See also* Death penalty

Death penalty, 2; relevance of disgust of jury to, 49–52; role of remorse in, 180–81, 187, 190